Structural Econometric Modeling in Industrial Organization and Quantitative Marketing

Structural Econometric Modeling in Industrial Organization and Quantitative Marketing

THEORY AND APPLICATIONS

ALI HORTAÇSU AND JOONHWI JOO

PRINCETON UNIVERSITY PRESS
PRINCETON & OXFORD

Published by Princeton University Press
41 William Street, Princeton, New Jersey 08540
99 Banbury Road, Oxford OX2 6JX

press.princeton.edu

Library of Congress Cataloging-in-Publication Data

Names: Hortaçsu, Ali, author. | Joo, Joonhwi, 1986– author.
Title: Structural econometric modeling in industrial organization and quantitative marketing : theory and applications / Ali Hortaçsu and Joonhwi Joo.
Description: Princeton : Princeton University Press, [2023] | Includes bibliographical references and index.
Identifiers: LCCN 2023003868 (print) | LCCN 2023003869 (ebook) | ISBN 9780691243467 (hardback) | ISBN 9780691251004 (ebook)
Subjects: LCSH: Econometric models—Case studies. | Industrial organization (Economic theory)—Econometric models—Case studies. | Marketing—Mathematical models. | BISAC: BUSINESS & ECONOMICS / Economics / Microeconomics | BUSINESS & ECONOMICS / Economics / Theory
Classification: LCC HB141 .H673 2023 (print) | LCC HB141 (ebook) | DDC 330.01/5195—dc23/eng/20230417
LC record available at https://lccn.loc.gov/2023003868
LC ebook record available at https://lccn.loc.gov/2023003869

British Library Cataloging-in-Publication Data is available

Editorial: Joe Jackson, Emma Wagh
Jacket: Wanda España
Production: Lauren Reese
Publicity: William Pagdatoon
Copyeditor: Susan McClung

Jacket Credit: santima suksawat / Alamy Stock Photo

This book has been composed in Arno Pro

10 9 8 7 6 5 4 3 2 1

CONTENTS

PREFACE

This book is prepared for a course on structural econometric methods used in empirical industrial organization and quantitative marketing. The targeted readers are second-year PhD students, who are assumed to have basic knowledge of first-year microeconomics and econometrics. We tried to give a concise and coherent overview of the literature, while not losing the key insights and features of the important structural econometric models and the associated estimation methods.

The purpose of this manuscript is to provide a compact overview of toolkits that can be used for a structural empirical analysis in industrial organization, quantitative marketing, and other related fields. Treatments on the subjects are far from complete, although we tried to include as detailed list of references as possible. The references at the end of each chapter include all the cited works in the body, and some additional readings related to the topic. We recommend that readers interested in a particular topic consult the references listed at the end of each chapter, and the relevant handbook chapters as well. We focus more on the formulations of economic and econometric models, estimation methods, and estimation algorithms. In many instances, we abstract away from concrete empirical applications. We emphasize that this is not because we think the applications are unimportant, but due to the limited scope of this volume.

We are grateful to Terry Culpepper and Steve (Haoran) Li, who helped prepare the manuscript. Jin Miao, Eric Richert, Jinyeong Son, and two anonymous reviewers read the manuscript very carefully and helped root out several errors and expositional problems. Hortaçsu would like to thank Rana, Suna, and Mina for their unwavering support throughout the project. Joo is grateful to Jean-Pierre Dubé for his continued guidance and support.

The authors' names are in alphabetical order and each contributed equally.

Structural Econometric Modeling in Industrial Organization and Quantitative Marketing

1

Introduction: Structural Econometric Modeling

Structural econometric modeling is a set of approaches that rely extensively on economic theory to explicitly specify and test the relationships among distinct economic phenomena. The terminology defines three parts: structure, econometrics, and model. In what follows, we first discuss what each part of the terminology entails, in reverse order. Then we touch upon the debate around the structural econometric modeling approach against its reduced-form counterpart.

1.1 Model

This section discusses what an economic model is. Then we articulate when a model should be considered as capturing only correlations and when a model can be considered as capturing causality as well. We begin our discussion in a broader context of how models are built and tested in science.

1.1.1 Scientific Model and Economic Model

A scientific model consists of abstractions and simplifications of the real world, selecting and incorporating only the relevant aspects of the world that a researcher is analyzing. Scientific models are most commonly formulated using mathematical language. One of the major strengths of utilizing a model in science comes from its logic of establishing the relations among distinct variables: build a model and test the predictions from that model using real-world data. The main goal of building a model is to specify hypothetical relationship among distinct phenomena, summarized in the form of variables, in a testable form. Once a model is built, predictions from that model are subject to tests using statistical methods applied to real-world data. A statistical test of a scientific model is expressed in terms of testing the null and alternative hypotheses. Very roughly, the probability that the null hypothesis is not true given the data boils down to the p-value. That is, the p-value is gives the probability that a test statistic is obtained just by coincidence, given that (1) the null and alternative hypotheses are set up correctly, and (2) an adequate estimation method is used to compute the p-value. If the real-world data do not support the predictions from a model, the model is rejected. Models that are rejected less often are considered more reliable, and more reliable models are considered to provide more reliable predictions.

Economics stands on the same ground. Economists build economic models and test model predictions using data with econometric methods. An immediate question might arise: what defines a model as an economic model? We suggest that there are two key ingredients of an economic model: (1) optimizing behaviors of (2) the rational agent(s).[1] Economic theory begins from preferences, technology, information, and various equilibrium concepts. As a result of the optimizing behavior of one or multiple rational agents, observable/testable equilibrium outcomes are derived in the form of mathematical statements. Those outcomes are tested using real-world data with appropriate econometric methods.

1.1.2 Predictive Model and Causal Model

A model generally makes testable predictions about correlations between distinct variables. Such correlations can sometimes imply causal relationships between the variables of interest, generally under much more stringent conditions and assumptions. In this subsection, we discuss when a model can be interpreted as implying a causal relationship between distinct variables. We begin our discussion with the following two simple examples. Both examples involve linear models between explanatory and explained variables.

Example 1.1.1. Suppose that one has collected data on the height and weight of a randomly selected group in the population. Let y_i be the weight, and let x_i be the height of each individual. The researcher runs the following regression:

$$y_i = \beta_1 + \beta_2 x_i + \epsilon_i. \tag{1.1.1}$$

The OLS estimate $\hat{\beta}_2$ turns out to be positive and highly statistically significant. Does this finding imply a causal relationship between height and weight?

1. Recent advances in several fields such as behavioral economics allow for violations of those two key ingredients. For instance, rationality might be bounded or optimization might be imperfect. Although we focus mostly on conventional microeconomic theory here, we do consider advances in behavioral economics as important progress in the profession.

Example 1.1.2. Suppose that one conducted a repeated Hooke's experiment and recorded the results. Let y_i be the length of the spring, and let x_i be the randomly assigned weight of the pendulum. Again, the researcher runs the following regression:

$$y_i = \gamma_1 + \gamma_2 x_i + \epsilon_i. \tag{1.1.2}$$

The OLS estimate $\hat{\gamma}_2$ is positive and highly statistically significant. Does this finding imply a causal relationship between the weight of the pendulum and the length of the spring?

The answer to the first question is definitely no.[2] But the answer to the second question is possibly yes. A positive and highly statistically significant $\hat{\gamma}_2$ estimate may be taken as evidence of a causal relationship—that is, x_i causes y_i. The structures of the two thought experiments seem to be quite similar at a glance; both equations (1.1.1) and (1.1.2) represent a linear model between x_i and y_i,[3] a data set is collected, a simple linear regression is run, and the coefficient estimates have the same sign and are statistically significant. But the implications on the causality can be starkly different. Where does this stark difference come from?

To answer this question, we first remind ourselves what regression reveals and what it does not. The slope coefficient estimate from a simple regression being positive (negative) is equivalent to the in-sample Pearson correlation coefficient between the explanatory variable and the explained variable being positive (negative).[4] If the data used in the regression are randomly sampled from the target population, high statistical significance can be interpreted as the positive (negative) sample correlation revealed from regression implying the positive (negative) population correlation.

What regression per se does not reveal is causality between the explanatory variable(s) and the explained variable. The experimental variations during the data-generating process are what make the correlation evidence of causality. Returning our focus to the two illustrative examples, the data on x_i of the second experiment are generated by a randomized experiment, where the researcher took full control over x_i. By contrast, the data on weight and height are not generated from a randomized experiment. Another possibly exogenous factor, such as good nutrition, is likely to simultaneously affect both height and weight; those exogenous factors are contained in the error term ϵ_i and treated as unobservable to the econometrician in the model considered.

2. If you are not convinced, recall Procrustes, the stretcher, in the *Odyssey*. When Procrustes stretches the guest to fit him in his bed, will the guest's weight increase?

3. We relegate the discussion on the role of ϵ_i to section 1.2.

4. Recall from elementary econometrics that the ordinary least squares (OLS) slope coefficient estimate is the sample covariance of x_i and y_i scaled by the sample variance of x_i.

An experimental variation in the explanatory variable(s) is essential for identifying the corresponding explanatory variable as a cause for change in the explained variable. The intuition behind the importance of experimental variation in establishing causality between two variables can be more easily illustrated in the context of omitted-variable bias in linear regression. Suppose that a causal and linear relationship exists between the vector of explanatory variables (x_i, v_i) and y_i, where v_i is unobserved to a researcher. Furthermore, assume that the correlation between x_i and v_i is nonzero, which is usual. If the sign and magnitude of the causal effect of interest are about variable x_i, a researcher may be tempted to run the following OLS regression:

$$y_i = \beta_1 + \beta_2 x_i + \epsilon_i,$$

and claim $\hat{\beta}$ represents the causal effect of x_i on y_i. This claim is unarguably false unless the correlation between x_i and v_i is zero or the correlation between v_i and y_i is zero.[5] The problem with virtually any observational data is that infinitely many v_i's are possible that are not observed, and the best way to avoid this situation is to have x_i generated by an experiment, and therefore, it has zero correlation with any possible omitted variables.

The linear model in Example 1.1.2, once estimated using experimental data on length and weight as described previously, can be used to predict a *causal* effect of the explanatory variable(s) on the explained variable. A model that has causal interpretation is often referred to as a *causal model*. On the contrary, the linear model in Example 1.1.1, after being estimated using observational data on height and weight, cannot be used to predict a causal relation. However, it does not prevent one from using the model to predict a correlation between the explanatory variable(s) and the explained variable. A model that can only be used to predict the behavior of the explained variable using the explanatory variable is often referred to as a *predictive model*. The usefulness of a causal model is its capability to answer the questions related to *counterfactual* experiments; with only a predictive model, it is generally not possible to answer questions regarding counterfactuals. Counterfactuals are the ultimate goal of building and calibrating a structural econometric model. We will discuss more about counterfactuals in section 1.3.

1.2 Econometrics

Economic (theory) models often do not readily incorporate real-world data without an added stochasticity that is necessary to estimate and/or test the model. The key characteristic that discerns an econometric model from an economic model is

5. See any undergraduate-level econometrics textbook for the reasoning behind this point.

whether the model can directly incorporate relevant data. To incorporate relevant data, additional statistical structure should be added to an economic model. As is often the case, the added statistical structure is imposed in the form of added unobservable (both to the econometrician and/or to economic agents) variable(s) to the economic model of interest. The error terms ϵ_i in Examples 1.1.1 and 1.1.2, respectively, are examples of added unobservables; ϵ_i captures anything other than the assumed linear relationship between x_i and y_i, and it is impossible to rationalize data without the error term. We note that an economic model and an econometric model are sometimes indistinguishable because in some stochastic economic models, the unobservables (to the economic agents) are inherent in the economic model.

Conceptually, econometric models have three kinds of error terms. The first is due to researcher uncertainty, which is sometimes referred to as the "structural error" or "unobserved heterogeneity." This kind of error term is observable to the economic agent, but not to the econometrician. The structural errors affect the decision of the economic agents in the same way that the observables do. The second is driven by agent uncertainty. It is observable to neither the economic agent nor the econometrician. However, the variable may affect the economic agent's decision, often in terms of ex ante expectations. The third is the error term that is added merely for the rationalization of the data or the tractability of estimation. This type of error term may include measurement errors. Distinguishing between these concepts during the estimation is sometimes difficult or even impossible. However, being clear about these conceptual distinctions in the modeling stage is very important because the distinctions may affect the counterfactuals critically.

1.3 Structure

Conducting a counterfactual policy[6] experiment is one of the most important goals of building and calibrating/estimating an econometric model. Through counterfactual policy experiments, a researcher can answer questions related to changes in economic outcomes *caused* by hypothetical changes in a policy that affects economic agents. The key ingredients of an economic model explained in section 1.2, optimizing behaviors of rational agents involved and possible changes in the equilibrium, need to be accounted for during the counterfactual policy experiments; they need to be explicitly formulated in the econometric model to evaluate and quantify the causal effect of a change in policy.

6. The term "policy" is used in a broad sense here. It can be a firm's conduct, government regulation, consumers' choice environment, and so on; it does not necessarily mean public policy.

For a valid counterfactual policy experiment, certain aspects of the corresponding econometric model should be taken as invariant to possible changes in a policy; such invariant aspects are referred to as the *structure* of the model. Structure in a model is a set of restrictions how variables behave. For example, in the simple causal linear model discussed in Example 1.1.2, the key structure imposed is that y_i responds linearly to a change in x_i.[7] The model parameters of the econometric model, (γ_1, γ_2), are set free during the stages of calibration/estimation. Once the model parameters (γ_1, γ_2) are estimated, the parameter estimates are also taken as a part of the structure during predictions and counterfactual experiments.

Economic theory is the main source of the structure in a structural econometric model. The structure of many structural econometric models is nonlinear because most underlying economic models specify nonlinear relationships between the variables of interest up to the set of unknown parameters. By estimating a structural econometric model using real-world data, a researcher can obtain the magnitude of the parameters, in addition to their signs, in the underlying economic model. In turn, the magnitude of the effects resulting from a hypothetical change in a policy can be quantified; in contrast, it is often the case that only signs of the effects from a hypothetical policy change can be identified from the reduced-form counterparts of structural econometric models. However, the ability of quantifying the effects associated with a hypothetical policy change comes with its costs: the nonlinearity from explicitly specifying the possible relationships generally makes the structural econometric approach much more difficult to implement than its reduced-form counterpart.

Formulating and estimating a structural econometric model typically follow the following steps: (1) Formulate a well-defined economic model of the environment under consideration; (2) add a sufficient number of stochastic unobservables to the economic model; (3) identify and estimate the model parameters; and (4) verify the adequacy of the resulting structural economic model as a description of the observed data. In step (2), a researcher should decide whether to fully specify the distribution of the unobservables. Related to steps (2) and (3), estimation of structural econometric models often boils down to obtaining the point-identified, finite-dimensional, and policy-invariant model parameters.[8] A few possibilities

7. The econometric model in equation (1.1.2) is a structural model to the extent that the linearity is taken as coming from a valid theory that specifies the causal linear relationship between x_i and y_i. Note that it is also possible to interpret the econometric model in equation (1.1.2) as an approximation of a possibly nonlinear causal relationship between x_i and y_i. More discussions of the interpretation of the linear models follow in section 1.4.

8. The literature on the partially identified or nonparametric structural econometric models is growing. We study some examples of them in subsequent chapters.

exist for step (4). For example, the researcher can split the sample, estimate the model using only a subset of the sample, and examine the accuracy of the out-of-sample prediction. Another way of validating the structural models is to match the predictions of structural models with the data from a randomized experiment. We think an appropriate model validation is crucial to the credibility of the results from estimating a structural econometric model and conducting counterfactual policy experiments using the estimated structural model. A simple sensitivity analysis alone may not be enough to persuade the audience that the model is a credible and realistic approximation of the world.

1.4 Debate around the Structural Econometric Modeling Approach

Broadly, there are two ends of building an econometric model from an economic model: reduced-form and structural econometric models in a narrow sense.[9] There has been a debate in the literature between the structural and reduced-form approaches in econometric modeling.

Reduced-form econometric models abstract away from rational agents, optimization, and equilibria. They specify the simple relationships between the variables of interest and use relevant estimation methods to back out the parameters. Their econometric specifications are mostly linear, which has a justification that linear functions are a first-order approximation of any smooth functions. The strengths of reduced-form econometric models are their simplicity and relative robustness to the model misspecifications. On the other hand, a structural econometric model begins by explicitly stating the economic model specifications, such as the objective functions, the optimizing variable, the equilibrium concept, the degree of information of the agents and of the econometrician, and the possible source of endogeneity. Then, the model is solved step by step. As a result, the relations between the variables are specified in terms of the moment (in)equalities, likelihoods, or quantile restrictions. Finally, the relevant estimation methods for such specifications are used to back out the model parameters.

By explicitly specifying the economic models, structural econometric modeling enables one to make in-sample and out-of-sample predictions and policy counterfactuals. Specifically, the ability to make out-of-sample causal predictions is one of the greatest strengths of a structural econometric model. For instance,

9. In a wide sense, even the linear instrumental-variable model is a structural econometric model, implicitly imposing a very specific structure on how the instrumental variables affect the outcome variables. This point has been thoroughly investigated by Heckman and Vytlacil (2005).

a reduced-form model of merger identified using retrospective analysis may be enough to predict a merger impact if the analyst is interested in predicting the effect of counterfactual merger with similar attributes to retrospective ones. However, if one is interested in simulating mergers under a different market environment, a linear extrapolation is likely to be a poor fit. Furthermore, the linear shape and even the direction of the merger impact suggested by the reduced-form model may not be valid anymore under some counterfactual policy experiments, subject to the "Lucas critique" (see Lucas 1976). By explicitly specifying and estimating the policy-invariant nonlinear economic relationships between the market environment and the equilibrium outcomes of a merger, structural econometric modeling allows one to make predictions out-of-sample.

A disadvantage of structural econometric modeling is that the predictions or policy counterfactuals can be sensitive to model misspecifications. The possibility of model misspecification is considered one of the greatest weaknesses in the structural econometric modeling approach, especially because structural econometric models generally take sophisticated nonlinear causal relationships between variables, inherited from the underlying economic theory, as given and fixed a priori. Ideally, every ingredient in a structural econometric model could be tested by running carefully designed, randomized experiments, but it is generally very difficult when the subject of study is the economic behavior of individuals or organizations.

Taking either approach does not exclude the other, and much successful research has used one approach to inform work with the other. That said, we view the reduced-form approach and structural approach to econometric modeling as complements with different strengths, not substitutes, as explained previously.

1.5 Outline of This Book

Modern empirical industrial organization and quantitative marketing rely extensively on the structural econometric modeling approach using observational data. The goal of this textbook is to give an overview of how the various streams of literature in empirical industrial organization and quantitative marketing use structural econometric modeling to estimate the model parameters, give economic-model-based predictions, and conduct policy counterfactuals.

This book consists of six chapters and an appendix. We discuss the basics of single-agent static and dynamic discrete choice in chapter 2, which is now a standard baseline modeling framework in empirical industrial organization, quantitative marketing, and many other adjacent fields. In chapter 3, we move on to study demand estimation with market data, where we introduce demand-estimation methods in the product space and characteristics space, respectively. In chapter 4, we focus on strategic interactions of firms in the static and dynamic setup. We then move our focus back to consumers to study the empirical frameworks of consumer search in chapter 5. Finally, we study the theory and empirics of auctions in chapter 6. For completeness, we also summarize basic features of the most commonly used baseline estimation frameworks in the appendix.

The book does not cover many interesting relevant topics, such as production function estimation methods and Bayesian learning models. We refer the readers to relevant survey papers and handbook chapters to learn more about these topics.[10]

Bibliography

Ackerberg, D., C. L. Benkard, S. Berry, & A. Pakes (2007). Chapter 63, "Econometric tools for analyzing market outcomes." In vol. 6A of *Handbook of Econometrics*, 4171–4276. Amsterdam: Elsevier.

Angrist, J. D., & J.-S. Pischke (2010). "The credibility revolution in empirical economics: How better research design is taking the con out of econometrics." *Journal of Economic Perspectives*, 24, 3–30.

Blundell, R. (2010). "Comments on: Michael P. Keane 'Structural vs. atheoretic approaches to econometrics'," *Journal of Econometrics*, 156, 25–26.

Ching, A. T., T. Erdem, & M. P. Keane (2013). "Learning models: An assessment of progress, challenges, and new developments," *Marketing Science*, 32, 913–938.

Ching, A. T., T. Erdem, & M. P. Keane (2017). Chapter 8, "Empirical models of learning dynamics: A survey of recent developments." In *Handbook of Marketing Decision Models*, 223–257. Springer.

Deaton, A. (2010). "Instruments, randomization, and learning about development." *Journal of Economic Literature*, 48, 424–455.

de Loecker, J., & C. Syverson (2021). Chapter 3, "An industrial organization perspective on productivity." In vol. 4 of *Handbook of Industrial Organization*, 141–223. Amsterdam: Elsevier.

Heckman, J. J., & E. Vytlacil (2005). "Structural equations, treatment effects, and econometric policy evaluation." *Econometrica*, 73, 669–738.

Imbens, G. W. (2010). "Better LATE than nothing: Some comments on Deaton (2009) and Heckman and Urzua (2009)." *Journal of Economic Literature*, 48, 399–423.

Keane, M. P. (2010). "Structural vs. atheoretic approaches to econometrics." *Journal of Econometrics*, 156, 3–20.

Keane, M. P., P. E. Todd, & K. I. Wolpin (2011). Chapter 4, "The structural estimation of behavioral models: Discrete choice dynamic programming methods and applications." In vol. 4a of *Handbook of Labor Economics*, 331–461. Amsterdam: Elsevier.

Laibson, D., & J. A. List (2015). "Principles of (behavioral) economics." *American Economic Review: Papers and Proceedings*, 105, 385–390.

Leamer, E. E. (1983). "Let's take the con out of econometrics." *American Economic Review*, 73, 31–43.

Low, H., & C. Meghir (2017). "The use of structural models in econometrics." *Journal of Economic Perspectives*, 31, 33–58.

Lucas, R. E. (1976). "Econometric policy evaluation: A critique." In *Carnegie-Rochester Conference Series on Public Policy*, vol. 1, 19–46. Amsterdam: Elsevier.

10. For production function estimation methods, see, e.g., de Loecker and Syverson (2021), and for Bayesian learning models, see, e.g., Ching, Erdem, and Keane (2013, 2017).

Nevo, A., & M. D. Whinston (2010). "Taking the dogma out of econometrics: Structural modeling and credible inference." *Journal of Economic Perspectives*, 24, 69–82.

Reiss, P. C., & F. A. Wolak (2007). Chapter 64, "Structural econometric modeling: Rationales and examples from industrial organization." In vol. 6A of *Handbook of Econometrics*, 4277–4415. Amsterdam: Elsevier.

Rust, J. (2010). "Comments on: "Structural vs. atheoretic approaches to econometrics" by Michael Keane." *Journal of Econometrics*, 156, 21–24.

Rust, J. (2014). "The limits of inference with theory: A review of Wolpin (2013)." *Journal of Economic Literature*, 52, 820–850.

Wolpin, K. I. (2013). *The limits of inference without theory*. Cambridge, MA: MIT Press.

2

Static and Dynamic Discrete Choice

The discrete-choice framework, often referred to as "qualitative response models," has become a major workhorse in diverse contexts of empirical industrial organization and other fields in applied microeconomics. In this chapter, we review the basic theory on the binary choice and multiple discrete-choice models. Then we proceed to study the dynamic discrete-choice models pioneered by Rust (1987); Hotz and Miller (1993), and Hotz et al. (1994) to study how the discrete-choice framework incorporates the forward-looking behavior of an economic agent. Throughout this chapter, we assume that individual choice data on a finite set of alternatives are available. We focus mostly on the fully parametric setup, of which the main goal often boils down to deriving the likelihood function for the maximum-likelihood estimation.

2.1 Binary Choice

2.1.1 *Motivation: Linear Probability Model*

In this section, we consider the binary choice data of individuals indexed by $i \in \mathcal{I} := \{1, 2, \ldots, I\}$, for alternatives indexed by $j \in \mathcal{J} := \left\{1, 2, \ldots, J\right\}$. Throughout this section, we assume that data for each consumer's choice on each alternative are available where the set of alternatives $\mathcal{J}$ is not exclusive. Let $y_{i,j}$ be a discrete outcome variable with only two possibilities, 0 and 1. If consumer i chooses to buy product j, $y_{i,j} = 1$; otherwise, $y_{i,j} = 0$. For notational convenience, our discussion focuses on a single individual i.

Consider the following linear estimation equation:

$$y_{i,j} = \delta_j + \eta_{i,j},$$

in which $\eta_{i,j}$ is an error term and $\delta_j = \mathbf{x}_j'\boldsymbol{\theta}$, where $\mathbf{x}_j$ is a vector of covariates that shifts the choice probability, observable to the econometrician.[1]

The ordinary least squares (OLS) estimator $\hat{\boldsymbol{\theta}}_{OLS}$ is consistent for $\boldsymbol{\theta}$ and asymptotically normal. The model is called the "linear probability model" because the prediction $\hat{y}_j$ is such that

$$\hat{y}_{i,j} = \hat{\mathbb{E}}\left[y_{i,j}|\mathbf{x}_j\right] = \hat{\Pr}\left(y_{i,j}=1|\mathbf{x}_j\right) = \mathbf{x}_j'\hat{\boldsymbol{\theta}}_{OLS}.$$

Because this model has the prediction $\hat{y}_{i,j} = \mathbf{x}_j'\hat{\boldsymbol{\theta}}_{OLS}$, the OLS estimator provides us with an easy interpretation of the marginal effects: A one-unit increase in $x_j^{(l)}$ will increase the predicted conditional probability $\hat{\Pr}\left(y_{i,j}=1|\mathbf{x}_j\right)$ by $\hat{\theta}_{OLS}^{(l)}$. The implied constant marginal effects follow from construction of the linear probability model. An immediate drawback of this approach is that the constant marginal effect assumption is likely invalid in any discrete-choice model. It yields a poor fit when $\hat{y}_{i,j}$ is close to 0 or 1, and it eventually leads the model to predict $\hat{y}_{i,j} > 1$ or $\hat{y}_{i,j} < 0$. It motivates the choice of $G(\cdot)$ to be a legitimate probability distribution with an unrestricted support, as we study in this chapter.[2]

2.1.2 *Binary Logit and Binary Probit Model*

Let us formalize the setup. Consider a latent utility $y_{i,j}^*$ specified by

$$y_{i,j}^* = \delta_j + \epsilon_{i,j} \qquad \epsilon_{i,j} \sim \text{i.i.d. } G(\cdot) \tag{2.1.1}$$

$$y_{i,j} = \begin{cases} 1 & \text{if } y_{i,j}^* \geq 0 \\ 0 & \text{if } y_{i,j}^* < 0 \end{cases},$$

where δ_j is the mean utility index that represents the observable component of $y_{i,j}^*$ to the econometrician; and $\epsilon_{i,j}$ represents the idiosyncratic shocks on the latent utility that are unobservable to the econometrician, which is fully known to the consumer. We assume that δ_j and $\epsilon_{i,j}$ are orthogonal.

1. Throughout chapter 2, we index the vector of characteristics $\mathbf{x}$ only by j, which implies that $\mathbf{x}$ can vary only with the alternatives, not with individuals. However, this restriction is purely for notational convenience. In principle, $\mathbf{x}$ can be indexed by both i and j.

2. We focus on the parametric methods in this section. Note that there are semiparametric index models that do not require a researcher to specify the shape of $G(\cdot)$. See, for example, Klein and Spady (1993) and Blundell and Powell (2004).

The two parametric specifications of $G(\cdot)$ used most often are standard Gaussian and logistic $(0,1)$. Assume that $g(.)$, the probability density function of $G(.)$, is symmetric around 0. This is indeed the case for the standard Gaussian and the logistic distribution with location parameter 0. Consider the following conditional probability:

$$\begin{aligned}\Pr\left(y_{i,j}=1|\mathbf{x}_j\right) &= \Pr\left(\mathbf{x}_j'\boldsymbol{\theta}+\epsilon_{i,j}>0\right)\\ &= \Pr\left(\epsilon_{i,j}>-\mathbf{x}_j'\boldsymbol{\theta}\right)\\ &= 1-\Pr\left(\epsilon_{i,j}\le-\mathbf{x}_j'\boldsymbol{\theta}\right)\\ &= \Pr\left(\epsilon_{i,j}\le\mathbf{x}_j'\boldsymbol{\theta}\right)\\ &= G\left(\mathbf{x}_j'\boldsymbol{\theta}\right).\end{aligned}$$

The next-to-last equality follows from $1-\Pr\left(\epsilon_{i,j}\le-\mathbf{x}_j'\boldsymbol{\theta}\right)=\Pr\left(\epsilon_{i,j}\le\mathbf{x}_j'\boldsymbol{\theta}\right)$ by the symmetry of $g(.)$. The Probit model assumes $\epsilon_{i,j}\sim$ i.i.d. $\mathcal{N}(0,1)$, and the logit model assumes $\epsilon_{i,j}\sim$ i.i.d. logistic $(0,1)$.[3] In both models, either the scale of $\boldsymbol{\theta}$ or $G(\cdot)$'s scale parameter σ cannot be identified. To see why, consider the following:

$$\begin{aligned}\Pr\left(y_{i,j}=1|\mathbf{x}_j\right) &= \Pr\left(\frac{\epsilon_{i,j}}{\sigma}>-\frac{\mathbf{x}_j'\boldsymbol{\theta}}{\sigma}\right)\\ &= \Pr\left(\epsilon_{i,j}\le\mathbf{x}_j'\boldsymbol{\theta}\right).\end{aligned}$$

So long as $\sigma>0$, any change in σ does not affect the choice probability. The convention is to set $\sigma=1$ rather than adjusting the scale of $\boldsymbol{\theta}$.

Fix i. Suppose that we have the observations $\left\{y_{i,j},\mathbf{x}_j\right\}_{j=1}^J$. The likelihood function of the binary choice models for individual i is

$$\begin{aligned}L_i\left(\left\{y_{i,j},\mathbf{x}_j\right\}_{j=1}^J|\boldsymbol{\theta}\right) &= \prod_{j=1}^J\left[\Pr\left(y_{i,j}=1|\mathbf{x}_j\right)\right]^{\mathbf{1}(y_{i,j}=1)}\left[\Pr\left(y_{i,j}=0|\mathbf{x}_j\right)\right]^{\mathbf{1}(y_{i,j}=0)}\\ &= \prod_{j=1}^J\left[G\left(\mathbf{x}_j'\boldsymbol{\theta}\right)\right]^{y_{i,j}}\left[1-G\left(\mathbf{x}_j'\boldsymbol{\theta}\right)\right]^{(1-y_{i,j})}. \qquad (2.1.2)\end{aligned}$$

3. That is, $\Pr\left(y_{i,j}=1|\mathbf{x}_j\right)=G\left(\mathbf{x}_j'\boldsymbol{\theta}\right)=\frac{\exp\left(\mathbf{x}_j'\boldsymbol{\theta}\right)}{1+\exp\left(\mathbf{x}_j'\boldsymbol{\theta}\right)}$.

The log-likelihood function follows by taking the logarithm

$$l_i\left(\left\{y_{i,j},\mathbf{x}_j\right\}_{j=1}^{J}|\boldsymbol{\theta}\right)=\sum_{j=1}^{J}\left\{y_{i,j}\ln G\left(\mathbf{x}_j'\boldsymbol{\theta}\right)+\left(1-y_{i,j}\right)\ln\left[1-G\left(\mathbf{x}_j'\boldsymbol{\theta}\right)\right]\right\}. \quad (2.1.3)$$

Taking derivatives with respect to the parameter vector $\boldsymbol{\theta}$ on equation (2.1.3) yields the sum of the scores:

$$\begin{aligned}\mathbf{s}_i\left(\left\{y_{i,j},\mathbf{x}_j\right\}_{j=1}^{J}|\boldsymbol{\theta}\right)&=\sum_{j=1}^{J}\left\{\frac{y_{i,j}}{G\left(\mathbf{x}_j'\boldsymbol{\theta}\right)}g\left(\mathbf{x}_j'\boldsymbol{\theta}\right)-\frac{1-y_{i,j}}{1-G\left(\mathbf{x}_j'\boldsymbol{\theta}\right)}g\left(\mathbf{x}_j'\boldsymbol{\theta}\right)\right\}\mathbf{x}_j\\&=\sum_{j=1}^{J}\left\{\frac{g\left(\mathbf{x}_j'\boldsymbol{\theta}\right)}{G\left(\mathbf{x}_j'\boldsymbol{\theta}\right)\left[1-G\left(\mathbf{x}_j'\boldsymbol{\theta}\right)\right]}\left[y_{i,j}-G\left(\mathbf{x}_j'\boldsymbol{\theta}\right)\right]\right\}\mathbf{x}_j.\end{aligned} \quad (2.1.4)$$

Setting equation (2.1.4) to $\mathbf{0}$ yields the first-order condition for the maximum-likelihood estimation for the binary choice models. The $\frac{g\left(\mathbf{x}_j'\boldsymbol{\theta}\right)}{G\left(\mathbf{x}_j'\boldsymbol{\theta}\right)\left[1-G\left(\mathbf{x}_j'\boldsymbol{\theta}\right)\right]}$ term can be interpreted as a weighting function; and $\left[y_{i,j}-G\left(\mathbf{x}_j'\boldsymbol{\theta}\right)\right]$ is the prediction error, the expectation of which is zero.

In the logit model, the first-order condition $\mathbf{s}_i\left(\left\{y_{i,j},\mathbf{x}_j\right\}_{j=1}^{J}|\boldsymbol{\theta}\right)=\mathbf{0}$ simplifies further, using the fact that $\forall z\in\mathbb{R}$, $\frac{g(z)}{G(z)[1-G(z)]}=1$.[4] Combining the fact with

4. For a logistic probability density function $g(\cdot)$ with location parameter 0 and scale parameter 1, the following holds:

$$\begin{aligned}g(z)&=\frac{\exp(z)}{1+\exp(z)}-\frac{\exp(2z)}{\left[1+\exp(z)\right]^2}\\&=\frac{\left[1+\exp(z)\right]\exp(z)-\exp(2z)}{\left[1+\exp(z)\right]^2}\\&=\frac{\exp(z)+\exp(2z)-\exp(2z)}{\left[1+\exp(z)\right]^2}\\&=\frac{\exp(z)}{\left[1+\exp(z)\right]^2}\end{aligned}$$

and

$$G(z)\left[1-G(z)\right]=\frac{\exp(z)}{1+\exp(z)}\left[\frac{1}{1+\exp(z)}\right].$$

Taking the ratio yields $\frac{g(z)}{G(z)[1-G(z)]}=1$.

equation (2.1.4), the first-order condition for the maximum likelihood problem with the first-order condition simplifies as

$$\mathbf{s}_i\left(\left\{y_{i,j},\mathbf{x}_j\right\}_{j=1}^{J}|\boldsymbol{\theta}\right)=\mathbf{0}$$

$$\Rightarrow\sum_{j=1}^{J}\left[y_{i,j}-G\left(\mathbf{x}_j'\boldsymbol{\theta}\right)\right]\mathbf{x}_j=\mathbf{0}.$$

If $\mathbf{x}_j$ contains 1 in its row, the first-order condition also contains $\bar{y}=\overline{G\left(\mathbf{x}_j'\boldsymbol{\theta}\right)}$.

2.1.3 Marginal Effects

The marginal effect of the binary choice model, $\frac{\partial \Pr(y_{i,j}=1|\mathbf{x}_j)}{\partial \mathbf{x}_j^{(l)}}$, is

$$\frac{\partial \Pr\left(y_{i,j}=1|\mathbf{x}_j\right)}{\partial x_j^{(l)}}=\frac{\partial G\left(\mathbf{x}_j'\boldsymbol{\theta}\right)}{\partial x_j^{(l)}}$$

$$=g\left(\mathbf{x}_j'\boldsymbol{\theta}\right)\theta^{(l)}. \qquad (2.1.5)$$

Unlike the linear probability model, the marginal effect varies across observations. Heterogeneity in responses exists in this model because of the nonlinearity of $G(\cdot)$. One may report equation (2.1.5) for each observation j in principle. Alternatively, one can consider either (1) the average marginal effect $\frac{1}{J}\sum_{j=1}^{J} g\left(\mathbf{x}_j'\hat{\boldsymbol{\theta}}\right)\hat{\theta}^{(l)}$ or (2) the marginal effect on average (or median) observation $g\left(\bar{\mathbf{x}}'\hat{\boldsymbol{\theta}}\right)\hat{\theta}^{(l)}$. It is acceptable to report either (1) or (2) as the summary measure of marginal effects; the researcher must be transparent about which summary measure is being reported.

2.2 Multiple Choice: Random Utility Maximization Framework

To model a discrete choice over multiple alternatives, we introduce the simple logit model and the nested logit model developed in a series of works by McFadden, (1974, 1978, 1981) and McFadden and Train (2000), among others. The random utility maximization (RUM) framework is the major workhorse in diverse contexts of applied microeconomics when multiple mutually exclusive alternatives exist. A common way to derive the logistic choice probabilities is to begin from the additive i.i.d. type I extreme-value-distributed idiosyncratic utility shocks. We present some preliminary results on type I extreme value distribution in section 2.2.1, and then present our main results in the subsections that follow.

2.2.1 Preliminary Results: Type I Extreme Value Distribution and Its Properties

Definition. *(Type I Extreme Value Distribution)* $\epsilon_i \sim T1EV(\alpha)$ if ϵ_i follows the cumulative distribution function

$$\begin{aligned}\Pr(\epsilon_i \leq \epsilon) &= F_\alpha(\epsilon) \\ &= \exp\left[-\exp\left[-(\epsilon-\alpha)\right]\right].\end{aligned}$$

Note that this distribution is also referred to as a "Gumbel distribution" or "double exponential distribution."[5] When $\alpha=0$, the expectation of a type I extreme value random variable is the Euler-Mascheroni constant $\gamma \approx 0.5772$. Note that throughout this book, we will take a location shift by $-\gamma \approx -0.5772$ when it represents an econometric error term in order to make it a mean-zero random variable.

Lemma 2.2.1. *(Density Function of Type I Extreme Value Distribution)* Let $F_\alpha(\epsilon)$ be the cumulative distribution function of $T1EV(\alpha)$. Then the probability density function $f_\alpha(\epsilon) = \exp(\alpha-\epsilon)\, F_\alpha(\epsilon)$.

Lemma 2.2.2. *(Distribution of Maximum over Independently Distributed T1EV Random Variables)* Let $\epsilon_{i,j} \sim T1EV(\alpha_j)$, where $\epsilon_{i,j}$ are independent over j. Let $\alpha = \ln\left[\sum_{j=1}^{J} \exp(\alpha_j)\right]$. Then,

$$\max_j \{\epsilon_{i,j}\} \sim T1EV(\alpha).$$

5. In principle, type I extreme value distribution is a two-parameter distribution, location, and scale. If the scale parameter is denoted by σ, then the cumulative distribution function would be $\Pr(\epsilon_i \leq \epsilon) = \exp[-\exp[-(\epsilon-\alpha)/\sigma]]$. We normalize the scale parameter to 1 because it cannot be identified in general.

Proof. Let $\epsilon \in \mathbb{R}$. We have

$$
\begin{aligned}
\Pr\left(\max_{j\in\mathcal{J}}\left\{\epsilon_{i,j}\right\} \leq \epsilon\right) &= \prod_{j=1}^{J} \Pr\left(\epsilon_{i,j} \leq \epsilon\right) \\
&= \prod_{j=1}^{J} \exp\left[-\exp\left[-\left(\epsilon - \alpha_j\right)\right]\right] \\
&= \exp\left[-\sum_{j=1}^{J} \exp\left[-\left(\epsilon - \alpha_j\right)\right]\right] \\
&= \exp\left[-\exp\left(-\epsilon\right)\sum_{j=1}^{J} \exp\left(\alpha_j\right)\right] \\
&= \exp\left[-\exp\left(-\epsilon\right)\exp\left(\alpha\right)\right] \\
&= F_\alpha\left(\epsilon\right).
\end{aligned}
$$

The first equality follows from the maximum order statistic for a sample size of J. □

Corollary. *(Expectation of Maximum over T1EV Random Variables)* Let $j \in \mathcal{J}$. Let $\epsilon_{i,j} \sim T1EV\ (0)$. Let $u_{i,j} = \delta_j + \epsilon_{i,j}$ where δ_j is the additive deterministic component of choice j. Then,

$$
\mathbb{E}\left[\max_{j\in\mathcal{J}}\left\{u_{i,j}\right\}\right] = \ln\left[\sum_{j\in\mathcal{J}} \exp\left(\delta_j\right)\right] + \gamma,
$$

where the Euler-Mascheroni constant $\gamma \approx 0.5772$.

Lemma 2.2.3. *(Subtraction of Two Independent T1EV Random Variables)* Suppose that $u_{i,j} \sim T1EV\left(\delta_j\right)$ and $u_{i,k} \sim T1EV\left(\delta_k\right)$ where $u_{i,j} \perp\!\!\!\perp u_{i,k}$. Then, $u_{i,j} - u_{i,k} \sim \text{Logistic}\left(\delta_j - \delta_k\right)$.

Proof. Let $F\left(u_j\right)$ be the cumulative distribution function of $T1EV\left(\delta_j\right)$, and let $f_{\delta_j}\left(u_j\right)$ be the corresponding probability density function. By lemma 2.2.1,

$$
\begin{aligned}
f_{\delta_k}\left(u_k\right) &= \exp\left[-\left(u_k - \delta_k\right)\right] F_{\delta_k}\left(u_k\right) \\
&= \exp\left[-\left(u_k - \delta_k\right)\right] \exp\left[-\exp\left[-\left(u_k - \delta_k\right)\right]\right].
\end{aligned}
$$

Thus,

$$
\begin{aligned}
&\Pr\left(u_j - u_k < u\right) \\
&= \Pr\left(u_j < u_k + u\right) \\
&= \int_{-\infty}^{\infty} \left\{ \int_{-\infty}^{u_k+u} f_{\delta_j}\left(u_j\right) du_j \right\} f_{\delta_k}\left(u_k\right) du_k \\
&= \int_{-\infty}^{\infty} f_{\delta_k}\left(u_k\right) F_{\delta_j}\left(u_k + u\right) du_k \\
&= \int_{-\infty}^{\infty} \exp\left[-\left(u_k - \delta_k\right)\right] F_{\delta_k}\left(u_k\right) F_{\delta_j}\left(u_k + u\right) du_k \\
&= \int_{-\infty}^{\infty} \exp\left[-\left(u_k - \delta_k\right)\right] \exp\left[-\exp\left[-\left(u_k - \delta_k\right)\right]\right] \\
&\quad \exp\left[-\exp\left[-\left(u_k + u - \delta_j\right)\right]\right] du_k \\
&= \int_{-\infty}^{\infty} \exp\left[-\left(u_k - \delta_k\right)\right] \exp\left[-\exp\left[-\left(u_k - \delta_k\right)\right]\right. \\
&\quad \left. - \exp\left[-\left(u_k + u - \delta_j\right)\right]\right] du_k \\
&= \int_{-\infty}^{\infty} \exp\left[-\left(u_k - \delta_k\right)\right] \exp\left[-\exp\left[-\left(u_k - \delta_k\right)\right]\right. \\
&\quad \left. - \exp\left[-\left(u_k - \delta_k + u + \delta_k - \delta_j\right)\right]\right] du_k \\
&= \int_{-\infty}^{\infty} \exp\left[-\left(u_k - \delta_k\right)\right] \exp\left[-\exp\left[-\left(u_k - \delta_k\right)\right]\right. \\
&\quad \left. \left\{1 + \exp\left[-\left(u + \delta_k - \delta_j\right)\right]\right\}\right] du_k .
\end{aligned}
$$

Denote $a := \left\{1 + \exp\left[-\left(u + \delta_k - \delta_j\right)\right]\right\}$ for notational simplicity:

$$
\begin{aligned}
&\int_{-\infty}^{\infty} \exp\left[-\left(u_k - \delta_k\right)\right] \exp\left[-a \exp\left[-\left(u_k - \delta_k\right)\right]\right] du_k \\
&= \frac{1}{a} \int_{-\infty}^{\infty} a \exp\left[-\left(u_k - \delta_k\right)\right] \exp\left[-a \exp\left[-\left(u_k - \delta_k\right)\right]\right] du_k \\
&= \frac{1}{1 + \exp\left[-\left(u + \delta_k - \delta_j\right)\right]} \qquad (2.2.1) \\
&= \frac{\exp\left(u - \left(\delta_j - \delta_k\right)\right)}{\exp\left(u - \left(\delta_j - \delta_k\right)\right) + 1},
\end{aligned}
$$

which is a logistic cumulative distribution function with mean $(\delta_j - \delta_k)$. Note that equation (2.2.1) follows because

$$\exp\left[-a\left(u_k-\delta_k\right)\right]\exp\left[-\exp\left[-a\left(u_k-\delta_k\right)\right]\right]$$

is the probability density function of a type I extreme value distribution with scale parameter a^{-1}, which integrates to 1. □

2.2.2 *The Simple Logit Model*

Let i denote an individual, and let j denote an alternative where $j \in \mathcal{J} := \{1, 2, \ldots, J\}$. Consumer i is assumed to choose up to one product in the set of alternatives $\mathcal{J}$. That is, now the consumer's choice is exclusive over the set of alternatives.[6] $\mathcal{J}$ may contain product 0, which is most commonly interpreted as choosing an outside option. The outside option, when included, is often interpreted as representing all other commodities that are not explicitly included in the choice set.

The latent utility is modeled as

$$u_{i,j} = \delta_j + \epsilon_{i,j}, \tag{2.2.2}$$

where δ_j is the utility from the observed product characteristics of product j[7] and $\epsilon_{i,j}$ represents the unobserved idiosyncratic utility shocks. The most common functional form used is the linear utility specification $\delta_j = \mathbf{x}_j'\boldsymbol{\theta}$. When $\mathcal{J}$ contains the outside option, normalizing $\mathbf{x}_0 = \mathbf{0}$ so that the mean utility of an outside option δ_0 is zero is common. Then, the utility levels of all other inside options are defined and identified against the outside option's utility level, normalized as zero.

Analogous with the binary choice model, the probability of individual i choosing product j is

$$\begin{aligned}\Pr\left(i \text{ chooses } j\right) &= \Pr\left(u_{i,j} > u_{i,k}, \forall k \neq j\right)\\ &= \Pr\left(\delta_j + \epsilon_{i,j} > \delta_k + \epsilon_{i,k}, \forall k \neq j\right)\end{aligned}$$

6. The setup and the assumptions on data availability are different from the binary choice model discussed in section 2.1. In the binary choice model, the choice over the set of alternatives was not exclusive—we assumed that the choice data on each alternative are available in the form of $\{0, 1\}$. Using the fact that the difference between two i.i.d. type I extreme-value random variables follows the logistic distribution, binary choice can be recast in the form of multiple choice with two alternatives $\{0, 1\}$.

7. Note that δ_j may include the unobserved (to the econometrician) attributes of alternative j. We discuss including the unobserved attributes in chapter 3. For now, we take δ_j to be composed only of the observed attributes.

$$= \Pr\left(\delta_j + \epsilon_{i,j} > \max_{k \neq j}\left\{\delta_k + \epsilon_{i,k}\right\}\right)$$

$$= \Pr\left(\mathbf{x}_j'\boldsymbol{\theta} + \epsilon_{i,j} > \max_{k \neq j}\left\{\mathbf{x}_k'\boldsymbol{\theta} + \epsilon_{i,k}\right\}\right), \tag{2.2.3}$$

where the last equality used the functional form $\delta_j = \mathbf{x}_j'\boldsymbol{\theta}$.

For the estimation, we assume the following to derive the closed-form probability of individual i choosing alternative j:

MLM(1) $\forall i, \forall k \neq j, \epsilon_{i,j} \perp\!\!\!\perp \epsilon_{i,k}$.
MLM(2) $\epsilon_{i,j} \sim T1EV\ (0)$.

Note MLM(1) and MLM(2) are often jointly abbreviated as $\epsilon_{i,j} \sim i.i.d.\ T1EV\ (0)$.

Theorem 2.2.1. *(Simple Logit Likelihood over Multiple Choice)* Suppose that *MLM(1)* and *MLM(2)* hold. Then,

$$\Pr\left(i \text{ chooses } j\right) = \frac{\exp\left(\mathbf{x}_j'\boldsymbol{\theta}\right)}{\sum_{k \in \mathcal{J}} \exp\left(\mathbf{x}_k'\boldsymbol{\theta}\right)}. \tag{2.2.4}$$

Proof. Let $u_{i,j} = \delta_j + \epsilon_{i,j}$, $u_{i,-j} = \max_{k \neq j}\left\{\delta_k + \epsilon_{i,k}\right\}$. Let $\delta_{-j} = \ln\left[\sum_{k \neq j} \exp\left(\delta_k\right)\right]$. From lemma 2.2.2, we know that $u_{i,-j} \sim T1EV\left(\delta_{-j}\right)$. Under MLM(1) and MLM(2), we have

$$\begin{aligned}
\Pr\left(\delta_j + \epsilon_{i,j} \geq \max_k\left\{\delta_k + \epsilon_{i,k}\right\}\right) &= \Pr\left(u_{i,j} \geq u_{i,-j}\right) \\
&= \Pr\left(u_{i,-j} - u_{i,j} \leq 0\right) \\
&= \frac{\exp\left(\delta_j\right)}{\exp\left(\delta_{-j}\right) + \exp\left(\delta_j\right)} \qquad (2.2.5) \\
&= \frac{\exp\left(\delta_j\right)}{\sum_{k \in \mathcal{J}} \exp\left(\delta_k\right)}.
\end{aligned}$$

Equation (2.2.5) is derived by applying equation (2.2.1) with $u = 0$. Substituting $\delta_k = \mathbf{x}_k'\boldsymbol{\theta}\ \forall k$, we get the desired result.[8] □

8. Consider the odds ratios of the choice set $\mathcal{J} = \{0, 1\}$ with $\delta_0 = \epsilon_{i,0}$, $\delta_1 = \mathbf{x}_1'\boldsymbol{\theta} + \epsilon_{i,1}$, where $\epsilon_{i,j} \sim$ i.i.d. $T1EV\ (0)$. Lemma 2.2.3 yields that $\epsilon_{i,1} - \epsilon_{i,0}$ follows standard logistic distribution.

It is straightforward from equation (2.2.3) that when $\mathcal{J} = \{0, 1\}$ and $\mathbf{x}_0 = \mathbf{0}$, the equation boils down to the logit likelihood.

Corollary. *(Simple Logit Likelihood with Nonzero Mean Parameter)* Suppose that *MLM(1)* holds. Suppose that *MLM(2)* is replaced with $\epsilon_{i,j} \sim T1EV\left(\alpha_j\right)$. Then,

$$\Pr\left(i \text{ Chooses } j\right) = \frac{\exp\left(\mathbf{x}_j'\boldsymbol{\theta} + \alpha_j\right)}{\sum_{k \in \mathcal{J}} \exp\left(\mathbf{x}_k'\boldsymbol{\theta} + \alpha_k\right)}.$$

The individual choice probability equation (2.2.4) derived from the i.i.d. additive type I extreme-value shocks on the preferences plays a central role in many contexts. The choice probability itself can be used as the likelihood for the maximum-likelihood estimation or it can be equated with data that approximate the individual choice probabilities. We study the models of the latter type in depth in section 3.2.

Now suppose that we have the individual choice data $\left\{y_{i,j}, \mathbf{x}_j\right\}_{i \in \mathcal{I}, j \in \mathcal{J}}$. The likelihood of observing the data is

$$L\left(\left\{y_{i,j}, \mathbf{x}_j\right\}_{i \in \mathcal{I}, j \in \mathcal{J}} | \boldsymbol{\theta}\right) = \prod_{i \in \mathcal{I}} \left\{\prod_{j \in \mathcal{J}} \Pr\left(i \text{ chooses } j\right)^{\mathbf{1}\left(i \text{ chooses } j\right)}\right\},$$

where $\Pr\left(i \text{ chooses } j\right)$ is as in equation (2.2.4). The log-likelihood and score function, which are required for the maximum-likelihood estimation, can be derived as usual. We emphasize that the model parameter $\boldsymbol{\theta}$ can be estimated using maximum likelihood only when δ_j in equation (2.2.2) contains no unknowns or unobservables. A more sophisticated method is required when an unobservable is included. We discuss some of those instances in section 2.3.4, and also in chapter 3.

2.2.3 *Independence of Irrelevant Alternatives and the Nested Logit Model*

Consider the ratio of simple logit choice probabilities:

$$\frac{\Pr\left(i \text{ chooses } j\right)}{\Pr\left(i \text{ chooses } k\right)} = \frac{\exp\left(\delta_j\right)}{\exp\left(\delta_k\right)} = \frac{\exp\left(\mathbf{x}_j'\boldsymbol{\theta}\right)}{\exp\left(\mathbf{x}_k'\boldsymbol{\theta}\right)}. \tag{2.2.6}$$

The ratio in equation (2.2.6), often referred to as the "odds ratio of choices j and k," is constant regardless of the average utility from other choices. The property is called the "independence of irrelevant alternatives (IIA) property," which is pioneered by Luce (1959). IIA substantially restricts the substitution pattern over the alternatives. We study further how and why IIA may not be desirable in section 3.2.3, in the context of demand estimation. What we want to emphasize at this point is that, given that the mean utility $\delta_j = \mathbf{x}_j'\boldsymbol{\theta}$, the individual choice probability equation (2.2.4) is the only legitimate choice probability equation that satisfies equation (2.2.6) for each alternative in $\mathcal{J}$ and sums to 1. In that sense, the individual choice probability equation (2.2.4) can also be derived from (2.2.6) instead of the additive, idiosyncratic, type I, extreme-value distributed shocks.

One might question why the specific functional form of the ratios between the exponentiated mean utilities are used to characterize the IIA. In principle, any function that satisfies the following three conditions can be used instead of $\exp(\delta_j)$: (1) the function maps the entire real line onto the positive real numbers, (2) the function is strictly increasing in its domain, and (3) the function does not take δ_k for $k \neq j$ as its argument. The exponential function is the simplest elementary function that satisfies these three conditions. Notably, when the idiosyncratic preference shocks $\epsilon_{i,j}$ are i.i.d. across alternative j, then it would be possible to obtain a different functional form than the $\exp(\cdot)$ used in the characterization in equation (2.2.6). Put another way, the source of IIA is not the shape of type I extreme-value distribution, but the i.i.d. preference shocks across alternatives.

IIA may not be very appealing in the multiple discrete-choice contexts where a third alternative may affect the choice-probability ratios of the two alternatives under consideration. A popular workaround in the literature when individual choice-level data are available is nesting the choice set and modeling the individual's choice in multiple stages. Suppose that the choice set $\mathcal{J}$ can be divided into S disjoint subsets, which we call "modules." Each module is denoted by $\mathcal{B}_s$, where $s \in \{1, 2, \ldots, S\}$. If the joint distribution of $\{\epsilon_{i,j}\}_{j\in\mathcal{J}}$ takes the form

$$F\left(\{\epsilon_j\}_{j\in\mathcal{J}}\right) = \exp\left\{-\sum_{s=1}^{S} \alpha_s \left[\sum_{j\in\mathcal{B}_s} \exp\left(-\rho_s^{-1}\epsilon_j\right)\right]^{\rho_s}\right\},$$

it can be shown that the individual choice probabilities have the following closed-form formula:

$$\Pr\left(i \text{ chooses } \mathcal{B}_s\right) = \frac{\alpha_s \left(\sum_{k\in\mathcal{B}_s} \exp\left(\rho_s^{-1}\delta_k\right)\right)^{\rho_s}}{\sum_{\tau=1}^{S} \alpha_\tau \left(\sum_{k\in\mathcal{B}_\tau} \exp\left(\rho_\tau^{-1}\delta_k\right)\right)^{\rho_\tau}} \tag{2.2.7}$$

$$\Pr\left(i \text{ chooses } j | i \text{ chooses } \mathcal{B}_s\right) = \frac{\exp\left(\rho_s^{-1}\delta_j\right)}{\sum_{k\in\mathcal{B}_s}\exp\left(\rho_s^{-1}\delta_k\right)} \tag{2.2.8}$$

$$\Pr\left(i \text{ chooses } j\right) = \Pr\left(i \text{ chooses } j | i \text{ chooses } \mathcal{B}_s\right) \Pr\left(i \text{ chooses } \mathcal{B}_s\right). \tag{2.2.9}$$

$\{\alpha_s, \rho_s\}_{s=1}^S$ are the parameters to be estimated. The nesting structures can also be extended to more than two stages in an analogous way.

Given the utility specification $\delta_j = \mathbf{x}_j'\boldsymbol{\theta} + \epsilon_{i,j}$, the nested logit model in equations (2.2.7)–(2.2.9) can be estimated either by the full maximum likelihood or by the two-stage method. Although both methods yield the consistent estimates, the asymptotic variance formulas are different. For further discussions of implementing nested logit with the two-stage methods, see, e.g., McFadden (1981).

Nested logit allows a more complex choice structure than the simple logit, but two major weaknesses remain in the model in equations (2.2.7)–(2.2.9). First, it does not exhibit IIA across modules, but it still exhibits IIA within a module. Next, to implement the nested logit model, the econometrician has to impose prior knowledge on the choice structures, and thus on the composition of modules.

Another possible way to get around of the IIA property is the correlated probit. A benefit of using the correlated probit is that the Gaussian error term naturally allows the correlation of errors across alternatives. However, it leads to greater computational burden than the simple logit because the likelihood has no closed-form solution, and it usually involves evaluating the integral numerically. Furthermore, it is often questioned what variation in data identifies the cross-alternative covariance term of the idiosyncratic preference shocks. These are the major reasons why the somewhat restrictive simple logit model is still the major workhorse in practice.

2.2.4 Discussion

Historically, the development of the simple logit and nested logit models has gone in the opposite direction of our presentation. The type I extreme value distribution is carefully reverse engineered to yield the odds ratio of the form in equation (2.2.4). McFadden (1981) and Cardell (1997) generalized the simple logit model to a broader class called the generalized extreme-value class models.[9] The generalized extreme-value class choice models are often referred to as the "RUM model" to emphasize the connection between the resulting choice

9. The generalized extreme-value class includes nested logit model.

probabilities and the axioms of stochastic choice, which is a set of axioms used to rationalize a stochastic choice.

The simple logit model over the multiple alternatives examined thus far is often referred to as the "conditional logit model" in the literature. There is another class of simple logit model, referred to as the "multinomial logit model." The multinomial logit likelihood is given by

$$\Pr\left(i \text{ Chooses } j\right) = \frac{\exp\left(\mathbf{x}'\boldsymbol{\theta}_j + \alpha_j\right)}{1 + \sum_{k=2}^{J} \exp\left(\mathbf{x}'\boldsymbol{\theta}_k + \alpha_k\right)}.$$

Note that the key differences between the multinomial logit model and the conditional logit model are (1) whether the choice likelihood contains the attribute vector that varies over alternatives and (2) whether the slopes are varying over alternatives.

Anderson, de Palma, and Thisse (1992) presents a classic reference to the theory of static discrete choice, which provides an extensive treatment of establishing the connection between the discrete choice framework and differentiated-product demand framework. We will study some aspects of the discrete choice framework as an aggregate consumer-demand framework in chapter 3. Train (2009) provides a detailed treatment of the microfoundation and estimation of discrete-choice models.

2.3 Single-Agent Dynamic Discrete Choice

Economic agents exhibit forward-looking behavior when the current state variables affect the current and future payoffs and the payoff streams change with respect to accumulation flow on the state variables. In this section, we study single-agent dynamic discrete-choice models, a combination of discrete choice with forward-looking economic agents. We focus on the setups in which the modeled dynamics are stationary, so the value function boils down to a two-period Bellman equation.

We first study the method of Rust (1987)'s bus-engine-replacement problem, which has become the standard baseline dynamic discrete-choice framework applied to discrete-choice data. Then we discuss the key ideas of Hotz and Miller (1993); Hotz et al. (1994), which is based on inverting the conditional choice probabilities. Then we study the nested pseudo-likelihood method by Aguirregabiria and Mira (2002), which is based on finding the dual problem of the value function fixed-point equations in the conditional choice probability space. Finally, we overview Arcidiacono and Miller (2011)'s method to accommodate unobserved state variables into Rust (1987)'s framework. The single-agent dynamic discrete-choice framework studied in this section will be extended and applied to richer settings in the later chapters of this book.

2.3.1 Full-Solution Method with Fixed-Point Iteration

2.3.1.1 FORMULATION

In this subsection, we study the full maximum-likelihood method developed by Rust (1987). Consider an infinite-horizon stochastic stationary dynamic utility-maximization problem, which has a two-period Bellman equation representation. The agent maximizes the discounted sum of the utilities. Let $\mathcal{J} = \{1, \ldots, J\}$ be the set of alternatives, where the agent's action $a_t \in \mathcal{J}$.[10] Let $\mathbf{s}_t$ ($\in \mathcal{S}$) be a state vector that has both an observed component x_t ($\in \mathcal{X}$) and an unobserved component $\boldsymbol{\epsilon}_t \equiv \left(\epsilon_{j,t}\right)_{j\in\mathcal{J}}$ to the econometrician; $\boldsymbol{\epsilon}_t$ is observed to the agent. That is, the agent fully observes the realization of $\boldsymbol{\epsilon}_t$ before she takes the action in each period t. We assume that $\mathcal{X}$, the support of x_t, is finite, that is, $\mathcal{X} = \{1, 2, \ldots, X\}$.[11] For each j, t pair, a corresponding observed component and the unobserved utility shock exist, and thus the state vector is $\mathbf{s}_t = \left(x_t, \epsilon_{1,t}, \ldots, \epsilon_{J,t}\right)$. The agent solves

$$\max_{\{a_t\}_{t=1}^{\infty}} \mathbb{E}\left[\sum_{t=1}^{\infty} \beta^{t-1} u\left(x_t, a_t, \boldsymbol{\epsilon}_t; \boldsymbol{\theta}\right)\right], \tag{2.3.1}$$

where $\beta \in (0, 1)$ is the discount factor, which has to be a prior knowledge of the econometrician.[12] Two sets of parameter vectors, $\boldsymbol{\theta}$ and $\boldsymbol{\varphi}$, exist. $\boldsymbol{\theta}$ is the parameter vector that governs the utility function of the agent, and $\boldsymbol{\varphi}$ is the parameter vector that governs the state-transition probability $\Pr\left(x_{t+1}, \boldsymbol{\epsilon}_{t+1} | x_t, \boldsymbol{\epsilon}_t, a_t; \boldsymbol{\varphi}\right)$. Both parameter vectors $(\boldsymbol{\theta}, \boldsymbol{\varphi})$ are known to the agent, the consistent estimation of which is our goal. The following assumptions on the unobserved state vector are imposed henceforth.

10. Rust (1987) considered only the binary choice set, but we allow for finite alternatives. The extension from binary to finite alternatives is straightforward, as we studied before in sections 2.1 and 2.2.

11. The discrete state space assumption is useful not only because it simplifies the illustration, but also because it simplifies the estimation algorithm. We note that the assumption can be relaxed to the compact support with the continuous value function. However, an approximation has to be taken during the estimation when the state space is continuous. Such an approximation may complicate the estimation algorithm and incur an additional source of error that needs to be accounted for during the statistical inference on the estimates.

12. Usually, β is not separately identified from the data. We discuss this point later in section 2.3.5.

DDC(1) (Additive Separability of Preferences in $\epsilon_{j,t}$) Let $u\left(\mathbf{s}_t, a_t = j; \boldsymbol{\theta}\right)$ be the utility of choosing action j at state $\mathbf{s}_t$. Then,

$$u\left(\mathbf{s}_t, a_t = j; \boldsymbol{\theta}\right) = \bar{u}_j\left(x_t; \boldsymbol{\theta}\right) + \epsilon_{j,t}$$

and $\bar{u}_j\left(x_t; \boldsymbol{\theta}\right)$ is bounded and monotone in x_t.

DDC(2) ($\boldsymbol{\epsilon}_t$ is i.i.d. over t) $\forall \boldsymbol{\epsilon}_t \left(\in \mathbb{R}^J\right)$,

$$\Pr\left(\boldsymbol{\epsilon}_{t+1} | \boldsymbol{\epsilon}_t\right) = \Pr\left(\boldsymbol{\epsilon}_{t+1}\right).$$

DDC(3) (Conditional Independence of State-Transition Probabilities) Given (x_t, a_t) observed, $x_{t+1} \perp\!\!\!\perp (\boldsymbol{\epsilon}_t, \boldsymbol{\epsilon}_{t+1})$, which implies

$$\begin{aligned}\Pr\left(x_{t+1}, \boldsymbol{\epsilon}_{t+1} | x_t, \boldsymbol{\epsilon}_t, a_t; \boldsymbol{\varphi}\right) &\equiv \Pr\left(\boldsymbol{\epsilon}_{t+1} | x_{t+1}, x_t, \boldsymbol{\epsilon}_t, a_t; \boldsymbol{\varphi}\right) \Pr\left(x_{t+1} | x_t, \boldsymbol{\epsilon}_t, a_t; \boldsymbol{\varphi}\right) \\ &= \Pr\left(\boldsymbol{\epsilon}_{t+1}\right) \Pr\left(x_{t+1} | x_t, a_t; \boldsymbol{\varphi}\right).\end{aligned}$$

Roughly stated, the assumptions are imposed to restrict the influence of $\boldsymbol{\epsilon}_t$ on $(x_{t+1}, \boldsymbol{\epsilon}_{t+1})$ such that $\boldsymbol{\epsilon}_t$ affects x_{t+1} only through a_t, and it does not affect $\boldsymbol{\epsilon}_{t+1}$ at all. It allows us to derive a conditional choice probability of the form later shown in equation (2.3.2).

As in the static discrete-choice problem, our goal is to derive the closed-form likelihood using the properties of the i.i.d. type I extreme-value, distributed utility shocks. To that end, we expect the conditional choice probability that action j is chosen in period t to be

$$\Pr\left(a_t = j | x_t; \boldsymbol{\theta}, \boldsymbol{\varphi}\right) = \frac{\exp\left(\bar{v}_j\left(x_t; \boldsymbol{\theta}, \boldsymbol{\varphi}\right)\right)}{\sum_{k \in \mathcal{J}} \exp\left(\bar{v}_k\left(x_t; \boldsymbol{\theta}, \boldsymbol{\varphi}\right)\right)} \tag{2.3.2}$$

$$= \frac{\exp\left(\bar{u}_j\left(x_t; \boldsymbol{\theta}\right) + \beta \mathbb{E}\left[v\left(x_{t+1}, \boldsymbol{\epsilon}_{t+1}; \boldsymbol{\theta}, \boldsymbol{\varphi}\right) | a_t = j, x_t, \boldsymbol{\epsilon}_t; \boldsymbol{\varphi}\right]\right)}{\sum_{k \in \mathcal{J}} \exp\left(\bar{u}_k\left(x_t; \boldsymbol{\theta}\right) + \beta \mathbb{E}\left[v\left(x_{t+1}, \boldsymbol{\epsilon}_{t+1}; \boldsymbol{\theta}, \boldsymbol{\varphi}\right) | a_t = k, x_t, \boldsymbol{\epsilon}_t; \boldsymbol{\varphi}\right]\right)}, \tag{2.3.3}$$

where $\bar{v}_j(\cdot)$ is the choice-specific expected value function, and $\bar{u}_j(\cdot)$ is the choice-specific expected utility function. The likelihood of observing the single time-series data $\{(x_t, a_t)\}_{t \in \mathcal{T}}$, where $\mathcal{T} = \{1, 2, \ldots, T\}$, is

$$\prod_{t=2}^{T} \left\{ \prod_{j \in \mathcal{J}} \Pr\left(a_t = j | x_t; \boldsymbol{\theta}, \boldsymbol{\varphi}\right)^{\mathbf{1}(a_t = j)} \right\} \Pr\left(x_t | x_{t-1}, a_{t-1}; \boldsymbol{\varphi}\right), \tag{2.3.4}$$

where $\Pr(x_{t+1}|x_t, a_t; \boldsymbol{\varphi})$ is the stationary transition probability of the state variables. We assume $\Pr(x_{t+1}|x_t, a_t; \boldsymbol{\varphi})$ is known to the econometrician up to parameter $\boldsymbol{\varphi}$. As we shall see next, $\Pr(x_{t+1}|x_t, a_t; \boldsymbol{\varphi})$ boils down to a state-transition matrix when $\mathcal{X}$ and $\mathcal{J}$ are both discrete and finite, in which case $\boldsymbol{\varphi}$ is simply the elements of the state-transition matrix.

2.3.1.2 INFORMATION AND TIMELINE

We summarize the informational assumption and the timeline of the decision here. The agent and the econometrician both know the shapes of $u(x_t, a_t, \boldsymbol{\epsilon}_t; \boldsymbol{\theta})$, $\Pr(\boldsymbol{\epsilon}_{t+1})$, and $\Pr(x_{t+1}|x_t, a_t; \boldsymbol{\varphi})$, respectively. β is also known to both the agent and the econometrician. The value of $(\boldsymbol{\theta}, \boldsymbol{\varphi})$ and the realization of $\boldsymbol{\epsilon}_t$ are not known to the econometrician but are known to the agent. At the beginning of each period t, the agent observes x_t and the full realization of $\boldsymbol{\epsilon}_t$ and then makes decision a_t.

2.3.1.3 THE BELLMAN-EQUATION REPRESENTATION

Assumptions DDC(1) through DDC(3) yield the stationary, Markov state-transition probability $\Pr(x_{t+1}|x_t, a_t; \boldsymbol{\varphi})$. Under the regularity conditions, including the infinite time horizons and $\beta < 1$, Blackwell's theorem asserts that a stationary and Markov decision rule exists that depends only on $(x_t, \boldsymbol{\epsilon}_t)$, and such a decision rule is unique.[13]

In addition to DDC(2), assume that $\epsilon_{j,t}$ follows the mean-zero i.i.d. type I extreme value distribution.[14] Assuming that the regularity conditions for the stochastic dynamic programming are satisfied,[15] the problem has a Bellman-equation representation:

$$\begin{aligned} & v(x_t, \boldsymbol{\epsilon}_t; \boldsymbol{\theta}, \boldsymbol{\varphi}) \\ & \quad = \max_{a_t \in \mathcal{J}} \{u(x_t, a_t, \boldsymbol{\epsilon}_t; \boldsymbol{\theta}) + \beta \mathbb{E}[v(x_{t+1}, \boldsymbol{\epsilon}_{t+1}; \boldsymbol{\theta}, \boldsymbol{\varphi}) | a_t, x_t, \boldsymbol{\epsilon}_t; \boldsymbol{\varphi}]\} \end{aligned} \tag{2.3.5}$$

13. Blackwell's theorem states the sufficient conditions for an operator to be a contraction mapping. The conditions, adapted to our context, are such that (1) the expected value function $\mathbb{E}[v(x_t, \boldsymbol{\epsilon}_t; \boldsymbol{\theta}, \boldsymbol{\varphi})]$ is monotone in x_t, and (2) there exists a positive number κ such that

$$u(x_t, a_t, \boldsymbol{\epsilon}_t; \boldsymbol{\theta}) + \beta \mathbb{E}[v(x_{t+1}, \boldsymbol{\epsilon}_{t+1}; \boldsymbol{\theta}, \boldsymbol{\varphi}) | a_t, x_t, \boldsymbol{\epsilon}_t; \boldsymbol{\varphi}] \le u(x_t, a_t, \boldsymbol{\epsilon}_t; \boldsymbol{\theta}) + \beta\kappa$$

for a $\beta < 1$. (i) follows by the assumed monotonicity of the per-period utility. Point (2) follows by the fact that per-period utility being bounded, and hence, the maximized value of equation (2.3.1) is also finite. For readers interested in mathematical details, see, for example, Rust (1994) and the references therein.

14. It does not mean the location parameter zero. Recall that the location parameter zero type I extreme-value distribution has mean$\approx$ 0.5772.

15. These include the stationarity of the transition probability among others. For details, see, for instance, Stokey and Lucas (1989).

$$= \max_{a_t \in \mathcal{J}} \left\{ u\left(x_t, a_t, \boldsymbol{\epsilon}_t; \boldsymbol{\theta}\right) + \beta \int \int v\left(x_{t+1}, \boldsymbol{\epsilon}_{t+1}; \boldsymbol{\theta}, \boldsymbol{\varphi}\right) \Pr\left(d\boldsymbol{\epsilon}_{t+1}\right) \right.$$

$$\left. \Pr\left(dx_{t+1} | x_t, a_t; \boldsymbol{\varphi}\right) \right\} \tag{2.3.6}$$

$$= \max_{j \in \mathcal{J}} \left\{ \bar{u}_j\left(x_t; \boldsymbol{\theta}\right) + \epsilon_{j,t} + \beta \int \int v\left(x_{t+1}, \boldsymbol{\epsilon}_{t+1}; \boldsymbol{\theta}, \boldsymbol{\varphi}\right) \Pr\left(d\boldsymbol{\epsilon}_{t+1}\right) \right.$$

$$\left. \Pr\left(dx_{t+1} | x_t, a_t = j; \boldsymbol{\varphi}\right) \right\} \tag{2.3.7}$$

$$\equiv \max_{j \in \mathcal{J}} \left\{ \bar{v}_j\left(x_t; \boldsymbol{\theta}, \boldsymbol{\varphi}\right) + \epsilon_{j,t} \right\}. \tag{2.3.8}$$

Note that we invoked DDC(3) and DDC(2) in equation (2.3.6), and DDC(1) in equation (2.3.7). Equation (2.3.8) follows from defining $\bar{v}_j\left(x_t; \boldsymbol{\theta}, \boldsymbol{\varphi}\right)$ as the deterministic part of the choice-specific value function.[16] Then the mean-zero i.i.d. type I extreme-value assumption on $\epsilon_{j,t}$ yields

$$\bar{v}_j\left(x_t; \boldsymbol{\theta}, \boldsymbol{\varphi}\right)$$

$$= \bar{u}_j\left(x_t; \boldsymbol{\theta}\right) + \beta \int \int v\left(x_{t+1}, \boldsymbol{\epsilon}_{t+1}; \boldsymbol{\theta}, \boldsymbol{\varphi}\right) \Pr\left(d\boldsymbol{\epsilon}_{t+1}\right) \Pr\left(dx_{t+1} | x_t, a_t = j, \boldsymbol{\varphi}\right)$$

$$= \bar{u}_j\left(x_t; \boldsymbol{\theta}\right) + \beta \int \int \max_{a_{t+1} \in \mathcal{J}} \left\{ v_j\left(x_{t+1}, \epsilon_{j,t+1}; \boldsymbol{\theta}, \boldsymbol{\varphi}\right) \right\} \Pr\left(d\boldsymbol{\epsilon}_{t+1}\right)$$

$$\Pr\left(dx_{t+1} | x_t, a_t = j, \boldsymbol{\varphi}\right)$$

$$= \bar{u}_j\left(x_t; \boldsymbol{\theta}\right) + \beta \int \ln\left(\sum_{k \in \mathcal{J}} \exp \bar{v}_k\left(x_{t+1}; \boldsymbol{\theta}, \boldsymbol{\varphi}\right) \right) \Pr\left(dx_{t+1} | x_t, a_t = j, \boldsymbol{\varphi}\right). \tag{2.3.9}$$

Equation (2.3.9) follows from the corollary to lemma 2.2.2 and is a fixed-point equation; solving it yields the value of $\bar{v}_j\left(x_t; \boldsymbol{\theta}, \boldsymbol{\varphi}\right)$ for each possible x_t given $(\boldsymbol{\theta}, \boldsymbol{\varphi})$. To see this fact more clearly, consider the stacked matrix form of equation (2.3.9)

16. The existing literature often denote the choice-specific value function as $\bar{v}_j\left(x_t; \boldsymbol{\theta}, \boldsymbol{\varphi}\right) + \epsilon_{j,t} - \bar{u}_j\left(x_t; \boldsymbol{\theta}\right)$ in our notation. If one wants to follow the conventional notation, the conditional choice probabilities and the fixed-point equation that we give next should be adjusted accordingly. In particular, the fixed-point equation should be altered to numerically solve for the functions $\bar{w}\left(\cdot; \boldsymbol{\theta}, \boldsymbol{\varphi}\right)$ in our notation. This was the original algorithm of Rust (1987), and it was followed by many others.

over the alternatives $\mathcal{J}$ and the possible states $\mathcal{X}$:

$$\operatorname{vec}\begin{pmatrix} \bar{v}_1(1;\boldsymbol{\theta},\boldsymbol{\varphi}) & \cdots & \bar{v}_J(1;\boldsymbol{\theta},\boldsymbol{\varphi}) \\ \vdots & \ddots & \vdots \\ \bar{v}_1(X;\boldsymbol{\theta},\boldsymbol{\varphi}) & \cdots & \bar{v}_J(X;\boldsymbol{\theta},\boldsymbol{\varphi}) \end{pmatrix} = \operatorname{vec}\begin{pmatrix} \bar{u}_1(1;\boldsymbol{\theta}) & \cdots & \bar{u}_J(1;\boldsymbol{\theta}) \\ \vdots & \ddots & \vdots \\ \bar{u}_1(X;\boldsymbol{\theta}) & \cdots & \bar{u}_J(X;\boldsymbol{\theta}) \end{pmatrix}$$
$$+\beta\mathbf{P}(x_{t+1}|x_t,a_t;\boldsymbol{\varphi})\operatorname{vec}\begin{pmatrix} \bar{w}(1;\boldsymbol{\theta},\boldsymbol{\varphi}) & \cdots & \bar{w}(1;\boldsymbol{\theta},\boldsymbol{\varphi}) \\ \vdots & \ddots & \vdots \\ \bar{w}(X;\boldsymbol{\theta},\boldsymbol{\varphi}) & \cdots & \bar{w}(X;\boldsymbol{\theta},\boldsymbol{\varphi}) \end{pmatrix},^{17} \quad (2.3.10)$$

where $\mathbf{P}(x_{t+1}|x_t,a_t;\boldsymbol{\varphi})$ returns the state-transition probability matrix given (x_t,a_t),[18] and $\bar{w}(x_t;\boldsymbol{\theta},\boldsymbol{\varphi})=\ln\left(\sum_{k\in\mathcal{J}}\exp\bar{v}_k(x_t;\boldsymbol{\theta},\boldsymbol{\varphi})\right)$. Because $\beta<1$, the fixed-point equation (2.3.10) has a solution, which is unique as well. Solving equation (2.3.10) for $\bar{v}_j(x_t;\boldsymbol{\theta},\boldsymbol{\varphi})$ and plugging back into equation (2.3.4) for each $(\boldsymbol{\theta},\boldsymbol{\varphi})$ fully specifies the likelihood.

Note that the additive i.i.d. type I extreme-value assumption simplifies the derivation of the log-likelihood in the following equation (2.3.11) substantially in two distinct aspects: (1) the conditional choice probability equation (2.3.2) has such a simple closed-form solution and (2) the expected value function in equation (2.3.9) also has a simple closed form.

2.3.1.4 ESTIMATION ALGORITHMS: NESTED FIXED POINT (NFP) AND MATHEMATICAL PROGRAMMING WITH EQUILIBRIUM CONSTRAINTS (MPEC)

The goal of maximum-likelihood estimation is to find the parameter values $(\boldsymbol{\theta},\boldsymbol{\varphi})$ such that

$$\left(\hat{\boldsymbol{\theta}},\hat{\boldsymbol{\varphi}}\right)=\arg\max_{(\boldsymbol{\theta},\boldsymbol{\varphi})}\prod_{t=2}^{T}\left\{\prod_{j\in\mathcal{J}}\Pr\left(a_t=j|x_t;\boldsymbol{\theta},\boldsymbol{\varphi}\right)^{\mathbf{1}(a_t=j)}\right\}\Pr\left(x_t|x_{t-1},a_{t-1};\boldsymbol{\varphi}\right)$$

17. vec $(\cdot)$ operator vectorizes a matrix to a column vector.
18. This should be a sort of block-diagonal matrix, such that

$$\begin{pmatrix} \mathbf{P}(x_{t+1}|x_t,a_t=1;\boldsymbol{\varphi}) & \mathbf{O} & \cdots & \mathbf{O} \\ \mathbf{O} & \mathbf{P}(x_{t+1}|x_t,a_t=2;\boldsymbol{\varphi}) & \cdots & \mathbf{O} \\ \vdots & \vdots & \ddots & \vdots \\ \mathbf{O} & \mathbf{O} & \cdots & \mathbf{P}(x_{t+1}|x_t,a_t=J;\boldsymbol{\varphi}) \end{pmatrix},$$

where each $\mathbf{P}(x_{t+1}|x_t,a_t=j;\boldsymbol{\varphi})$ is a $J\times X$ matrix.

$$= \arg\max_{(\boldsymbol{\theta},\boldsymbol{\varphi})} \sum_{t=2}^{T} \left\{ \sum_{j\in\mathcal{J}} \mathbf{1}\left(a_t = j\right) \ln \Pr\left(a_t = j | x_t; \boldsymbol{\theta}, \boldsymbol{\varphi}\right) \right\}$$

$$+ \sum_{t=2}^{T} \ln \Pr\left(x_t | x_{t-1}, a_{t-1}; \boldsymbol{\varphi}\right)$$

$$= \arg\max_{(\boldsymbol{\theta},\boldsymbol{\varphi})} \sum_{t=2}^{T} \left\{ \sum_{j\in\mathcal{J}} \mathbf{1}\left(a_t = j\right) \ln \left(\frac{\exp\left(\bar{v}_j\left(x_t; \boldsymbol{\theta}, \boldsymbol{\varphi}\right)\right)}{\sum_{k\in\mathcal{J}} \exp\left(\bar{v}_k\left(x_t; \boldsymbol{\theta}, \boldsymbol{\varphi}\right)\right)} \right) \right\}$$

$$+ \sum_{t=2}^{T} \ln \Pr\left(x_t | x_{t-1}, a_{t-1}; \boldsymbol{\varphi}\right) \tag{2.3.11}$$

holds. We emphasize again that $\Pr\left(x_t | x_{t-1}, a_{t-1}; \boldsymbol{\varphi}\right)$ is known up to $\boldsymbol{\varphi}$.

The original nested fixed-point (NFP) algorithm suggested by Rust (1987) is based on computing the likelihood value $\Pr\left(a_t = j | x_t; \boldsymbol{\theta}, \boldsymbol{\varphi}\right)$ at each guess of $(\boldsymbol{\theta}, \boldsymbol{\varphi})$ by solving the set of fixed-point equations (2.3.10). The inner loop of NFP consists of iterating over the values of $\bar{v}_j\left(x_t; \boldsymbol{\theta}, \boldsymbol{\varphi}\right)$ for a given guess of $(\boldsymbol{\theta}, \boldsymbol{\varphi})$. The outer loop consists of guessing a new value of $(\boldsymbol{\theta}, \boldsymbol{\varphi})$ to maximize the objective function. As one may easily imagine, the process is computationally very intensive, especially when β is close to 1 and the size of the state space is large.[19]

Recent development of modern derivative-based numerical optimizers provided another solution that may prove advantageous. The key idea is to convert the unconstrained likelihood maximization problem in equation (2.3.11) to the constrained maximization problem by adding more parameters $\left\{\bar{v}_j\left(x\right)\right\}_{\forall j\in\mathcal{J}, x\in\mathcal{X}}$ that the optimizer may freely adjust. To that end, the problem may be converted to

$$\arg \max_{\left(\boldsymbol{\theta},\boldsymbol{\varphi},\left\{\bar{v}_j(x)\right\}_{\forall j\in\mathcal{J},x\in\mathcal{X}}\right)} \sum_{t=2}^{T} \left\{ \sum_{j\in\mathcal{J}} \mathbf{1}\left(a_t = j\right) \ln \left(\frac{\exp\left(\bar{v}_j\left(x_t = x\right)\right)}{\sum_{k\in\mathcal{J}} \exp\left(\bar{v}_k\left(x_t = x\right)\right)} \right) \right\}$$

$$+ \sum_{t=2}^{T} \ln \Pr\left(x_t | x_{t-1}, a_{t-1}; \boldsymbol{\varphi}\right)$$

$$\text{s.t.} \qquad \bar{v}_j\left(x_t = x\right) = \bar{u}_j\left(x_t = x; \boldsymbol{\theta}\right) + \beta \int \ln \left(\sum_{k\in\mathcal{J}} \exp \bar{v}_k\left(x_{t+1} = x'\right) \right)$$

$$\Pr\left(dx_{t+1} = x' | x_t = x, a_t = j; \boldsymbol{\varphi}\right) \qquad \forall j \in \mathcal{J}, x, x' \in \mathcal{X},$$

19. Recall that the fixed-point equation is the contraction mapping of modulus β.

which yields the same solution as equation (2.3.11). This approach is referred to as mathematical programming with equilibrium constraints (MPEC), developed by Su and Judd (2012). MPEC conducts the maximum-likelihood optimization in one step, which does not require iterating over inner and outer loops. This removes numerical errors of the inner loop that propagate to the outer loop. Notice the number of control variables has drastically increased because $\bar{v}_j\ (x_t = x)$ are treated as free parameters, which the optimizer can adjust. But this does not necessarily increase computation time, and in fact it can even reduce it, sometimes drastically. The speed advantage of MPEC comes from not iterating the fixed-point equation at every guess of $(\boldsymbol{\theta}, \boldsymbol{\varphi})$. Unlike in the NFP algorithm, the fixed-point equation has to be satisfied only at the optimum, and modern numerical optimizers allow constraint violations during the trajectory. Su and Judd (2012) report that the speed advantage can be an order of 10^3. That being said, Iskhakov et al. (2016) report that the NFP algorithms combined with Newton-Kantorovich iterations can be as fast as MPEC.[20] Finding a faster and more reliable algorithm for this type of problem is an ongoing area of research. We will revisit the use of this constrained optimization approach in section 3.2.2.3 of chapter 3, in the context of demand estimation.

2.3.2 *Estimation with Conditional Choice Probability Inversion*

2.3.2.1 CHOICE PROBABILITY INVERSION

Evaluating the fixed-point equation can be very intensive. The choice probability inversion theorem and the estimators for finite-horizon models were developed by Hotz and Miller (1993). The major advantage of their method is that evaluating the fixed-point equation may not be necessary at all. We review a simplified version here to illustrate this point.

Recall the conditional choice probability equation (2.3.2) under the type I extreme-value assumption:

$$\Pr\left(a_t = j | x_t; \boldsymbol{\theta}, \boldsymbol{\varphi}\right) = \frac{\exp\left(\bar{v}_j\left(x_t; \boldsymbol{\theta}, \boldsymbol{\varphi}\right)\right)}{\sum_{k \in \mathcal{J}} \exp\left(\bar{v}_k\left(x_t; \boldsymbol{\theta}, \boldsymbol{\varphi}\right)\right)}. \tag{2.3.12}$$

The major challenge associated with this conditional choice probability equation is the difficulty and computational intensity of estimating the continuation values $\mathbb{E}\left[v\left(x_{t+1}, \epsilon_{t+1}; \boldsymbol{\theta}, \boldsymbol{\varphi}\right) | a_t = k, x_t, \epsilon_t; \boldsymbol{\varphi}\right]$ for each possible choice k.

20. See Iskhakov et al. (2016) for details about Newton-Kantorovich iterations.

The innovation of Hotz and Miller (1993) comes from the observation that a sample analog of $\Pr\left(a_t = j|x_t; \boldsymbol{\theta}, \boldsymbol{\varphi}\right)$ can be observed from the data under the stationarity assumption. Given that a sufficiently long time series of choices is observed, those conditional choice probabilities can be approximated from data. Denote $\hat{\Pr}\left(a_t = j|x_t\right)$ and $\hat{v}_j\left(x_t\right)$ to be the sample analog of $\Pr\left(a_t = j|x_t; \boldsymbol{\theta}, \boldsymbol{\varphi}\right)$ and $\bar{v}_j\left(x_t; \boldsymbol{\theta}, \boldsymbol{\varphi}\right)$, respectively.[21,22] Then, we can formulate a sample analog of equation (2.3.12) as

$$\hat{\Pr}\left(a_t = j|x_t\right) = \frac{\exp\left(\hat{v}_j\left(x_t\right)\right)}{\sum_{k\in\mathcal{J}} \exp\left(\hat{v}_k\left(x_t\right)\right)}.$$

Denote J as the reference choice, or the outside option, of which the choice-specific expected value $\bar{v}_J\left(x_t; \boldsymbol{\theta}, \boldsymbol{\varphi}\right)$ is normalized to 0. We have

$$\ln\left(\frac{\hat{\Pr}\left(a_t = j|x_t\right)}{\hat{\Pr}\left(a_t = J|x_t\right)}\right) = \hat{v}_j\left(x_t\right) - 0 \tag{2.3.13}$$

for each possible state x_t. This reveals the values of $\hat{v}_j\left(x_t\right)$ relative to $\hat{v}_J\left(x_t\right)$ for each j, which will be taken as data during the estimation. Note that the level of $\hat{v}_j\left(x_t\right)$'s cannot be identified because the conditional choice probability is invariant to the uniform location shift of $\hat{v}_j\left(x_t\right)$. We return to the identification problem of these models in section 2.3.5.

2.3.2.2 MAXIMUM-LIKELIHOOD AND MINIMUM DISTANCE ESTIMATORS

To obtain $\bar{v}_j\left(x_t; \boldsymbol{\theta}, \boldsymbol{\varphi}\right) - \bar{v}_J\left(x_t; \boldsymbol{\theta}, \boldsymbol{\varphi}\right)$, one possibility is to iterate the value function once by plugging $\hat{v}_j\left(x_t\right)$ from equation (2.3.13) back into the expectations. It gives

$$\begin{aligned}
&\bar{\hat{v}}_j\left(x_t; \boldsymbol{\theta}, \boldsymbol{\varphi}\right) - \bar{\hat{v}}_J\left(x_t; \boldsymbol{\theta}, \boldsymbol{\varphi}\right) \\
&= \bar{u}_j\left(x_t; \boldsymbol{\theta}\right) - \bar{u}_J\left(x_t; \boldsymbol{\theta}\right) \\
&\quad + \beta \int \ln\left(\sum_{k\in\mathcal{J}} \exp \hat{v}_k\left(x_{t+1}\right)\right) \left\{\Pr\left(dx_{t+1}|x_t, a_t = j, \boldsymbol{\varphi}\right)\right. \\
&\quad \left. - \Pr\left(dx_{t+1}|x_t, a_t = J, \boldsymbol{\varphi}\right)\right\}.
\end{aligned} \tag{2.3.14}$$

21. Note that $\hat{\Pr}\left(a_t = j|x_t\right)$ and $\hat{v}_j\left(x_t\right)$ are no longer functions of $\boldsymbol{\theta}, \boldsymbol{\varphi}$, because we consider them to be directly observable from data.

22. Several possibilities exist for forming these, including a simple frequency estimator and Nadaraya-Watson-type kernel-smoothing estimator.

Then, one can proceed with either maximum likelihood or with moment matching and minimum distance estimation. The maximum-likelihood estimator is

$$\left(\hat{\theta},\hat{\varphi}\right)=\arg\max_{\theta,\varphi}\prod_{t}\prod_{j\in\mathcal{J}}\left\{\frac{\exp\left(\bar{\hat{v}}_j\left(x_t;\theta,\varphi\right)\right)}{\sum_{k\in\mathcal{J}}\exp\left(\bar{\hat{v}}_k\left(x_t;\theta,\varphi\right)\right)}\right\}^{\mathbf{1}\left(a_t=j|x_t\right)}. \quad (2.3.15)$$

The moment-matching estimator is

$$\left(\hat{\theta},\hat{\varphi}\right)=\arg\min_{\theta,\varphi}\sum_{t}\left\{\ln\left(\frac{\hat{\Pr}\left(a_t=j|x_t\right)}{\hat{\Pr}\left(a_t=J|x_t\right)}\right)-\bar{\hat{v}}_j\left(x_t;\theta,\varphi\right)\right\}^2, \quad (2.3.16)$$

or alternatively,

$$\left(\hat{\theta},\hat{\varphi}\right)=\arg\min_{\theta,\varphi}\sum_{t}\left\{\frac{\exp\left(\bar{\hat{v}}_j\left(x_t;\theta,\varphi\right)\right)}{\sum_{k\in\mathcal{J}}\exp\left(\bar{\hat{v}}_k\left(x_t;\theta,\varphi\right)\right)}-\mathbf{1}\left(a_t=j|x_t\right)\right\}^2. \quad (2.3.17)$$

The estimators defined in equations (2.3.15)–(2.3.17) will be $\sqrt{T}$-consistent and asymptotically normal estimators, given that the mean-zero i.i.d. type I error assumption is valid and the errors from the first-stage estimators $\hat{v}_j\left(x_t\right)$ vanish at a fast enough rate.

2.3.2.3 DISCUSSION

Hotz et al. (1994) suggest forward simulation to find the right-hand side of equation (2.3.14). The discreteness of the action set is essential in both Hotz and Miller (1993) and Hotz et al. (1994) because they compute the discounted sum of utilities using the tree structure. Although we assume that $\epsilon_{j,t}$ follows the i.i.d. type I extreme-value distribution, the inversion result holds for more general distributions supported on the entire real line. This idea to invert the choice probabilities has been exploited in diverse contexts, including demand estimation and static/dynamic game model estimation that we cover in later chapters of this book.

That being said, although the Hotz and Miller (1993) inversion makes the implementation substantially simpler, it comes with its own costs. In a finite sample, the additional uncertainty involved in estimating $\hat{\Pr}\left(a_t=j|x_t\right)$ out of data would incur measurement error. Since the measurement error enters nonlinearly into the model, it cannot easily be addressed using standard techniques. Furthermore, the efficiency of the estimation procedure, summarized by the standard error of the estimator, is lower than the full-solution method explained in section 2.3.1.

2.3.3 Nested Pseudo-Likelihood Estimation

2.3.3.1 DUALITY OF DYNAMIC DISCRETE-CHOICE MODELS: INVERTING THE VALUE-FUNCTION FIXED-POINT EQUATION IN PROBABILITY TERMS

Aguirregabiria and Mira (2002) further elaborate on the idea of inverting the choice probabilities. They consider inverting the value-function fixed-point equation of Rust (1987) in terms of the conditional choice probabilities. Although the setup and the assumption are the same as in Rust (1987), Aguirregabiria and Mira's arguments apply to a generic error-term distribution instead of just an i.i.d. type I extreme value.

We work with a slightly different notion of value function here. Consider the ex ante expected value function:

$$\begin{aligned}
&\bar{\bar{v}}\left(x_t; \boldsymbol{\theta}, \boldsymbol{\varphi}\right) \\
&:= \int \max_{j\in\mathcal{J}} \left\{ \bar{u}_j\left(x_t; \boldsymbol{\theta}\right) + \epsilon_{j,t} + \beta \int\int v\left(x_{t+1}, \boldsymbol{\epsilon}_{t+1}; \boldsymbol{\theta}, \boldsymbol{\varphi}\right) \Pr\left(d\boldsymbol{\epsilon}_{t+1}\right) \right. \\
&\qquad \left. \Pr\left(dx_{t+1} | x_t, a_t = j; \boldsymbol{\varphi}\right) \right\} \Pr\left(d\boldsymbol{\epsilon}_t\right) \\
&= \int \max_{j\in\mathcal{J}} \left\{ \bar{u}_j\left(x_t; \boldsymbol{\theta}\right) + \epsilon_{j,t} + \beta \int \bar{\bar{v}}\left(x_{t+1}; \boldsymbol{\theta}, \boldsymbol{\varphi}\right) \Pr\left(dx_{t+1} | x_t, a_t = j; \boldsymbol{\varphi}\right) \right\} \\
&\qquad \Pr\left(d\boldsymbol{\epsilon}_t\right) \\
&= \sum_{j\in\mathcal{J}} \Pr\left(a_t = j | x_t; \boldsymbol{\theta}, \boldsymbol{\varphi}\right) \left\{ \bar{u}_j\left(x_t; \boldsymbol{\theta}\right) + E\left[\epsilon_{j,t} | a_t = j, x_t\right] \right. \\
&\qquad \left. + \beta \sum_{x'\in\mathcal{X}} \bar{\bar{v}}\left(x_{t+1} = x'; \boldsymbol{\theta}, \boldsymbol{\varphi}\right) \Pr\left(x_{t+1} = x' | x_t, a_t = j; \boldsymbol{\varphi}\right) \right\}.^{23}
\end{aligned} \tag{2.3.18}$$

It can be shown that for a given $(\boldsymbol{\theta}, \boldsymbol{\varphi})$, the value function $\bar{\bar{v}}\left(x_t; \boldsymbol{\theta}, \boldsymbol{\varphi}\right)$ satisfying equation (2.3.18) is a unique fixed point. Next, note that

23. Note the difference between $\bar{\bar{v}}\left(x_t; \boldsymbol{\theta}, \boldsymbol{\varphi}\right)$ and the choice-specific expected value function $\bar{v}_j\left(x_t; \boldsymbol{\theta}, \boldsymbol{\varphi}\right)$ that we worked with earlier in this chapter.

$$\mathbb{E}\left[\epsilon_{j,t}|a_t = j, x_t\right] = -\ln \Pr\left(a_t = j|x_t; \boldsymbol{\theta}, \boldsymbol{\varphi}\right) \tag{2.3.19}$$

holds, where $\epsilon_{j,t}$ is the jth element of $\boldsymbol{\epsilon}_t$.[24] Substituting back, equation (2.3.18) becomes

$$\begin{aligned}\bar{\bar{v}}\left(x_t; \boldsymbol{\theta}, \boldsymbol{\varphi}\right) = \sum_{j\in\mathcal{J}} \Pr\left(a_t = j|x_t; \boldsymbol{\theta}, \boldsymbol{\varphi}\right) \Big\{\bar{u}_j\left(x_t; \boldsymbol{\theta}\right) - \ln \Pr\left(a_t = j|x_t; \boldsymbol{\theta}, \boldsymbol{\varphi}\right) \\ + \beta \sum_{x'\in\mathcal{X}} \bar{\bar{v}}\left(x_{t+1} = x'; \boldsymbol{\theta}, \boldsymbol{\varphi}\right) \Pr\left(x_{t+1} = x'|x_t, a_t = j; \boldsymbol{\varphi}\right)\Big\}.\end{aligned} \tag{2.3.22}$$

We stack the fixed-point equations (2.3.22) to express them in terms of the conditional choice probabilities $\Pr\left(a_t|x_t; \boldsymbol{\theta}, \boldsymbol{\varphi}\right)$ and the state-transition probabilities $\Pr\left(x_{t+1}|x_t, a_t; \boldsymbol{\varphi}\right)$. As an illustration, consider the case $x_t = 1$:

24. We invoked the mean-zero i.i.d. type I extreme-value assumption in equation (2.3.19). By the corollary to lemma 2.2.2, we know that

$$\begin{aligned}&\ln\left(\sum_{j\in\mathcal{J}} \exp\left(\bar{v}_j\left(x_t; \boldsymbol{\theta}, \boldsymbol{\varphi}\right)\right)\right)\\ &= \int \max_{j\in\mathcal{J}} \left\{\bar{v}_j\left(x_t; \boldsymbol{\theta}, \boldsymbol{\varphi}\right) + \epsilon_{j,t}\right\} \Pr\left(d\boldsymbol{\epsilon}_t\right)\\ &= \sum_{j\in\mathcal{J}} \Pr\left(a_t = j|x_t; \boldsymbol{\theta}, \boldsymbol{\varphi}\right) \left\{\bar{v}_j\left(x_t; \boldsymbol{\theta}, \boldsymbol{\varphi}\right) + \mathbb{E}\left[\epsilon_{j,t}|a_t = j, x_t\right]\right\}.\end{aligned} \tag{2.3.20}$$

On the other hand,

$$\begin{aligned}&\sum_{j\in\mathcal{J}} \Pr\left(a_t = j|x_t; \boldsymbol{\theta}, \boldsymbol{\varphi}\right) \left\{\bar{v}_j\left(x_t; \boldsymbol{\theta}, \boldsymbol{\varphi}\right) - \ln \Pr\left(a_t = j|x_t; \boldsymbol{\theta}, \boldsymbol{\varphi}\right)\right\}\\ &= \sum_{j\in\mathcal{J}} \Pr\left(a_t = j|x_t; \boldsymbol{\theta}, \boldsymbol{\varphi}\right) \left\{\bar{v}_j\left(x_t; \boldsymbol{\theta}, \boldsymbol{\varphi}\right) - \ln \frac{\exp\left(\bar{v}_j\left(x_t; \boldsymbol{\theta}, \boldsymbol{\varphi}\right)\right)}{\sum_{k\in\mathcal{J}} \exp\left(\bar{v}_k\left(x_t; \boldsymbol{\theta}, \boldsymbol{\varphi}\right)\right)}\right\}\\ &= \left\{\ln\left(\sum_{k\in\mathcal{J}} \exp\left(\bar{v}_k\left(x_t; \boldsymbol{\theta}, \boldsymbol{\varphi}\right)\right)\right)\right\} \sum_{j\in\mathcal{J}} \Pr\left(a_t = j|x_t; \boldsymbol{\theta}, \boldsymbol{\varphi}\right)\\ &= \ln\left(\sum_{j\in\mathcal{J}} \exp\left(\bar{v}_j\left(x_t; \boldsymbol{\theta}, \boldsymbol{\varphi}\right)\right)\right).\end{aligned} \tag{2.3.21}$$

Combining equations (2.3.20) and (2.3.21) yields the desired conclusion.

$$\bar{\bar{v}}(1;\boldsymbol{\theta},\boldsymbol{\varphi}) = \mathbf{p}(a_t|1;\boldsymbol{\theta},\boldsymbol{\varphi})' \begin{pmatrix} \bar{u}_1(1;\boldsymbol{\theta}) - \ln \Pr(a_t = 1|1;\boldsymbol{\theta},\boldsymbol{\varphi}) \\ \bar{u}_2(1;\boldsymbol{\theta}) - \ln \Pr(a_t = 2|1;\boldsymbol{\theta},\boldsymbol{\varphi}) \\ \vdots \\ \bar{u}_J(1;\boldsymbol{\theta}) - \ln \Pr\left(a_t = J|1;\boldsymbol{\theta},\boldsymbol{\varphi}\right) \end{pmatrix} + \beta \mathbf{p}(a_t|1;\boldsymbol{\theta},\boldsymbol{\varphi})' \mathbf{P}(x_{t+1}|1,a_t;\boldsymbol{\varphi}) \begin{pmatrix} \bar{\bar{v}}(1;\boldsymbol{\theta},\boldsymbol{\varphi}) \\ \bar{\bar{v}}(2;\boldsymbol{\theta},\boldsymbol{\varphi}) \\ \vdots \\ \bar{\bar{v}}(X;\boldsymbol{\theta},\boldsymbol{\varphi}) \end{pmatrix},$$

where

$$\mathbf{p}(a_t|1;\boldsymbol{\theta},\boldsymbol{\varphi}) = \begin{pmatrix} \Pr(1|1;\boldsymbol{\theta},\boldsymbol{\varphi}) \\ \Pr(2|1;\boldsymbol{\theta},\boldsymbol{\varphi}) \\ \vdots \\ \Pr\left(J|1;\boldsymbol{\theta},\boldsymbol{\varphi}\right) \end{pmatrix}$$

$$\mathbf{P}(x_{t+1}|1,a_t;\boldsymbol{\varphi}) = \begin{pmatrix} \Pr(1|1,1;\boldsymbol{\varphi}) & \Pr(2|1,1;\boldsymbol{\varphi}) & \cdots & \Pr(X|1,1;\boldsymbol{\varphi}) \\ \Pr(1|1,2;\boldsymbol{\varphi}) & \Pr(2|1,2;\boldsymbol{\varphi}) & \cdots & \Pr(X|1,2;\boldsymbol{\varphi}) \\ \vdots & \vdots & \ddots & \vdots \\ \Pr\left(1|1,J;\boldsymbol{\varphi}\right) & \Pr\left(2|1,J;\boldsymbol{\varphi}\right) & \cdots & \Pr\left(X|1,J;\boldsymbol{\varphi}\right) \end{pmatrix}.$$ [25]

Notice that $\mathbf{p}(a_t|1;\boldsymbol{\theta},\boldsymbol{\varphi})' \mathbf{P}(x_{t+1}|1,a_t;\boldsymbol{\varphi})$ yields a $1 \times X$ vector. An analogous observation leads us to form an $X \times X$ unconditional state-transition probability matrix $\mathbf{P}(x_{t+1}|x_t;\boldsymbol{\theta},\boldsymbol{\varphi})$. Define

$$\bar{\mathbf{u}}(x_t = x;\boldsymbol{\theta}) := \begin{pmatrix} \bar{u}_1(x;\boldsymbol{\theta}) \\ \bar{u}_2(x;\boldsymbol{\theta}) \\ \vdots \\ \bar{u}_J(x;\boldsymbol{\theta}) \end{pmatrix}.$$

By stacking $\bar{\bar{v}}(x_t;\boldsymbol{\theta},\boldsymbol{\varphi})$, we get

$$\begin{pmatrix} \bar{\bar{v}}(1;\boldsymbol{\theta},\boldsymbol{\varphi}) \\ \bar{\bar{v}}(2;\boldsymbol{\theta},\boldsymbol{\varphi}) \\ \vdots \\ \bar{\bar{v}}(X;\boldsymbol{\theta},\boldsymbol{\varphi}) \end{pmatrix} = \begin{pmatrix} \mathbf{p}(a_t|1;\boldsymbol{\theta},\boldsymbol{\varphi})' \left(\bar{\mathbf{u}}(x_t = 1;\boldsymbol{\theta}) - \ln \mathbf{p}(a_t|1;\boldsymbol{\theta},\boldsymbol{\varphi})\right) \\ \mathbf{p}(a_t|2;\boldsymbol{\theta},\boldsymbol{\varphi})' \left(\bar{\mathbf{u}}(x_t = 2;\boldsymbol{\theta}) - \ln \mathbf{p}(a_t|2;\boldsymbol{\theta},\boldsymbol{\varphi})\right) \\ \vdots \\ \mathbf{p}(a_t|X;\boldsymbol{\theta},\boldsymbol{\varphi})' \left(\bar{\mathbf{u}}(x_t = X;\boldsymbol{\theta}) - \ln \mathbf{p}(a_t|X;\boldsymbol{\theta},\boldsymbol{\varphi})\right) \end{pmatrix}$$

25. In practice, one should let free only $J-1$ of the conditional choice probabilities.

$$+\beta\mathbf{P}\left(x_{t+1}|x_t;\boldsymbol{\theta},\boldsymbol{\varphi}\right)\begin{pmatrix}\bar{\bar{v}}\left(1;\boldsymbol{\theta},\boldsymbol{\varphi}\right)\\ \bar{\bar{v}}\left(2;\boldsymbol{\theta},\boldsymbol{\varphi}\right)\\ \vdots\\ \bar{\bar{v}}\left(X;\boldsymbol{\theta},\boldsymbol{\varphi}\right)\end{pmatrix}. \tag{2.3.23}$$

We invert equation (2.3.23), which yields

$$\begin{pmatrix}\bar{\bar{v}}\left(1;\boldsymbol{\theta},\boldsymbol{\varphi}\right)\\ \bar{\bar{v}}\left(2;\boldsymbol{\theta},\boldsymbol{\varphi}\right)\\ \vdots\\ \bar{\bar{v}}\left(X;\boldsymbol{\theta},\boldsymbol{\varphi}\right)\end{pmatrix}=\left[\mathbf{I}-\beta\mathbf{P}\left(x_{t+1}|x_t;\boldsymbol{\theta},\boldsymbol{\varphi}\right)\right]^{-1}$$

$$\begin{pmatrix}\mathbf{p}\left(a_t|1;\boldsymbol{\theta},\boldsymbol{\varphi}\right)'\left(\bar{\mathbf{u}}\left(x_t=1;\boldsymbol{\theta}\right)-\ln\mathbf{p}\left(a_t|1;\boldsymbol{\theta},\boldsymbol{\varphi}\right)\right)\\ \mathbf{p}\left(a_t|2;\boldsymbol{\theta},\boldsymbol{\varphi}\right)'\left(\bar{\mathbf{u}}\left(x_t=2;\boldsymbol{\theta}\right)-\ln\mathbf{p}\left(a_t|2;\boldsymbol{\theta},\boldsymbol{\varphi}\right)\right)\\ \vdots\\ \mathbf{p}\left(a_t|X;\boldsymbol{\theta},\boldsymbol{\varphi}\right)'\left(\bar{\mathbf{u}}\left(x_t=X;\boldsymbol{\theta}\right)-\ln\mathbf{p}\left(a_t|X;\boldsymbol{\theta},\boldsymbol{\varphi}\right)\right)\end{pmatrix}. \tag{2.3.24}$$

The right-hand side of equation (2.3.24) involves only the model primitives $\{\beta,\bar{u}\left(x_t;\boldsymbol{\theta}\right)\}$, the state-transition probabilities $\Pr\left(x_{t+1}|x_t,a_t;\boldsymbol{\varphi}\right)$, and the conditional choice probabilities $\Pr\left(a_t|x_t;\boldsymbol{\theta},\boldsymbol{\varphi}\right)$. We write equation (2.3.24) compactly in matrix notation as

$$\bar{\bar{\mathbf{v}}}\left(x_t;\boldsymbol{\theta},\boldsymbol{\varphi}\right)=\left[\mathbf{I}-\beta\mathbf{P}\left(x_{t+1}|x_t;\boldsymbol{\theta},\boldsymbol{\varphi}\right)\right]^{-1}\mathbf{w}\left(a_t,x_t;\boldsymbol{\theta},\boldsymbol{\varphi}\right), \tag{2.3.25}$$

where

$$\mathbf{w}\left(a_t,x_t;\boldsymbol{\theta},\boldsymbol{\varphi}\right):=\begin{pmatrix}\mathbf{p}\left(a_t|1;\boldsymbol{\theta},\boldsymbol{\varphi}\right)'\left(\bar{\mathbf{u}}\left(x_t=1;\boldsymbol{\theta}\right)-\ln\mathbf{p}\left(a_t|1;\boldsymbol{\theta},\boldsymbol{\varphi}\right)\right)\\ \mathbf{p}\left(a_t|2;\boldsymbol{\theta},\boldsymbol{\varphi}\right)'\left(\bar{\mathbf{u}}\left(x_t=2;\boldsymbol{\theta}\right)-\ln\mathbf{p}\left(a_t|2;\boldsymbol{\theta},\boldsymbol{\varphi}\right)\right)\\ \vdots\\ \mathbf{p}\left(a_t|X;\boldsymbol{\theta},\boldsymbol{\varphi}\right)'\left(\bar{\mathbf{u}}\left(x_t=X;\boldsymbol{\theta}\right)-\ln\mathbf{p}\left(a_t|X;\boldsymbol{\theta},\boldsymbol{\varphi}\right)\right)\end{pmatrix}.$$ [26]

2.3.3.2 *K*-STAGE POLICY-ITERATION ESTIMATOR

Now we get to the pseudo-likelihood estimation. First, it is assumed that $\hat{\boldsymbol{\varphi}}$, a consistent estimator for the parameters of state-transition probabilities, can be obtained separately. Plugging $\hat{\boldsymbol{\varphi}}$ back into the conditional choice probabilities

26. Chiong, Galichon, and Shum (2016) also derive equation (2.3.25) through simpler steps using the concept of McFadden's (1974, 1981) social surplus function and its differentials.

yields

$$\Pr\left(a_t = j | x_t; \boldsymbol{\theta}, \hat{\boldsymbol{\varphi}}\right) = \frac{\exp\left(\bar{v}_j\left(x_t; \boldsymbol{\theta}, \hat{\boldsymbol{\varphi}}\right)\right)}{\sum_{k \in \mathcal{J}} \exp\left(\bar{v}_k\left(x_t; \boldsymbol{\theta}, \hat{\boldsymbol{\varphi}}\right)\right)}, \tag{2.3.26}$$

and

$$\bar{v}_j\left(x_t; \boldsymbol{\theta}, \hat{\boldsymbol{\varphi}}\right) = \bar{u}_j\left(x_t; \boldsymbol{\theta}\right) + \beta \sum_{x' \in \mathcal{X}} \bar{\bar{v}}\left(x_{t+1} = x'; \boldsymbol{\theta}, \hat{\boldsymbol{\varphi}}\right) \Pr\left(x_{t+1} = x' | x_t, a_t = j; \hat{\boldsymbol{\varphi}}\right). \tag{2.3.27}$$

Substituting equation (2.3.24) into equation (2.3.27) for all possible pairs of (a_t, x_t, x_{t+1}), and then again substituting into equation (2.3.26), we get

$$\mathbf{P}\left(a_t | x_t; \boldsymbol{\theta}, \hat{\boldsymbol{\varphi}}\right) = \Psi\left(\mathbf{P}\left(a_t | x_t; \boldsymbol{\theta}, \hat{\boldsymbol{\varphi}}\right)\right),$$

where $\Psi(\cdot)$ is what we define as the policy-iteration operator.

The estimation algorithm proceeds as follows. Begin from an initial guess $\mathbf{P}^0\left(a_t | x_t; \boldsymbol{\theta}, \hat{\boldsymbol{\varphi}}\right)$. The initial guess can be, for example, obtained by the Hotz and Miller (1993) inversion. The first stage is to obtain

$$\hat{\boldsymbol{\theta}}^K = \arg\max_{\boldsymbol{\theta}} \prod_i \mathcal{L}_i\left(\Psi\left(\mathbf{P}^{K-1}\left(a_t | x_t; \boldsymbol{\theta}, \hat{\boldsymbol{\varphi}}\right)\right)\right),$$

where $\mathcal{L}_i(\cdot)$ denotes the likelihood induced by the argument and i denotes the data.[27] The second stage is to update $\mathbf{P}\left(a_t | x_t; \boldsymbol{\theta}, \hat{\boldsymbol{\varphi}}\right)$ using the right-hand side of equation (2.3.24), and then plugging the results back into equations (2.3.27) and (2.3.26) sequentially. To that end, we have

$$\mathbf{P}^K\left(a_t | x_t; \boldsymbol{\theta}, \hat{\boldsymbol{\varphi}}\right) = \Psi\left(\mathbf{P}^{K-1}\left(a_t | x_t; \hat{\boldsymbol{\theta}}^K, \hat{\boldsymbol{\varphi}}\right)\right).$$

It can be shown that the Hotz-Miller estimator can be nested as a special case of this estimator when $K = 1$. When $K \to \infty$, the estimator is equivalent to Rust's full solution, provided that $\hat{\boldsymbol{\theta}}^K$ converges. This nested pseudo-likelihood (NPL) estimator can achieve the potential accuracy gain over Hotz-Miller when the first-stage estimator is imprecise. Furthermore, it can achieve some speed advantage over Rust's full-solution method because the researcher can decide the stopping criterion. As in MPEC, the speed advantage comes from the fact that iterating over the

27. This will take the usual form:

$$\prod_{x,j,t} \Pr\left(a_{i,t} = j | x_{i,t} = x; \boldsymbol{\theta}, \hat{\boldsymbol{\varphi}}\right)^{\mathbf{1}\left(a_{i,t} = j | x_{i,t} = x\right)}.$$

fixed point at each iteration is unnecessary. The authors show that if the sequence $\hat{\boldsymbol{\theta}}^K$ converges, it is $\sqrt{T}$-consistent, asymptotically normal, and asymptotically equivalent to the full-solution MLE. They also report that solving Rust's original problem does not seem to lead to much accuracy gain for $K > 3$.

2.3.4 Extension to Incorporate Unobserved State Variables

The dynamic discrete-choice models that we have examined thus far do not allow an unobserved state variable. That is, they de facto assume that the agent and the econometrician have the same degree of ex ante information,[28] which is often unrealistic.

An agent may observe persistent state variables that are not observable to the econometrician. Such state variables may or may not be invariant over time. In this subsection, we study the estimation method developed by Arcidiacono and Miller (2011), which may incorporate unobserved heterogeneity into dynamic discrete-choice models. Arcidiacono and Miller allow unobserved heterogeneity that has the following two properties: (1) a finite number of possible unobserved states exist, and (2) either the unobserved states are time invariant (i.e., they are simply fixed effects) or they follow the first-order stationary Markov chain. Property (2) is a sufficient condition for the distribution of the unobserved states to be stationary. The assumption of the hidden state following a stationary Markov chain allows the econometrician to ignore initial conditions, ensuring the tractability of the estimation framework. The estimation combines the Hotz and Miller (1993) inversion with the expectation-maximization algorithm. The setup we study next simplifies Property (2), where we assume the unobserved state variable h_t is i.i.d. over time.

2.3.4.1 FORMULATION

Denote $\mathbf{z}_t := (x_t, h_t)$ as the state vector at time t, where x_t is observable to the econometrician and h_t is unobservable. All other notations are the same as before. The state space is assumed to be a finite set. We denote $x_t \in \mathcal{X} := \{1, 2, \ldots, X\}$, $h_t \in \mathcal{H} := \{1, 2, \ldots, H\}$, and $a_t \in \mathcal{J} := \{1, 2, \ldots, J\}$. The flow utility $\bar{u}_j(\mathbf{z}_t; \boldsymbol{\theta})$ is now a function of the unobserved state h_t, as well as of the observed state x_t, and it is assumed that the functional form is known up to the parameter vector $\boldsymbol{\theta}$. The econometrician observes the evolution of x_t but the evolution of h_t is hidden to the econometrician.

The idea is to implement the Hotz and Miller (1993) inversion in equation (2.3.14) to form the likelihood; that is,

28. By ex ante information, we mean the information right before the realization of ϵ_t.

$$
\begin{aligned}
&\bar{v}_j(\mathbf{z}_t;\boldsymbol{\theta},\boldsymbol{\varphi}) - \bar{v}_J(\mathbf{z}_t;\boldsymbol{\theta},\boldsymbol{\varphi}) \\
&= \bar{u}_j(\mathbf{z}_t;\boldsymbol{\theta}) - \bar{u}_J(\mathbf{z}_t;\boldsymbol{\theta}) \\
&\quad + \beta \int \ln\left(\sum_{k\in\mathcal{J}} \exp \hat{v}_k(\mathbf{z}_{t+1})\right)\left\{\Pr\left(d\mathbf{z}_{t+1}|\mathbf{z}_t, a_t=j,\boldsymbol{\varphi}\right)\right. \\
&\quad \left. - \Pr\left(d\mathbf{z}_{t+1}|\mathbf{z}_t, a_t=J,\boldsymbol{\varphi}\right)\right\}, \qquad (2.3.28)
\end{aligned}
$$

with

$$
\ln\left(\frac{\hat{\Pr}\left(a_t=j|\mathbf{z}_t\right)}{\hat{\Pr}\left(a_t=J|\mathbf{z}_t\right)}\right) = \hat{v}_j(\mathbf{z}_t) - \hat{v}_J(\mathbf{z}_t). \qquad (2.3.29)
$$

The problem here is that the econometrician cannot observe the sample analogs of $\Pr\left(\mathbf{z}_{t+1}|\mathbf{z}_t, a_t=j,\boldsymbol{\varphi}\right)$ and $\hat{\Pr}\left(a_t=j|\mathbf{z}_t\right)$. The econometrician can only observe $\Pr\left(x_{t+1}|x_t, a_t=j,\boldsymbol{\varphi}\right)$ and $\Pr\left(a_t=j|x_t\right)$.

2.3.4.2 EXPECTATION-MAXIMIZATION (EM) ALGORITHM

The likelihood contribution with the observed data $\left\{a_t=j, x_t=x\right\}$ is

$$
L\left(\left\{a_t=j, x_t=x\right\}|\boldsymbol{\theta},\boldsymbol{\varphi}\right) = \mathbb{E}_{h_t}\left[L\left(\left\{a_t=j, x_t=x, h_t\right\}|\boldsymbol{\theta},\boldsymbol{\varphi}\right)\right]. \qquad (2.3.30)
$$

However, the product of equation (2.3.30) over t cannot be directly maximized because h_t is hidden and $\boldsymbol{\varphi}$ is initially unknown to the econometrician, subject to being estimated. In turn, the sample analog of the conditional choice probability $\Pr\left(a_t=j|\mathbf{z}_t\right)$, the state-transition probability $\Pr(\mathbf{z}_{t+1}|\mathbf{z}_t, a_t,\boldsymbol{\varphi})$, and the mean utility $\bar{u}_j(\mathbf{z}_t;\boldsymbol{\theta})$ are also unknown, even if we know the parameter $\boldsymbol{\theta}$. Therefore, we proceed with the expectation-maximization (EM) algorithm applied to the dynamic discrete-choice problem, taking h_t as the hidden state that is unobserved to the econometrician but observed to the agent. For notational simplicity, we assume that $\boldsymbol{\varphi}$ is the H-dimensional vector such that $\varphi_{(h)} = \Pr(h_t=h)$, and no other variable is included in $\boldsymbol{\varphi}$.

Suppose that the iteration is at the mth stage, so we have $\hat{\boldsymbol{\theta}}^{(m)}$ and $\hat{\boldsymbol{\varphi}}^{(m)}$. We begin the mth iteration by assuming that $\hat{\Pr}^{(m)}\left(a_t=j|x_t,h_t\right)$ is known, which will be updated in step 4.

Step 1. Formulate the likelihood By combining equations (2.3.28), (2.3.29), and (2.3.30), it is immediate that we can formulate the likelihood contribution conditional on the current observed state $x_t = x$ and hidden state $h_t = h$:

$$L\left(\left\{a_t = j, x_t = x, h_t = h\right\} | \hat{\boldsymbol{\theta}}^{(m)}, \hat{\boldsymbol{\varphi}}^{(m)}\right) = \frac{\exp\left(\bar{v}_j\left(x_t = x, h_t = h; \hat{\boldsymbol{\theta}}^{(m)}, \hat{\boldsymbol{\varphi}}^{(m)}\right)\right)}{\sum_{k \in \mathcal{J}} \exp\left(\bar{v}_k\left(x_t = x, h_t = h; \hat{\boldsymbol{\theta}}^{(m)}, \hat{\boldsymbol{\varphi}}^{(m)}\right)\right)}. \tag{2.3.31}$$

Step 2. Update $\hat{\Pr}^{(m)}\left(h_t = h | a_t, x_t; \hat{\boldsymbol{\theta}}^{(m)}, \hat{\boldsymbol{\varphi}}^{(m)}\right)$ Next, we find $\hat{\Pr}^{(m+1)}\left(h_t = h | a_t, x_t; \hat{\boldsymbol{\theta}}^{(m)}, \hat{\boldsymbol{\varphi}}^{(m)}\right)$ by using Bayes's rule:

$$\hat{\Pr}^{(m+1)}\left(h_t = h | a_t = j, x_t = x; \hat{\boldsymbol{\theta}}^{(m)}, \hat{\boldsymbol{\varphi}}^{(m)}\right) = \frac{\hat{\varphi}_h^{(m)} L\left(\left\{a_t = j, x_t = x, h_t = h\right\} | \hat{\boldsymbol{\theta}}^{(m)}, \hat{\boldsymbol{\varphi}}^{(m)}\right)}{\sum_{h' \in \mathcal{H}} \hat{\varphi}_{h'}^{(m)} L\left(\left\{a_t = j, x_t = x, h_t = h'\right\} | \hat{\boldsymbol{\theta}}^{(m)}, \hat{\boldsymbol{\varphi}}^{(m)}\right)}. \tag{2.3.32}$$

Step 3. Update $\hat{\boldsymbol{\varphi}}^{(m)}$ In this step, we update $\hat{\boldsymbol{\varphi}}^{(m)}$ to $\hat{\boldsymbol{\varphi}}^{(m+1)}$. By definition,

$$\hat{\varphi}_h^{(m+1)} = \frac{1}{N_{j,x}} \sum_{j \in \mathcal{J}} \sum_{x \in \mathcal{X}} \hat{\Pr}^{(m+1)}\left(h_t = h | a_t = j, x_t = x; \hat{\boldsymbol{\theta}}^{(m)}, \hat{\boldsymbol{\varphi}}^{(m)}\right), \tag{2.3.33}$$

where $N_{j,x}$ is the observed sample size for action j and state x.

Step 4. Update $\hat{\Pr}^{(m)}\left(a_t = j | x_t, h_t\right)$ Similarly, we also update $\hat{\Pr}^{(m)}\left(a_t = j | x_t, h_t\right)$ as

$$\hat{\Pr}^{(m+1)}\left(a_t = j | x_t, h_t = h\right) = \frac{\sum_{x \in \mathcal{X}} \mathbf{1}\left(a_t = j, x_t = x\right) \hat{\Pr}^{(m+1)}\left(h_t = h | a_t = j, x_t = x; \hat{\boldsymbol{\theta}}^{(m)}, \hat{\boldsymbol{\varphi}}^{(m)}\right)}{\sum_{x \in \mathcal{X}} \mathbf{1}\left(x_t = x\right) \hat{\Pr}^{(m+1)}\left(h_t = h | a_t = j, x_t = x; \hat{\boldsymbol{\theta}}^{(m)}, \hat{\boldsymbol{\varphi}}^{(m)}\right)}.$$

Step 5. Update $\hat{\boldsymbol{\theta}}^{(m)}$ Using $\hat{\Pr}^{(m+1)}\left(a_t = j | x_t, h_t\right)$, form the updated likelihood by substituting $\hat{\boldsymbol{\varphi}}^{(m+1)}$ back into equation (2.3.31) and solving the likelihood maximization problem to update $\hat{\boldsymbol{\theta}}^{(m)}$:

$$\hat{\boldsymbol{\theta}}^{(m+1)} = \arg\max_{\boldsymbol{\theta}} \sum_{t} \sum_{h \in \mathcal{H}} \mathbf{1}\left(a_t = j | x_t = x\right)$$
$$\ln\left\{\mathbb{E}_{h_t}^{(m+1)}\left[L\left(\left\{a_t = j, x_t = x, h_t\right\} | \boldsymbol{\theta}, \hat{\boldsymbol{\varphi}}^{(m+1)}\right)\right]\right\}, \tag{2.3.34}$$

where

$$\mathbb{E}_{h_t}^{(m+1)}\left[L\left(\left\{a_t = j, x_t = x, h_t\right\} | \boldsymbol{\theta}, \hat{\boldsymbol{\varphi}}^{(m+1)}\right)\right]$$
$$= \sum_{h \in \mathcal{H}} \hat{\varphi}_h^{(m+1)} \frac{\exp\left(\bar{v}_j\left(x_t = x, h_t = h; \boldsymbol{\theta}, \hat{\boldsymbol{\varphi}}^{(m+1)}\right)\right)}{\sum_{k \in \mathcal{J}} \exp\left(\bar{v}_k\left(x_t = x, h_t = h; \boldsymbol{\theta}, \hat{\boldsymbol{\varphi}}^{(m+1)}\right)\right)}.$$

Iterating over steps 1–5 will give the consistent and asymptotically normal estimator for $\boldsymbol{\theta}$ and $\boldsymbol{\varphi}$.

2.3.4.3 DISCUSSION AND FURTHER READING

The EM algorithm illustrated here implicitly assumes that the hidden state h_t is stationary so that the model parameters can be consistently estimated with a single time series. It can be easily extended to a setup where the hidden state follows a first-order Markov chain or is persistent over all periods,[29] which will in general require a panel data for identification and estimation.

Incorporating unobservable state variables into dynamic econometric models is an ongoing area of research. Connault (2016), Hu and Shum (2012), Hu et al. (2017), and Kasahara and Shimotsu (2009) provide identification results under different setups. Notably, Kasahara and Shimotsu (2009) provide identification results when the unobserved heterogeneity is time invariant, which Arcidiacono

29. This way, the problem boils down to estimating the Markov transition matrix along with the model parameters. The estimation algorithm should be modified to update the transition matrix Ξ and initialization probability $\boldsymbol{\Pi}$. Ξ is a matrix of which the (h, τ)'th entry is the transition probability from state h to state τ; that is,

$$\Xi_{h,\tau} := \Pr\left(h_{t+1} = \tau | h_t = h\right).$$

$\boldsymbol{\Pi}$ is a matrix of which the (x, h)th entry is the conditional probability of h_1 given x_1; that is,

$$\Pi_{x,h} := \Pr\left(h_1 = h | x_1 = x\right).$$

Now, $\boldsymbol{\varphi}$ contains Ξ, $\boldsymbol{\Pi}$, and $\Pr\left(h_t = h\right)$, but otherwise the estimation routine is similar to what was described earlier in this chapter.

and Miller (2011) build upon. Imai, Jain, and Ching (2009) develop an estimation procedure based on the Bayesian perspective, which merges the successive approximation algorithm of solving a dynamic programming problem with a Markov chain, Monte Carlo, Bayesian estimation algorithm. Norets (2009) extends the framework of Imai et al. (2009) to account for time-varying unobserved heterogeneity.

2.3.5 (Non)-identification of the Discount Factor

Magnac and Thesmar (2002) study the identification problem of the dynamic discrete-choice framework. The parameter vector $\boldsymbol{\theta}$ of interest is identified if the observed joint distribution of data $\Pr(a_t|x_t)$[30] and the structural restrictions of the economic model uniquely pin down $\boldsymbol{\theta}$.[31] To put the conclusions first, Magnac and Thesmar show that the model is generically underidentified. Identification of the model parameters requires prior knowledge of (1) the discount factor β, (2) the state-transition probability $\Pr(x_{t+1}|x_t, a_t)$, and (3) functional forms of the current utility and the value function for at least one reference alternative. Here, (2) and (3) do not pose a concern when the functional forms of the current utility and the transition probability distribution are specified. Yet the nonidentifiability of β is a difficult problem to resolve even in fully parametric dynamic discrete-choice models.

A heuristic argument for the nonidentifiability of β is given here. Assume that $\epsilon_t \sim$ i.i.d. $T1EV$ and

$$\bar{u}(x_t, a_t; \theta) = \begin{cases} 0 & \text{if } a_t = 1 \\ x_t\theta & \text{if } a_t = 2 \end{cases}.$$

We have shown that the conditional choice probability takes the following form:

$$\begin{aligned} \Pr(a_t = 1|x_t) &= \frac{\exp(\beta\bar{w}_1(x_t))}{\exp(\beta\bar{w}_1(x_t)) + \exp(x_t\theta + \beta\bar{w}_2(x_t))} \\ &= \frac{1}{1 + \exp(x_t\theta + \beta(\bar{w}_2(x_t) - \bar{w}_1(x_t)))}. \end{aligned}$$

Furthermore, suppose that we know the exact value of $\bar{w}_2(x_t) - \bar{w}_1(x_t)$ for all possible values of x_t. Now the problem boils down to finding (θ, β) by inverting the

30. It is essentially assuming a situation where an econometrician has an infinite amount of data.

31. In the context of dynamic discrete-choice models, the functional form of $\bar{u}(x_t, a_t; \boldsymbol{\theta})$ and the fact that the agent is engaging in the dynamic optimization problem are the main structural restrictions under consideration.

conditional cumulative distribution function $F_{a_t|x_t}(a=1|x)$, which turns out to be impossible. To see why, fix $x_t = x$ and assume that we have infinitely many data, so the value $\Pr(a_t = 1|x_t = x)$ can be pinned down exactly from the data. We can always find some $\alpha_1 \neq 1$ and $\alpha_2 \neq 1$ such that the following holds:

$$\begin{aligned}\Pr(a_t = 1|x_t = x) &= \frac{1}{1+\exp(x\theta + \beta(\bar{w}_2(x) - \bar{w}_1(x)))} \\ &= \frac{1}{1+\exp(\alpha_1 x\theta + \alpha_2\beta(\bar{w}_2(x) - \bar{w}_1(x)))}.\end{aligned} \tag{2.3.35}$$

In this equation, $\alpha_2\beta$ can be taken as corresponding to another discount factor. Therefore, uniquely pinning down the discount factor by inverting $F_{a_t|x_t}(1|x)$ is impossible. In this example, (θ, β) and $(\alpha_1\theta, \alpha_2\beta)$ are *observationally equivalent*, in that they both result in the same probability distribution of observable data. Point identification of the model parameters requires that the observationally equivalent set is a singleton.[32] For this reason, we specified the value of β ex ante, often with some a priori knowledge.[33]

A common solution for identifying β is to impose an exclusion restriction. Different authors suggest different schemes for the exclusion restriction. Magnac and Thesmar (2002) suggest finding two states x and x' such that $\beta(\bar{w}_2(x) - \bar{w}_1(x)) = \beta(\bar{w}_2(x') - \bar{w}_1(x'))$, but $x\theta \neq x'\theta$. θ is then identified in a straightforward manner, from which β would follow. Dalton, Gowrisankaran, and Town (2020) employ Magnac and Thesmar's idea to test myopic behavior versus forward-looking behavior with exponential discounting. Abbring and Daljord (2020) suggest imposing restrictions on the current utility $\bar{u}(x, a; \theta)$, to find two different states x and x' such that $\bar{u}(x, a; \theta) = \bar{u}(x', a; \theta)$. Then, differencing $\bar{u}(x, a; \theta)$ out would leave $\beta\{(\bar{w}_2(x) - \bar{w}_1(x)) - (\bar{w}_2(x') - \bar{w}_1(x'))\}$ as nonzero, and inverting this against the differences of observed conditional choice probabilities yields the identified value of β. Ching and Osborne (2020) and Kong, Dubé, and Daljord (2022) apply Abbring and Daljord's invertibility result to a consumer stockpiling model and a consumer brand loyalty model, respectively.

Another possibility of identifying β using an exclusion restriction would be to find another state variable that only affects either the current flow utility or the continuation value. However, finding an extra state variable that satisfies such an exclusion restriction is generally a difficult problem, and this possibility would depend on the individual empirical context being studied.

32. When the observationally equivalent set is nonempty and not a singleton, the parameter is said to be partially identified or set identified as opposed to point identified.

33. For example, the most usual choice of β is 0.95 when the data are recorded yearly.

Bibliography

Abbring, J. H., & Ø. Daljord (2020). "Identifying the discount factor in dynamic discrete choice models." *Quantitative Economics*, 11, 471–501.

Aguirregabiria, V., & P. Mira (2002). "Swapping the nested fixed point algorithm: A class of estimators for discrete Markov decision models." *Econometrica*, 70, 1519–1543.

Aguirregabiria, V., & P. Mira (2010). "Dynamic discrtete choice structural models: A survey." *Journal of Econometrics*, 156, 38–67.

Anderson, S. P., A. de Palma, & J.-F. Thisse (1992). *Discrete choice theory of product differentiation*. Cambridge, MA: MIT Press.

Arcidiacono, P., & R. A. Miller (2011). "Conditional choice probability estimation of dynamic discrete choice models with unobserved heterogeneity." *Econometrica*, 79, 1823–1867.

Blundell, R., & J. L. Powell (2004). "Endogeneity in semiparametric binary response models." *Review of Economic Studies*, 71, 655–679.

Cardell, N. S. (1997). "Variance components structures for the extreme-value and logistic distributions with application to models of heterogeneity." *Econometric Theory*, 13, 185–213.

Ching, A., & M. Osborne (2020). "Identification and estimation of forward-looking behavior: The case of consumer stockpiling." *Marketing Science*, 39, 707–726.

Chiong, K. X., A. Galichon, & M. Shum (2016). "Duality in dynamic discrete-choice models." *Quantitative Economics*, 7, 83–115.

Connault, B. (2016). "Hidden rust models." Working paper, University of Pennsylvania.

Dalton, C. M., G. Gowrisankaran, & R. J. Town (2020). "Salience, myopia, and complex dynamic incentives: Evidence from Medicare part D." *Review of Economic Studies*, 87, 822–869.

Dubin, J. A., & D. McFadden (1984). "An econometric analysis of residential electric appliance holdings and consumption." *Econometrica*, 52, 345–362.

Fang, H., & Y. Wang (2015). "Estimating dynamic discrete choice models with hyperbolic discounting, with an application to mammography decisions." *International Economic Review*, 56, 565–596.

Honoré, B. E., & J. L. Powell (2005). Chapter 22, "Identification and inference for econometric models." In *Pairwise difference estimators for nonlinear models*, 520–553. Cambridge, UK: Cambridge University Press.

Hotz, V. J., & R. A. Miller (1993). "Conditional choice probabilities and the estimation of dynamic models." *Review of Economic Studies*, 60, 497–529.

Hotz, V. J., R. A. Miller, S. Sanders, & J. Smith (1994). "A simulation estimator for dynamic models of discrete choice." *Review of Economic Studies*, 61, 265–289.

Hu, Y., & M. Shum (2012). "Nonparametric identification of dynamic models with unobserved state variables." *Journal of Econometrics*, 171, 32–44.

Hu, Y., M. Shum, W. Tan, & R. Xiao (2017). "A simple estimator for dynamic models with serially correlated unobservables." *Journal of Eonometric Methods*, 6, 1–16.

Imai, S., N. Jain, & A. Ching (2009). "Bayesian estimation of dynamic discrete choice models." *Econometrica*, 77, 1865–1899.

Iskhakov, F., J. Lee, J. Rust, B. Schjerning, & K. Seo (2016). "Constrained optimization approaches to estimation of structural models: Comment." *Econometrica*, 84, 365–370.

Kasahara, H., & K. Shimotsu (2009). "Nonparametric identification of finite mixture models of dynamic discrete choices." *Econometrica*, 77, 135–175.

Klein, R. W., & R. H. Spady (1993). "An efficient semiparametric estimator for binary response models." *Econometrica*, 61, 387–421.

Kong, X., J.-P. Dubé, & O. Daljord (2022). "Nonparametric estimation of habitual brand loyalty." Working paper, University of Chicago.

Luce, R. D. (1959). *Individual choice Behavior: A theoretical analysis*. New York: Wiley.

Magnac, T., & D. Thesmar (2002). "Identifying dynamic discrete decision processes." *Econometrica*, 70, 801–816.

McFadden, D. (1974). Chapter 4, "Conditional logit analysis of qualitative choice behavior." In *Frontiers in Econometrics*, 105–142. Cambridge: Academic Press.

McFadden, D. (1978). Chapter 3, "Modelling the choice of residential location." In Vol. 3 of *Spatial interaction theory and planning models*, A. Karlqvist, L. Lundqvist, F. Snickars, and J. W. Weibull (Eds.), 75–96. Amsterdam: North Holland Publishing.

McFadden, D. (1981). Chapter 5, "Structural analysis of discrete data with econometric applications." In *Econometric models of probabilistic choice*, 198–272. Cambridge, MA: MIT Press.

McFadden, D. (2001). "Economic choices." *American Economic Review*, 91, 351–378.

McFadden, D., & K. Train (2000). "Mixed MNL models for discrete response." *Journal of Applied Econometrics*, 15, 447–470.

Norets, A. (2009). "Inference in dynamic discrete choice models with serially correlated unobserved state variables." *Econometrica*, 77, 1665–1682.

Rust, J. (1987). "Optimal replacement of GMC bus engines: An empirical model of Harold Zurcher." *Econometrica*, 55, 999–1033.

Rust, J. (1994). *Structural estimation of Markov decision processes*. Chapter 51 in Vol. 4 of *Handbook of Econometrics*, 3081–3143. Amsterdam: Elsevier.

Small, K. A., & H. S. Rosen (1981). "Applied welfare economics with discrete choice models." *Econometrica*, 49, 105–130.

Stokey, N. L., & R. E. Lucas (1989). *Recursive methods in economic dynamics*. Cambridge, MA: Harvard University Press.

Su, C.-L., & K. L. Judd (2012). "Constrained optimization approaches to estimation of structural models." *Econometrica*, 80, 2213–2230.

Train, K. E. (2009). *Discrete choice methods with simulation*, 2nd ed. Cambridge: Cambridge University Press.

3

Demand Estimation Using Market-Level Data

In this chapter, we study estimation methods of demand systems derived under various assumptions on the consumer preferences and optimization structures. According to conventional consumer theory, Marshallian and Hicksian demand systems are derived as a result of the consumers' budget-constrained optimization problem. However, a modern approach to empirical demand systems begins from a discrete-choice problem of consumers and aggregates the individual choice probabilities to form market demand.

An empirical demand system has certain restrictions to be imposed, which are inherent from the consumers' respective optimization problem. Those restrictions are empirically tested or imposed as a priori model structures. We also study how different setups on the consumer preferences and optimization problems lead to various empirical demand systems and restrictions imposed on them and how they can be estimated or tested.

Demand estimation has been a central problem in the modern empirical industrial organization literature and quantitative marketing because it is fundamental to structural analyses in diverse contexts that involve consumer demand. The primary aim of demand estimation is to estimate the own- and cross-price elasticities. Combined with cost-parameter estimates of an industry, they can be used for applied analyses, including computing price-cost margins, merger analysis, and welfare changes due to the introduction of a new product, and so on.

Throughout the chapter, we assume that only market-level data on the prices, quantities, and other product characteristics of an alternative in the choice set are available to an econometrician. Although not reviewed in this chapter, remarkably, recent advances in the literature make extensive use of individual-level purchase data, taking individual-level heterogeneity more seriously.

3.1 Product-Space Approach

The product-space approach, from which we begin our discussion on demand systems, attempts to directly estimate the own- and cross-price elasticities of a demand system. In a sense, the product-space approach is more flexible than the characteristics-space approach, at a cost of a rapidly increasing number of parameters to be estimated. The approach is often referred to as "estimating the reduced-form demand systems."

3.1.1 Linear and Log-Linear Demand Model

We start with the simplest linear demand model. Let j and k denote alternatives. In the linear demand model, the market demand for product j is specified as

$$q_j = a_j + \sum_{k=1}^{J} \beta_{j,k} p_k + \epsilon_j. \tag{3.1.1}$$

Equation (3.1.1) can be interpreted as a first-order approximation of any demand system. In that regard, $\epsilon_{j,k}$ can be an approximation error or a measurement error. Each product j has its own intercept, a_j. Summing over k for each fixed j also allows the nonzero cross-price elasticities. However, this model can predict even a negative market demand q_j, which is problematic.

A straightforward modification of equation (3.1.1) is the following log-linear specification:

$$\ln q_j = a_j + \sum_{k=1}^{J} \beta_{j,k} \ln p_k + \epsilon_j. \tag{3.1.2}$$

Because $\varepsilon_{j,k} := \frac{d \ln q_j}{d \ln p_k} = \beta_{j,k}$ is the cross-price elasticity between products j and k, it is immediate that the own- and cross-price elasticities in this empirical specification are constant.

3.1.2 The Almost Ideal Demand System

Deaton and Muellbauer (1980a) elaborate on the reduced-form demand estimation problem in the context of the aggregation theory of Walrasian demand systems. The motivation for the development of the Almost Ideal Demand System (AIDS)[1] was to rationalize the aggregate consumer demand as if it were the outcome of a single representative utility-maximizing consumer.

1. This AIDS (1980) was developed before the other AIDS was first discovered (1981).

Consider the following form of the individual expenditure function:

$$c_i(\mathbf{p}, u_i) = \kappa_i \left(a(\mathbf{p})^\alpha (1 - u_i) + b(\mathbf{p})^\alpha u_i\right)^{\frac{1}{\alpha}},$$

where the real-valued functions $a(\mathbf{p})$ and $b(\mathbf{p})$ are concave and homogeneous of degree 1 in $\mathbf{p}$. This form of expenditure function belongs to a class called the "price-independent generalized linear (PIGL)" form, which is price independent in the sense that the associated income function in the budget shares is independent of price.[2] PIGL is the only form of expenditure function that allows an exact non-linear aggregation of the expenditure function across heterogeneous households, regardless of the price vector $\mathbf{p}$ and income distribution.[3] That is, it can be shown that there exists the representative consumer's expenditure function:

$$c(\mathbf{p}, u) = \left(a(\mathbf{p})^\alpha (1 - u) + b(\mathbf{p})^\alpha u\right)^{\frac{1}{\alpha}},$$

which aggregates c_i in a certain nonlinear way. Sending α to zero and taking logarithms yield the price-independent generalized log-linear (PIGLOG) expenditure function, which is

$$\ln c(\mathbf{p}, u) = (1 - u)\ln a(\mathbf{p}) + u \ln b(\mathbf{p}). \tag{3.1.3}$$

The AIDS specification begins from equation (3.1.3). The following functional form specification allows a second-order approximation of an arbitrary expenditure function:

$$\ln a(\mathbf{p}) = a_0 + \sum_k a_k \ln p_k + \frac{1}{2}\sum_k \sum_j \gamma^*_{k,j} \ln p_k \ln p_j$$

$$\ln b(\mathbf{p}) = \ln a(\mathbf{p}) + \beta_0 \exp\left(\sum_k \beta_k \ln p_k\right).$$[4]

2. Formally, the associated budget shares $w_{i,j}(\mathbf{p}, y_i)$ take the following functional form:

$$w_{i,j}(\mathbf{p}, y_i) = y_i^{-\eta} A_j(\mathbf{p}) + B_j(\mathbf{p}),$$

where the functions $A_j(\mathbf{p})$ and $B_j(\mathbf{p})$ are homogeneous of degree 0 and they satisfy $\sum_{j\in\mathcal{J}} A_j(\mathbf{p}) = 0$, $\sum_{j\in\mathcal{J}} B_j(\mathbf{p}) = 1$.

3. PIGL is equivalent to the Gorman polar form under mild conditions. See Muellbauer (1975, 1976) for a detailed argument and proof.

Substituting these back to equation (3.1.3), the AIDS expenditure function is given by

$$\ln c(\mathbf{p}, u) = a_0 + \sum_k a_k \ln p_k + \frac{1}{2}\sum_k \sum_j \gamma^*_{k,j} \ln p_k \ln p_j$$

$$+ u\beta_0 \exp\left(\sum_k \beta_k \ln p_k\right). \tag{3.1.4}$$

Our goal is to derive an estimation equation for the associated demand system in terms of the expenditure share and income level by eliminating the utility level u.

Let us first differentiate the left-hand side of equation (3.1.4) with respect to $\ln p_j$. It gives the expenditure share of product j:

$$\frac{\partial \ln c(\mathbf{p}, u)}{\partial \ln p_j} = \frac{\partial c(\mathbf{p}, u)}{\partial p_j}\frac{p_j}{c(\mathbf{p}, u)} = \frac{p_j q_j}{c(\mathbf{p}, u)} = w_j,$$

where we invoked Shephard's lemma in the second equality. Differentiating the right-hand side of equation (3.1.4) with respect to $\ln p_j$ and equating with the above display equation gives

$$w_j = \alpha_j + \sum_k \gamma_{j,k} \ln p_k + \beta_j u \beta_0 \exp\left(\sum_k \beta_k \ln p_k\right), \tag{3.1.5}$$

where we define $\gamma_{j,k} = \frac{1}{2}\left(\gamma^*_{j,k} + \gamma^*_{k,j}\right)$.

The next step is to eliminate u from equation (3.1.5). Let us further define the AIDS price index as

$$\ln P = a_0 + \sum_k a_k \ln p_k + \frac{1}{2}\sum_k \sum_j \gamma^*_{k,j} \ln p_k \ln p_j,$$

which can be estimated either in its exact form or in a first-order approximation. Substituting $c(\mathbf{p}, u) = w$ back into equation (3.1.4) and rearranging gives

$$u = \frac{\ln\left(\frac{w}{P}\right)}{\beta_0 \exp\left(\sum_k \beta_k \ln p_k\right)}. \tag{3.1.6}$$

4. It shall become clear that the functional form $\beta_0 \exp\left(\sum_k \beta_k \ln p_k\right)$ is reverse engineered such that it is canceled out but β_j is left in the estimation equation.

Substituting equation (3.1.6) back into equation (3.1.5) gives the AIDS estimation equation:

$$w_j = \alpha_j + \sum_k \gamma_{j,k} \ln p_k + \beta_j \ln\left(\frac{w}{P}\right). \tag{3.1.7}$$

Equation (3.1.7) is the AIDS demand function in the expenditure-share form, given that the following testable parameter restrictions are met: (1) $\sum_j \alpha_j = 1$ and $\sum_j \gamma^*_{k,j} = \sum_k \gamma^*_{k,j} = \sum_j \beta_j = 0$ for equation (3.1.4) to be a legitimate expenditure function, and (2) $\gamma_{k,j} = \gamma_{j,k}$ for Slutsky symmetry. If these restrictions are met, equation (3.1.7) represents a system of Marshallian demand functions that add up to the total expenditure. The Marshallian and Hicksian price elasticities and the income elasticity have the following expressions:

$$\varepsilon^M_{j,k} = -\mathbf{1}\,(j=k) + \left(\frac{\gamma_{j,k}}{w_j}\right) - \left(\frac{\beta_j}{w_j}\right) w_k.$$

$$\varepsilon^H_{j,k} = \varepsilon^M_{j,k} + \eta_j w_k.$$

$$\eta_j = 1 + \left(\frac{\beta_j}{w_j}\right).$$

As an arbitrary second-order approximation to any PIGLOG class of demand systems, AIDS has several theoretically desirable properties. Furthermore, estimating the system looks simple, so it has been popular in the literature. Exemplar applications include Hausman, Leonard, and Zona (1994) and Chaudhuri, Goldberg, and Jia (2006). Major challenges for the estimation include the number of parameters and the number of instruments for a consistent estimation. Specifically, the number of endogenous variables to be estimated increases on the order of J^2.

3.1.3 Further Discussion of the Product-Space Approach

The product-space approach has two major limitations. First, a curse-of-dimensionality problem exists, originating from the flexibility that all the cross-price elasticities should be estimated. It is generally a difficult problem to tackle because not only does the number of the parameters to be estimated increase, but also the number of instrumental variables should increase. The solution for this curse of dimensionality problem would be imposing a structure on the substitution pattern, which is a primary motivation of the characteristics space approach that we study in this chapter. Note that within the product space approach, Pinkse, Slade, and Brett (2002) and Pinkse and Slade (2004) have developed a method to address the curse of dimensionality by taking the cross-price elasticity as a function of the "distance" between the product attributes. Second, the product space approach does not allow for some interesting counterfactuals, such as the response of the market when a new product is introduced. These two major shortcomings were the motivations for the development of the characteristics-space approach, which we discuss in section 3.2.

We mention two potential problems that persist in the characteristics-space approach here. The first is the endogeneity of the prices. The observed market data are from the supply-demand equilibrium. Although none of the works mentioned here pay explicit attention to what the error term includes, the price and the error term are likely to be positively correlated. An upward-sloping demand curve is often estimated when this type of endogeneity is not appropriately taken into account. A common solution is to find a cost shifter as an instrument. Second, in log-log/multiplicative models, zero demand is inherently ruled out. Rationalizing zeroes in multiplicative models[5] is an ongoing area of research (see, e.g., Dubé, Hortaçsu, and Joo, 2021; Gandhi, Lu, and Shi, 2019).

Deaton and Muellbauer (1980b) is a classic reference of the product-space approach to aggregate demand estimation, which provides a thorough treatment on the derivation of an empirical demand system from preference relations. Although the product-space approach in demand estimation was developed in the context of the classical Marshallian demand framework where utility maximization under a binding budget constraint of a representative consumer is assumed, the approach is flexible enough to be applied to the world where the budget constraint is not binding.

3.2 Characteristics-Space Approach I: Static Logit Demand Models

In the characteristics-space approach, a product is defined by a bundle of observed and unobserved product characteristics. It reduces the parameter dimensions substantially and allows counterfactual analyses such as consumer welfare changes by new product entry. It has become the de facto standard method for demand estimation since Berry (1994) and Berry, Levinsohn, and Pakes (1995).

3.2.1 Microfoundation: Discrete-Choice Random Utility Maximization

In the characteristics-space approach, a product is decomposed into the bundle of characteristics $(\mathbf{x}_j, p_j, \xi_j)$, where $(\mathbf{x}_j, p_j)$ is observed but ξ_j is unobserved

5. This applies not only to the demand models, but also to the gravity models in the international trade literature.

to an econometrician. Demand-estimation literature based on this approach has been developed upon the discrete-choice random utility maximization (RUM) framework that we studied in section 2.2 in chapter 2. We briefly review the discrete-choice RUM approach in the context of demand estimation.

Consumer *i*'s utility from consuming product *j* is given by

$$u_{i,j}=\alpha_i\left(w_i-p_j\right)+\mathbf{x}_j'\boldsymbol{\beta}_i+\xi_j+\epsilon_{i,j}, \qquad (3.2.1)$$

where w_i is the consumer's income; p_j is the price of product j; $\mathbf{x}_j$ is the observed characteristics of product j; ξ_j represents utility from the unobserved (only to the econometrician—consumers observe ξ_j fully) characteristics of product j; and $\epsilon_{i,j}$ denotes the idiosyncratic utility shocks.[6] The explicit distinction between the two error terms ξ_j and $\epsilon_{i,j}$ was one of the key breakthroughs made by Berry (1994) and Berry et al. (1995). Note also that we allowed coefficients $\left(\alpha_i, \boldsymbol{\beta}_i\right)$ to vary over individual i. The detailed implications of these features are discussed later in this chapter, in section 3.2.2.

Individual i chooses product j if the product maximizes the utility over the finite choice set $\mathcal{J}_t$; that is,

$$j=\arg\max_{k\in\mathcal{J}_t}\left\{u_{i,k}\right\} \qquad (3.2.2)$$

$$=\arg\max_{k\in\mathcal{J}_t}\left\{u_{i,k}-\alpha_i w_i\right\}. \qquad (3.2.3)$$

The solution for the unconstrained utility-maximization problem in equation (3.2.2) is invariant to a location adjustment. Because we have assumed that $u_{i,j}$ is linear in $\alpha_i w_i$, we made a location adjustment in equation (3.2.3) to eliminate the income effect.[7] We also note that $\mathcal{J}_t$ must include the numeraire denoted by product 0 for the demand system derived from the choice problem in equation (3.2.3) to be sensible, and also for the identification purposes that we discuss later. If the numeraire is not included, a price increase of an alternative would induce an individual to switch to another alternative in the set of alternatives, and the extensive margin would be completely ruled out. Alternative 0 is often interpreted as the *composite outside goods*. Here, p_0, $\mathbf{x}_0$, and ξ_0 are normalized to zero, so that $E\left[u_{i,0}\right]=0$.

As studied in section 2.2, we obtain the following expression of the individual choice probability $\Pr\left(i \text{ chooses } j\right)$ by assuming that $\epsilon_{i,j}$ follows the mean-zero i.i.d. type I extreme value distribution:

6. We interpret $u_{i,j}$ as direct utility from choosing alternative j, and relegate the discussion about the interpretation of $u_{i,j}$ as "conditional indirect utility" to section 3.2.3.4.

7. As such, the linearity of $u_{i,j}$ in income is not an innocuous assumption. We further discuss the consequences of the assumption on the functional forms of the utility specification in section 3.2.3.4.

$$\Pr\left(i \text{ chooses } j\right) = \frac{\exp\left(-\alpha_i p_j + \mathbf{x}_j'\boldsymbol{\beta}_i + \xi_j\right)}{\sum_{k\in\mathcal{J}_t}\exp\left(-\alpha_i p_k + \mathbf{x}_k'\boldsymbol{\beta}_i + \xi_k\right)}. \tag{3.2.4}$$

This individual choice probability equation, which shall be equalized with the predicted individual quantity shares and combined with a few approximation assumptions, completely specifies the logit demand system.[8]

3.2.2 *Logit Demand Models with Aggregate Market Data*

We assume that an econometrician has data on market shares, prices, some characteristics, and the availability of each product in each market. We also assume the existence of suitable instruments to correct for the endogeneity of prices. Throughout the section, we denote s_j as the observed market share and π_j as the predicted market share of alternative j, respectively.

We begin our discussion by distinguishing between the two error terms, ξ_j and $\epsilon_{i,j}$. These terms are included in the model for different reasons; ξ_j represents the product characteristics that are not observable to the econometrician. Because ξ_j directly enters into the consumer's utility specification, it might be regarded as consumers' mean valuations of the product characteristics that are unobservable to the econometrician. On the suppliers' side, ξ_j captures the quality of a product, which is highly likely to be correlated with the firms' pricing decision. For this reason, we need to correct for the endogeneity of ξ_j using the instruments. On the other hand, $\epsilon_{i,j}$, which is often referred to as the idiosyncratic utility shocks, is included to derive a tractable expression for the choice probability equation. It allows us to derive the individual choice probability equation in terms of the other model parameters, so it is washed out in equation (3.2.4). Inclusion of $\epsilon_{i,j}$ is the reason why the framework formulated in equations (3.2.1)–(3.2.3) is called "discrete-choice *random* utility."

3.2.2.1 HOMOGENEOUS LOGIT MODEL OF DEMAND

We study Berry (1994)'s homogeneous logit model of demand first. Suppose that $\boldsymbol{\beta}_i = \boldsymbol{\beta}$, $\alpha_i = \alpha$ for all i. That is, we are removing all the structural heterogeneity over individuals in the utility specification in equation (3.2.1), and thus from

8. If a researcher has individual choice-level data, then equation (3.2.4) can be used as a building block for the likelihood expressed in equation (2.2.4) in section 2.2.2 of chapter 2. Maximum likelihood estimation, however, may not be as straightforward when possible endogeneity in some of the covariates $(p_j, \mathbf{x}_j)$ needs to be addressed.

equation (3.2.4) as well. We relax this homogeneity assumption later in this discussion. Under this homogeneity assumption, the individual choice probability equation (3.2.4) reduces to

$$\Pr\left(i \text{ chooses } j\right) = \frac{\exp\left(-\alpha p_j + \mathbf{x}_j'\boldsymbol{\beta} + \xi_j\right)}{\sum_{k\in\mathcal{J}_t}\exp\left(-\alpha p_k + \mathbf{x}_k'\boldsymbol{\beta} + \xi_k\right)}.$$

If infinitely many consumers are in a market, we may equate the individual choice probability $\Pr\left(i \text{ chooses } j\right)$ with the predicted market share π_j, and then approximate it with the observed market share s_j. Therefore, we have

$$s_j \simeq \pi_j \tag{3.2.5}$$

$$= \frac{\exp\left(-\alpha p_j + \mathbf{x}_j'\boldsymbol{\beta} + \xi_j\right)}{\sum_{k\in\mathcal{J}_t}\exp\left(-\alpha p_k + \mathbf{x}_k'\boldsymbol{\beta} + \xi_k\right)} \tag{3.2.6}$$

for each product j, which is often referred to as the "market share equation."[9] By taking the ratios s_j/s_0 and logarithms, and then invoking the normalization assumption on $\left(p_0, \mathbf{x}_0, \xi_0\right)$, we obtain

$$\ln\left(\frac{s_j}{s_0}\right) = -\alpha p_j + \mathbf{x}_j'\boldsymbol{\beta} + \xi_j. \tag{3.2.7}$$

Equation (3.2.7) is the estimation equation for the homogeneous logit model of demand. With a suitable set of instruments $\mathbf{z}_j$[10] to correct for the endogeneity of ξ_j, we can estimate the model parameters $(\alpha, \boldsymbol{\beta})$ consistently by using generalized method of moments (GMM) with the moment condition $\mathbb{E}\left[\xi_j|\mathbf{z}_j\right] = 0$. In section 3.2.3, we discuss the choice of suitable instruments.

3.2.2.2 RANDOM COEFFICIENTS LOGIT MODEL OF DEMAND

In the random coefficients logit model developed by Berry et al. (1995) (BLP), the coefficients in the individual choice probability equation may vary over i. For tractability, distributions of $\left(\alpha_i, \boldsymbol{\beta}_i\right)$ are assumed to be known up to finite-dimensional parameters $\boldsymbol{\Pi}$ and $\boldsymbol{\Sigma}$. To that end, BLP assume that individual i's utility of choosing product j is specified as

9. Note the distinction between the market share equation and the individual choice probability equation. This market share equation is a result of aggregation, approximation, and equating with observed data on the left-hand side.

10. Here, $\mathbf{z}_j$ includes all the exogenous components of $\mathbf{x}_j$.

$$
\begin{aligned}
u_{i,j} &= \alpha_i\left(w_i - p_j\right) + \mathbf{x}_j'\boldsymbol{\beta}_i + \xi_j + \epsilon_{i,j} \qquad \epsilon_{i,j} \sim \text{i.i.d. } T1EV \\
\begin{pmatrix}\alpha_i \\ \boldsymbol{\beta}_i\end{pmatrix} &= \begin{pmatrix}\alpha \\ \boldsymbol{\beta}\end{pmatrix} + \boldsymbol{\Pi}\mathbf{q}_i + \boldsymbol{\Sigma}\mathbf{v}_i \\
&= \begin{pmatrix}\alpha \\ \boldsymbol{\beta}\end{pmatrix} + \begin{pmatrix}\boldsymbol{\Pi}_\alpha \\ \boldsymbol{\Pi}_\beta\end{pmatrix}\mathbf{q}_i + \begin{pmatrix}\boldsymbol{\Sigma}_\alpha \\ \boldsymbol{\Sigma}_\beta\end{pmatrix}\begin{pmatrix}v_{\alpha,i} \\ \mathbf{v}_{\beta,i}\end{pmatrix},
\end{aligned} \tag{3.2.8}
$$

where $\mathbf{q}_i$ is the demographic variables and $\mathbf{v}_i$ is an idiosyncratic taste shock, $\boldsymbol{\Pi}$ represents the correlation between demographics and the coefficients, and $\boldsymbol{\Sigma}$ is the correlation between the taste shocks $\mathbf{v}_i$ and the coefficients. We assume that the distribution of $\mathbf{q}_i$ and $\mathbf{v}_i$ are fully known. For the idiosyncratic shocks $\mathbf{v}_i$, the assumption that $\mathbf{v}_i \sim \mathcal{N}\left(\mathbf{0}, \mathbf{I}_{\dim(\mathbf{v}_i)}\right)$ is common.[11] The demographics $\mathbf{q}_i$ can be drawn from the population distribution, such as population census data. See Nevo (2001); Petrin (2002) and Berry, Levinsohn, and Pakes (2004a) for discussions and examples of which variables can be included in $\mathbf{q}_i$.

When we allow coefficients to vary across individuals, the right-hand side of the market share equation should involve the expectation over i. Specifically,

$$
\begin{aligned}
s_j &\simeq \pi_j && (3.2.9)\\
&= \mathbb{E}\left[\Pr\left(i \text{ chooses } j\right)\right] && (3.2.10)\\
&= \int_{\mathbf{v}_i}\int_{\mathbf{q}_i} \Pr\left(i \text{ chooses } j\right) dF\left(\mathbf{q}_i\right) dF\left(\mathbf{v}_i\right) && (3.2.11)\\
&= \int_{\mathbf{v}_i}\int_{\mathbf{q}_i} \frac{\exp\left(-\alpha_i p_j + \mathbf{x}_j'\boldsymbol{\beta}_i + \xi_j\right)}{\sum_{k\in\mathcal{J}_t}\exp\left(-\alpha_i p_k + \mathbf{x}_k'\boldsymbol{\beta}_i + \xi_k\right)} dF\left(\mathbf{q}_i\right) dF\left(\mathbf{v}_i\right) && (3.2.12)\\
&\simeq \frac{1}{n_s}\sum_{i=1}^{n_s} \frac{\exp\left(-\alpha_i p_j + \mathbf{x}_j'\boldsymbol{\beta}_i + \xi_j\right)}{\sum_{k\in\mathcal{J}_t}\exp\left(-\alpha_i p_k + \mathbf{x}_k'\boldsymbol{\beta}_i + \xi_k\right)}.^{12} && (3.2.13)
\end{aligned}
$$

Now the inversion does not have a simple closed-form formula as in equation (3.2.7). In fact, the invertibility of equation (3.2.12) itself to recover $(\alpha, \boldsymbol{\beta})$ is not trivial, the proof of which is one of the major contributions of Berry (1994) and

11. Including nonzero covariance terms is not impossible, but it incurs a serious challenge to identification. See section 3.2.3.3 for further details.

12. Note that we implicitly assume $\mathbf{q}_i \perp\!\!\!\perp \mathbf{v}_i$ in equation (3.2.11).

Berry et al. (1995).[13] In the random coefficients logit demand model, the market share inversion should be done numerically in the estimation, which we discuss next.

Equation (3.2.13) is added to approximate the values of the integrals in equation (3.2.12) because the closed-form formula for the integral is not available in general. BLP's solution to this problem was to approximate the exact integral using a simulation integral. Because we assume that the distribution $F(\mathbf{q}_i)$ and $F(\mathbf{v}_i)$ are fully known, the distribution of $\mathbf{q}_i$ and $\mathbf{v}_i$ can be simulated. Combined with equation (3.2.8), we can simulate the distribution of $\Pr(i \text{ chooses } j)$ for any given set of parameter values $(\alpha, \boldsymbol{\beta}, \boldsymbol{\Pi}, \boldsymbol{\Sigma})$. It leads us to equation (3.2.13), which approximate the integral $\mathbb{E}\left[\Pr(i \text{ chooses } j)\right]$ with the average of n_s numbers of simulation draws.[14] We take both *approximations* (3.2.11) and (3.2.13) as *exact* during the estimation.

Two dimensions of approximations, equations (3.2.9) and (3.2.13), are involved in the market share equation of BLP. In principle, the errors from both approximations should be considered in the inference, but they are ignored in most of the applications. In theory, the approximation error from taking equation (3.2.13) as an equality is considered to be less of a problem because n_s can be set as an arbitrarily large number, provided that the computing power and time allow. Different asymptotics are applied in different circumstances for the simulation error to wash out. Berry, Linton, and Pakes (2004b) show n_s should be of an order of $\sqrt{|\mathcal{J}_t|} + \eta$ for some $\eta > 0$ when only one market exists and $|\mathcal{J}_t|$ is growing to infinity. Freyberger (2015) shows that when the number of markets T grows to infinity with a finite $|\mathcal{J}_t|$, n_s should be of an order of $T^2 + \eta$. We note that the upper bound of n_s seems to be several thousand in most applications.

Taking equation (3.2.9) as equality may cause a more serious conceptual problem. Freyberger (2015) shows that when the number of markets T grows to infinity, the number of consumers $|\mathcal{I}|$ should grow with an order of $T^2 + \eta$ for the approximation error from taking equation (3.2.9) as equality to disappear at least asymptotically. It can be more problematic when only a finite number of consumers are making the underlying discrete choices. Gandhi, Lu, and Shi (2019) argue that any finite approximation that takes equation (3.2.9) as equality is uninformative for the probability distribution of the parameters.

13. The most general version of the demand-system invertibility theorem to date can be found in Berry, Gandhi, and Haile (2013). Berry and Haile (2014) study the identification of the random coefficients $(\alpha_i, \boldsymbol{\beta}_i)$ based on Berry, Gandhi, and Haile's invertibility results.

14. It would be also possible to approximate the integrals using quadratures, importance sampling, or Halton sequences. Conlon and Gortmaker (2020) provides a discussion of the benefits and costs of various methods to simulate the integrals.

3.2.2.3 ESTIMATION OF THE RANDOM COEFFICIENTS LOGIT MODEL OF DEMAND

The objective of the BLP estimation is essentially the same with the homogeneous logit model: GMM estimation with the moment condition $\mathbb{E}\left[\xi_j|\mathbf{z}_j\right]=0$. All the extra complications during the estimation routine arise from the nontrivial invertibility of the market share equation (3.2.12).

Let t denote different markets, labeled from 1 to T. What we want to do is find the parameter values of $(\alpha, \boldsymbol{\beta}, \boldsymbol{\Pi}, \boldsymbol{\Sigma})$ to minimize the following GMM objective function:

$$\sum_{j,t}\left(\xi_{j,t}\mathbf{z}_{j,t}\right)'\boldsymbol{\Omega}\left(\xi_{j,t}\mathbf{z}_{j,t}\right),$$

where $\boldsymbol{\Omega}$ is a GMM weighting matrix. Consider the unobservable $\xi_{j,t}$, which would be some function of the parameters $(\alpha, \boldsymbol{\beta}, \boldsymbol{\Pi}, \boldsymbol{\Sigma})$ and the data $\left(p_{j,t}, \mathbf{x}_{j,t}, \mathbf{q}_i, \mathbf{v}_i\right)$. Denote the function by $\xi_{j,t}\left(\alpha, \boldsymbol{\beta}, \boldsymbol{\Pi}, \boldsymbol{\Sigma}\,|p_{j,t}, \mathbf{x}_{j,t}, \mathbf{q}_i, \mathbf{v}_i\right)$. In the homogeneous logit model,

$$\begin{aligned}
\xi_{j,t} &\equiv \xi_{j,t}\left(\alpha, \boldsymbol{\beta}, \boldsymbol{\Pi}, \boldsymbol{\Sigma}\,|p_{j,t}, \mathbf{x}_{j,t}, \mathbf{q}_i, \mathbf{v}_i\right) \\
&= \xi_{j,t}\left(\alpha, \boldsymbol{\beta}\,|p_{j,t}, \mathbf{x}_{j,t}\right) \\
&= \ln\left(\frac{s_j}{s_0}\right) - \left(-\alpha p_{j,t} + \mathbf{x}_{j,t}'\boldsymbol{\beta}\right),
\end{aligned}$$

which is linear. However, in the random coefficients logit model, a closed-form expression for inversion no longer exists. What can be shown is only that such a function $\xi_{j,t}\left(\alpha, \boldsymbol{\beta}, \boldsymbol{\Pi}, \boldsymbol{\Sigma}\,|p_{j,t}, \mathbf{x}_{j,t}, \mathbf{q}_i, \mathbf{v}_i\right)$ exists and the value at each parameter value can be calculated in a certain nonlinear way. To that end, the optimization problem that BLP solves is

$$\begin{aligned}
\min_{\alpha,\boldsymbol{\beta},\boldsymbol{\Pi},\boldsymbol{\Sigma}} &\sum_{j,t}\left(\xi_{j,t}\left(\alpha, \boldsymbol{\beta}, \boldsymbol{\Pi}, \boldsymbol{\Sigma}\,|p_{j,t}, \mathbf{x}_{j,t}, \mathbf{q}_i, \mathbf{v}_i\right)\mathbf{z}_{j,t}\right)' \\
&\boldsymbol{\Omega}\left(\xi_{j,t}\left(\alpha, \boldsymbol{\beta}, \boldsymbol{\Pi}, \boldsymbol{\Sigma}\,|p_{j,t}, \mathbf{x}_{j,t}, \mathbf{q}_i, \mathbf{v}_i\right)\mathbf{z}_{j,t}\right). \qquad (3.2.14)
\end{aligned}$$

The original BLP paper suggested the nested fixed point (NFP) algorithm to calculate $\delta_{j,t}$, and in turn $\xi_{j,t}$, at each possible parameter value. The NFP algorithm solves the fixed-point equation to find $\xi_{j,t}$ for each candidate parameter value $(\alpha, \boldsymbol{\beta}, \boldsymbol{\Pi}, \boldsymbol{\Sigma})$ at each iteration. Evaluating the fixed-point equations is computationally expensive, and therefore, the NFP algorithm with a contraction-mapping iteration originally proposed by Berry (1994); Berry et al. (1995) can be computationally very heavy. Conlon and Gortmaker (2020) note that applying quasi-Newton methods to the fixed-point iteration would reduce the computational burden substantially.

Recent developments on the numerical optimization techniques led to the mathematical programming under equality constraints (MPEC) approach, which is much faster and more reliable. The optimization problem in equation (3.2.14) can be rewritten as

$$\min_{\{\xi_{j,t},\boldsymbol{\zeta}_{j,t}\}_{j\in\mathcal{J}_t,t\in\mathcal{T}},\alpha,\boldsymbol{\beta},\boldsymbol{\Pi},\boldsymbol{\Sigma}} \sum_{j,t} \boldsymbol{\zeta}'_{j,t}\boldsymbol{\Omega}\boldsymbol{\zeta}_{j,t}$$

$$\text{s.t.} \quad s_{j,t} = \frac{1}{n_s}\sum_{i=1}^{n_s} \frac{\exp\left(-\alpha_i p_{j,t} + \mathbf{x}'_{j,t}\boldsymbol{\beta}_i + \xi_{j,t}\right)}{\sum_{k\in\mathcal{J}_t}\exp\left(-\alpha_i p_{k,t} + \mathbf{x}'_{k,t}\boldsymbol{\beta}_i + \xi_{k,t}\right)} \tag{3.2.15}$$

$$\boldsymbol{\zeta}_{j,t} = \xi_{j,t}\mathbf{z}_{j,t} \qquad \forall j,t. \tag{3.2.16}$$

Dube et al. (2012) show equation (3.2.15) is equivalent to equation (3.2.14); that is, they both yield the same solution. Notice that equation (3.2.15) is an implicit function of $\xi_{j,t}$, and the optimizer adjusts around all the $\xi_{j,t}$ as if they were variables. In a sense, MPEC leaves the nonlinear fixed-point inversion problem of finding $\delta_{j,t}$ to the numerical optimizers. The major speed advantage of MPEC comes from the fact that the optimizer does not need to solve for the fixed point at every candidate parameter value. MPEC requires the fixed-point equation to be satisfied only at the optimum. For further details about the estimation, we encourage readers to refer to the online appendices of Dube et al. (2012).

3.2.3 Further Discussion of the Static Logit Demand Models

3.2.3.1 IDENTIFICATION 1: PRICE ENDOGENEITY AND THE CHOICE OF THE INSTRUMENTS FOR PRICES

Recall the utility specification and the estimation equation of the homogeneous logit model of demand:

$$u_{i,j} = \alpha\left(w - p_j\right) + \mathbf{x}'_j\boldsymbol{\beta} + \xi_j + \epsilon_{i,j}$$

$$\ln\left(\frac{\pi_j}{\pi_0}\right) = -\alpha p_j + \mathbf{x}'_j\boldsymbol{\beta} + \xi_j, \tag{3.2.17}$$

where ξ_j represents the quality of product j, which is not captured by the utility from observable product characteristics $\mathbf{x}'_j\boldsymbol{\beta}$. The assumption that different characteristics of a product are independent of each other could be plausible in many empirical contexts. The observable product characteristics $\mathbf{x}_j$ can be taken as exogenous when we consider the consumer's choice. Thus, we can assume that $\mathbf{x}_j \perp\!\!\!\perp \xi_j$, or at least $Cov\left(\mathbf{x}_j, \xi_j\right) = \mathbf{0}$.[15]

However, it is unlikely that $Cov\left(p_j, \xi_j\right) = 0$. To see why, recall first that ξ_j represents the quality of option j from product attributes that are unobserved to the econometrician, but observed to the consumer.[16] Consumers prefer products with higher ξ_j. On the other hand, it is also likely that producing a high-quality product would incur a high cost of production, which is reflected in the pricing decisions of firms. Put differently, firms will charge higher prices for products that exhibit higher (marginal) costs of production, and the costs tend to increase with the unobserved quality term ξ_j. Furthermore, firms would want to set high prices for products with high ξ_j. Because price p_j is some function of $\mathbf{x}_j$ and ξ_j, an immediate consequence is that a strong endogeneity is involved for term p_j in the estimation equation (3.2.17). Therefore, it is highly likely that

$$\mathbb{E}\left[\xi_j | \mathbf{x}_j, p_j\right] > 0 \tag{3.2.18}$$

holds. Provided that $\mathbf{x}_j$ is exogenous, equation (3.2.18) leads to $Cov\left(\xi_j, p_j\right) > 0$,[17] which makes estimating equation (3.2.17) using least squares implausible. And the nature of the problem persists when we consider a random-coefficients specification.

Finding an instrument to correct for the endogeneity in prices has been a major challenge in the literature. In estimating the price coefficients of consumer demand systems, the classic choice of instrument is a cost shifter that is uncorrelated with the demand shocks. However, firms' cost shifters are not directly observable in most empirical contexts, which has been in fact one of the major motivations for estimating consumer demand systems first when analyzing industry structure. Therefore, researchers have tried to find some proxies for cost shifters to use as instruments for price endogeneity. Suitable instruments differ by empirical context, individual case, and data availability. No general solution exists for the problem of finding a suitable instrument. We introduce two examples that serve as proxies for cost shifters next.

Hausman, Leonard, and Zona (1994) use the averages of other cities' prices for the same product as a proxy for the cost shifter. Their identifying assumption is

15. Incorporating endogenous product characteristics is an ongoing area of research. See, for example, Fan (2013).

16. See, for example, Trajtenberg (1989) for an example of upward sloping demand caused for example,omitted attributes in discrete choice modeling.

17. Note that we assume the level of ξ_j is absorbed into the intercept term; in other words, we are implicitly assuming that $\mathbf{x}_j$ includes 1 as its element.

the following: Consider a set of geographically segregated markets. The valuations of each product may vary over markets (demand side), but the marginal cost of a product should be the same (supply side). Because the marginal costs are reflected in the prices of other markets concurrently, the means of other markets' prices can be used as a proxy for the cost shifters. Berry et al. (1995) use the sums of the values of the same characteristics of other products by the same firm, as well as the sums of the values of the same characteristics of products by other firms. The identifying assumption is similar but slightly different: some common *markup*-shifter component should exist in the summand.

3.2.3.2 OWN- AND CROSS-PRICE ELASTICITIES: IMPLICATIONS OF THE INDEPENDENCE OF IRRELEVANT ALTERNATIVES PROPERTY

Let $\pi_{i,j,t} := \Pr\left(i \text{ chooses } j|t\right)$ be the individual predicted quantity shares in market t. The own- and cross-price elasticities of the demand system specified by equation (3.2.12) are

$$\begin{aligned} \varepsilon_{jk,t} &= \frac{\partial \pi_{j,t}}{\partial p_{k,t}} \frac{p_{k,t}}{\pi_{j,t}} \\ &= \begin{cases} -\frac{p_{j,t}}{\pi_{j,t}} \int_{\mathbf{v}_i} \int_{\mathbf{q}_i} \alpha_i \pi_{i,j,t} \left(1 - \pi_{i,j,t}\right) dF\left(\mathbf{q}_i\right) dF\left(\mathbf{v}_i\right) & \text{if } j = k \\ \frac{p_{k,t}}{\pi_{j,t}} \int_{\mathbf{v}_i} \int_{\mathbf{q}_i} \alpha_i \pi_{i,j,t} \pi_{i,k,t} dF\left(\mathbf{q}_i\right) dF\left(\mathbf{v}_i\right) & \text{otherwise.} \end{cases} \end{aligned} \tag{3.2.19}$$

Consider the homogeneous consumers case (i.e., $\alpha_i = \alpha$, $\boldsymbol{\beta}_i = \boldsymbol{\beta}$. Equation (3.2.19) simplifies to

$$\varepsilon_{jk,t} = \begin{cases} -\alpha p_{j,t}\left(1 - \pi_{j,t}\right) & \text{if } j = k \\ \alpha p_{k,t} \pi_{k,t} & \text{otherwise.}^{18,19} \end{cases} \tag{3.2.20}$$

The elasticity expression in equation (3.2.20) can be problematic because the own- and cross-price elasticities depend only on the prices and market shares. In particular, the form of the cross-price elasticities may restrict the substitution pattern in an unrealistic manner because the cross-price elasticity depends only

18. The price elasticities here could be calculated either by using the estimated model parameters or by substituting the observed market shares $s_{j,t}$ back into $\pi_{j,t}$. The former method is especially relevant when a researcher is conducting policy counterfactuals.

19. Note these elasticity expressions change with respect to the functional form of the utility $u_{i,j}$, especially how price $p_{j,t}$ enters in $u_{i,j}$. We provide further discussion about the functional forms in section 3.2.3.4.

on α and $p_{k,t}q_{k,t}$.[20] To see how unrealistic a substitution pattern such a cross-price elasticity may generate, consider a market where only three car brands exist: KIA, Mercedes, and BMW. Assume that KIA is priced at \$50,000 and its market share $s_{k,t} = 0.5$; Mercedes and BMW are priced at \$100,000 with market shares $s_{k,t} = 0.25$, respectively; and ignore the outside option for simplicity. If the price of Mercedes increases by 1 percent, the quantity demand of BMW and KIA will increase by exactly the same percentage points; the extent dictated solely by the price coefficient α and the aggregate expenditure $p_{k,t}q_{k,t}$ of BMW and KIA, respectively. This substitution pattern is very unrealistic because in reality, BMW is more likely to be a substitute product for Mercedes than KIA. The restrictive substitution pattern is a direct implication of taking the choice probabilities as market shares, which exhibits the independence of irrelevant alternatives (IIA) properties explained in section 2.2.3 in chapter 2.[21]

The primary motivation for the extension to the random coefficients logit model from the homogeneous logit model was to overcome this restrictive substitution pattern caused by the IIA property. IIA is resolved in equation (3.2.19) at least in the market level. Yet such a solution comes at its own cost: possible issues in the identification of the random coefficients, increased complication in the estimation, computational burden, and possible numerical instability of the estimators. Furthermore, although the IIA is overcome at the market level in the random coefficients logit model, the problem persists within an individual. Another way to avoid IIA is to assume a correlated error structure such as nested logit. For an example of this, Goldberg (1995) and Goldberg and Verboven (2001) study the car market using the aggregate nested logit demand model.

3.2.3.3 IDENTIFICATION 2: IDENTIFICATION OF THE RANDOM COEFFICIENTS

The restrictive substitution pattern implied by IIA can be avoided at the market level by introducing random coefficients in the logit demand. However, such a workaround incurs a fundamental problem of identifying the random coefficients out of market data. To illustrate why, consider a version of the alternative-specific

20. To see this, recall that $s_{k,t} = \frac{q_{k,t}}{\sum_{j\in\mathcal{J}} q_{j,t}}$ and the denominator $\sum_{j\in\mathcal{J}} q_{j,t}$ is common to all the alternatives.

21. We note again that the source of IIA is not the shape of the T1EV distribution, but by the i.i.d. assumption of $\epsilon_{i,j}$ across js. The IIA property will persist when we assume, for example, that $\epsilon_{i,j} \sim i.i.d. \mathcal{N}(0, 1)$.

Also note that the form of equation (3.2.20) depends on the functional form of the alternative-specific utility in equation (3.2.17). For example, if price enters the alternative-specific utility log-linearly, then the price elasticities depend only on the quantity market shares. The IIA of the underlying choice probability still places an unrealistic restriction in the substitution pattern when the alternative-specific utility is log-linear in price.

utility specification where $\mathbf{\Pi} = \mathbf{O}$ (i.e., the distribution of demographics is not included in the specification), which is the most commonly used empirical specification in applications. The utility specification is as follows:

$$u_{i,j,t} = \alpha_i \left(w_{i,t} - p_{j,t}\right) + \mathbf{x}'_{j,t}\boldsymbol{\beta}_i + \xi_{j,t} + \epsilon_{i,j,t} \qquad \epsilon_{i,j,t} \sim i.i.d.\ T1EV$$

$$\begin{pmatrix} \alpha_i \\ \boldsymbol{\beta}_i \end{pmatrix} = \begin{pmatrix} \alpha \\ \boldsymbol{\beta} \end{pmatrix} + \boldsymbol{\Sigma}\mathbf{v}_i \qquad \mathbf{v}_i \sim \mathcal{N}\left(\mathbf{0}, \mathbf{I}_L\right),$$

where $L = \dim\left(\left(\alpha_i, \boldsymbol{\beta}'_i\right)'\right)$ and $\mathbf{I}_L$ is the $L \times L$ identity matrix. In principle, $\boldsymbol{\Sigma}$ can be a Cholesky decomposition of any covariance matrix, which allows nonzero covariance between the elements of $\left(\alpha_i, \boldsymbol{\beta}'_i\right)'$. For reasons that shall become clear next, we restrict $\boldsymbol{\Sigma}$ to be a diagonal matrix, nonzero elements of which correspond to the standard deviation of each element of $\left(\alpha_i, \boldsymbol{\beta}'_i\right)'$. Thus, $\boldsymbol{\Sigma}$ also has L nonzero elements.

An immediate consequence of this simplest random-coefficients specification is that there are $2L$ parameters to be identified and estimated in the model. Turning to the unconditional GMM moment condition $\mathbb{E}\left[\xi_{j,t}\mathbf{z}_{j,t}\right] = \mathbf{0}$, having to identify and estimate $2L$ parameters requires $\dim\left(\mathbf{z}_{j,t}\right) \geq 2L$. Even after taking into account the fact that $\mathbf{z}_{j,t}$ typically includes all the exogenous covariates $\mathbf{x}_{j,t}$ $\left(\in \mathbb{R}^{L-1}\right)$ and assuming that we found an instrument for price endogeneity that we discussed in section 3.2.3.1, we are still short at least L instruments. These L instruments should have the power to identify the elements of $\boldsymbol{\Sigma}$, the dispersion parameters of the random coefficients.

To find a suitable candidate for instrumenting $\boldsymbol{\Sigma}$, we need to first clarify what $\boldsymbol{\Sigma}$ captures. Consider a version of the market share equation of the random-coefficients logit demand system:

$$s_{j,t} = \mathbb{E}_{\boldsymbol{\Sigma}}\left[\frac{\exp\left(-\alpha_i p_{j,t} + \mathbf{x}'_{j,t}\boldsymbol{\beta}_i + \xi_{j,t}\right)}{\sum_{k \in \mathcal{J}_t} \exp\left(-\alpha_i p_{k,t} + \mathbf{x}'_{k,t}\boldsymbol{\beta}_i + \xi_{k,t}\right)}\right].$$

Suppose that σ_α, the standard deviation parameter of α_i, is 0. Then, the market-level substitution pattern with respect to changes in $p_{j,t}$ would exhibit IIA since the log odds-ratio is constant.[22] On the contrary, when $\sigma_\alpha > 0$, the substitution pattern with respect to changes in $p_{j,t}$ would deviate from the constant-log-odds-ratio. The same argument applies to all other standard deviation parameters for $\boldsymbol{\beta}_i$.

22. Recall equation (2.2.6) in section 2.2.3 in chapter 2.

Thus, the instruments to identify the parameters in $\mathbf{\Sigma}$ should include the data-side variations of the nonlogit substitution patterns for each of the elements in $\left(p_{j,t}, \mathbf{x}'_{j,t}\right)'$. The conventional choice in the literature when the exogenous covariates $\mathbf{x}_{j,t}$ and the price instrument $\tilde{z}_{j,t}$ are all continuous is to take a nonlinear transformation of $\left(\tilde{z}_{j,t}, \mathbf{x}'_{j,t}\right)'$, such as taking squares. To see why such seemingly arbitrary nonlinear transformations can be valid as instruments to identify $\mathbf{\Sigma}$, we begin our somewhat heuristic argument from the nature of the identification problem. The identification problem is, very roughly, to find a mapping from the distribution of data to parameters, taking the structures of the model as given. Nonzero elements in $\mathbf{\Sigma}$ can be taken as representing the market-level nonlogit substitution pattern in data. $\mathbf{\Sigma}$ as parameters capture the remainder of the data variation of the simple logit functional form of the individual-choice-probability expression. The raw instrument variables $\left(\tilde{z}_{j,t}, \mathbf{x}'_{j,t}\right)'$ are used to identify the linear parameters $\left(\alpha, \boldsymbol{\beta}'\right)'$ that generates the logit-form substitution pattern; the nonlinear transformation of $\left(\tilde{z}_{j,t}, \mathbf{x}'_{j,t}\right)'$ is used to identify the nonlinear parameters $\mathbf{\Sigma}$ that generate the violation of the logit-form substitution pattern. The reason why the usual empirical specification does not include the nonzero off-diagonal covariance term in $\mathbf{\Sigma}$ is now clear; it is challenging to find instruments for the diagonal elements of $\mathbf{\Sigma}$ already. And it is even more challenging to find a reasonable instrument that has an identifying power over the cross-substitution pattern across attributes. The same argument applies as to why introducing the correlation between coefficients and the population distribution has not been popular in the applications: one needs to find a suitable instrument for each nonzero element of $\mathbf{\Pi}$.

That being said, finding instruments for $\mathbf{\Sigma}$ by taking a nonlinear transformation on the raw instrument variables $\left(\tilde{z}_{j,t}, \mathbf{x}'_{j,t}\right)'$ would not work when some of its elements are binary, which is very often the case in the applications. Also, such nonlinear transformations generally suffer from low instrument power, very often leading to zero estimates of $\mathbf{\Sigma}$ with a very high standard error of the estimates. As such, Gandhi and Houde (2021) recently developed another class of nonlinear instruments, referred to as "product differentiation instruments." Product differentiation instruments exploit the attribute-level competition structure in a market. The idea is to measure where j is located in the attribute space and to use the summary measure of the distance from all other alternatives in a market as a nonlinear instrument. Recent applications of random-coefficients logit demand models report that product differentiation instruments work better than simply taking a nonlinear transformation on the raw instrument variables. Another solution that the literature has employed to supplement the cost instruments and product-differentiation instruments is to use "micro-moments" (e.g., Berry et al.,

2004a; Petrin, 2002; Goolsbee and Petrin, 2004). It exploits the individual or household-level information in the data as identifying variation for the nonlogit substitution pattern.

To sum up, *identification of the random-coefficients using market-level data comes from the functional form assumption on the idiosyncratic preference shock distribution* $\epsilon_{i,j,t}$. Some papers in the literature have established nonparametric identification results that do not rely on the i.i.d. T1EV assumption on $\epsilon_{i,j,t}$ (see, e.g., Berry and Haile, 2014). However, the usual criticisms of the nonparametric identification literature apply—it is difficult to implement in practice and requires much more data than the parametric approach outlined throughout this section. In empirical contexts where market-level IIA does not matter much, using Berry (1994)'s homogeneous logit demand model would be advisable; it avoids the problem of finding nonlinear instruments, implementation is much simpler, and the estimates are numerically much more stable.

3.2.3.4 SPECIFICATION ISSUES: FUNCTIONAL FORM OF THE ALTERNATIVE-SPECIFIC UTILITY AND INCLUSION OF THE NUMERAIRE IN THE SET OF ALTERNATIVES

Throughout this chapter, we have made a functional form assumption that the alternative-specific utility $u_{i,j}$ is linear in $\alpha_i\left(w_i - p_j\right)$, and interpreted $u_{i,j}$ as the direct utility of choosing j. This functional form assumption is not innocuous and is in fact related closely to the interpretation of the alternative-specific utility as a conditional indirect utility.

Pioneers of the discrete choice literature (e.g., McFadden, 1974, 1981; Small and Rosen, 1981; Dubin and McFadden, 1984) interpreted $u_{i,j}$ in equation (3.2.1) as the indirect utility conditional on choosing j, emphasizing the connection between discrete-choice demand systems and Marshallian demand systems.[23] The empirical context considered therein is as follows. The set of alternatives that a household chooses among contains one discrete alternative and several continuous alternatives. Once the choice over discrete alternative is made, the remaining disposable budget $w_i - p_j$ is spent on the continuous alternatives. It is implicitly assumed that households solve the usual budget-constrained utility maximization problem over continuous alternatives using the disposable budget $w_i - p_j$, which is the reason why $u_{i,j}$ is referred to as the "conditional indirect utility." A relationship akin to Roy's identity in the Marshallian demand system holds as well. Another

23. By Marshallian demand systems, we refer to the demand systems derived from solving a budget-constrained utility maximization problem, where commodities are infinitely divisible and the utility function represents the preference relation that satisfies textbook axioms.

justification for interpreting $u_{i,j}$ as indirect utility function is that it contains utility from money (i.e., disutility from high price) as an argument, which textbook direct utility functions should not.

In this conditional indirect utility interpretation of $u_{i,j}$, the term $(w_i - p_j)$ should be included in $u_{i,j}$, either linearly or nonlinearly. When $(w_i - p_j)$ is included linearly, the w_i term can be eliminated (since subtracting it is just a monotonic transformation). Two immediate consequences then follow. First, the own- and cross-price elasticity expressions are restricted exactly to the form of equation (3.2.19) in section 3.2.3.2. Second, the level of income/wealth does not affect the resulting demand system at all (i.e., the income effect is absent in the resulting discrete-choice demand system). As the level of income w_i is not observed to a researcher in many empirical contexts, this specification has its own appeal in practice. However, in contexts wherein the level of wealth is of central interest in the resulting demand system, w_i may need to be explicitly included. This is the reason why, for example, Berry et al. (1995) specified $u_{i,j}$ as linear in $\ln(w_i - p_j)$.

Suppose that a researcher wants to specify $u_{i,j}$ as linear to some other function, such as

$$u_{i,j} = -\alpha_i f(p_j) + \mathbf{x}_j'\boldsymbol{\beta} + \xi_j + \epsilon_{i,j}, \tag{3.2.21}$$

where $f(\cdot)$ is a possibly nonlinear function. So long as one does not attempt to interpret this $u_{i,j}$ as a conditional indirect utility, this specification is completely legitimate, which is one of the reasons why we have been interpreting $u_{i,j}$ as the direct utility of choosing j throughout this chapter. Furthermore, the direct utility interpretation of $u_{i,j}$ provides a wide variety of possibilities in the functional form of $f(p_j)$, which has a direct impact on the resulting elasticity expressions and welfare functions. The only possible conceptual problem is that the utility includes "disutility from price" in its argument. However, as it is widely perceived nowadays that money-metric utility or quasi-linear utility can be legitimate direct utility functions, we consider that including $p_{i,j}$ in the direct utility is not very problematic.

Another important issue in specification of the discrete-choice demand system is the inclusion of the numeraire (outside option). Consider the individual choice probability equation (3.2.4). The set of alternatives $\mathcal{J}_t$ must include the numeraire, both for conceptual reasons and for identification purposes. Conceptually, if the numeraire is not included in the set of alternatives, the extensive margin is eliminated in the resulting demand system. A price increase of product j will only lead to switching to other products in the choice set $\mathcal{J}_t$; that is, no one will exit the market as a result of a price increase. Furthermore, without the numeraire, demand will not change at all when the prices of all the products in the set of alternatives increase, which is very unrealistic in most empirical contexts. In the identification aspect, the level of utility is not identified from inverting the choice probabilities.[24] Put differently, the choice probability system conveys information about only the utility differences from a reference option. Thus, the utility level of one alternative should be normalized (e.g., 0). Inclusion of the numeraire in the set of alternatives and setting the utility level from choosing the numeraire to 0 make the solution to this problem straightforward. Otherwise, a researcher needs to select one of the alternatives as the reference option; utility levels of all other alternatives are identified only relative to the reference option.

Of course, inclusion of the numeraire comes at a cost. In the context of demand estimation using market data, the market share of the numeraire s_0, which is often referred to as the "outside shares," needs to be imputed by the researcher. One imminent challenge is that the researcher has to either know or be able to estimate the *potential* market size. The other tentative problem is that the magnitude of the extensive margin is in a sense also imputed by the researcher through the magnitude of s_0.[25]

3.2.3.5 CONSUMER WELFARE ANALYSIS USING DISCRETE CHOICE DEMAND SYSTEMS

Economists are often interested in consumer-welfare effects of a policy change[26] that leads to changes in the equilibrium prices or attributes of products offered in a market. There are three measures of consumer-welfare changes: compensating variation (CV), Marshallian consumer surplus (CS), and equivalent variation (EV). The compensating variation (CV) and the equivalent variation (EV) have been the primary welfare parameters of interest in the literature because they easily quantify the utility change with respect to the changes of the prices and/or the choice set. McFadden (1981) and Small and Rosen (1981) provide formulas to calculate the compensating variations in the discrete-choice demand models. In the utility-maximization-problem context, compensating variations and equivalent variations are defined such that

$$v\left(\mathbf{p}^0, w^0\right) = v\left(\mathbf{p}^1, w^0 + CV\right)$$
$$v\left(\mathbf{p}^0, w^0 - EV\right) = v\left(\mathbf{p}^1, w^0\right)$$

24. This fact can be most easily seen by adding or subtracting the same positive constant in the mean utilities δ_j of the logit choice probabilities. The resulting choice probabilities are identical—level adjustments of the mean utilities δ_j yield observationally equivalent choice probabilities. The implication from the simple logit carries over to any discrete-choice probability expression generated from an additive RUM problem.

25. Recall, for example, the price elasticities of the homogeneous logit model in equation (3.2.20). The magnitude of the extensive margin in this context, where the utility is linear in $w_i - p_j$, is the cross-price elasticity between product j and product 0, which is dictated by the magnitude of $\pi_{0,t}$.

26. We emphasize again that the term "policy" is used in a broad sense.

hold, where $v(\cdot,\cdot)$ is the indirect utility function. The superscripts 0 and 1 denote the values before and after the price/choice set change, respectively.

Next, we show that $CV = CS = EV$ in the Walrasian consumer theory when income effect is absent, and an analogous result can be shown in the context of discrete choice demand when $u_{i,j}$ is linear in $w_i - p_j$. We stick to the indirect utility interpretation of $u_{i,j}$ for now, assuming that $u_{i,j}$ includes $(w_i - p_j)$ linearly. Recall the indirect utility specification of the homogeneous logit model that is linear in $(w_i - p_j)$:

$$u_{i,j} = \alpha\left(w_i - p_j\right) + \mathbf{x}_j'\boldsymbol{\beta} + \xi_j + \epsilon_{i,j} \qquad \epsilon_{i,j} \sim i.i.d.\ T1EV,$$

and the consumers solve the following problem:

$$\max_{j\in\mathcal{J}}\left\{\alpha\left(w_i - p_j\right) + \mathbf{x}_j'\boldsymbol{\beta} + \xi_j + \epsilon_{i,j}\right\}.$$

Now suppose that there has been a change in prices and the choice set from $(\mathbf{p}^0, \mathcal{J}^0)$ to $(\mathbf{p}^1, \mathcal{J}^1)$. By definition of the compensating variation, the following equality holds:

$$\begin{aligned}&\max_{j\in\mathcal{J}^0}\left\{\alpha\left(w_i - p_j^0\right) + \mathbf{x}_j'\boldsymbol{\beta} + \xi_j + \epsilon_{i,j}\right\}\\ &\quad= \max_{j\in\mathcal{J}^1}\left\{\alpha\left(w_i + CV_i - p_j^1\right) + \mathbf{x}_j'\boldsymbol{\beta} + \xi_j + \epsilon_{i,j}\right\}.\end{aligned}$$

Rearranging and taking the expectation yield

$$\begin{aligned}\mathbb{E}_{\epsilon_i}\left[CV_i\right] &= -\frac{1}{\alpha}\mathbb{E}_{\epsilon_i}\left[\max_{j\in\mathcal{J}^1}\left\{\alpha\left(w_i - p_j^1\right) + \mathbf{x}_j'\boldsymbol{\beta} + \xi_j + \epsilon_{i,j}\right\}\right]\\ &\quad+\frac{1}{\alpha}\mathbb{E}\left[\max_{j\in\mathcal{J}^0}\left\{\alpha\left(w_i - p_j^0\right) + \mathbf{x}_j'\boldsymbol{\beta} + \xi_j + \epsilon_{i,j}\right\}\right]\\ &= \frac{1}{\alpha}\left\{\ln\left(\sum_{j\in\mathcal{J}^0}\exp\left(\alpha\left(w_i - p_j^0\right) + \mathbf{x}_j'\boldsymbol{\beta} + \xi_j\right)\right)\right.\\ &\quad\left.-\ln\left(\sum_{j\in\mathcal{J}^1}\exp\left(\alpha\left(w_i - p_j^1\right) + \mathbf{x}_j'\boldsymbol{\beta} + \xi_j\right)\right)\right\}.^{27}\end{aligned} \tag{3.2.22}$$

Define $CV = \mathbb{E}_{\epsilon_i}[CV_i]$ and $EV = \mathbb{E}_{\epsilon_i}[EV_i]$. It is immediate that $CV = EV$ under this linear indirect utility specification. It can be further shown that $CV = \mathbb{E}_{\epsilon_i}[\Delta CS_i] = EV$ (i.e., compensating variation and equivalent variation are the same as the changes in the area left to the demand function in the discrete choice demand when the indirect utility is linear in $w_i - p_j$). Motivated by this equivalence, the function

$$W(\boldsymbol{\delta}) := \mathbb{E}_{\epsilon_i}\left[\max_{j\in\mathcal{J}}\{\delta_j + \epsilon_{i,j}\}\right] \tag{3.2.23}$$

is named as the social surplus function (e.g., McFadden, 1981; Anderson, de Palma, and Thisse 1992). Also note that when δ_j is linear in p_j, taking partial derivatives with respect to p_j gives the choice probability of j. This fact is often called the "Williams-Daly-Zachary theorem" in the literature (Williams, 1977; Daly and Zachary, 1978).[28]

When the income effect is present in the discrete choice demand system, possibly by the nonlinearity of utility in income net of prices, the exact compensating variation and equivalent variation should be calculated according to the Hicksian demand system implied by the discrete-choice probabilities (see, e.g., Hausman and Newey, 1995, 2016; Herriges and Kling, 1999; Dagsvik and Karlström, 2005; Bhattacharya, 2015). However, EV and CV still can be calculated using simulation. See Herriges and Kling (1999) for details about the simulation methods in practice. As in any counterfactual analysis, consumer welfare analysis is generally sensitive to the utility specification and how the preferences are aggregated.

27. We used the fact that when $\epsilon_{i,j} \sim$ i.i.d. $T1EV$,

$$\mathbb{E}\left[\max_j\{\delta_j + \epsilon_{i,j}\}\right] = \ln\left[\sum_{j=1}^{J}\exp(\delta_j)\right] + C,$$

where the Euler-Mascheroni constant $C \approx 0.5772$.

28. The equivalence $CV = \mathbb{E}_{\epsilon_i}[\Delta CS_i] = EV$ when δ_j is linear in p_j can be easily shown using the Williams-Daly-Zachary theorem, which establishes $W(\boldsymbol{\delta})$ is the potential function of a conservative vector field that maps $\boldsymbol{\delta} \to \Pr(i \text{ chooses } j; \boldsymbol{\delta})$. When there is a change of mean utility from $\boldsymbol{\delta}^0$ to $\boldsymbol{\delta}^1$, the fundamental theorem of calculus of line integrals asserts

$$W(\boldsymbol{\delta}^1) - W(\boldsymbol{\delta}^0) = \int_{\partial} \sum_{j\in\mathcal{J}\setminus 0} \Pr(i \text{ chooses } j; \boldsymbol{\delta})\, \mathrm{d}\boldsymbol{\delta}, \tag{3.2.24}$$

where ∂ denotes a path from $\boldsymbol{\delta}^0$ to $\boldsymbol{\delta}^1$. Note that we explicitly excluded the outside option to avoid the integrand being a constant. We know that the left-hand side of equation (3.2.24) is $CV = EV$ scaled by the constant price coefficient $-\alpha$. By recalling the fact that we take $\Pr(i \text{ chooses } j; \boldsymbol{\delta})$ as the predicted market shares $\pi_{i,j}$, and in turn as the normalized demand function, the right-hand side of equation (3.2.24) is the sum of area changes left to the normalized demand function $\pi_{i,j}$ across alternatives. Using the fact that δ_j is linear in p_j, taking the appropriate scale adjustment by the price coefficient $-\alpha$ gives the desired result.

The final remark in this discussion is about the interpretation of the function $W(\boldsymbol{\delta})$ defined in equation (3.2.23). Regardless of whether a researcher includes w_i in the alternative-specific utility, the function can be interpreted as the expected benefits of engaging in the discrete choice problem. Therefore, even when we adopt the direct utility interpretation of $u_{i,j}$, changes in $W(\boldsymbol{\delta})$ with respect to a policy change can be interpreted as the changes in the expected benefits of consumers making a choice. The compatibility of the consumer-welfare function $W(\boldsymbol{\delta})$ to the direct utility interpretation of $u_{i,j}$ ensures wider applicability of the discrete choice demand models and the associated consumer-welfare evaluation methods discussed thus far. Recent studies often take $W(\boldsymbol{\delta})$ as the beginning point of the consumer welfare evaluation.

3.3 Characteristics-Space Approach II: Extensions of the Static Logit Demand Models

This section introduces extensions of the homogeneous and random-coefficients logit demand models. We discuss how to accommodate zero observed market shares in section 3.3.1. Then we provide an explicit connection between logit demand models and constant elasticity of substitution (CES) demand models in section 3.3.2. Empirical demand models derived from the budget-constrained CES utility maximization problem have been used extensively in the macro/trade literature. The connection explained herein provides a possibility of logit demand models to be applied in a broader context outside the industrial organization or quantitative marketing literature.

3.3.1 Accommodating Zero Market Shares

Zero market shares are often observed in demand data. The assumptions of the aggregate discrete-choice demand systems—that the choice probabilities are strictly positive and there are infinitely many underlying consumers—are inconsistent with zero market shares. When the observed market shares are zero for some alternatives, the implied utility of those alternatives should be negative infinity, which is problematic. Thus, two papers in the literature provide solutions to accommodate zero observed market shares.

The first approach, by Gandhi, Lu, and Shi (2019), is to treat zero observed market shares as a result of measurement errors caused by a small number in the underlying consumer population. Gandhi et al. first pushes the observed market shares s_j into $(0, 1)$ using the Laplace correction factor and then uses set identification and bound estimation methods developed by Manski and Tamer

(2002); Imbens and Manski (2004); Chernozhukov, Hong, and Tamer (2007); and Ciliberto and Tamer (2009), among others.

The second approach, by Dubé, Hortaçsu, and Joo (2021), considers zero observed market shares to be a result of consumer selection, which can cause products to enter or be excluded from consumers' choice sets. Let d_j be an indicator function such that the value is 1 when $s_j > 0$ and 0 when $s_j = 0$. When there is selection on unobservables, then ξ_j, the original GMM moment condition imposed by Berry et al. (1995) after dropping the alternatives with zero observed market shares, $E\left[\xi_j|\mathbf{z}_j, d_j = 1\right]$, is not zero anymore even when $E\left[\xi_j|\mathbf{z}_j\right] = 0$. Ignoring the selection may bias the demand parameter estimates.

Dubé et al. (2021) consider an alternative GMM moment condition based on the pairwise-difference estimation literature (e.g., Ahn and Powell, 1993; Blundell and Powell, 2004; Aradillas-Lopez et al., 2007; Aradillas-Lopez, 2012). Let μ_j denote the continuously-distributed propensity score for alternative j not being selected. First, rewrite the demand shocks as follows:

$$\xi_j = \iota\left(\mu_j\right) + \zeta_j,$$

with $\mathbb{E}\left[\zeta_j|\mu_j, \mathbf{z}_j\right] = 0$ and $\iota(\cdot)$ being a smooth, monotonically increasing function. Then consider the following moment condition based on differences between the demand shocks of two goods i and j:

$$E\left[\xi_i - \xi_j|\mathbf{z}_i, \mathbf{z}_j, \mu_i = \mu_j, d_i = d_j = 1\right] = 0.$$

The moment condition here is based on differencing out the selection propensities. To illustrate, consider a pair of products i and j with the same $\mu_i = \mu_j$, and hence $\iota(\mu_i) = \iota\left(\mu_j\right)$ in the homogeneous logit model:

$$\ln\left(\frac{s_i}{s_0}\right) = -\alpha p_i + \mathbf{x}_i'\boldsymbol{\beta} + \iota(\mu_i) + \zeta_i$$
$$\ln\left(\frac{s_j}{s_0}\right) = -\alpha p_j + \mathbf{x}_j'\boldsymbol{\beta} + \iota\left(\mu_j\right) + \zeta_j.$$

Taking differences yields

$$\ln\left(\frac{s_i}{s_0}\right) - \ln\left(\frac{s_j}{s_0}\right) = -\alpha\left(p_i - p_j\right) + \left(\mathbf{x}_i - \mathbf{x}_j\right)'\boldsymbol{\beta} + \left(\zeta_i - \zeta_j\right).$$

Then the following conditional moment condition can be derived:

$$\begin{aligned} 0 &= E\left[\zeta_i - \zeta_j | \mathbf{z}_i, \mathbf{z}_j, \mu_i = \mu_j, d_i = d_j = 1\right] \\ &= E\left[\xi_i - \xi_j | \mathbf{z}_i, \mathbf{z}_j, \mu_i = \mu_j, d_i = d_j = 1\right]. \end{aligned} \tag{3.3.1}$$

The same moment condition applies to the random-coefficients logit demand model.

Equation (3.3.1) leads to the GMM objective function and constraints based on pairwise-difference:

$$\frac{2}{n(n-1)} \sum_{i=1}^{n-1} \sum_{j=i+1}^{n} \hat{\omega}_{i,j} \left\{\Delta \mathbf{z}_{i,j} \Delta \xi_{i,j}\right\}' \boldsymbol{\Omega} \left\{\Delta \mathbf{z}_{i,j} \Delta \xi_{i,j}\right\},$$

where $\hat{\omega}_{i,j}$ is the estimated nonparametric kernel-weights that place more weights on the pair of observations where μ_i and μ_j are close. The kernel weights are introduced because event $\mu_i = \mu_j$ occurs with probability 0 in theory. The same set of market share equations should be imposed either as constraints (MPEC) or as inner loops (NFP), as in the Berry et al. (1995) estimation.

3.3.2 Characteristics-Space Approach without Random Utility Shocks

Bajari and Benkard (2005) and Berry and Reiss (2007) develop demand-estimation frameworks in the characteristics space that do not rely on idiosyncratic preference shocks on the alternative-specific utility. In line with Bajari and Benkard and Berry and Reiss, Dubé et al. (2021) derive the same market share equation of the homogeneous and random-choice logit demand models from the budget-constrained CES utility-maximization problem, implying that the CES Marshallian demand system is just as rich as the logit demand system and is able to incorporate product characteristics and demographics. Furthermore, the identification results and estimation methods developed for logit demand systems can be readily applied to estimate the CES Marshallian demand systems. We briefly review Dubé et al.'s equivalence result here.

3.3.2.1 EQUIVALENCE OF THE PREDICTED MARKET SHARES DERIVED FROM THE CES MARSHALLIAN DEMAND SYSTEM AND THE LOGIT DEMAND SYSTEM

Consider a differentiated-products market denoted by subscript t and composed of homogeneous consumers with a CES preference. The representative consumer solves

$$\max_{\{q_{j,t}\}_{j\in\mathcal{J}_t}} \left(\sum_{j\in\mathcal{J}_t} \left\{ \chi\left(\mathbf{x}_{j,t}, \xi_{j,t}, \mathbf{w}_{j,t}, \eta_{j,t}\right) \right\}^{\frac{1}{\sigma}} q_{j,t}^{\frac{\sigma-1}{\sigma}} \right)^{\frac{\sigma}{\sigma-1}} \quad \text{s.t.} \quad \sum_{j\in\mathcal{J}_t} p_{j,t} q_{j,t} = w_t. \tag{3.3.2}$$

Here, $\mathcal{J}_t$ is a set of alternatives in the category, which might include the numeraire/outside option; $q_{j,t}$ is the quantity of product j consumed in market t; $\chi\left(\mathbf{x}_{j,t}, \xi_{j,t}, \mathbf{w}_{j,t}, \eta_{j,t}\right)$, defined as the quality kernel, is a nonnegative function of observed and unobserved product characteristics; $\mathbf{x}_{j,t}$ and $\mathbf{w}_{j,t}$ are vectors of product j's characteristics in market t, which are observable to the econometrician; $\xi_{j,t}$ and $\eta_{j,t}$ are scalars that represent utility from product j's characteristics that are unobservable to the econometrician; $\mathbf{w}_{j,t}$ and $\eta_{j,t}$ are extensive-margin shifters that the representative consumer considers whether to buy the product; and $\mathbf{x}_{j,t}$ and $\xi_{j,t}$ are intensive margin shifters that determine the level of utility when a consumer buys a product. In this equation, $\mathbf{w}_{j,t}$ and $\mathbf{x}_{j,t}$ might have common components, but we can require an exclusion restriction on $\mathbf{w}_{j,t}$ for semiparametric identification when the extensive margin matters. In such a case, $\mathbf{w}_{j,t}$ must contain at least one component that is not in $\mathbf{x}_{j,t}$. Finally, we assume the existence of price instruments $\mathbf{z}_{j,t}$.

It is immediate that the Marshallian demand system is

$$q_{j,t} = w_t \left\{ \frac{\chi\left(\mathbf{x}_{j,t}, \xi_{j,t}, \mathbf{w}_{j,t}, \eta_{j,t}\right) p_{j,t}^{-\sigma}}{\sum_{k\in\mathcal{J}_t} \chi\left(\mathbf{x}_{k,t}, \xi_{k,t}, \mathbf{w}_{k,t}, \eta_{k,t}\right) p_{k,t}^{1-\sigma}} \right\} \quad \forall j \in \mathcal{J}_t, \tag{3.3.3}$$

which leads to the predicted quantity market shares $\pi_{j,t}$ as

$$\begin{aligned} \pi_{j,t} &\equiv \frac{q_{j,t}}{\sum_{k\in\mathcal{J}_t} q_{k,t}} \\ &= \frac{\chi\left(\mathbf{x}_{j,t}, \xi_{j,t}, \mathbf{w}_{j,t}, \eta_{j,t}\right) p_{j,t}^{-\sigma}}{\sum_{k\in\mathcal{J}_t} \chi\left(\mathbf{x}_{k,t}, \xi_{k,t}, \mathbf{w}_{k,t}, \eta_{k,t}\right) p_{k,t}^{-\sigma}}. \end{aligned} \tag{3.3.4}$$

Now consider a functional form for $\chi(\cdot)$:

$$\chi\left(\mathbf{x}_{j,t}, \xi_{j,t}, \mathbf{w}_{j,t}, \eta_{j,t}\right) = \exp\left(\alpha + \mathbf{x}_{j,t}'\boldsymbol{\beta} + \xi_{j,t}\right). \tag{3.3.5}$$

Equation (3.3.4) becomes

$$\pi_{i,j} = \frac{\exp\left(-\sigma \ln p_j + \mathbf{x}_j'\boldsymbol{\beta} + \xi_j\right)}{\sum_{k\in\mathcal{J}_t} \exp\left(-\sigma \ln p_k + \mathbf{x}_k'\boldsymbol{\beta} + \xi_k\right)}, \tag{3.3.6}$$

which is the predicted market share equation of the logit demand where the prices are replaced by the logarithm of the prices. Taking the logarithm of the prices can be taken as a scale adjustment of the utility of each alternative.[29] If we allow the model parameters $(\sigma, \boldsymbol{\beta})$ to vary across individuals i, we obtain the Berry et al. (1995) predicted individual share equation:

$$\pi_{i,j} = \frac{\exp\left(-\sigma_i \ln p_j + \mathbf{x}_j' \boldsymbol{\beta}_i + \xi_j\right)}{\sum_{k \in \mathcal{J}_t} \exp\left(-\sigma_i \ln p_k + \mathbf{x}_k' \boldsymbol{\beta}_i + \xi_k\right)}. \tag{3.3.7}$$

Aggregating equation (3.3.7) over individuals and equating with observed market shares yields the estimation equation of Berry et al. (1995).

3.3.2.2 MARSHALLIAN AND HICKSIAN PRICE ELASTICITIES AND INCOME ELASTICITY

Usually, the first-order goal of demand estimation is to find the price and income elasticities. Even though the identification results and estimation methods developed by many authors, including Berry (1994), Berry et al. (1995), and Berry and Haile (2014), can be directly implemented for the model parameters $\left(\sigma_i, \boldsymbol{\beta}_i\right)$, the elasticity expressions of the CES Marshallian demand system are different from the logit demand system.

Let $b_{j,t}$ be the budget share of product j in market t. Consider the homogeneous coefficients case. Denote $\varepsilon_{jc,t}^M$ and $\varepsilon_{jc,t}^H$ to be the Marshallian and Hicksian cross-price elasticities between alternatives j and c, respectively. We have the following simple closed-form formulas for the Marshallian and the Hicksian own- and cross-price elasticities:

$$\begin{aligned} \varepsilon_{jj,t}^M &= -\sigma + (\sigma - 1)\, b_{j,t} \\ \varepsilon_{jc,t}^M &= (\sigma - 1)\, b_{c,t} \\ \varepsilon_{jj,t}^H &= -\sigma \left(1 - b_{j,t}\right) \\ \varepsilon_{jc,t}^H &= \sigma\, b_{c,t}, \end{aligned} \tag{3.3.8}$$

and the income elasticity is 1. When budget shares are observed in the data or calculated from the data, these elasticities can be calculated easily. From these elasticity expressions, it can be immediately noticed that a version of the IIA property holds; the substitution pattern depends solely on the budget shares

29. Note again that the "indirect utility" interpretation of the discrete-choice utility no longer holds if we use the logarithm of the prices instead of the raw prices.

of corresponding products. Welfare counterfactuals should be done accordingly, following the formulas from the CES Marshallian demand system.

3.3.2.3 AGGREGATION AND INTEGRABILITY OF DISCRETE-CHOICE DEMAND SYSTEMS

One might question whether the equivalence akin to what we discussed in section 3.3.2 holds between a broader class of discrete choice demand systems and Marshallian demand systems.[30] The difficulty is that the classical integrability theorem by Hurwicz and Uzawa (1971) does not apply because one of the critical conditions for their theorem to hold is that demand is zero whenever income is zero.[31] This condition is a direct implication of the binding budget constraint in the commodity space. A binding budget constraint can be appealing because it leads to the Slutsky equation, the central result of Walrasian consumer theory that establishes the systematic relationship between the substitution effects and income effects. To date, a general result of equivalence between discrete choice demand systems and Marshallian demand systems derived under a binding budget constraint does not exist.

In the world where the budget is not binding, Nocke and Schutz (2017) suggested a general quasi-linear integrability theorem, which can rationalize the discrete-choice demand systems as resulting from a representative consumer's "budget-constrained" quasi-linear utility-maximization problem. We note, however, that the direct utility function that can rationalize discrete-choice demand systems does not have all the desired properties for a direct utility function in the following aspects: (1) It takes possibly negative money (numeraire) as a direct argument, (2) the budget constraint does not bind in general in the commodity space, (3) the utility function may not be defined on a nontrivial subset of the commodity space,[32] and (4) a nontrivial subset of the commodity space can be composed of satiation points.

Bibliography

Ackerberg, D., C. L. Benkard, S. Berry, & A. Pakes (2007). Chapter 63, "Econometric tools for analyzing market outcomes." In Vol. 6A of *Handbook of Econometrics*, 4171–4276. Amsterdam: Elsevier.

Ahn, H., & J. L. Powell (1993). "Semiparametric estimation of censored selection models with a nonparametric selection mechanism." *Journal of Econometrics*, 58, 3–29.

30. See also Anderson, de Palma, and Thisse (1987, 1992) and Verboven (1996), wherein the demand systems are derived from solving a discrete-continuous choice problem akin to Hanemann (1984).

31. For discrete-choice demand systems, the sum of the demand is fixed at a positive level even when the income is zero.

32. Or, equivalently, some commodity bundles should yield a utility of negative infinity.

Anderson, S. P., A. de Palma, & J.-F. Thisse (1987). "The CES is a discrete choice model?" *Economics Letters*, 24, 139–140.

Anderson, S. P., A. de Palma, & J. F. Thisse (1992). *Discrete choice theory of product differentiation*. Cambridge, MA: MIT Press.

Aradillas-Lopez, A. (2012). "Pairwise-difference estimation of incomplete information games." *Journal of Econometrics*, 168, 120–140.

Aradillas-Lopez, A., B. E. Honoré, & J. L. Powell (2007). "Pairwise difference estimation with nonparametric control variables." *International Economic Review*, 48, 1119–1158.

Bajari, P., & C. L. Benkard (2005). "Demand estimation with heterogeneous consumers & unobserved product characteristics: A hedonic approach." *Journal of Political Economy*, 113, 1239–1276.

Berry, S. (1994). "Estimating discrete-choice models of product differentiation." *RAND Journal of Economics*, 25, 242–262.

Berry, S., A. Gandhi, & P. Haile (2013). "Connected substitutes and invertibility of demand." *Econometrica*, 81, 2087–2111.

Berry, S., J. Levinsohn, & A. Pakes (1995). "Automobile prices in market equilibrium." *Econometrica*, 63, 841–890.

Berry, S., J. Levinsohn, & A. Pakes (2004a). "Differentiated products demand systems from a combination of micro and macro data: The new car market." *Journal of Political Economy*, 112, 68–105.

Berry, S., O. B. Linton, & A. Pakes (2004b). "Limit theorems for estimating the parameters of differentiated product demand systems." *Review of Economic Studies*, 71, 613–654.

Berry, S. T., & P. A. Haile (2014). "Identification in differentiated products markets using market level data." *Econometrica*, 82, 1749–1797.

Berry, S., & P. Reiss (2007). Chapter 29, "Empirical models of entry and market structure." In vol. 3, *Handbook of Industrial Organization*, 1845–1886. Amsterdam: Elsevier.

Bhattacharya, D. (2015). "Nonparametric welfare analysis for discrete choice." *Econometrica*, 83, 617–649.

Blundell, R. W., & J. L. Powell (2004). "Endogeneity in semiparametric binary response models." *Review of Economic Studies*, 71, 655–679.

Chaudhuri, S., P. K. Goldberg, & P. Jia (2006). "Estimating the effects of global patent protection in pharmaceuticals: A case study of Quinolones in India." *American Economic Review*, 96, 1477–1514.

Chernozhukov, V., H. Hong, & E. Tamer (2007). "Estimation and confidence regions for parameter sets in econometric models." *Econometrica*, 75, 1243–1284.

Ciliberto, F., and E. Tamer (2009). "Market structure and multiple equilibria in airline markets." *Econometrica*, 77, 1791–1828.

Conlon, C., & J. Gortmaker (2020). "Best practices for differentiated products demand estimation with PyBLP." *RAND Journal of Economics*, 51, 1108–1161.

Dagsvik, J. K., & A. Karlström (2005). "Compensating variation and Hicksian choice probabilities in random utility models that are nonlinear in income." *Review of Economic Studies*, 72, 57–76.

Daly, A., & S. Zachary (1978). "Improved multiple choice models." *Determinants of Travel Choice*, Identifying and Measuring the Determinants of Mode Choice.

Deaton, A., & J. Muellbauer (1980a). "An almost ideal demand system." *American Economic Review*, 70, 312–326.

Deaton, A., & J. Muellbauer (1980b). *Economics and consumer behavior*. Cambridge, UK: Cambridge University Press.

Dube, J.-P., J. T. Fox, & C.-L. Su (2012). "Improving the numerical performance of static and dynamic aggregate discrete choice random coefficients demand estimation." *Econometrica*, 80, 2231–2267.

Dubé, J.-P., A. Hortaçsu, & J. Joo (2021). "Random-coefficients logit demand estimation with zero-valued market shares." *Marketing Science*, 40(4), 637–660.

Dubin, J. A., & D. McFadden (1984). "An econometric analysis of residential electric appliance holdings and consumption." *Econometrica*, 52, 345–362.

Fan, Y. (2013). "Ownership consolidation of product characteristics: A study of the US daily newspaper market." *American Economic Review*, 103, 1598–1628.

Freyberger, J. (2015). "Asymptotic theory for differentiated products demand models with many markets." *Journal of Econometrics*, 185, 162–181.

Gandhi., A, & J.-F. Houde (2021). "Measuring substitution patterns in differentiated products industries." Working paper, University of Wisconsin-Madison.

Gandhi, A., Z. Lu, & X. Shi (2019). "Estimating demand for differentiated products with zeroes in market share data." Unpublished manuscript.

Goldberg, P. K. (1995). "Product differentiation and oligopoly in international markets: The case of the U.S. automobile industry." *Econometrica*, 63, 891–951.

Goldberg, P. K., & F. Verboven (2001). "The evolution of price dispersion in the European car market." *Review of Economic Studies*, 68, 811–848.

Goolsbee, A., & A. Petrin (2004). "The consumer gains from direct broadcast satellites and the competition with cable TV." *Econometrica*, 72, 351–381.

Hanemann, W. M. (1984). "Discrete/continuous models of consumer demand." *Econometrica*, 52, 541–561.

Hansen, L. P. (1982). "Large sample properties of generalized method of moments estimators." *Econometrica*, 50, 1029–1054.

Hausman, J., G. Leonard, & J. D. Zona (1994). "Competitive analysis with differentciated products." *Annales D'Economie et de Statistique*, 34, 159–180.

Hausman, J. A., & W. K. Newey (1995). "Nonparametric estimation of exact consumers surplus and dead-weight loss." *Econometrica*, 63, 1445–1476.

Hausman, J. A., & W. K. Newey (2016). "Individual heterogeneity and average welfare." *Econometrica*, 84, 1225–1248.

Hendel, I., & A. Nevo (2006a). "Measuring the implications of sales and consumer inventory behavior." *Econometrica*, 74, 1637–1673.

Hendel, I., & A. Nevo (2006b). "Sales and consumer inventory." *RAND Journal of Economics*, 37, 543–561.

Herriges, J. A., & C. L. Kling (1999). "Nonlinear income effects in random utility models." *Review of Economics and Statistics*, 81, 62–72.

Hurwicz, L., & H. Uzawa (1971). Chapter 6, "Preferences, utlity, and demand." In *the integrability of demand functions*, 114–148, New York: Harcourt Brace Jovanovich.

Imbens, G. W., & C. F. Manski (2004). "Confidence intervals for partially identified parameters." *Econometrica*, 72, 1845–1857.

Lee, J., & K. Seo (2015). "A computationally fast estimator for random coefficients logit demand models using aggregate data." *RAND Journal of Economics*, 46, 86–102.

Manski, C. F., & E. Tamer (2002). "Inference on regressions with interval data on a regressor or outcome." *Econometrica*, 70, 519–546.

McFadden, D. (1974). Chapter 4, "Conditional logit analysis of qualitative choice behavior." In *Frontiers in Econometrics*, 105–142. Cambridge: Academic Press.

McFadden, D. (1981). Chapter 5, "Structural analysis of discrete data with econometric applications." In *Econometric models of probabilistic choice*, 198–272, Cambridge, MA: MIT Press.

Muellbauer, J. (1975). "Aggregation, income distribution and consumer demand." *Review of Economic Studies*, 42, 525–543.

Muellbauer, J. (1976). "Community preferences and the representative consumer." *Econometrica*, 44, 979–999.

Nevo, A. (2000). "A practitioner's guide to estimation of random-coefficients logit models of demand." *Journal of Economics and Management Strategy*, 9, 513–548.

Nevo, A. (2001). "Measuring market power in the ready-to-eat cereal industry." *Econometrica*, 69, 307–342.

Nocke, V., & N. Schutz (2017). "Quasi-linear integrability." *Journal of Economic Theory*, 169, 603–628.

Petrin, A. (2002). "Quantifying the benefits of new products: The case of the minivan." *Journal of Political Economy*, 110, 705–729.

Pinkse, J., & M. E. Slade (2004). "Mergers, brand competition, and the price of a pint." *European Economic Review*, 48, 617–643.

Pinkse, J., M. E. Slade, & C. Brett (2002). "Spatial price competition: a semiparametric approach." *Econometrica*, 70, 1111–1153.

Reiss, P. C., & F. A. Wolak (2007). Chapter 64, "Structural econometric modeling: Rationales and examples from industrial organization." In Vol. 6A, *Handbook of Econometrics*, 4277–4415. Amsterdam: Elsevier.

Small, K. A., & H. S. Rosen (1981). "Applied welfare economics with discrete choice models." *Econometrica*, 49, 105–130.

Trajtenberg, M. (1989). "The welfare analysis of product innovations, with an application to computed tomography scanners." *Journal of Political Economy*, 97, 444–479.

Verboven, F. (1996). "The nested logit model and representative consumer theory." *Economics Letters*, 50, 57–73.

Williams, H. (1977). "On the formation of travel demand models and economic evaluation measures of user benefit." *Environment and Planning A: Economy and Space*, 9, 285–344.

4

Estimation of Discrete-Game Models

In this chapter, we study the problem of identifying and estimating model parameters that underlies a discrete game model. We specifically focus on the equilibrium firm entry game models. Entry game models are extensively studied in the empirical industrial organization literature, as firm entry and exit are among the primary factors that determine market structure and market power, the core themes of industrial organization. However, the methods covered in this chapter can be extended and applied to other contexts as well.

As in other structural econometric models, estimation of model parameters of a game typically assumes that the observed data are coming from a single equilibrium, which in this case is a pure-strategy Nash equilibrium, as well as its refinements. A common challenge is that the underlying game models often have multiple equilibria, and thus some measure to handle this problem must exist. Multiplicity of equilibria is problematic in the estimation of model parameters, as well as in the model predictions and counterfactuals. The measures taken in the literature are equilibrium refinement, the equilibrium-selection mechanism, and the set-identification approach (this is in contrast to point identification). We provide an overview of each of the measures in this chapter.

4.1 Estimation of Discrete-Game Models with Cross-Sectional Data

In this section, we study estimation of model parameters characterized by the pure-strategy Nash equilibria when cross-sectional data are available to the researcher. The models covered in this section do not involve dynamics, in the sense that the players are not forward looking at the time when the payoffs are realized.[1] We study the discrete games with complete and incomplete information, respectively. The

1. The games that we study in this section include the subgame perfect Nash equilibria.

literature has focused on the entry in the oligopolistic markets, which we focus on in our presentation as well.

4.1.1 Static Discrete Games with Complete Information

4.1.1.1 SIMULTANEOUS ENTRY

Setup and Equilibrium Estimation of static discrete-game models with complete information was pioneered by Bresnahan and Reiss (1990, 1991a). Our presentation closely follows their work. We consider the simplest setup for illustration: one-shot simultaneous complete information entry/exit games played by two players, denoted by $i \in \{1, 2\}$. The reduced-form, long-run, equilibrium monopoly profit function in market j is

$$\pi_{i,j} = \mathbf{x}'_{i,j}\boldsymbol{\alpha}_i + \epsilon_{i,j},$$

here $\epsilon_{i,j} \perp\!\!\!\perp \mathbf{x}_{i,j}$.[2] To that end, consider the following payoff matrix:

$$\begin{array}{ccc} & O_2 & E_2 \\ O_1 & (0,0) & \left(0, \mathbf{x}'_{2,j}\boldsymbol{\alpha}_2 + \epsilon_{2,j}\right) \\ E_1 & \left(\mathbf{x}'_{1,j}\boldsymbol{\alpha}_1 + \epsilon_{1,j}, 0\right) & \left(\mathbf{x}'_{1,j}\boldsymbol{\alpha}_1 - \delta_1 + \epsilon_{1,j}, \mathbf{x}'_{2,j}\boldsymbol{\alpha}_2 - \delta_2 + \epsilon_{2,j}\right). \end{array}$$

If only one firm enters, the firm enjoys the monopoly profit $\mathbf{x}'_{i,j}\boldsymbol{\alpha}_i + \epsilon_{i,j}$. If both enter, they enjoy duopoly profit $\mathbf{x}'_{i,j}\boldsymbol{\alpha}_i - \delta_i + \epsilon_{i,j}$. Here, $\epsilon_{i,j}$ is not observable to the econometrician, but both players know the realization of $\left(\epsilon_{1,j}, \epsilon_{2,j}\right)$ before making the entry decision. We assume that the econometrician knows $F\left(\epsilon_{1,j}, \epsilon_{2j}|\boldsymbol{\theta}\right)$, the joint cumulative distribution function of $\left(\epsilon_{1,j}, \epsilon_{2,j}\right)$ up to a finite-dimensional parameter $\boldsymbol{\theta}$. We only consider the pure-strategy Nash equilibria of the game. Note that we define δ_i to be the difference between the monopoly profit and the duopoly profit of firm i. A natural restriction in the context of entry game is $\delta_i > 0$ for $i = 1, 2$.[3] The model parameters subject to estimation are $(\boldsymbol{\alpha}_1, \boldsymbol{\alpha}_2, \delta_1, \delta_2, \boldsymbol{\theta})$. We suppress $\boldsymbol{\theta}$ for the sake of notational convenience unless it becomes necessary.

We assume that the observed data are coming from the pure-strategy Nash equilibrium. The pure-strategy Nash equilibrium realization depends on the

2. The equilibrium formulation studied in this subsection can be extended to finite players with finite actions.

3. Bresnahan and Reiss (1991a) note the possibility that either one or both δ_i can be negative. However, negative δ_i is not realistic for a noncooperative entry game, and thus the following literature is mostly focused only on positive δ_i.

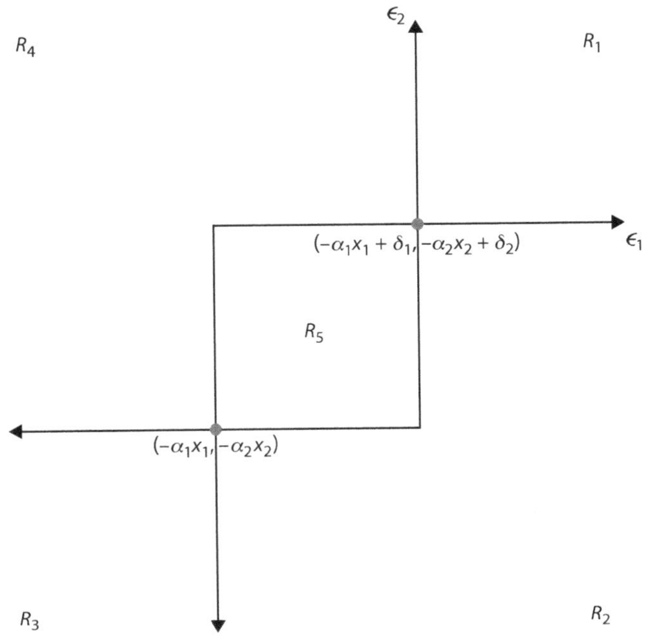

FIGURE 4.1.1. Equilibrium strategy plotted in the $(\epsilon_{1,j}, \epsilon_{2,j})$ plane when $\delta_1 > 0$ and $\delta_2 > 0$

parameters and the realizations of $\epsilon_{i,j}$. Firm i enters market j if it earns a nonnegative profit (i.e., $\mathbf{1}\left(\pi_{i,j} \geq 0\right)$). Hence, we can summarize the realizations of the Nash equilibrium and its corresponding region of $(\epsilon_{1,j}, \epsilon_{2,j})$ as follows:

- $\mathcal{R}_3 = \{(O_1, O_2) \text{ is observed}\} =$
  $\left\{\left(\epsilon_{1,j}, \epsilon_{2,j}\right) : \mathbf{x}_{1,j}'\boldsymbol{\alpha}_1 + \epsilon_{1,j} < 0 \text{ and } \mathbf{x}_{2,j}'\boldsymbol{\alpha}_2 + \epsilon_{2,j} < 0\right\}$;
- $\mathcal{R}_1 = \{(E_1, E_2) \text{ is observed}\} =$
  $\left\{\left(\epsilon_{1,j}, \epsilon_{2,j}\right) : \mathbf{x}_{1,j}'\boldsymbol{\alpha}_1 - \delta_1 + \epsilon_{1,j} > 0 \text{ and } \mathbf{x}_{2,j}'\boldsymbol{\alpha}_2 - \delta_2 + \epsilon_{2,j} > 0\right\}$;
- $\mathcal{R}_2 + \mathcal{R}_5 = \{(E_1, O_2) \text{ is observed}\} =$
  $\left\{\left(\epsilon_{1,j}, \epsilon_{2,j}\right) : \mathbf{x}_{1,j}'\boldsymbol{\alpha}_1 + \epsilon_{1,j} > 0 \text{ and } \mathbf{x}_{2,j}'\boldsymbol{\alpha}_2 - \delta_2 + \epsilon_{2,j} < 0\right\}$; and
- $\mathcal{R}_4 + \mathcal{R}_5 = \{(O_1, E_2) \text{ is observed}\} =$
  $\left\{\left(\epsilon_{1,j}, \epsilon_{2,j}\right) : \mathbf{x}_{1,j}'\boldsymbol{\alpha}_1 - \delta_1 + \epsilon_{1,j} < 0 \text{ and } \mathbf{x}_{2,j}'\boldsymbol{\alpha}_2 + \epsilon_{2,j} > 0\right\}$.

$\mathcal{R}_1, \ldots, \mathcal{R}_5$, the sets of possible realizations of $(\epsilon_{1,j}, \epsilon_{2,j})$, depend on the parameter $(\boldsymbol{\alpha}_1, \boldsymbol{\alpha}_2, \delta_1, \delta_2)$. Figure 4.1.1 plots $\mathcal{R}_1, \ldots, \mathcal{R}_5$ on the $(\epsilon_{1,j}, \epsilon_{2,j})$ plane.

The overlapping region $\mathcal{R}_5$ is problematic in the prediction of the model outcomes and in turn in the identification and estimation of model parameters. In terms of the prediction, suppose that we know the value of the model parameters $(\boldsymbol{\alpha}_1, \boldsymbol{\alpha}_2, \delta_1, \delta_2)$. If the realized value of $(\epsilon_{1,j}, \epsilon_{2,j})$ is in $\mathcal{R}_5$, it can either yield the outcome (E_1, O_2) or (O_1, E_2). In other words, $\mathcal{R}_5$ can rationalize both (E_1, O_2) and (O_1, E_2) as an equilibrium outcome, so prediction becomes impossible in this region of $(\epsilon_{1,j}, \epsilon_{2,j})$ realization. It becomes more problematic when we consider the identification and estimation of model parameters. Now suppose that $(\boldsymbol{\alpha}_1, \boldsymbol{\alpha}_2, \delta_1, \delta_2)$ is unknown, and we assume that we calculate the action probabilities as usual, ignoring the overlapping region. The sum of the probabilities exceeds 1, and the resulting likelihood is not legitimate. This example nicely illustrates how a fully specified econometric model can be incomplete, in the sense that for a given $(\epsilon_{1,i}, \epsilon_{2,i})$ a range of parameters $(\boldsymbol{\alpha}_1, \boldsymbol{\alpha}_2, \delta_1, \delta_2)$ can rationalize the same outcome of the model. The literature has suggested a few solutions to address this incompleteness problem, as we discuss next.

Incompleteness and Likelihoods Our primary goal in the estimation is to derive the legitimate likelihoods of observing the data $\left\{\mathbf{x}_{i,j}, \mathbf{1}\left(\pi_{i,j} > 0\right)\right\}_{i\in\{1,2\}, j\in\mathcal{J}}$. The original solution suggested by Bresnahan and Reiss (1990, 1991a) is to exploit only the number of firms in a market. When (δ_1, δ_2) are constants, we can estimate the model parameters $(\boldsymbol{\alpha}_1, \boldsymbol{\alpha}_2, \delta_1, \delta_2, \boldsymbol{\theta})$ using MLE. The likelihoods of observing 0, 1, and 2 firms are, respectively,

$$\mathcal{L}\left(0 \text{ firms enter}|\mathbf{x}_{1,j}, \mathbf{x}_{2,j}; \boldsymbol{\alpha}_1, \boldsymbol{\alpha}_2, \delta_1, \delta_2, \boldsymbol{\theta}\right) = \int_{\mathcal{R}_3} dF\left(\epsilon_{1,j}, \epsilon_{2,j}|\boldsymbol{\theta}\right)$$

$$\mathcal{L}\left(2 \text{ firms enter}|\mathbf{x}_{1,j}, \mathbf{x}_{2,j}; \boldsymbol{\alpha}_1, \boldsymbol{\alpha}_2, \delta_1, \delta_2, \boldsymbol{\theta}\right) = \int_{\mathcal{R}_1} dF\left(\epsilon_{1,j}, \epsilon_{2,j}|\boldsymbol{\theta}\right)$$

$$\mathcal{L}\left(1 \text{ firm enters}|\mathbf{x}_{1,j}, \mathbf{x}_{2,j}; \boldsymbol{\alpha}_1, \boldsymbol{\alpha}_2, \delta_1, \delta_2, \boldsymbol{\theta}\right)$$
$$= 1 - \int_{\mathcal{R}_1} dF\left(\epsilon_{1,j}, \epsilon_{2,j}|\boldsymbol{\theta}\right) - \int_{\mathcal{R}_3} dF\left(\epsilon_{1,j}, \epsilon_{2,j}|\boldsymbol{\theta}\right).$$

Bresnahan and Reiss (1990) further allow δ_1, δ_2 to be nonnegative random variables for more flexibility. To that end, they consider

$$\delta_{i,j} = g\left(\mathbf{z}_{i,j}'\boldsymbol{\gamma}_i\right) + \eta_{i,j} \tag{4.1.1}$$

for $i = 1, 2$, where $g(\cdot)$ is a parametric nonnegative function and $\eta_{i,j}$ is a nonnegative random variable.

This classic approach has three shortcomings: (1) Using only the number of entrants in a market is throwing away some information from data, (2) uniqueness in the number of entrants in the equilibrium does not always hold,[4] and (3) generalizing it is difficult when more than two potential entrants exist.

4. For example, consider when $\delta_1 < 0$ and $\delta_2 < 0$.

Kooreman (1994) suggests an ad-hoc solution to resolve point (1). The idea is to add a nuisance parameter, which is essentially the equilibrium-selection probability in region $\mathcal{R}_5$. As before, the likelihood of observing the samples (O_1, O_2), (E_1, E_2) can be written as

$$\begin{aligned}\mathcal{L}\left(\{O_1, O_2\} \mid \mathbf{x}_{1,j}, \mathbf{x}_{2,j}; \boldsymbol{\alpha}_1, \boldsymbol{\alpha}_2, \delta_1, \delta_2, \boldsymbol{\theta}\right) &= \Pr\left(\epsilon_{1,j} < -\mathbf{x}_{1,j}'\boldsymbol{\alpha}_1, \epsilon_{2,j} < -\mathbf{x}_{2,j}'\boldsymbol{\alpha}_2\right) \\ &= \int_{\mathcal{R}_3} dF\left(\epsilon_{1,j}, \epsilon_{2,j} \mid \boldsymbol{\theta}\right) \qquad (4.1.2)\end{aligned}$$

$$\begin{aligned}&\mathcal{L}\left(\{E_1, E_2\} \mid \mathbf{x}_{1,j}, \mathbf{x}_{2,j}; \boldsymbol{\alpha}_1, \boldsymbol{\alpha}_2, \delta_1, \delta_2, \boldsymbol{\theta}\right) \\ &= \Pr\left(\epsilon_{1,j} > -\mathbf{x}_{1,j}'\boldsymbol{\alpha}_1 + \delta_1, \epsilon_{2,j} < -\mathbf{x}_{2,j}'\boldsymbol{\alpha}_2 + \delta_2\right) \\ &= \int_{\mathcal{R}_1} dF\left(\epsilon_{1,j}, \epsilon_{2,j} \mid \boldsymbol{\theta}\right). \qquad (4.1.3)\end{aligned}$$

For the likelihood of observing the $\{E_1, O_2\}$ and $\{O_1, E_2\}$ pair, we add parameter $\lambda \in [0, 1]$, which can be jointly estimated. λ can be further parameterized as a function of covariates. The likelihood is legitimate now, which is

$$\begin{aligned}&\mathcal{L}\left(\{O_1, E_2\} \mid \mathbf{x}_{1,j}, \mathbf{x}_{2,j}; \boldsymbol{\alpha}_1, \boldsymbol{\alpha}_2, \delta_1, \delta_2, \boldsymbol{\theta}, \lambda\right) \\ &= \Pr\left(\epsilon_{1,j} < -\mathbf{x}_{1,j}'\boldsymbol{\alpha}_1 + \delta_1, \epsilon_{2,j} > -\mathbf{x}_{2,j}'\boldsymbol{\alpha}_2\right) \\ &= \int_{\mathcal{R}_4} dF\left(\epsilon_{1,j}, \epsilon_{2,j} \mid \boldsymbol{\theta}\right) + \lambda \int_{\mathcal{R}_5} dF\left(\epsilon_{1,j}, \epsilon_{2,j} \mid \boldsymbol{\theta}\right) \\ &\mathcal{L}\left(\{E_1, O_2\} \mid \mathbf{x}_{1,j}, \mathbf{x}_{2,j}; \boldsymbol{\alpha}_1, \boldsymbol{\alpha}_2, \delta_1, \delta_2, \boldsymbol{\theta}, \lambda\right) \\ &= \Pr\left(\epsilon_{1,j} > -\mathbf{x}_{1,j}'\boldsymbol{\alpha}_1, \epsilon_{2,j} < -\mathbf{x}_{2,j}'\boldsymbol{\alpha}_2 + \delta_2\right) \\ &= \int_{\mathcal{R}_2} dF\left(\epsilon_{1,j}, \epsilon_{2,j} \mid \boldsymbol{\theta}\right) + (1 - \lambda) \int_{\mathcal{R}_5} dF\left(\epsilon_{1,j}, \epsilon_{2,j} \mid \boldsymbol{\theta}\right).\end{aligned}$$

The nuisance parameter λ is the conditional probability of choosing $\{O_1, E_2\}$, given that the $\left(\epsilon_{1,j}, \epsilon_{2,j}\right)$ realization is in $\mathcal{R}_5$. The idea to add a data-driven equilibrium-selection rule is further elaborated in Bajari, Hong, and Ryan (2010). They allow λ to be a function of the properties of the equilibrium itself: λ can be a function of indicators of pure-strategy equilibrium, Pareto-dominated equilibrium, and joint-payoff-maximizing equilibrium, the coefficients of which are estimable from the data.

A modern approach to resolving the incompleteness of the underlying model is to exploit the moment inequalities, which leads to the bound estimates for the partially identified model parameters. Ciliberto and Tamer (2009) and Pakes et al. (2015) give full treatments of the problem, and we study Ciliberto and Tamer's framework here. Suppose that we have observed a sample of $\{O_1, E_2\}$. Denote the conditional probability of observing $\{O_1, E_2\}$ given $\left(\mathbf{x}_{1,j}, \mathbf{x}_{2,j}\right)$ by $\Pr\left(\{O_1, E_2\} \,|\mathbf{x}_{1,j}, \mathbf{x}_{2,j}\right)$,[5] which is bounded as

$$\begin{aligned}\int_{\mathcal{R}_4} dF\left(\epsilon_{1,j}, \epsilon_{2,j}|\boldsymbol{\theta}\right) &\leq \Pr\left(\{O_1, E_2\} \,|\mathbf{x}_{1,j}, \mathbf{x}_{2,j}\right)\\ &\leq \int_{\mathcal{R}_4} dF\left(\epsilon_{1,j}, \epsilon_{2,j}|\boldsymbol{\theta}\right) + \int_{\mathcal{R}_5} dF\left(\epsilon_{1,j}, \epsilon_{2,j}|\boldsymbol{\theta}\right). \end{aligned} \tag{4.1.4}$$

Similarly, $\Pr\left(\{E_1, O_2\} \,|\mathbf{x}_{1,j}, \mathbf{x}_{2,j}\right)$ is bounded as

$$\begin{aligned}\int_{\mathcal{R}_2} dF\left(\epsilon_{1,j}, \epsilon_{2,j}|\boldsymbol{\theta}\right) &\leq \Pr\left(\{E_1, O_2\} \,|\mathbf{x}_{1,j}, \mathbf{x}_{2,j}\right)\\ &\leq \int_{\mathcal{R}_2} dF\left(\epsilon_{1,j}, \epsilon_{2,j}|\boldsymbol{\theta}\right) + \int_{\mathcal{R}_5} dF\left(\epsilon_{1,j}, \epsilon_{2,j}|\boldsymbol{\theta}\right). \end{aligned} \tag{4.1.5}$$

We have two trivial bounds for $\Pr\left(\{O_1, O_2\} \,|\mathbf{x}_{1,j}, \mathbf{x}_{2,j}\right)$ and $\Pr\left(\{E_1, E_2\} \,|\mathbf{x}_{1,j}, \mathbf{x}_{2,j}\right)$ as

$$\int_{\mathcal{R}_3} dF\left(\epsilon_{1,j}, \epsilon_{2,j}|\boldsymbol{\theta}\right) \leq \Pr\left(\{O_1, O_2\} \,|\mathbf{x}_{1,j}, \mathbf{x}_{2,j}\right) \leq \int_{\mathcal{R}_3} dF\left(\epsilon_{1,j}, \epsilon_{2,j}|\boldsymbol{\theta}\right) \tag{4.1.6}$$

$$\int_{\mathcal{R}_1} dF\left(\epsilon_{1,j}, \epsilon_{2,j}|\boldsymbol{\theta}\right) \leq \Pr\left(\{E_1, E_2\} \,|\mathbf{x}_{1,j}, \mathbf{x}_{2,j}\right) \leq \int_{\mathcal{R}_1} dF\left(\epsilon_{1,j}, \epsilon_{2,j}|\boldsymbol{\theta}\right). \tag{4.1.7}$$

For simplicity of notation, let $\mathbf{y}$ denote the possible outcomes. Stack equations (4.1.4)–(4.1.7), and then denote the left-hand and the right-hand sides of the inequalities by $\mathbf{h}^l\left(\mathbf{x}_{1,j}, \mathbf{x}_{2,j}; \boldsymbol{\alpha}_1, \boldsymbol{\alpha}_2, \delta_1, \delta_2, \boldsymbol{\theta}\right)$ and $\mathbf{h}^u\left(\mathbf{x}_{1,j}, \mathbf{x}_{2,j}; \boldsymbol{\alpha}_1, \boldsymbol{\alpha}_2, \delta_1, \delta_2, \boldsymbol{\theta}\right)$, respectively. Collecting equations (4.1.4)–(4.1.7) yields 2^2 inequalities:

$$\mathbf{h}^l\left(\mathbf{x}_{1,j}, \mathbf{x}_{2,j}; \boldsymbol{\alpha}_1, \boldsymbol{\alpha}_2, \delta_1, \delta_2, \boldsymbol{\theta}\right) \leq \mathbf{Pr}\left(\mathbf{y}|\mathbf{x}_{1,j}, \mathbf{x}_{2,j}\right) \leq \mathbf{h}^u\left(\mathbf{x}_{1,j}, \mathbf{x}_{2,j}; \boldsymbol{\alpha}_1, \boldsymbol{\alpha}_2, \delta_1, \delta_2, \boldsymbol{\theta}\right).^{6} \tag{4.1.8}$$

5. Note the distinction of this conditional probability from the likelihoods defined here. The likelihoods are a function of the parameters as well, whereas the conditional probabilities here, which are taken to be directly observable from data, are not a function of parameters.

6. Although we focus on a two-player entry game, extension to a k-player entry game is straightforward. In general, we have 2^k inequalities.

The parameter vector $(\boldsymbol{\alpha}_1, \boldsymbol{\alpha}_2, \delta_1, \delta_2, \boldsymbol{\theta})$ satisfying equation (4.1.8) is not a singleton in general, even if $F\left(\epsilon_{1,j}, \epsilon_{2,j} | \boldsymbol{\theta}\right)$ has a well-behaved density. The parameter vector is only partially identified or set identified, as opposed to being point identified. Furthermore, as a result of being agnostic about the equilibrium selection, this approach to estimate only the bounds of the parameters may not be very informative in the model predictions and counterfactuals.

Estimation of the System Specified by Moment Inequalities For the sake of notational simplicity, denote $\boldsymbol{\omega} := (\boldsymbol{\alpha}_1, \boldsymbol{\alpha}_2, \delta_1, \delta_2, \boldsymbol{\theta})$. Equation (4.1.8) as the population moment inequalities. For estimation, we replace each term in the inequalities with its sample analog. To that end, the term $\mathbf{Pr}\left(\mathbf{y}|\mathbf{x}_{1,j}, \mathbf{x}_{2,j}\right)$ should be estimated first. Various nonparametric conditional cumulative distribution function estimators are available. Ciliberto and Tamer (2009) use the simple frequency estimator. More options can be found in, for example, Li and Racine (2007).

Let $\boldsymbol{\Omega}_0$ be the set such that for any equation $\boldsymbol{\omega} \in \boldsymbol{\Omega}_0$, equation (4.1.8) is satisfied for any $\left(\mathbf{x}_{1,j}, \mathbf{x}_{2,j}\right)$ with probability 1. Such a set $\boldsymbol{\Omega}_0$ is called the "identified set." The focus of Ciliberto and Tamer (2009) is to find a consistent set estimator $\hat{\boldsymbol{\Omega}}$ in the sense that $\hat{\boldsymbol{\Omega}} \subset \boldsymbol{\Omega}_0$ and $\boldsymbol{\Omega}_0 \subset \hat{\boldsymbol{\Omega}}$ with probability 1 as the sample size n grows to infinity. To that end, they consider the following objective function:

$$Q_n(\boldsymbol{\omega}) := \frac{1}{n} \sum_{j=1}^{n} \left\{ \left\| \min\left\{ \mathbf{0}, \mathbf{Pr}\left(\mathbf{y}|\mathbf{x}_{1,j}, \mathbf{x}_{2,j}\right) - \mathbf{h}^l\left(\mathbf{x}_{1,j}, \mathbf{x}_{2,j}; \boldsymbol{\omega}\right) \right\} \right\| \right.$$
$$\left. + \left\| \max\left\{ \mathbf{0}, \mathbf{Pr}\left(\mathbf{y}|\mathbf{x}_{1,j}, \mathbf{x}_{2,j}\right) - \mathbf{h}^u\left(\mathbf{x}_{1,j}, \mathbf{x}_{2,j}; \boldsymbol{\omega}\right) \right\} \right\| \right\}, \qquad (4.1.9)$$

where $\|\cdot\|$ is the Euclidian norm, and min and max operators inside $\|\cdot\|$ are taken elementwise. Notice each part of equation (4.1.9) penalizes the violation of the inequalities on only one side, and the objective function has some flat region where the inequalities in equation (4.1.8) are strict. By construction, it is clear that $Q(\boldsymbol{\omega}) \geq 0$ for any $\boldsymbol{\omega}$, and $Q(\boldsymbol{\omega}) = 0$ for $\boldsymbol{\omega} \in \boldsymbol{\Omega}_0$. Now, define the set estimator as

$$\hat{\boldsymbol{\Omega}} := \left\{ \boldsymbol{\omega} \in \boldsymbol{\Omega} : nQ_n(\boldsymbol{\omega}) \leq \nu_n \right\},$$

where $\nu_n \to \infty$ and $\nu_n / n \to 0$. Chernozhukov, Hong, and Tamer (2007) show consistency and asymptotic properties of the set estimator $\hat{\boldsymbol{\Omega}}$ defined here.

The remaining part is an algorithm to construct $\mathbf{h}^l\left(\mathbf{x}_{1,j}, \mathbf{x}_{2,j}; \boldsymbol{\omega}\right)$ and $\mathbf{h}^u\left(\mathbf{x}_{1,j}, \mathbf{x}_{2,j}; \boldsymbol{\omega}\right)$. They suggest using simulation, which is similar to Berry (1992), which we study next. The key steps are as follows: (1) Draw R numbers of $\left(\epsilon_{1,j}, \epsilon_{2,j}\right)$ for each j; (2) compute the profits of each potential entrant; and

(3) when the equilibrium is unique for a simulation draw, the corresponding element of both $\mathbf{h}^l\left(\mathbf{x}_{1,j}, \mathbf{x}_{2,j}; \boldsymbol{\omega}\right)$ and $\mathbf{h}^u\left(\mathbf{x}_{1,j}, \mathbf{x}_{2,j}; \boldsymbol{\omega}\right)$ is set at 1. When the equilibrium is not unique, add 1 only in $\mathbf{h}^u\left(\mathbf{x}_{1,j}, \mathbf{x}_{2,j}; \boldsymbol{\omega}\right)$. For example, the upper-bound estimate on the outcome probability $\Pr\left(\{E_1, E_1\} \mid \mathbf{x}_{1,j}, \mathbf{x}_{2,j}\right)$ is

$$\begin{aligned}
&\hat{h}^{u,(4)}\left(\mathbf{x}_{1,j}, \mathbf{x}_{2,j}; \boldsymbol{\omega}\right) \\
&= \frac{1}{R}\sum_{r=1}^{R}\mathbf{1}\left(\left\{\mathbf{x}_{1,j}'\boldsymbol{\alpha}_1 - \delta_1 + \epsilon_{1,j}^r > 0 \text{ and } \mathbf{x}_{2,j}'\boldsymbol{\alpha}_2 - \delta_2 + \epsilon_{2,j}^r > 0\right\}\right).
\end{aligned}$$

The simulation procedure is computationally very intensive, but it is parallelizable. Another computational challenge is that we cannot use the derivative-based optimizers due to the flat region of the objective function. Instead, the estimation algorithm should be essentially a grid search. Curse of dimensionality becomes a serious problem in a grid search.

4.1.1.2 SEQUENTIAL ENTRY WITH MORE THAN TWO POTENTIAL ENTRANTS

The two-player discrete-game models studied in subsection 4.1.1.1 have a straightforward extension to multiple players. When the number of potential entrants is larger than two, the incompleteness problem becomes much more complicated. Some classical works, which we review in this subsection, rule out this potential multiple-equilibria problem by assuming sequential entry. We review Bresnahan and Reiss (1991a,b) and Berry (1992) here.

The basic idea of this equilibrium refinement is described in Bresnahan and Reiss (1991a). In a two-player entry game, when the entry is assumed to be sequential, region $\mathcal{R}_5$ in figure 4.1.1 only allows for the first mover's entry in the pure-strategy, subgame perfect Nash equilibrium. The idea can readily be generalized to a game with more than two potential entrants.

Bresnahan and Reiss (1991b) assume the nonnegative-profit condition with sequential entry and homogeneous firms. In market j, n_j number of entrants are observed when $\pi_j\left(n_j\right) \geq 0$ and $\pi_j\left(n_j+1\right) < 0$ hold. The reduced-form profit function is

$$\begin{aligned}
\pi_j\left(n_j\right) &= \left(\mathbf{q}_j'\boldsymbol{\lambda}\right)\left(\alpha_1 + \mathbf{x}_j'\boldsymbol{\beta} - \sum_{k=2}^{n_j}\alpha_k\right) - \left(\gamma_1 + \mathbf{w}_j'\boldsymbol{\delta} + \sum_{k=2}^{n_j}\gamma_k\right) + \epsilon_j \\
&=: \bar{\pi}_j\left(n_j\right) + \epsilon_j,
\end{aligned}$$

where $\mathbf{q}_j$ is the demographics of the region in which firm j is located, $\mathbf{x}_j$ is the variable-cost shifter, and $\mathbf{w}_j$ is the fixed-cost shifter. The assumption on the error term is $\epsilon_j \sim$ i.i.d. $\mathcal{N}(0,1)$. The model parameters to be estimated are $(\boldsymbol{\lambda}, \boldsymbol{\alpha}, \boldsymbol{\gamma}, \boldsymbol{\delta})$. The i.i.d. normal assumption on the error term allows ordered Probit estimation. To that end, consider the likelihood of observing n_j firms:

$$\begin{aligned}
\Pr\left(n_j \text{ firms observed}\right) &= \Pr\left(\pi_j\left(n_j\right) \geq 0, \pi_j\left(n_j+1\right) < 0\right) \\
&= \Pr\left(\bar{\pi}_j\left(n_j\right) + \epsilon_j \geq 0, \bar{\pi}_j\left(n_j+1\right) + \epsilon_j < 0\right) \\
&= \Pr\left(-\bar{\pi}_j\left(n_j\right) \leq \epsilon_j < -\bar{\pi}_j\left(n_j+1\right)\right) \\
&= \Phi\left(-\bar{\pi}_j\left(n_j+1\right)\right) - \Phi\left(-\bar{\pi}_j\left(n_j\right)\right).
\end{aligned}$$

Maximum-likelihood estimation will yield the consistent, asymptotically normal estimators as usual.

Berry (1992) allows firm-level heterogeneity in the fixed cost of the potential entrants. The model is again a complete-information, oligopolistic entry game to a market. Only the pure-strategy equilibrium is considered. To that end, define the reduced-form profit function of a potential entrant i in market j as

$$\pi_{i,j}\left(n_j\right) = \mathbf{x}_j'\boldsymbol{\beta} - \delta \ln\left(n_j\right) + \mathbf{z}_{i,j}'\boldsymbol{\alpha} + \rho\epsilon_j + \sqrt{1-\rho^2}\epsilon_{i,j}, \tag{4.1.10}$$

where n_j is the equilibrium number of firms in market j, $\mathbf{x}_j$ is the market-level variable-profit, shifter, $\mathbf{z}_{i,j}$ is the firm-level, fixed-cost shifter. Market-specific heterogeneity is reflected in the term $\mathbf{z}_{i,j}'\boldsymbol{\alpha} + \sqrt{1-\rho^2}\epsilon_{i,j}$. Firm i enters market j if $\pi_{i,j}\left(n_j\right) > 0$.[7] It is assumed that ϵ_j and $\epsilon_{i,j}$ both follow i.i.d. standard normal distribution. Thus, within a market, the joint distribution of the composite error term $\mathbf{u}_j := \rho\epsilon_j + \sqrt{1-\rho^2}\boldsymbol{\epsilon}_j$ is

$$\begin{pmatrix} u_{1,j} \\ u_{2,j} \\ \vdots \\ u_{N,j} \end{pmatrix} \sim \mathcal{N}\left(\mathbf{0}, \begin{pmatrix} 1 & \rho & \cdots & \rho \\ \rho & 1 & \vdots & \rho \\ \vdots & \cdots & \ddots & \vdots \\ \rho & \rho & \cdots & 1 \end{pmatrix}\right).$$

Furthermore, if we assume that the firms enter in the order of profitability and operate with nonnegative profits, we can show that the equilibrium number of firms in a market is determined uniquely.

7. Because Berry (1992) studies the domestic airline market, a market is naturally defined by the city pair. Then, the potential entrant is defined by any airline that is operating in either of the end points. Identifying who is a potential entrant and who is not is generally a difficult problem.

The goal is to estimate the model parameters $(\boldsymbol{\beta}, \boldsymbol{\alpha}, \delta, \rho)$ in equation (4.1.10) consistently. However, even though we specify the model up to the distribution of error term, MLE is still practically infeasible because the likelihood of observing $1, 2, \ldots, N$ entrants should be computed for each data point. For each $\Pr\left(n_j^* = n | \mathbf{x}_j, \mathbf{z}_{i,j}; \boldsymbol{\beta}, \boldsymbol{\alpha}, \delta, \rho\right)$, evaluation of approximately N times the integral is necessary, which is computationally expensive. Another difficult problem arises because n_j is endogenous, in that the number of players observed in the market is determined by the players' decision. Berry (1992) suggests GMM with simulated moment conditions. To implement GMM estimation, we must first specify the moment conditions. First, fix j and consider the equilibrium condition for the number of players in the market:

$$n_j^* = \sum_i \mathbf{1}\left(\pi_{i,j}\left(n_j^*\right) > 0 \middle| \mathbf{x}_j, \mathbf{z}_{i,j}; \boldsymbol{\beta}, \boldsymbol{\alpha}, \delta, \rho\right).$$

Taking expectation gives

$$n_j^* = \sum_i \mathbb{E}_{u_{i,j}}\left[\mathbf{1}\left(\pi_{i,j}\left(n_j\right) > 0 \middle| \mathbf{x}_j, \mathbf{z}_{i,j}; \boldsymbol{\beta}, \boldsymbol{\alpha}, \delta, \rho\right)\right]. \tag{4.1.11}$$

The corresponding moment condition is

$$\mathbb{E}\left[n_j^* - \sum_i \Pr\left(\pi_{i,j}\left(n_j\right) > 0 \middle| \mathbf{x}_j, \mathbf{z}_{i,j}\right) \middle| \boldsymbol{\beta}, \boldsymbol{\alpha}, \delta, \rho\right] = 0. \tag{4.1.12}$$

The right-hand-side object of equation (4.1.11) is difficult to evaluate exactly. We employ a simulation approach, which is similar to Berry, Levinsohn, and Pakes (1995) studied in chapter 3. First, simulate many enough $\boldsymbol{\epsilon}_j$ and store the simulated $\boldsymbol{\epsilon}_j$ in the memory. Then, for each candidate $(\boldsymbol{\beta}, \boldsymbol{\alpha}, \delta, \rho)$, calculate the simulation analog of $\sum_i \Pr\left(\pi_{i,j}\left(n_j\right) > 0 | \mathbf{x}_j, \mathbf{z}_{i,j}\right)$. Iterate over $(\boldsymbol{\beta}, \boldsymbol{\alpha}, \delta, \rho)$ to find the parameter values that minimize the GMM objective function corresponding to the moment condition in equation (4.1.12).

The uniqueness of the equilibrium relies on the assumption that firms enter sequentially and the information is perfect.[8] We assume that the firms enter in the order of profitability in Berry (1992), in which the actual sequence of entry is not observed. Note that the estimated model parameter may vary substantially if we

8. It can be shown that in an extensive-form game with perfect information and a finite number of nodes, a unique sequential equilibrium exists. See theorem 4.7 of Myerson (1991).

assume a different order of entry, especially when the potential entrants are similar in terms of profitability. For further discussions on the assumed order of entry and robustness of the estimators, see Ellickson and Misra (2011).

4.1.1.3 SIMULTANEOUS ENTRY WITH MULTIPLE MARKETS

Jia (2008) allows multiple location entry decisions by two firms. Consider two retail discount chains, Walmart and Kmart. Both chains decide whether to enter many markets simultaneously to maximize the chainwide profit. The profit functions of each chain store $i \in \{K, W\}$ at market j are given by

$$\pi_{i,j}\left(\mathbf{d}_i, d_{-i,j}; \mathbf{x}_j, \mathbf{l}_j, \epsilon_j, \epsilon_{i,j}\right)$$
$$= d_{i,j}\left(\mathbf{x}_j'\boldsymbol{\beta}_i + \delta_{i,-i} d_{-i,j} + \delta_{i,i} \sum_{k \neq j} \frac{d_{i,k}}{l_{j,k}} + \rho\epsilon_j + \sqrt{1-\rho^2}\epsilon_{i,j}\right),$$

where $d_{i,j} \in \{0, 1\}$ is the endogenous (at equilibrium) entry-decision variable and $l_{j,k}$ is the physical distance between market j and k. The problem becomes complicated because each chain maximizes the profit over the sum over all the markets. To that end, the chainwide profit-maximization problem of chain i is

$$\max_{\{d_{i,1}, d_{i,2}, \ldots, d_{i,J}\} \in \{0,1\}^J} \sum_{j=1}^{J} d_{i,j}\left(\mathbf{x}_j'\boldsymbol{\beta}_i + \delta_{i,-i} d_{-i,j} + \delta_{i,i} \sum_{k \neq j} \frac{d_{i,k}}{l_{j,k}} + \rho\epsilon_j + \sqrt{1-\rho^2}\epsilon_{i,j}\right). \tag{4.1.13}$$

Solving this problem is complicated because (1) the number of decision variables 2^J increases exponentially over the number of markets, and (2) the decision variable is discrete.

Jia (2008) simplifies the solution of the problem substantially, using the lattice structure of the choice variables. She uses the lattice fixed-point theorem, which states that under certain conditions,[9] the optimal decision $\left\{d_{i,1}^*, d_{i,2}^*, \ldots, d_{i,J}^*\right\}$ can be bounded elementwise. As an illustrative example, suppose that $J = 3$ and the equilibrium entry decision is $\left\{d_{i,1}^*, d_{i,2}^*, d_{i,3}^*\right\} = \{0, 1, 0\}$. The lattice fixed-point theorem provides an algorithm that gives the upper and lower bound for the equilibrium entry decision, such as $\{0, 0, 0\}$ and $\{0, 1, 1\}$. Then the degree of freedom for numerical search being left is reduced by half in this example.

9. The key condition is that $\left(\mathbf{x}_j'\boldsymbol{\beta}_i + \delta_{i,-i} d_{-i,j} + \delta_{i,i} \sum_{k \neq j} \frac{d_{i,k}}{l_{j,k}} + \rho\epsilon_j + \sqrt{1-\rho^2}\epsilon_{i,j}\right)$ is increasing in each $d_{i,k}$ (i.e., $\delta_{i,i} \geq 0$).

The remaining estimation step is done by the method of simulated moments, as in Berry (1992). For each candidate parameter, find the simulated profits as described here, and iterate over to minimize the objective function. The equilibrium-selection criteria are not the focus of Jia (2008), and they are arbitrary in a sense. Jia (2008) chooses the equilibrium that best predicts the observed pattern of the chain store locations, and conducts some sensitivity analysis over various equilibrium-selection rules.

4.1.2 *Static Discrete Games with Incomplete Information*

4.1.2.1 PRIVATE INFORMATION AND BAYESIAN NASH EQUILIBRIUM

The baseline discrete-game model pioneered by Bresnahan and Reiss (1991a) raises the fundamental problem of multiple equilibria. As we discussed previously, the literature has developed four solutions: (1) Aggregate the possible outcomes to the form that makes the model coherent; (2) specify an equilibrium-selection rule as a nuisance parameter and estimate it from the data; (3) abandon the point identification and exploit the moment inequalities, which essentially leads only to the set identification; and (4) refine the equilibrium concepts.

Refining the Nash equilibria by introducing private information and employing the relevant equilibrium concept falls into solution (4). The Bayesian Nash equilibrium, which requires that the belief probabilities of the players line up with the strategies of each corresponding player, partly addresses the multiple-equilibria problem by refining the Nash equilibria. The Bayesian Nash equilibrium refinement, however, does not guarantee the uniqueness of the equilibrium. Although the degree of multiplicity shrinks substantially, the equilibrium-selection problem persists. In this section, we focus on the estimation of discrete games where the cross-sectional data are assumed to be generated from pure-strategy Bayesian Nash equilibria. Then, we discuss the recent developments on allowing more flexibility in the information structures.

Baseline Two-Player Simultaneous Entry Model with Additive i.i.d. Logit Errors Consider the entry game studied in section 4.1.1.1. We keep restricting our attention to the two-player entry game for simplicity. Let $y_{i,j}$ be an indicator such that $y_{i,j} = 1$ if firm $i \in \{1, 2\}$ entered market j, and $y_{i,j} = 0$ otherwise. When the realization of $(\epsilon_{1,j}, \epsilon_{2,j})$ was known to both firms, the following equations characterized the Nash equilibrium of this static entry game:

$$y_{1,j} = \mathbf{1}\left(\mathbf{x}_{1,j}'\boldsymbol{\alpha}_1 - \delta_1 y_{2,j} + \epsilon_{1,j} \geq 0\right)$$

$$y_{2,j} = \mathbf{1}\left(\mathbf{x}_{2,j}'\boldsymbol{\alpha}_2 - \delta_2 y_{1,j} + \epsilon_{2,j} \geq 0\right).$$

The key idea of Seim (2006) is to assume that the realization of $\epsilon_{i,j}$ is the private information and the distribution of $\epsilon_{i,j}$ is the common knowledge. Players know only the realization of their own $\epsilon_{i,j}$. For tractability, we assume that $\epsilon_{i,j}$ follows i.i.d. logistic distribution.[10]

The Bayesian Nash equilibrium is defined as the strategy profiles and belief systems of each player such that, given (1) each player's posterior belief on other players' type[11] and (2) other players' strategy, each player's strategy maximizes the expected payoff. Because we normalized the expected payoff of the exit option as zero, each player's strategy boils down to

$$\begin{aligned} y_{i,j} &= \mathbf{1}\left(\mathbf{x}_{i,j}'\boldsymbol{\alpha}_i - \delta_i \mathbb{E}\left[y_{-i,j} | \mathbf{x}_{-i,j}\right] + \epsilon_{i,j} \geq 0\right) \\ &= \mathbf{1}\left(\mathbf{x}_{i,j}'\boldsymbol{\alpha}_i - \delta_i p_{-i,j} + \epsilon_{i,j} \geq 0\right), \end{aligned} \tag{4.1.14}$$

where $p_{-i,j} := E\left[y_{-i,j} | \mathbf{x}_{-i,j}\right] = \Pr\left(y_{-i,j} = 1 | \mathbf{x}_{-i,j}\right)$. Because $\epsilon_{i,j}$ is i.i.d., stacking equation (4.1.14) for $i = 1, 2$ and taking expectations yield

$$p_{i,j} = 1 - F_\epsilon\left(-\mathbf{x}_{i,j}'\boldsymbol{\alpha}_i + \delta_i p_{-i,j}\right). \tag{4.1.15}$$

Invoking the logit error assumption, equation (4.1.15) becomes the set of equilibrium fixed-point equations as

$$p_{1,j} = \frac{\exp\left(\mathbf{x}_{1,j}'\boldsymbol{\alpha}_1 - \delta_1 p_{2,j}\right)}{1 + \exp\left(\mathbf{x}_{1,j}'\boldsymbol{\alpha}_1 - \delta_1 p_{2,j}\right)} \tag{4.1.16}$$

$$p_{2,j} = \frac{\exp\left(\mathbf{x}_{2,j}'\boldsymbol{\alpha}_2 - \delta_2 p_{1,j}\right)}{1 + \exp\left(\mathbf{x}_{2,j}'\boldsymbol{\alpha}_2 - \delta_2 p_{1,j}\right)}. \tag{4.1.17}$$

10. Alternatively, we can assume

$$\begin{aligned} y_{1,j} &= \mathbf{1}\left(\mathbf{x}_{1,j}'\boldsymbol{\alpha}_1 - \delta_1 y_{2,j} + \epsilon_{1,j} \geq \epsilon_{1,j}'\right) \\ y_{2,j} &= \mathbf{1}\left(\mathbf{x}_{2,j}'\boldsymbol{\alpha}_2 - \delta_2 y_{1,j} + \epsilon_{2,j} \geq \epsilon_{2,j}'\right), \end{aligned}$$

with $\epsilon_{i,j}$ and $\epsilon_{i,j}'$ both following i.i.d. type I extreme value distribution.

11. In this context, a player's type is synonymous to the player's private information.

That is, the Bayesian Nash equilibrium data-generating assumption implies the probability of entry must satisfy these fixed-point equations (4.1.16) and (4.1.17). In other words, $p_{i,j} = \Pr\left(y_{i,j} = 1 | \mathbf{x}_{i,j}, \mathbf{x}_{-i,j}, p_{-i,j}; \boldsymbol{\omega}\right)$, where $\boldsymbol{\omega} := \left(\boldsymbol{\alpha}_1, \boldsymbol{\alpha}_2, \delta_1, \delta_2\right)$.

Maximum-Likelihood Estimation Again, the likelihood is

$$\mathcal{L}\left(\left\{y_{i,j}, \mathbf{x}_{i,j}\right\}_{i\in\{1,2\}, j\in\mathcal{J}}; \boldsymbol{\omega}\right)$$

$$= \prod_{j\in\mathcal{J}} \prod_{i=1}^{2} \Pr\left(y_{i,j} = 1 | \mathbf{x}_{i,j}, \mathbf{x}_{-i,j}, p_{-i,j}; \boldsymbol{\omega}\right)^{y_{i,j}}$$

$$\left\{1 - \Pr\left(y_{i,j} = 1 | \mathbf{x}_{i,j}, \mathbf{x}_{-i,j}, p_{-i,j}; \boldsymbol{\omega}\right)\right\}^{1-y_{i,j}}.$$

The problem in implementation is that the solution of equations (4.1.16)–(4.1.17) might not be unique. The number of different solutions is at most finitely many. That is, the model parameters may not be point identified, but the cardinality of the identified set is finite, as opposed to a positive Lebesgue measure set in $\mathbb{R}^2$. This reduction can be regarded as one of the results of the equilibrium refinement by imposing the specific information structure.

A more serious problem in the implementation of MLE is that the number of solutions depends on the candidate parameter values $\boldsymbol{\omega}$. The likelihood as a function of $\boldsymbol{\omega}$ may have kinks, which prevents the derivative-based optimization routine from being used. Vitorino (2012) and Su (2014) convert the optimization problem to an equality-constrained one—namely, mathematical programming with equilibrium constraints (MPEC)—and addresses the multiplicity problem by trying many starting values. To this end, the problem can be restated as

$$\max_{\left\{p_{i,j}\right\}_{i\in\{1,2\}, j\in\mathcal{J}}, \boldsymbol{\omega}} \prod_{j\in\mathcal{J}} \prod_{i=1}^{2} p_{i,j}^{y_{i,j}} \left\{1 - p_{i,j}\right\}^{1-y_{i,j}}$$

$$s.t. \qquad p_{i,j} = \Pr\left(y_{i,j} = 1 | \mathbf{x}_{i,j}, \mathbf{x}_{-i,j}, p_{-i,j}; \boldsymbol{\omega}\right) \qquad i = 1, 2 \quad j \in \mathcal{J}.$$

This constrained maximization problem is feasible because equations (4.1.16)–(4.1.17) are smooth in $\left(\boldsymbol{\omega}, p_{1,j}, p_{2,j}\right)$, and the Jacobian of the constraints is of full rank. Su (2014) argues that when the Bayesian Nash equilibrium is not unique, the one that yields the highest likelihood value should be the data-generating equilibrium. This global maximum of the likelihood serves as a data-driven equilibrium-selection criterion.

Two-Stage GMM Estimation Pesendorfer and Schmidt-Dengler (2008) suggest a two-stage GMM method, which is computationally lighter than the maximum-likelihood estimation because it does not need to exactly satisfy the fixed-point equation in the second-stage parameter estimation. Consider again equations (4.1.16)–(4.1.17). The key idea is to replace $(p_{1,j}, p_{2,j})$ with its consistent estimators $(\hat{p}_{1,j}, \hat{p}_{2,j})$, and then form the moment conditions

$$\mathbb{E}\left[\hat{p}_{1,j} - \frac{\exp\left(\mathbf{x}_{1,j}'\boldsymbol{\alpha}_1 - \delta_1\hat{p}_{2,j}\right)}{1+\exp\left(\mathbf{x}_{1,j}'\boldsymbol{\alpha}_1 - \delta_1\hat{p}_{2,j}\right)}\right] = 0$$

$$\mathbb{E}\left[\hat{p}_{2,j} - \frac{\exp\left(\mathbf{x}_{2,j}'\boldsymbol{\alpha}_2 - \delta_2\hat{p}_{1,j}\right)}{1+\exp\left(\mathbf{x}_{2,j}'\boldsymbol{\alpha}_2 - \delta_2\hat{p}_{1,j}\right)}\right] = 0$$

for $j \in \mathcal{J}$. The second-stage estimation can be done relatively easily using the nonlinear GMM. Assuming the players' strategies corresponds to a single equilibrium, $(\hat{p}_{1,j}, \hat{p}_{2,j})$ will converge to the true probabilities $(p_{1,j}, p_{2,j})$ as the sample size grows to infinity.

The first-stage consistent estimator $(\hat{p}_{1,j}, \hat{p}_{2,j})$ can be a simple frequency estimator, a Nadaraya-Watson-type smoothing estimator, or a partial maximum-likelihood estimator. Note that the error of the first-stage estimates propagates to the second-stage parameter estimates, which means that the asymptotic variances of the second-stage parameter estimates have to be corrected for this additional uncertainty.[12] Su (2014) reports that the finite-sample properties of the two-stage estimators can be worse than the full maximum-likelihood estimator.

4.1.2.2 FLEXIBLE INFORMATION STRUCTURES

The set of possible equilibria shrinks more as the assumption imposed on the information structures becomes stronger. What we have studied thus far is the two extremes; that is, the realization of $\boldsymbol{\epsilon}_{-i,j}$ is either fully known to player i or completely unknown to that player. Furthermore, we assume that $\epsilon_{i,j}$ is i.i.d. over i and j. Recent advances in the literature relax these extreme assumptions on the information structures.

Grieco (2014) introduces both private and public shocks on the player's payoff functions. That analysis is based on the pure-strategy Bayesian Nash equilibrium,

12. A full treatment on this subject when the first-stage estimator is $\sqrt{n}$-consistent can be found in Newey and McFadden (1994).

whereas the model parameters might be only partially identified due to the existence of public shocks in the payoff functions. Wan and Xu (2014) and Liu, Vuong, and Xu (2017) study the estimation of discrete games with incomplete information when players' private information is possibly correlated, assuming that the data are generated by a single Bayesian Nash equilibrium.

Aradillas-Lopez (2010) investigates semiparametric identification and estimation when the distribution of $\epsilon_{i,j}$'s are unknown to the researcher, assuming that the data are generated from correlated equilibria developed by Aumann (1987). Magnolfi and Roncoroni (2020) employ the Bayes-correlated equilibrium concept by Bergemann and Morris (2013, 2016), which is an extension of Aumann (1987) to games with incomplete information. In Magnolfi and Roncoroni's setup, player i receives a signal about the realization of $\boldsymbol{\epsilon}_{-i,j}$, which can be either informative or uninformative. If the signal is not informative at all, the Bayes-correlated equilibrium boils down to the Bayesian Nash equilibrium, and if it is fully informative, it boils down to the complete-information, pure-strategy Nash equilibrium. The researchers characterize the sharp identified set, and in their application, the set is small enough to be informative. Because the sharp identified set is much larger than what is characterized by the pure-strategy Nash equilibria, whether the informativeness can be generalized to other contexts remains an open question.

4.1.3 Further Discussion of the Estimation of Game Models with Cross-Sectional Data

We studied the estimation of model parameters of a discrete-game model with cross-sectional data by assuming that the observed data come from one or more of the Nash equilibria or their refinement. The fundamental issue in this literature is the incompleteness of the baseline economic model that yields the multiplicity of equilibria. If an econometrician wants to maintain the assumption that the data are generated by a single equilibrium, some equilibrium-selection criteria must exist. We reviewed that the equilibrium-selection criteria can be imposed in two ways: equilibrium refinement or the data-driven equilibrium-selection rule. One can choose to drop some information from the data, which was the original approach of Bresnahan and Reiss (1990, 1991a). The last possible choice is partial identification. This sophisticated method, however, often lacks the prediction, and thus it may not be very useful to conduct policy counterfactuals.

We overviewed the estimation of complete-information-game models and incomplete-information-game models thus far. One can immediately question which is the more adequate concept. One possible argument is that complete-information-game models are more adequate for the markets that are under a long-run equilibrium.

Further discussions on this subject can be found in Berry and Tamer (2006) and Berry and Reiss (2007). Berry and Tamer (2006) study the identification conditions for various oligopoly entry models under the presence of multiple equilibria, focusing more on mixed-strategy equilibria. Surveys on the estimation of discrete-game models with cross-sectional data can be found in Ellickson and Misra (2011) and de Paula (2013).

4.2 Estimation of Dynamic Discrete-Game Models

In this section, we study the estimation of dynamic game models. We first briefly discuss the general framework of Markov-perfect industry dynamics developed by Ericson and Pakes (1995), and then move on to methods to estimate the model parameters of a dynamic game under Markov state-transition probabilities and Markov decision rules. Estimation frameworks of the dynamic games under Markov assumptions are pioneered by Aguirregabiria and Mira (2007); Bajari, Benkard, and Levin (2007); Pakes, Ostrovsky, and Berry (2007) and Pesendorfer and Schmidt-Dengler (2008). We go over their key ideas in this section.

The dynamic game model estimation frameworks presented in this section are extensions of the single-agent dynamics studied in section 2.3; in chapter 2 in a sense, single-agent dynamics can be regarded as a game against nature. Furthermore, in all of the dynamic games we study in this section, each player has private information. Therefore, the games could also be regarded as an extension of the static games with incomplete information studied in section 4.1.2.

4.2.1 Industry Dynamics in an Oligopolistic Market and the Markov Perfect Equilibrium

Ericson and Pakes (1995) develop a theoretical framework of industry dynamics, which is general enough to encompass most of the empirical frameworks used in the literature thus far. We review only the key features of the model here, leaving out most of the technical details. We assume that all the regularity conditions required for the Markov perfect Nash equilibria hold.

4.2.1.1 SETUP

Consider ex ante homogeneous firms. Firms differ only by productivity level $\omega\ (\in \Omega \subseteq \mathbb{Z})$, where $\mathbb{Z}$ denotes the set of integers; ω represents the producer-specific heterogeneity; and ω^0, the state at the entry, is drawn from a set of states $\Omega^e\ (\subseteq \Omega)$. For the entrants, only the distribution $\Pr\left(\omega^0\right)$ over Ω^e is common prior knowledge. Potential entrants must pay the sunk cost of entry x^e to draw the initial level of productivity ω^0.

Industry structure is summarized by $\mathbf{s} \in \mathbb{Z}_{+}$, which gives a count of the number of firms at each ω. Here, $\mathbf{s}$ can be regarded as the summary measure of the competitiveness in the industry. Note that firms' prospects are completely summarized by the $(\omega, \mathbf{s})$ pair. Each period, firms make investment decision $x \in \mathbb{R}_{+}$, given knowledge of $(\omega, \mathbf{s})$ and the state-space evolution probability.

Firms have a common salvage value ϕ, which can be interpreted as the opportunity cost of being in the industry. In every period, a stochastic negative shift occurs in all incumbent firms' ω (one explanation could be the progress outside the industry). The negative shifts are large enough that all firms will exit eventually, absent any investment.

Let $R(\omega, \mathbf{s}; x) = A(\omega, \mathbf{s}) - c(\omega)\, x$ be the per-period net profit function. $A(\omega, \mathbf{s})$ is the per-period gross profit, x is the period investment, and $c(\omega)$ is the unit cost of 1 unit of investment. The state-transition rule is $\omega' = \omega + \tau + \eta$. Here, τ, the stochastic outcome of investment decision, is $\tau \sim \pi(\omega, x)$, and η is the stochastic negative shift of ω. In this, $x = 0$ implies $\tau = 0$. Note that the future states are stochastically affected only by the current investment.

4.2.1.2 VALUE FUNCTIONS, FIRM DYNAMICS, AND MARKOV PERFECT NASH EQUILIBRIA

Incumbent firms choose either to operate or to scrap the firm and get ϕ. The incumbent firms' value function is as follows:

$$V(\omega, \mathbf{s}) = \max \left[\sup_{x \geq 0} \left\{ R(\omega, \mathbf{s}; x) + \beta \sum_{\eta'} \sum_{\mathbf{s}'} \sum_{\omega'} V(\omega', \mathbf{s}')\, p(\omega' | \omega, x, \eta) \right.\right.$$

$$\left.\left. q_{\omega}(\mathbf{s}' | \mathbf{s}, \eta')\, p_{\eta'} \right\}, \phi \right], \tag{4.2.1}$$

where $p_{\eta'}$ is the stochastic shift and $q_{\omega}(\mathbf{s}'|\mathbf{s}, \eta')$ produces the belief about the evolution of $\mathbf{s}$. Let the superscript e denote an entrant. The entrant's productivity evolution, $\pi^{e}(\omega^{0} - \eta'; 0, 0)$, is defined by $\pi^{e}(\omega^{0} - \eta'; 0, 0) := p^{e}(\omega'|\omega, 0, \eta')$. At the beginning of each period, the entrant firm pays a sunk cost of entry x^{e} to enter the market, draws the initial level of productivity ω^{0}, and gets nothing in the period of entry. The entrant firms' value function is

$$V^{e}(\mathbf{s}, m) = \beta \sum_{\eta'} \sum_{\mathbf{s}'} \sum_{\hat{\omega}_m} \sum_{\omega^{0}} V\left(\omega^{0}, \mathbf{s}' + \mathbf{e}_{\omega^{0}} + \sum_{j=1}^{m-1} \mathbf{e}_{\omega_j^{0}}\right) \pi^{e}(\omega^{0} - \eta'; 0, 0)$$

$$\prod_{j=1}^{m-1} \pi^{e}\left(\omega_j^{0} - \eta'; 0, 0\right) q^{0}(\mathbf{s}'|\mathbf{s}, \eta')\, p_{\eta'}, \tag{4.2.2}$$

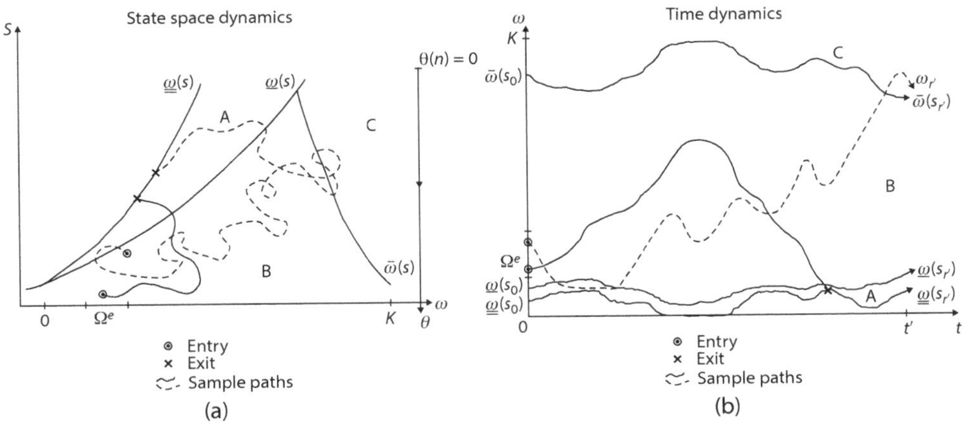

FIGURE 4.2.1. Examples of simulated firm dynamics, adopted from Ericson and Pakes (1995)

where the number of entrants $m(\mathbf{s})$ is endogenously given by

$$m(\mathbf{s}) = \min\left\{0, \arg\min_{m\in\mathbb{Z}_+}\left\{V^e(\mathbf{s}, m) > x^e_m, V^e(\mathbf{s}, m+1) \leq x^e_{m+1}\right\}\right\}. \quad (4.2.3)$$

Here, $\mathbf{e}_{\omega^0}$ is the unit vector with 1 in the ω^0th place. Equations (4.2.1)–(4.2.3) summarize the entire dynamics of this economy.

Figure 4.2.1 depicts some simulated firm dynamics. In both panels, $\underline{\underline{\omega}}(\mathbf{s})$ denotes the threshold for exit, and $\underline{\omega}(\mathbf{s})$ and $\bar{\omega}(\mathbf{s})$ are the no-investment threshold. A denotes the no-investment region due to too-low productivity, while C denotes the no-investment region due to a too-high cost. In B, investment occurs to improve the chance of moving to the higher states in the future. The set Ω^e is also depicted, which is a subset of all possible states Ω.

A Markov-perfect Nash equilibrium is defined by (1) the set of beliefs of each player regarding other players' unobservables, (2) a Markov strategy profile[13] that maps the set of beliefs and the set of states to the set of own actions, and (3) each player's belief coinciding with other players' actual action probability and the actual state-transition probability. Doraszelski and Satterthwaite (2010) prove the existence of a Markov perfect Nash equilibrium in the setup of Ericson and Pakes (1995) by introducing firms' private information on the cost shock that has full support. The existence of the equilibrium allows for empirical frameworks that employ or simplify this setup by assuming the data come from a Markov perfect

13. This is meant in the sense that the mapping depends only on the current states and the current beliefs. Note that without the Markov requirement, the equilibrium concept boils down to the perfect Bayesian Nash equilibrium.

equilibrium. Most empirical frameworks focus on the algorithms for finding the equilibria with the equilibrium-selection rules.

Weintraub, Benkard, and van Roy (2008) develop a new equilibrium concept, the oblivious equilibrium, in a setup similar to Ericson and Pakes (1995). In the oblivious equilibrium, players' strategies depend only on their own states and the long-run average industry state. The authors claim that it is easier to compute than the Markov perfect Nash equilibrium. They further show the oblivious equilibrium is a limiting approximation to the Markov perfect Nash equilibrium under certain conditions.

4.2.2 Estimation Frameworks of Dynamic Discrete Games

4.2.2.1 SETUP AND ASSUMPTIONS

Let $i\ (\in \mathcal{I} = \{1, 2, \ldots, I\})$ denote a firm that plays the repeated game in periods $t = 0, 1, 2, \ldots, \infty$. Let $a_{i,t}\ \left(\in \mathcal{J} = \{1, 2, \ldots, J\}\right)$ be the action that firm i takes in period t. Let $\mathbf{s}_{i,t} := \left(x_{i,t}, \boldsymbol{\epsilon}_{i,t}\right)$ be the state vector that has an observed component $x_{i,t}\ (\in \mathcal{X} = \{1, 2, \ldots, X\})$ and an unobserved component $\boldsymbol{\epsilon}_{i,t} \equiv \left(\epsilon_{i,j,t}\right)_{j\in\mathcal{J}}$. The sets $\mathcal{I}, \mathcal{J}, \mathcal{X}$ are taken as fixed.[14] For tractability, we assume that $\epsilon_{i,j,t}$ follows the mean-zero i.i.d. type I extreme value distribution throughout the section unless noted otherwise.

Let $u_i\left(a_{i,t}, \mathbf{s}_{i,t}, \mathbf{a}_{-i,t}, \mathbf{s}_{-i,t}; \boldsymbol{\theta}\right) \equiv u_i\left(\mathbf{a}_t, \mathbf{s}_t; \boldsymbol{\theta}\right)$ be agent i's per-period utility function. Note that agent i's utility is affected not only by its own state and action, but also by other players' states and actions. Define $\boldsymbol{\sigma}\left(\mathbf{s}_t\right) = \left(\sigma_i\left(\mathbf{x}_t, \boldsymbol{\epsilon}_{i,t}\right)\right)_{i\in\mathcal{I}}$ as the stationary Markov pure strategy of the players.[15] We impose the following assumptions, which are analogous to DDC(1)–DDC(3) in section 2.3.1 of chapter 2. Although these assumptions are not the most general ones required, they encompass most empirical applications.

DDG(1) *(Additive Separability of Preferences)* Let $u_i\left(a_{i,t} = j, \mathbf{s}_{i,t}, \mathbf{a}_{-i,t}, \mathbf{s}_{-i,t}; \boldsymbol{\theta}\right)$ be the utility of agent i choosing action j at state $\mathbf{s}_t$. Then,

$$u_i\left(a_{i,t} = j, \mathbf{s}_{i,t}, \mathbf{a}_{-i,t}, \mathbf{s}_{-i,t}; \boldsymbol{\theta}\right) = \bar{u}_{i,j}\left(x_{i,t}, \mathbf{s}_{-i,t}, \mathbf{a}_{-i,t}; \boldsymbol{\theta}\right) + \epsilon_{i,j,t}.$$

14. We allow some players in $\mathcal{I}$ to be potentially inactive.

15. There is an important distinction in the notations. When the utility function $u_i\left(a_{i,t}, \mathbf{s}_{i,t}, \boldsymbol{\sigma}_{-i}\left(\mathbf{s}_t\right), \mathbf{s}_{-i,t}; \boldsymbol{\theta}\right)$ or the value function $v_i\left(\boldsymbol{\sigma}\left(\mathbf{s}_t\right), \mathbf{s}_t; \boldsymbol{\theta}, \boldsymbol{\varphi}\right)$ is conditioned on other players' strategies, it denotes the expected utility or expected value over other players' actions. That is,

$$u_i\left(a_{i,t}, \mathbf{s}_{i,t}, \boldsymbol{\sigma}_{-i}\left(\mathbf{s}_t\right), \mathbf{s}_{-i,t}; \boldsymbol{\theta}\right) := \int u_i\left(a_{i,t}, \mathbf{s}_{i,t}, \mathbf{a}_{-i,t}, \mathbf{s}_{-i,t}; \boldsymbol{\theta}\right) d\Pr\left(\mathbf{a}_{-i,t}\right).$$

However, player i's own strategy $\sigma_i\left(\mathbf{x}_t, \boldsymbol{\epsilon}_{i,t}\right)$ and own action a_i can be used interchangeably because they are observationally equivalent when players employ pure strategies.

DDG(2) *($\epsilon_{i,t}$ is i.i.d. over t)* $\forall \epsilon_{i,t} \left(\in \mathbb{R}^J\right)$,

$$\Pr\left(\epsilon_{i,t+1} | \epsilon_{i,t}\right) = \Pr\left(\epsilon_{i,t+1}\right).$$

DDG(3) *($\epsilon_{i,t}$ is i.i.d. over i)* $\forall \epsilon_{i,t} \left(\in \mathbb{R}^J\right)$,

$$\Pr\left(\epsilon_t\right) = \prod_{i \in \mathcal{I}} \Pr\left(\epsilon_{i,t}\right).$$

DDG(4) *(Conditional Independence of State-Transition Probabilities)* Given that $(\mathbf{x}_t, \mathbf{a}_t)$ is observed,

$$\begin{aligned} \Pr\left(\mathbf{x}_{t+1}, \epsilon_{t+1} | \mathbf{x}_t, \epsilon_t, \mathbf{a}_t; \boldsymbol{\varphi}\right) &\equiv \Pr\left(\epsilon_{t+1} | \mathbf{x}_{t+1}, \mathbf{x}_t, \epsilon_t, \mathbf{a}_t; \boldsymbol{\varphi}\right) \Pr\left(\mathbf{x}_{t+1} | \mathbf{x}_t, \epsilon_t, \mathbf{a}_t; \boldsymbol{\varphi}\right) \\ &= \Pr\left(\epsilon_{t+1}\right) \Pr\left(\mathbf{x}_{t+1} | \mathbf{x}_t, \mathbf{a}_t; \boldsymbol{\varphi}\right). \end{aligned}$$

DDG(2) and DDG(3) establish that unobservable states over t and over i have the i.i.d. property. DDG(4) establishes the Markov state-transition probability, such that the state transition is affected directly only by the current observed states and actions. As in the single-agent problem, the unobservable states ϵ_t can affect the future states $\mathbf{x}_{t+1}$ only via the current action $\mathbf{a}_t$.

At each period t, each player's expected discounted utility is

$$\mathbb{E}_t \left[\sum_{s=t}^{\infty} \beta^{s-t} u_i \left(a_{i,s}, \mathbf{s}_{i,s}, \mathbf{a}_{-i,s}, \mathbf{s}_{-i,s}; \boldsymbol{\theta}\right) \middle| \{\mathbf{x}_l\}_{l=1}^{t}, \left\{\epsilon_{i,l}\right\}_{l=1}^{t} \right], \tag{4.2.4}$$

where $\beta \in (0, 1)$ is the discount factor. At each period t, each player observes the history of observed state variables $\left\{x_{i,l}\right\}_{l=1}^{t}$ for all the players and the history of own unobserved state variables $\left\{\epsilon_{i,l}\right\}_{l=1}^{t}$, and then makes decision $a_{i,t}$. Assuming that DDG(1)–DDG(4) and all the agents employ the stationary Markov decision rule $\boldsymbol{\sigma}(\mathbf{s}_t) = \left(\sigma_i\left(\mathbf{x}_t, \epsilon_{i,t}\right)\right)_{i \in \mathcal{I}}$, the dynamic utility-maximization problem associated with equation (4.2.4) can be written recursively as follows:

$$\begin{aligned} v_i\left(\boldsymbol{\sigma}(\mathbf{s}_t), \mathbf{s}_t; \boldsymbol{\theta}, \boldsymbol{\varphi}\right) = \max_{\sigma_i\left(\mathbf{x}_t, \epsilon_{i,t}\right)} \Big\{ & u_i\left(\sigma_i\left(\mathbf{x}_t, \epsilon_{i,t}\right), \boldsymbol{\sigma}_{-i}(\mathbf{s}_t), \mathbf{s}_t; \boldsymbol{\theta}, \boldsymbol{\varphi}\right) \\ & + \beta \int v_i\left(\boldsymbol{\sigma}(\mathbf{s}_{t+1}), \mathbf{s}_{t+1}; \boldsymbol{\theta}, \boldsymbol{\varphi}\right) d \Pr\left(\mathbf{x}_{t+1} | \mathbf{x}_t, \boldsymbol{\sigma}(\mathbf{s}_t); \boldsymbol{\varphi}\right) \Big\}. \end{aligned}$$

Analogous to the single-agent problem, we define the choice-specific value function $\bar{v}_{i,j}\left(\mathbf{x}_t; \boldsymbol{\sigma}_{-i}(\mathbf{s}_t), \boldsymbol{\theta}, \boldsymbol{\varphi}\right)$ and the integrated Bellman equation $\bar{\bar{v}}_i\big(\sigma_i\left(\mathbf{x}_t, \epsilon_{i,t}\right), \mathbf{x}_t; \boldsymbol{\sigma}_{-i}(\mathbf{s}_t), \boldsymbol{\theta}, \boldsymbol{\varphi}\big)$ as

$$\bar{v}_{i,j}\left(\mathbf{x}_t;\boldsymbol{\sigma}_{-i}\left(\mathbf{s}_t\right),\boldsymbol{\theta},\boldsymbol{\varphi}\right)$$
$$:=\bar{u}_{i,j}\left(\mathbf{x}_t;\boldsymbol{\sigma}_{-i}\left(\mathbf{s}_t\right),\boldsymbol{\theta},\boldsymbol{\varphi}\right)+\beta\int v_i\left(\boldsymbol{\sigma}\left(\mathbf{s}_{t+1}\right),\mathbf{s}_{t+1};\boldsymbol{\theta},\boldsymbol{\varphi}\right)d\Pr\left(\mathbf{x}_{t+1}|\mathbf{x}_t,\boldsymbol{\sigma}\left(\mathbf{s}_t\right);\boldsymbol{\varphi}\right)$$
$$\bar{\bar{v}}_i\left(\sigma_i\left(\mathbf{x}_t,\boldsymbol{\epsilon}_{i,t}\right),\mathbf{x}_t;\boldsymbol{\sigma}_{-i}\left(\mathbf{s}_t\right),\boldsymbol{\theta},\boldsymbol{\varphi}\right)$$
$$:=\mathbb{E}\left[v_i\left(\boldsymbol{\sigma}\left(\mathbf{s}_t\right),\mathbf{s}_t;\boldsymbol{\theta},\boldsymbol{\varphi}\right)\right].$$

The definitions of the choice-specific value function $\bar{v}_{i,j}\left(\mathbf{x}_t;\boldsymbol{\sigma}_{-i}\left(\mathbf{s}_t\right),\boldsymbol{\theta},\boldsymbol{\varphi}\right)$ and the integrated Bellman equation $\bar{\bar{v}}_i\left(\sigma_i\left(\mathbf{x}_t,\boldsymbol{\epsilon}_{i,t}\right),\mathbf{x}_t;\boldsymbol{\sigma}_{-i}\left(\mathbf{s}_t\right),\boldsymbol{\theta},\boldsymbol{\varphi}\right)$ parallel the corresponding objects in the single-agent dynamic discrete choice studied in section 2.3 in chapter 2. Here, $\bar{v}_{i,j}\left(\mathbf{x}_t;\boldsymbol{\sigma}_{-i}\left(\mathbf{s}_t\right),\boldsymbol{\theta},\boldsymbol{\varphi}\right)$ represents the expected value of action j conditional on choosing action j at period t (i.e., conditioning on both $\mathbf{s}_t$ and $a_t=j$); and $\bar{\bar{v}}_i\left(\sigma_i\left(\mathbf{x}_t,\boldsymbol{\epsilon}_{i,t}\right),\mathbf{x}_t;\boldsymbol{\sigma}_{-i}\left(\mathbf{s}_t\right),\boldsymbol{\theta},\boldsymbol{\varphi}\right)$ represents the ex-ante expected value before engaging in the action but after state $\mathbf{s}_t$ is realized at period t. Notice that $\bar{v}_{i,j}\left(\mathbf{x}_t;\boldsymbol{\sigma}_{-i}\left(\mathbf{s}_t\right),\boldsymbol{\theta},\boldsymbol{\varphi}\right)$ and $\bar{\bar{v}}_i\left(\sigma_i\left(\mathbf{x}_t,\boldsymbol{\epsilon}_{i,t}\right),\mathbf{x}_t;\boldsymbol{\sigma}_{-i}\left(\mathbf{s}_t\right),\boldsymbol{\theta},\boldsymbol{\varphi}\right)$ are conditioned on other players' strategies $\boldsymbol{\sigma}_{-i}\left(\mathbf{s}_t\right)$.

The pure-strategy stationary Markov perfect Nash equilibrium $\boldsymbol{\sigma}^*\left(\mathbf{s}_t\right)$ is defined by the set of strategy profiles $\sigma_i\left(\mathbf{x}_t,\boldsymbol{\epsilon}_{i,t}\right)$, such that for all $i\in\mathcal{I}$,

$$\sigma_i^*\left(\mathbf{x}_t,\boldsymbol{\epsilon}_{i,t}\right)=\arg\max_{j\in\mathcal{J}}\left\{\bar{v}_{i,j}\left(\mathbf{x}_t;\boldsymbol{\sigma}_{-i}^*\left(\mathbf{s}_t\right),\boldsymbol{\theta},\boldsymbol{\varphi}\right)+\epsilon_{i,j,t}\right\}. \tag{4.2.5}$$

As is common in other Nash equilibrium concepts, the Markov perfect Nash equilibrium requires each player's strategy to be the best response for other players' strategies.[16] As shown by Pesendorfer and Schmidt-Dengler (2008) and Doraszelski and Satterthwaite (2010), the Markov perfect Nash equilibrium exists in the setup under some regularity conditions.

Existence of the equilibrium does not tell us much about the multiplicity of the equilibrium. When the data are generated by different equilibria that the econometrician cannot distinguish among, estimation and policy counterfactuals might be pointless. All the estimation methods studied in this chapter get around the problem by simply assuming that the data come from a single pure-strategy Markov perfect equilibrium. Such an assumption is more suitable if the econometrician uses the data of a single time series with fixed players.

16. To be precise, strategy $\sigma_i^*\left(\mathbf{x}_t,\boldsymbol{\epsilon}_{i,t}\right)$ returns the best-response action given player i's belief (in terms of the expectations) about the unobservables and other players' strategies. Then, at the Markov perfect Nash equilibrium, the belief should coincide with the actual conditional choice probabilities of other players. The Markov perfect Nash equilibrium is a direct extension of the Bayesian Nash equilibrium to infinite-horizon dynamic games under Markov assumptions.

4.2.2.2 TWO-STAGE FORWARD-SIMULATION ESTIMATION

Bajari et al. (2007) develop the two-stage estimation procedure, which extends the idea of forward simulation originally developed by Hotz et al. (1994) in the context of a single agent's dynamic problem. In the first stage, the choice-specific value functions $\bar{v}_{i,j}(\mathbf{x}_t; \boldsymbol{\sigma}_{-i}(\mathbf{s}_t), \boldsymbol{\theta}, \boldsymbol{\varphi})$ and the state-transition probabilities $\Pr(\mathbf{x}_{t+1} | \mathbf{x}_t, \boldsymbol{\sigma}(\mathbf{s}_t); \boldsymbol{\varphi})$ are estimated, and then the value functions $v_i\left(\sigma_i^*\left(\mathbf{x}_t, \epsilon_{i,t}\right), \mathbf{s}_t; \boldsymbol{\sigma}_{-i}^*(\mathbf{s}_t), \boldsymbol{\theta}, \boldsymbol{\varphi}\right)$ are simulated. In the second stage, the model parameter $\boldsymbol{\theta}$ is estimated.

Our presentation follows the reverse order: we first illustrate how the model parameter $\boldsymbol{\theta}$ can be estimated in the second stage. Then we present how the policy functions and value functions can be estimated and simulated in the first stage.

Second-Stage Parameter Estimation Let $\sigma_i\left(\mathbf{x}_t, \epsilon_{i,t}; \boldsymbol{\varphi}\right)$ be parameterized by a finite dimensional parameter vector $\boldsymbol{\varphi}$. Let $\hat{\boldsymbol{\varphi}}$ be the preliminary $\sqrt{N}$-consistent estimator of the parameter $\boldsymbol{\varphi}$.[17] If $\boldsymbol{\sigma}^*(\mathbf{s}_t)$ is an equilibrium strategy profile, it must be that

$$v_i\left(\sigma_i^*\left(\mathbf{x}_t, \epsilon_{i,t}\right), \mathbf{s}_t; \boldsymbol{\sigma}_{-i}^*(\mathbf{s}_t), \boldsymbol{\theta}, \hat{\boldsymbol{\varphi}}\right) \geq v_i\left(\sigma_i'\left(\mathbf{x}_t, \epsilon_{i,t}\right), \mathbf{s}_t; \boldsymbol{\sigma}_{-i}^*(\mathbf{s}_t), \boldsymbol{\theta}, \hat{\boldsymbol{\varphi}}\right) \quad (4.2.6)$$

for all $i \in \mathcal{I}$ and $\sigma_i'\left(\mathbf{x}_t, \epsilon_{i,t}\right)$. Equation (4.2.6) expresses the equilibrium inequalities that rationalize the strategy profile $\boldsymbol{\sigma}^*(\mathbf{s}_t)$. Let $\boldsymbol{\Theta}_0\left(\boldsymbol{\sigma}^*, \hat{\boldsymbol{\varphi}}\right)$ be the set of possible $\boldsymbol{\theta}$ such that given $\hat{\boldsymbol{\varphi}}$, equation (4.2.6) is satisfied for all possible $\left(\mathbf{s}_t, i, \sigma_i'\right)$. Suppose that the set $\boldsymbol{\Theta}_0\left(\boldsymbol{\sigma}^*, \hat{\boldsymbol{\varphi}}\right)$ is a singleton.[18] The true parameter value $\boldsymbol{\theta}_0 = \boldsymbol{\Theta}_0$ must satisfy the condition that

$$\begin{aligned}\min_{\boldsymbol{\theta}} \mathbb{E}\Big[\Big(\min\Big\{& v_i\left(\sigma_i^*\left(\mathbf{x}_t, \epsilon_{i,t}\right), \mathbf{s}_t; \boldsymbol{\sigma}_{-i}^*(\mathbf{s}_t), \boldsymbol{\theta}, \hat{\boldsymbol{\varphi}}\right) \\ & - v_i\left(\sigma_i'\left(\mathbf{x}_t, \epsilon_{i,t}\right), \mathbf{s}_t; \boldsymbol{\sigma}_{-i}^*(\mathbf{s}_t), \boldsymbol{\theta}, \hat{\boldsymbol{\varphi}}\right), 0\Big\}\Big)^2\Big] = 0, \end{aligned} \quad (4.2.7)$$

where the expectation is taken over the $\left(\mathbf{s}_t, i, \sigma_i'\right)$ combination. Note that the term inside the expectation penalizes the violation of the inequality in equation (4.2.6), which is similar to Ciliberto and Tamer (2009), studied in chapter 3. The authors suggest minimizing the simulation analog of equation (4.2.7):

17. The state-transition probability $\Pr(\mathbf{x}_{t+1} | \mathbf{x}_t, \boldsymbol{\sigma}(\mathbf{s}_t); \boldsymbol{\varphi})$ and its parameter $\hat{\boldsymbol{\varphi}}$ can be easily estimated using, for example, MLE or a simple frequency estimator, depending on the specification.

18. The set $\boldsymbol{\Theta}_0\left(\boldsymbol{\sigma}^*, \hat{\boldsymbol{\varphi}}\right)$ may not be a singleton. In such a case, bound estimation can be used to recover the confidence region. For details on estimation and inference when $\boldsymbol{\theta}_0$ is not point identified, see Bajari et al. (2007).

$$\frac{1}{N_s}\sum_{k_s=1}^{N_s}\left(\min\left\{\hat{v}_{i,k_s}\left(\sigma^*_{i,k_s}\left(\mathbf{x}_{t,k_s},\epsilon_{i,t,k_s}\right),\mathbf{s}_{t,k_s};\boldsymbol{\sigma}^*_{-i,k_s}\left(\mathbf{s}_{t,k_s}\right),\boldsymbol{\theta},\hat{\boldsymbol{\varphi}}\right)\right.\right.$$

$$\left.\left.-\hat{v}_{i,k_s}\left(\sigma'_{i,k_s}\left(\mathbf{x}_{t,k_s},\epsilon_{i,t,k_s}\right),\mathbf{s}_{t,k_s};\boldsymbol{\sigma}^*_{-i,k_s}\left(\mathbf{s}_{t,k_s}\right),\boldsymbol{\theta},\hat{\boldsymbol{\varphi}}\right),0\right\}\right)^2, \qquad (4.2.8)$$

where k_s denotes the index for a randomly sampled $\left(\mathbf{s}_t, i, \sigma'_i\right)$ combination.

One possibility for choosing $\sigma'_i\left(\mathbf{x}_t, \epsilon_{i,t}\right)$ is to add a slight perturbation to the estimated optimal policy (i.e., $\sigma'_i\left(\mathbf{x}_t, \epsilon_{i,t}\right) = \sigma^*_i\left(\mathbf{x}_t, \epsilon_{i,t}\right) + \eta$). The authors note the choice of $\sigma'_i\left(\mathbf{x}_t, \epsilon_{i,t}\right)$ only affects the efficiency of the estimator, not the consistency. The estimator $\hat{\boldsymbol{\theta}}$ minimizing equation (4.2.8) is shown to be $\sqrt{N}$-consistent and asymptotically normal under suitable regularity conditions.

First-Stage Value Function Estimation The first stage is a combination of Hotz and Miller (1993) and Hotz et al. (1994). Consider the Hotz-Miller inversion:

$$\begin{aligned}&\bar{v}_{i,j}\left(\mathbf{x}_t;\boldsymbol{\sigma}^*_{-i}\left(\mathbf{s}_t\right),\boldsymbol{\theta},\hat{\boldsymbol{\varphi}}\right)-\bar{v}_{i,J}\left(\mathbf{x}_t;\boldsymbol{\sigma}^*_{-i}\left(\mathbf{s}_t\right),\boldsymbol{\theta},\hat{\boldsymbol{\varphi}}\right)\\&=\ln\left(\Pr\left(a_{i,j}|\mathbf{x}_t\right)\right)-\ln\left(\Pr\left(a_{i,J}|\mathbf{x}_t\right)\right).^{19}\end{aligned} \qquad (4.2.9)$$

Because the sample analog of the right-hand side is directly observed or can be easily estimated, we can obtain an estimate of all the choice-specific value differences for all possible observed states $\mathbf{x}_t$. These difference estimates are used to find the optimal $\sigma_i\left(\mathbf{x}_t, \epsilon_{i,t}\right)$ during the forward simulation, where at each simulated path, $\epsilon_{i,j,t}$ is taken as known.

The remaining model primitives are the value function estimates for each candidate parameter $\boldsymbol{\theta}$, with $\hat{\boldsymbol{\varphi}}$ fixed. Recall the definition of $v_i\left(\boldsymbol{\sigma}^*\left(\mathbf{s}_t\right), \mathbf{s}_t; \boldsymbol{\theta}, \hat{\boldsymbol{\varphi}}\right)$:

$$v_i\left(\boldsymbol{\sigma}^*\left(\mathbf{s}_t\right),\mathbf{s}_t;\boldsymbol{\theta},\hat{\boldsymbol{\varphi}}\right)=\mathbb{E}\left[\sum_{t=0}^{\infty}\beta^t u_i\left(a_{i,t},\mathbf{s}_{i,t},\mathbf{a}_{-i,t},\mathbf{s}_{-i,t};\boldsymbol{\theta}\right)\middle|\mathbf{x}_0,\epsilon_{i,0}\right]. \qquad (4.2.10)$$

We use forward simulation to compute $v_i\left(\boldsymbol{\sigma}^*\left(\mathbf{s}_t\right), \mathbf{s}_t; \boldsymbol{\theta}, \hat{\boldsymbol{\varphi}}\right)$. We impose the equilibrium assumption (or perturbation assumption) during the forward simulation. The steps are as follows:

1. Fix the candidate parameter $\boldsymbol{\theta}$. Start at a randomly drawn state $\mathbf{x}_t$. Draw $\boldsymbol{\epsilon}_{i,t}$ for each $i \in \mathcal{I}$.

19. Notice that we invoke the type I extreme value assumption here to simplify the inversion. The inversion, however, works for other distributions.

2. Compare the values of all $\bar{v}_{i,j}\left(\mathbf{x}_t; \boldsymbol{\sigma}^*_{-i}(\mathbf{s}_t), \boldsymbol{\theta}, \hat{\boldsymbol{\varphi}}\right) + \epsilon_{i,j,t}$ for all i and j pairs, which are obtained from equation (4.2.9), to find the optimal action $a_{i,t} \in \mathcal{J}$.
3. Compute $u_i\left(a_{i,t}, \mathbf{s}_{i,t}, \mathbf{a}_{-i,t}, \mathbf{s}_{-i,t}; \boldsymbol{\theta}\right)$ for the set of optimal actions.
4. Draw a new state $(\mathbf{x}_{t+1}, \boldsymbol{\epsilon}_{t+1})$ using the estimates of $\Pr\left(\mathbf{x}_{t+1} | \mathbf{x}_t, \boldsymbol{\sigma}^*(\mathbf{s}_t); \hat{\boldsymbol{\varphi}}\right)$, given the set of optimal actions.
5. Iterate over steps 1–4 until $\sum_{t=0}^{\infty} \beta^t u_i\left(a_{i,t}, \mathbf{s}_{i,t}, \mathbf{a}_{-i,t}, \mathbf{s}_{-i,t}; \boldsymbol{\theta}\right)$ converges for all $i \in \mathcal{I}$.
6. Upon convergence, save the converged value in memory.
7. Repeat steps 1–6 many times, and then take the mean for each i, respectively, which will construct the simulation analog of $v_i\left(\boldsymbol{\sigma}^*(\mathbf{s}_t), \mathbf{s}_t; \boldsymbol{\theta}, \hat{\boldsymbol{\varphi}}\right)$ for each candidate parameter $\boldsymbol{\theta}$.

If the utility function $u_i\left(a_{i,t}, \mathbf{s}_{i,t}, \mathbf{a}_{-i,t}, \mathbf{s}_{-i,t}; \boldsymbol{\theta}\right)$ is linear in $\boldsymbol{\theta}$—that is,

$$u_i\left(a_{i,t}, \mathbf{s}_{i,t}, \mathbf{a}_{-i,t}, \mathbf{s}_{-i,t}; \boldsymbol{\theta}\right) = h_i\left(a_{i,t}, \mathbf{s}_{i,t}, \mathbf{a}_{-i,t}, \mathbf{s}_{-i,t}\right) \cdot \boldsymbol{\theta}$$

for some h_i—then iterating 1–4 only once will be sufficient to obtain the values of $v_i\left(\boldsymbol{\sigma}^*(\mathbf{s}_t), \mathbf{s}_t; \boldsymbol{\theta}, \hat{\boldsymbol{\varphi}}\right)$ because $\boldsymbol{\theta}$ factors out as

$$\sum_{t=0}^{\infty} \beta^t u_i\left(a_{i,t}, \mathbf{s}_{i,t}, \mathbf{a}_{-i,t}, \mathbf{s}_{-i,t}; \boldsymbol{\theta}\right) = \left(\sum_{t=0}^{\infty} \beta^t h_i\left(a_{i,t}, \mathbf{s}_{i,t}, \mathbf{a}_{-i,t}, \mathbf{s}_{-i,t}\right)\right) \cdot \boldsymbol{\theta};$$

that is, step 5 is not necessary, but step 7 is.

4.2.2.3 ESTIMATION UNDER FIXED-POINT EQUILIBRIUM CHARACTERIZATION IN A PROBABILITY SPACE

Characterization of the Markov Perfect Nash Equilibrium as a Fixed Point of Conditional Choice Probabilities Recall the condition for the Markov perfect Nash equilibrium (4.2.5): For each i,

$$\max_{j \in \mathcal{J}} \left\{\bar{v}_{i,j}\left(\mathbf{x}_t; \boldsymbol{\sigma}^*_{-i}(\mathbf{s}_t), \boldsymbol{\theta}, \boldsymbol{\varphi}\right) + \epsilon_{i,j,t}\right\}.$$

Define $\bar{\bar{v}}_i\left(\mathbf{x}_t; \boldsymbol{\sigma}^*_{-i}(\mathbf{s}_t), \boldsymbol{\theta}, \boldsymbol{\varphi}\right)$ as

$$\bar{\bar{v}}_i\left(\mathbf{x}_t; \boldsymbol{\sigma}^*_{-i}(\mathbf{s}_t), \boldsymbol{\theta}, \boldsymbol{\varphi}\right) := \int \max_{j \in \mathcal{J}} \left\{\bar{v}_{i,j}\left(\mathbf{x}_t; \boldsymbol{\sigma}^*_{-i}(\mathbf{s}_t), \boldsymbol{\theta}, \boldsymbol{\varphi}\right) + \epsilon_{i,j,t}\right\} \Pr\left(d\boldsymbol{\epsilon}_{i,t}\right). \tag{4.2.11}$$

Assume that all the players employ the equilibrium strategy. As with the single-agent problem—specifically equation (2.3.25) in section 2.3.3.1 of chapter 2—we invert equation (4.2.11) in terms of the state-transition probability and the conditional choice probability. To that end, in an equilibrium, we have

$$\bar{\bar{\mathbf{v}}}_i\left(\mathbf{x}_t;\boldsymbol{\sigma}^*_{-i}(\mathbf{s}_t),\boldsymbol{\theta},\boldsymbol{\varphi}\right)=\left[\mathbf{I}-\beta\mathbf{P}\left(\mathbf{x}_{t+1}|\mathbf{x}_t;\boldsymbol{\sigma}^*(\mathbf{s}_t),\boldsymbol{\theta},\boldsymbol{\varphi}\right)\right]^{-1}\mathbf{w}_i\left(\boldsymbol{\sigma}^*(\mathbf{s}_t),\mathbf{x}_t;\boldsymbol{\theta},\boldsymbol{\varphi}\right) \tag{4.2.12}$$

for each $i\in\mathcal{I}$. Note that each element of $\mathbf{w}_i(\boldsymbol{\sigma}^*(\mathbf{s}_t),\mathbf{x}_t;\boldsymbol{\theta},\boldsymbol{\varphi})$ consists of

$$\mathbf{p}\left(a_{i,t}|\boldsymbol{\sigma}^*_{-i}(\mathbf{s}_t),\mathbf{x}_t;\boldsymbol{\theta},\boldsymbol{\varphi}\right)'\left(\bar{\mathbf{u}}_i\left(\mathbf{x}_t;\boldsymbol{\sigma}^*_{-i}(\mathbf{s}_t),\boldsymbol{\theta}\right)-\ln\mathbf{p}\left(a_{i,t}|\mathbf{x}_t;\boldsymbol{\sigma}^*_{-i}(\mathbf{s}_t),\boldsymbol{\theta},\boldsymbol{\varphi}\right)\right).$$ [20]

Combining

$$\Pr\left(a_{i,t}=j|\mathbf{x}_t;\boldsymbol{\sigma}^*_{-i}(\mathbf{s}_t),\boldsymbol{\theta},\boldsymbol{\varphi}\right)=\frac{\exp\left(\bar{v}_{i,j}\left(\mathbf{x}_t;\boldsymbol{\sigma}^*_{-i}(\mathbf{s}_t),\boldsymbol{\theta},\boldsymbol{\varphi}\right)\right)}{\sum_{k\in\mathcal{J}}\exp\left(\bar{v}_{i,k}\left(\mathbf{x}_t;\boldsymbol{\sigma}^*_{-i}(\mathbf{s}_t),\boldsymbol{\theta},\boldsymbol{\varphi}\right)\right)} \tag{4.2.13}$$

and

$$\begin{aligned}&\bar{v}_{i,j}\left(\mathbf{x}_t;\boldsymbol{\sigma}^*_{-i}(\mathbf{s}_t),\boldsymbol{\theta},\boldsymbol{\varphi}\right)\\&=\bar{u}_{i,j}\left(\mathbf{x}_t;\boldsymbol{\sigma}^*_{-i}(\mathbf{s}_t),\boldsymbol{\theta},\boldsymbol{\varphi}\right)\\&\quad+\beta\sum_{\mathbf{x}'\in\mathcal{X}^{\mathcal{I}}}\bar{\bar{\mathbf{v}}}_i\left(\mathbf{x}_{t+1}=\mathbf{x}';\boldsymbol{\sigma}^*_{-i}(\mathbf{s}_{t+1}),\boldsymbol{\theta},\boldsymbol{\varphi}\right)\Pr\left(\mathbf{x}_{t+1}=\mathbf{x}'|\mathbf{x}_t,\boldsymbol{\sigma}^*(\mathbf{s}_t);\boldsymbol{\varphi}\right)\end{aligned} \tag{4.2.14}$$

with equation (4.2.12) gives us the matrix-form, fixed-point equations in the probability space:

$$\mathbf{P}\left(a_{i,t}|\mathbf{x}_t;\boldsymbol{\sigma}^*_{-i}(\mathbf{s}_t),\boldsymbol{\theta},\boldsymbol{\varphi}\right)=\Psi\left(\mathbf{P}\left(a_{i,t}|\mathbf{x}_t;\boldsymbol{\sigma}^*_{-i}(\mathbf{s}_t),\boldsymbol{\theta},\boldsymbol{\varphi}\right)\right).$$ [21] (4.2.15)

Aguirregabiria and Mira (2007) and Pesendorfer and Schmidt-Dengler (2008) show the fixed-point mapping in equation (4.2.15) characterizes the Markov perfect Nash equilibrium of this dynamic game. To be specific, it is shown that equation (4.2.15) is the necessary and sufficient condition for the Markov perfect Nash equilibrium in this setup. Existence of the equilibrium follows by Brouwer's

20. The dimensionality is such that we vectorized all the possible observed states. Both sides of equation (4.2.12) will be $X\times I$ dimensional vectors. Equation (4.2.12) coincides with equation (2.3.25) in chapter 2 otherwise.

21. To be precise, operator $\Psi(\cdot)$ should have $(\boldsymbol{\theta},\boldsymbol{\varphi})$ as its argument as well. For brevity, we suppress it unless otherwise noted.

fixed-point theorem. Note, for a given $(\boldsymbol{\theta}, \boldsymbol{\varphi})$, multiple sets of conditional choice probabilities that satisfy equation (4.2.15) may be possible.

Nested Pseudo-Likelihood Estimation Aguirregabiria and Mira (2007) suggest that a nested pseudo-likelihood (NPL) estimation method, which is essentially an extension of Aguirregabiria and Mira (2002), which we studied in section 2.3.3 of chapter 2. We assume that $\hat{\boldsymbol{\varphi}}$, the consistent estimator for $\boldsymbol{\varphi}$, can be obtained separately. The estimation algorithm proceeds in two stages as follows. Begin from the initial guess $\mathbf{P}^0\left(a_{i,t}|\mathbf{x}_t; \boldsymbol{\sigma}^*_{-i}(\mathbf{s}_t), \boldsymbol{\theta}, \hat{\boldsymbol{\varphi}}\right)$. The first stage is to obtain

$$\hat{\boldsymbol{\theta}}^K = \arg\max_{\boldsymbol{\theta}} \prod_i \mathcal{L}_i\left(\mathbf{P}^K\left(a_{i,t}|\mathbf{x}_t; \boldsymbol{\sigma}^*_{-i}(\mathbf{s}_t), \boldsymbol{\theta}, \hat{\boldsymbol{\varphi}}\right)\right), \tag{4.2.16}$$

where $\mathcal{L}_i(\cdot)$ denotes the likelihood induced by the argument and i denotes the data. The second stage is to update $\mathbf{P}\left(a_{i,t}|\mathbf{x}_t; \boldsymbol{\sigma}^*_{-i}(\mathbf{s}_t), \boldsymbol{\theta}, \hat{\boldsymbol{\varphi}}\right)$ using the right-hand side of equation (4.2.12), and then plugging the result back into equations (4.2.14) and (4.2.13) sequentially. To that end, the K-stage pseudo-likelihood is updated as

$$\mathbf{P}^{K+1}\left(a_{i,t}|\mathbf{x}_t; \boldsymbol{\sigma}^*_{-i}(\mathbf{s}_t), \boldsymbol{\theta}, \hat{\boldsymbol{\varphi}}\right) = \Psi\left(\mathbf{P}^K\left(a_{i,t}|\mathbf{x}_t; \boldsymbol{\sigma}^*_{-i}(\mathbf{s}_t), \hat{\boldsymbol{\theta}}^K, \hat{\boldsymbol{\varphi}}\right)\right). \tag{4.2.17}$$

Iterating over K until convergence of $\left(\hat{\boldsymbol{\theta}}^K, \mathbf{P}^K\right)$ will yield the NPL estimator, and also the corresponding fixed point $\mathbf{P}^\infty\left(a_{i,t}|\mathbf{x}_t; \boldsymbol{\sigma}^*_{-i}(\mathbf{s}_t), \hat{\boldsymbol{\theta}}^\infty, \hat{\boldsymbol{\varphi}}\right)$.

When $K=0$ (i.e., when the econometrician does not iterate over K), the resulting estimator is called the two-step pseudo-maximum likelihood (PML) estimator. Given that the initial guess $\mathbf{P}^0\left(a_{i,t}|\mathbf{x}_t; \boldsymbol{\sigma}^*_{-i}(\mathbf{s}_t), \boldsymbol{\theta}, \hat{\boldsymbol{\varphi}}\right)$ is a consistent estimator, two-step PML estimators are consistent and asymptotically normal, but the finite sample properties can be worse than NPL estimators.

Multiple sets of fixed points $\left(\hat{\boldsymbol{\theta}}^\infty, \mathbf{P}^\infty\right)$ may exist that satisfy equation (4.2.17). In such a case, Aguirregabiria and Mira (2007) assert that the one that maximizes the right-hand side of equation (4.2.16) is the estimator $\hat{\boldsymbol{\theta}}^\infty$. $\hat{\boldsymbol{\theta}}^\infty$ is consistent only when it attains the global maximum of the pseudo-likelihood function. Thus, Aguirregabiria and Mira suggest that the econometrician try different $\mathbf{P}^0\left(a_{i,t}|\mathbf{x}_t; \boldsymbol{\sigma}^*_{-i}(\mathbf{s}_t), \boldsymbol{\theta}, \hat{\boldsymbol{\varphi}}\right)$'s to find "all" the possible convergence points of $\hat{\boldsymbol{\theta}}^\infty$, and then compare the pseudo-likelihood values.

However, such an algorithm may never converge to the true data-generating fixed points, regardless of the choice of the initial values. That is, although the NPL estimator is well defined, the algorithm suggested by Aguirregabiria and Mira may fail to converge to the true parameter.[22] Pesendorfer and Schmidt-Dengler (2010) show that the NPL iteration always converges, but only to stable fixed points. Thus, if the data come from an unstable equilibrium, the pseudo-likelihood iteration may fail to converge to the equilibrium that generates the data.

Kasahara and Shimotsu (2012) further show that the NPL algorithm converges only when the fixed-point mapping has the local contraction property. They suggest an alternative updating algorithm in equation (4.2.17) as follows:

$$\begin{aligned}\mathbf{P}^{K+1}\left(a_{i,t}|\mathbf{x}_t;\boldsymbol{\sigma}^*_{-i}(\mathbf{s}_t),\boldsymbol{\theta},\hat{\boldsymbol{\varphi}}\right) &= \left\{\Psi\left(\mathbf{P}^{K}\left(a_{i,t}|\mathbf{x}_t;\boldsymbol{\sigma}^*_{-i}(\mathbf{s}_t),\hat{\boldsymbol{\theta}}^{K},\hat{\boldsymbol{\varphi}}\right)\right)\right\}^{\lambda} \\ &\quad \circ \left\{\mathbf{P}^{K}\left(a_{i,t}|\mathbf{x}_t;\boldsymbol{\sigma}^*_{-i}(\mathbf{s}_t),\boldsymbol{\theta},\hat{\boldsymbol{\varphi}}\right)\right\}^{1-\lambda}\end{aligned}$$

for a small $\lambda \in (0, 1)$, where $\circ$ denotes the elementwise product and the exponents are taken elementwise. An optimal[23] λ cannot be known to the econometrician ex ante because it is a function of the model primitives. All the fixed points satisfying the local contraction property are more likely when λ is small. The trade-off of a small λ is that it will require more iterations until convergence is attained.

Constrained Full Maximum Likelihood Estimation Egesdal, Lai, and Su (2015) suggest the full maximum likelihood estimation, the possibility of which is also briefly mentioned by Aguirregabiria and Mira (2007). They consider the following constrained optimization problem:

$$\max_{\boldsymbol{\theta},\left\{\bar{\bar{\mathbf{v}}}_i\left(\mathbf{x}_t;\boldsymbol{\sigma}^*_{-i}(\mathbf{s}_t),\boldsymbol{\theta},\hat{\boldsymbol{\varphi}}\right)\right\}_{i\in\mathcal{I}},\left\{\mathbf{P}\left(a_{i,t}|\mathbf{x}_t;\boldsymbol{\sigma}^*_{-i}(\mathbf{s}_t),\boldsymbol{\theta},\hat{\boldsymbol{\varphi}}\right)\right\}_{i\in\mathcal{I}}} \prod_i \mathcal{L}_i\left(\mathbf{P}\left(a_{i,t}|\mathbf{x}_t;\boldsymbol{\sigma}^*_{-i}(\mathbf{s}_t),\boldsymbol{\theta},\hat{\boldsymbol{\varphi}}\right)\right),$$

such that equations (4.2.12), (4.2.13), (4.2.14), and (4.2.15) hold. In this constrained maximization problem, the objective function and all the constraints are smooth functions, so a derivative-based optimizer can find the local maxima as usual. When multiple local maxima exist, the researcher should try many starting values and find the global maximum. They report that this full maximum likelihood performs better than the two-step PML or NPL estimators.

Asymptotic Least-Squares Estimators Pesendorfer and Schmidt-Dengler (2008) take the fixed-point equilibrium characterization in equation (4.2.15) as a moment condition. Taking the expectation on equation (4.2.15) yields

22. One approach to circumvent the problem, taken by Sweeting (2013), is to use a tweak during the step (4.2.17) to not update other players' action probabilities.

23. It is optimal in the sense that it is a required minimum to guarantee the local contraction property to every fixed point.

$$\mathbb{E}\left[\operatorname{vec}\left\{\mathbf{P}\left(a_{i,t}|\mathbf{x}_t;\boldsymbol{\sigma}^*_{-i}(\mathbf{s}_t),\boldsymbol{\theta},\hat{\boldsymbol{\varphi}}\right)\right\}-\operatorname{vec}\left\{\Psi\left(\mathbf{P}\left(a_{i,t}|\mathbf{x}_t;\boldsymbol{\sigma}^*_{-i}(\mathbf{s}_t),\boldsymbol{\theta},\hat{\boldsymbol{\varphi}}\right)\right)\right\}\right]=\mathbf{0}.$$

To calculate the fixed-point iteration

$$\Psi\left(\mathbf{P}\left(a_{i,t}|\mathbf{x}_t;\boldsymbol{\sigma}^*_{-i}(\mathbf{s}_t),\boldsymbol{\theta},\hat{\boldsymbol{\varphi}}\right);\boldsymbol{\sigma}^*(\mathbf{s}_t),\boldsymbol{\theta},\hat{\boldsymbol{\varphi}}\right),$$

the state-transition probability $\mathbf{P}\left(\mathbf{x}_{t+1}|\mathbf{x}_t;\boldsymbol{\sigma}^*(\mathbf{s}_t),\boldsymbol{\theta},\hat{\boldsymbol{\varphi}}\right)$ and the conditional choice probabilities $\mathbf{P}\left(a_{i,t}|\mathbf{x}_t;\boldsymbol{\sigma}^*_{-i}(\mathbf{s}_t),\boldsymbol{\theta},\hat{\boldsymbol{\varphi}}\right)$ have to be taken as the argument of $\Psi\left(\cdot;\boldsymbol{\sigma}^*(\mathbf{s}_t),\boldsymbol{\theta},\hat{\boldsymbol{\varphi}}\right)$. They suggest a few possibilities. One of them is to use a consistent estimator $\left\{\hat{\mathbf{P}}\left(a_{i,t}|\mathbf{x}_t\right),\hat{\mathbf{P}}\left(\mathbf{x}_{t+1}|\mathbf{x}_t\right)\right\}$, such as simple frequency, and take it as data. Another possibility is to use

$$\mathbb{E}\left[\operatorname{vec}\left\{\mathbf{1}\left(a_{i,t}|\mathbf{x}_t\right)\right\}-\operatorname{vec}\left\{\Psi\left(\hat{\mathbf{P}}\left(a_{i,t}|\mathbf{x}_t\right);\boldsymbol{\sigma}^*(\mathbf{s}_t),\boldsymbol{\theta},\hat{\boldsymbol{\varphi}}\right)\right\}\right]=\mathbf{0}.$$

Either will yield the consistent estimates, but the asymptotic variance will be different; the authors derive the asymptotically efficient weighting matrix. The remaining estimation step is the usual one: impose the corresponding moment conditions and implement nonlinear GMM.

The two-step estimators of Bajari et al. (2007) and Pakes et al. (2007) can be characterized as a variant of asymptotic least-squares estimators, as using different conditional choice probabilities, different state-transition probabilities, or different weighting matrices in the nonlinear GMM estimation. An advantage of using these two-stage estimators is that they place less of a computational burden than the estimation methods that iterate over the fixed-point equation. However, a possible downside is that the two-stage estimators may suffer from a large finite-sample bias.

4.2.3 Further Issues and Discussion of Dynamic Game Models Estimation

4.2.3.1 UNOBSERVED HETEROGENEITY

All the estimation frameworks for the dynamic-game models that we studied thus far commonly assume no private information other than the i.i.d. idiosyncratic shocks $\boldsymbol{\epsilon}_t$. Such shocks are unobservable both to the other players in the game and to the econometrician. In that sense, the econometrician has the same degree of information as the players. This assumption can often be inadequate. Recently, attempts have been made to incorporate unobserved heterogeneity, which is possibly serially correlated, into the model.

Igami and Yang (2017) estimate a dynamic entry model of hamburger chains, which accommodates the unobserved heterogeneity, combining the estimation procedures suggested by Bajari et al. (2007) and Arcidiacono and Miller (2011), and building upon the identification results provided by Kasahara and Shimotsu (2009). They consider the time-invariant unobserved market types, where some markets can be more lucrative than others, which leads to some markets being more attractive for entry than others. The method is essentially a combination of Arcidiacono and Miller (2011) and Bajari et al. (2007). Kasahara and Shimotsu discretize the type of markets, estimate the conditional probability of each market belonging to a specific type, then compute the market-type-specific conditional choice probability of entry. The rest of the estimation procedure follows Bajari et al. (2007). Igami and Yang (2017) find that ignoring unobserved market heterogeneity attenuates the effect of competition on profits.

4.2.3.2 (UNDER)-IDENTIFICATION

Underidentification in dynamic games becomes much more serious than in the single-agent problem. Pesendorfer and Schmidt-Dengler (2008) show the degree of underidentification increases exponentially with the number of players in the game. The outline of the argument is as follows: Each agent has J possible actions. When I players are in the game, the combination of possible beliefs on the actions of all the players are $I \times J^I$.[24] But the dimension of the observed conditional choice probabilities are at most $I \times J$. Thus, the degree of underidentification $I \times J^I - I \times J$ increases exponentially with I.[25] One possible restriction that Pesendorfer and Schmidt-Dengler suggest to ensure identification is to impose the independence of the per-period utility of each player in the game.

Bajari et al. (2015) suggest imposing the exclusion restriction on per-period utility; that is, some of the state variables are excluded from player i's per-period choice-specific value function, which implies

$$\bar{v}_{i,j}\left(\mathbf{x}_t; \boldsymbol{\sigma}^*_{-i}(\mathbf{s}_t)\right) = \bar{v}_{i,j}\left(\mathbf{x}_{i,t}; \boldsymbol{\sigma}^*_{-i}(\mathbf{s}_t)\right)^{26}$$

where $\mathbf{x}_t \equiv \left(\mathbf{x}_{i,t}, \mathbf{x}_{-i,t}\right)$. Bajari et al. show that the nonparametric identification of $\bar{u}_{i,j}\left(\mathbf{x}_t; \boldsymbol{\sigma}^*_{-i}(\mathbf{s}_t)\right)$ can be achieved if (1) the conditional distribution of $\mathbf{x}_{-i,t}$, given $\mathbf{x}_{i,t}$, has more than J support points; and (2) the following J^{I-1} equations are linearly independent:

24. This is because each player $i \in I$ has a belief on each $j \in J$, leading to $I \times J^I$.

25. The argument is not exact because we do not consider the number of free equations, which is $J - 1$.

26. Here, $(\boldsymbol{\theta}, \boldsymbol{\varphi})$ are suppressed because we are considering the *nonparametric* identification problem. That is, we do not assume here that the per-period utility function is parameterized by $\boldsymbol{\theta}$.

$$\bar{u}_{i,j}\left(\mathbf{x}_t; \sigma^*_{-i}\left(\mathbf{s}_t\right)\right) = \sum_{\mathbf{a}_{-i} \in \mathcal{J}^{I-1}} \Pr\left(\mathbf{a}_{-i} | \mathbf{x}_t\right) \bar{u}_{i,j}\left(\mathbf{x}_{i,t}; \mathbf{a}_{-i,t}\right).$$

Aguirregabiria and Magesan (2020) extend this identification result to circumstances where players' beliefs are not in equilibrium.

With regard to the exclusion restriction, a recent advancement in the literature by Luo et al. (2022) establishes the identification results of the components of dynamic games under MPE with unobserved player heterogeneity. The components identified include the number of multiple equilibria, as well as other objects such as the equilibrium (conditional) action probabilities and state-transition probabilities studied previously. However, to the best of our knowledge, an estimation framework exploiting Luo et al.'s identification results does not exist yet.

4.2.3.3 DYNAMIC DISCRETE GAMES WITH EQUILIBRIUM CONCEPTS OTHER THAN MPE

Fershtman and Pakes (2012) develop a setup and framework that can accommodate unobserved actions and states in dynamic games. It is based on a new dynamic equilibrium concept that they introduce, which is called *experience-based equilibrium.*[27] In the Markov perfect equilibrium–based frameworks, accommodating unobserved actions or states is difficult, mainly because for each t, each player's belief should coincide with the actual conditional choice probabilities and the actual state-transition probabilities. An experience-based equilibrium relaxes this requirement, such that beliefs should coincide with the conditional choice probabilities only at the limiting recurrent states. In the experience-based equilibrium, each agent maximizes the sum of the expected discounted value, conditional on the limiting information sets that are observed to the corresponding players when the game is repeated infinitely many times. All the players in the game learn about other players' best responses as the game is repeated.

The experience-based equilibrium is a relaxation of the Markov perfect Nash equilibrium. If the Markov perfect Nash equilibrium exists in a setup being considered, the existence of an experience-based equilibrium is guaranteed. Fershtman and Pakes provide an algorithm to calculate experience-based equilibria under unobserved actions and/or states, and then conduct a simulation study. The framework is well suited to the environment where players' learning is involved because it naturally involves their learning process to calculate the equilibrium. Asker et al. (2020) and Doraszelski, Lewis, and Pakes (2018) apply the

27. The idea of such an equilibrium concept was first outlined in Pakes et al. (2007).

experience-based equilibrium framework to collusion in auctions and entry to the UK electricity system, respectively.

Igami (2017, 2018) assume a finite-horizon sequential entry/exit game with nonstationarity, in which firms are forward looking because of investment or innovation decisions. These studies estimate the corresponding dynamic game, assuming that the firms employ perfect Bayesian Nash equilibrium strategies.

Bibliography

Aguirregabiria, V., & C.-Y. Ho (2012). "A dynamic oligopoly game of the US airline industry: Estimation and policy experiments." *Journal of Econometrics*, 168, 156–173.

Aguirregabiria, V., & A. Magesan (2020). "Identification and estimation of dynamic games when players' beliefs are not in equilibrium." *Review of Economic Studies*, 87, 582–625.

Aguirregabiria, V., & P. Mira (2002). "Swapping the nested fixed point algorithm: A class of estimators for discrete Markov decision models." *Econometrica*, 70, 1519–1543.

Aguirregabiria, V., & P. Mira (2007). "Sequential estimation of dynamic discrete games." *Econometrica*, 75, 1–53.

Aguirregabiria, V., & P. Mira (2010). "Dynamic discrete choice structural models: A survey." *Journal of Econometrics*, 156, 38–67.

Aguirregabiria, V., P. Mira, & H. Roman (2007). "An estimable dynamic model of entry, exit, and growth in oligopoly retail markets." *American Economic Review: Papers and Proceedings*, 97, 449–454.

Aguirregabiria, V., & N. Suzuki (2014). "Identification and counterfactuals in dynamic models of market entry and exit." *Quantitative Marketing and Economics*, 12, 267–304.

Aradillas-Lopez, A. (2010). "Semiparametric estimation of a simultaneous game with incomplete information." *Journal of Econometrics*, 157, 409–431.

Arcidiacono, P., & R. A. Miller (2011). "Conditional choice probability estimation of dynamic discrete choice models with unobserved heterogeneity." *Econometrica*, 79, 1823–1867.

Asker, J., C. Fershtman, J. Jeon, & A. Pakes (2020). "A computational framework for analyzing dynamic auctions: The market impact of information sharing." *RAND Journal of Economics*, 51, 805–839.

Aumann, R. J. (1987). "Correlated equilibrium as an expression of Bayesian rationality." *Econometrica*, 55, 1–18.

Bajari, P., C. L. Benkard, & J. Levin (2007). "Estimating dynamic models of imperfect competition." *Econometrica*, 75, 1331–1370.

Bajari, P., V. Chernozhukov, H. Hong, & D. Nekipelov (2015). "Identification and efficient semiparametric estimation of a dynamic discrete game." NBER Working Paper, no. 21125.

Bajari, P., H. Hong, & S. P. Ryan (2010). "Identification and estimation of a discrete game of complete information." *Econometrica*, 78, 1529–1568.

Bergemann, D., & S. Morris (2013). "Robust predictions in games with incomplete information." *Econometrica*, 81, 1251–1308.

Bergemann, D., & S. Morris (2016). "Bayes correlated equilibrium and the comparison of information structures in games." *Theoretical Economics*, 11, 487–522.

Berry, S. (1992). "Estimation of a model of entry in the airline industry." *Econometrica*, 60, 889–917.

Berry, S., J. Levinsohn, & A. Pakes (1995). "Automobile prices in market equilibrium." *Econometrica*, 63, 841–890.

Berry, S., & P. Reiss (2007). Chapter 29, "Empirical models of entry and market structure, vol. 3 of Handbook of Industrial Organization." 1845–1886. Amsterdam: Elsevier.

Berry, S., & E. Tamer (2006). *Identification in models of oligopoly entry*, vol. 2 of *Advances in Economics and Econometrics, Ninth World Congress of the Econometric Society*, 46–85. Cambridge: Cambridge University Press.

Bhaskar, V., G. J. Mailath, & S. Morris (2013). "A foundation for Markov equilibria in sequential games with finite social memory." *Review of Economic Studies*, 80, 925–948.

Bresnahan, T. F., & P. C. Reiss (1990). "Entry in monopoly markets." *Review of Economic Studies*, 57, 531–553.

Bresnahan, T. F., & P. C. Reiss (1991a). "Empirical models of discrete games." *Journal of Econometrics*, 48, 57–81.

Bresnahan, T. F., & P. C. Reiss (1991b). "Entry and competition in concentrated markets." *Journal of Political Economy*, 99, 977–1009.

Chernozhukov, V., H. Hong, & E. Tamer (2007). "Estimation and confidence regions for parameter sets in econometric models." *Econometrica*, 75, 1243–1284.

Ciliberto, F., & E. Tamer (2009). "Market structure and multiple equilibria in airline markets." *Econometrica*, 77, 1791–1828.

de Paula, A. (2013). "Econometric analysis of games with multiple equilibria." *Annual Review of Economics*, 5, 107–131.

Doraszelski, U., G. Lewis, & A. Pakes (2018). "Just starting out: Learning and equilibrium in a new market." *American Economic Review*, 108, 565–615.

Doraszelski, U., & A. Pakes (2007). Chapter 30, "A framework for applied dynamic analysis in IO, vol. 3 of Handbook of Industrial Organization." 1887–1966. Amsterdam: Elsevier.

Doraszelski, U., & M. Satterthwaite (2010). "Computable Markov-perfect industry dynamics." *RAND Journal of Economics*, 41, 215–243.

Egesdal, M., Z. Lai, & C.-L. Su (2015). "Estimating dynamic discrete-choice games of incomplete information." *Quantitative Economics*, 6, 567–597.

Ellickson, P. B., & S. Misra (2011). "Estimating discrete games." *Marketing Science*, 30, 997–1010.

Epstein, L. G., H. Kaido, & K. Seo (2015). "Robust confidence regions for incomplete models." *Econometrica*, 84(5), 1799–1838.

Ericson, R., & A. Pakes (1995). "Markov-perfect industry dynamics: A framework for empirical work." *Review or Economic Studies*, 62, 53–82.

Fershtman, C., & A. Pakes (2012). "Dynamic games with asymmetric information: A framework for empirical work." *Quarterly Journal of Economics*, 127, 1611–1661.

Galichon, A., & M. Henry (2011). "Set identification in models with multiple equilibria." *Review of Economic Studies*, 78, 1264–1298.

Grieco, P. L. E. (2014). "Discrete games with flexible information structures: an application to local grocery markets." *RAND Journal of Economics*, 45, 303–340.

Hotz, V. J., & R. A. Miller (1993). "Conditional choice probabilities and the estimation of dynamic models." *Review of Economic Studies*, 60, 497–529.

Hotz, V. J., R. A. Miller, S. Sanders, & J. Smith (1994). "A simulation estimator for dynamic models of discrete choice." *Review of Economic Studies*, 61, 265–289.

Igami, M. (2017). "Estimating the innovator's dilemma: Structural analysis of creative destruction in the hard distk drive industry, 1981–1998." *Journal of Political Economy*, 125, 798–847.

Igami, M. (2018). "Industry dynamics of offshoring: The case of hard disk drives." *American Economic Journal: Microeconomics*, 10, 67–101.

Igami, M., & N. Yang (2017). "Unobserved heterogeneity in dynamic games: Cannibalization and preemptive entry of hamburger chains in Canada." *Quantitative Economics*, 7, 483–521.

Jia, P. (2008). "What happens when Wal-mart comes to town: An empirical analysis of the discount retailing industry." *Econometrica*, 76, 1263–1316.

Kasahara, H., & K. Shimotsu (2009). "Nonparametric identification of finite mixture models of dynamic discrete choices." *Econometrica*, 77, 135–175.

Kasahara, H., & K. Shimotsu (2012). "Sequential estimation of structural models with a fixed point constraint." *Econometrica*, 80, 2303–2319.

Kooreman, P. (1994). "Estimation of econometric models of some discrete games." *Journal of Applied Econometrics*, 9, 255–268.

Li, Q., & J. S. Racine (2007). *Nonparametric econometrics: Theory and practice*. Princeton, NJ: Princeton University Press.

Liu, N., Q. Vuong, & H. Xu (2017). "Rationalization and identification of binary games with correlated types," *Journal of Econometrics*, 201, 249–268.

Luo, Y., P. Xiao, & R. Xiao (2022). "Identification of dynamic games with unobserved heterogeneity and multiple equilibria." *Journal of Econometrics*, 226(2), 343–367.

Magnolfi, L., & C. Roncoroni (2020). "Estimation of discrete games with weak assumptions on information." *Review of Economic Studies*. Accessed: https://academic.oup.com/restud/advance-article-abstract/doi/10.1093/restud/rdac058/6670639?redirectedFrom=fulltext.

Manzel, K. (2016). "Inference for games with many players." *Review of Economic Studies*, 83(1), 306–337.

Maskin, E., & J. Tirole (1988). "A theory of dynamic oligopoly, I: Overview and quantity competition with large fixed costs." *Econometrica*, 56, 549–569.

Maskin, E., & J. Tirole (2001). "Markov perfect equilibrium: I. Observable actions." *Journal of Economic Theory*, 100, 191–219.

Mazzeo, M. J. (2002). "Product choice and oligopoly market structure." *RAND Journal of Economics*, 33, 221–242.

Myerson, R. B. (1991). *Game theory: Analysis of conflict*. Cambridge, MA: Harvard University Press.

Newey, W. K., & D. McFadden (1994). Chapter 36, "Large sample estimation and hypothesis testing." In Vol. 4, *Handbook of Econometrics*, 2111–2245. Amsterdam: Elsevier.

Pakes, A., M. Ostrovsky, & S. Berry (2007). "Simple estimators for the parameters of discrete dynamic games (with entry/exit examples)." *RAND Journal of Economics*, 38, 373–399.

Pakes, A., J. Porter, K. Ho, & J. Ishii (2015). "Moment inequalities and their application." *Econometrica*, 83, 315–334.

Pesendorfer, M., & P. Schmidt-Dengler (2008). "Asymptotic least squares estimators for dynamic games." *Review of Economic Studies*, 75, 901–928.

Pesendorfer, M., & P. Schmidt-Dengler (2010). "Sequential estimation of dynamic discrete games: A comment." *Econometrica*, 78, 833–842.

Seim, K. (2006). "An empirical model of firm entry with endogenous product-type choices." *RAND Journal of Economics*, 37, 619–640.

Su, C.-L. (2014). "Estimating discrete-choice games of incomplete information: Simple static examples." *Quantitative Marketing and Economics*, 12, 167–207.

Sweeting, A. (2009). "The strategic timing incentives of commercial radio stations: An empirical analysis using multiple equilibria." *RAND Journal of Economics*, 40, 710–742.

Sweeting, A. (2013). "Dynamic product positioning in differentiated product markest: The effect of fees for musical performance rights on the commercial radio industry." *Econometrica*, 81, 1763–1803.

Tamer, E. (2003). "Incomplete simultaneous discrete response model with multiple equilibria." *Review of Economic Studies*, 70, 147–165.

Vitorino, M. A. (2012). "Empirical entry games with complementarities: An application to the shopping center entry." *Journal of Marketing Research*, 49, 175–191.

Wan, Y., & H. Xu (2014). "Semiparametric identification of binary decision games of incomplete information with correlated private signals." *Journal of Econometrics*, 182, 235–246.

Weintraub, G. Y., C. L. Benkard, & B. van Roy (2008). "Markov perfect industry dynamics with many firms." *Econometrica*, 76, 1375–1411.

5

Empirical Frameworks of Consumer Search

Search is a major modeling framework reflecting friction in the information of an economic agent. In this chapter, we briefly overview the historical development of the theoretical frameworks of optimal consumer search and price dispersion. We then study empirical frameworks that combine data with the predictions from the search models such as optimal search sequence or search size.

Search models commonly derive the optimal size or degree of search under different setups. When the theory models of search is to be combined with empirics, availability of data becomes a primary concern. In an ideal world, an econometrician should be able to observe individual-level data of (1) consumers' thought process regarding the search-mode decision (simultaneous / sequential / mixed); (2) the set (or even better, sequence) of searched alternatives; and (3) the purchase decisions. Such detailed individual-level search data are not easily available, and earlier works developed empirical frameworks to identify and estimate the search-cost distribution out of market data on the observed price dispersion. In this chapter, we review the empirical frameworks on consumer search combining different degrees of data availability with theoretic models of consumer search. We note that to the best of our knowledge, none of the existing empirical works to date incorporate (1) directly.

5.1 Utility Specification and Some Preliminary Results

5.1.1 *Utility Specification in Consumer Search Models*

We focus on the price search of consumers within the context of a more general utility search. Consumers search over discrete alternatives to maximize the utility net of search cost. Let $u_{i,j}$ be consumer i's utility of purchasing $j \in \mathcal{J}$. The utility is given by

$$u_{i,j} := u\left(-p_j, \mathbf{x}_j, \xi_j, \epsilon_{i,j}\right). \tag{5.1.1}$$

The utility function in equation (5.1.1) takes price p_j, observed product characteristics $\mathbf{x}_j$, unobserved product characteristics ξ_j, and idiosyncratic utility shock $\epsilon_{i,j}$ as its argument. We put the negative sign on the price term p_j to emphasize that the utility is decreasing in the prices.

The utility specification in equation (5.1.1) is fairly general, encompassing most empirical setups that have been employed in the literature thus far. For example, if consumers search only for the prices for an identical product, the utility function is simply

$$u_{i,j} = -p_j.$$

This way, the problem of finding an alternative that yields the best utility can be directly converted to the problem of finding an alternative with the lowest price. In the context of differentiated-products markets, the search procedure can be thought of as consumers locking in to the characteristics first, and then search for the prices (e.g., all the classical search models covered in section 5.2, Honka (2014), and Honka and Chintagunta (2017)). Notice that a 1-unit increase of p_j cannot be compensated by any change of $\mathbf{x}_j$. The other extreme would be the linear utility; that is,

$$u_{i,j} := -\alpha p_j + \mathbf{x}_j'\boldsymbol{\beta} + \xi_j + \epsilon_{i,j},$$

where a price increase can be compensated linearly by an increase/decrease of $\mathbf{x}_j$ or ξ_j.

Throughout sections 5.1 and 5.2, we assume that the product is homogeneous; therefore, consumers search only for the lowest price unless otherwise noted. Consumers want to find a seller that offers the lowest price for the item, but search is costly. Consumers therefore optimize over the size and/or order of search to maximize the expected benefit net of search costs. Note that the results and implications derived in sections 5.1 and 5.2 apply directly to the utility search context where consumers search to maximize the utility net of search costs.

5.1.2 Some Preliminary Results on Stochastic Dominance

For quick reference, we present some equivalent statements for the first- and second-order stochastic dominance without proof. The following results are used extensively in the search literature.

Proposition 5.1.1. *(First-Order Stochastic Dominance)* Let $F(\cdot)$ and $G(\cdot)$ be two continuous cumulative distribution functions on $[0, \infty)$. The following statements are equivalent:

(i) $F(\cdot)$ first-order stochastically dominates $G(\cdot)$.
(ii) $\forall x \in [0, \infty), F(x) \le G(x)$.
(iii) For any nondecreasing function $u : \mathbb{R}^{+} \to \mathbb{R}$,

$$\int_0^{\infty} u(x)\, dF(x) \ge \int_0^{\infty} u(x)\, dG(x).$$

Proposition 5.1.2. *(Second-Order Stochastic Dominance)* Let $F(\cdot)$ and $G(\cdot)$ be two continuous cumulative distribution functions on $[0, \infty)$. The following statements are equivalent:

(i) $F(\cdot)$ second-order stochastically dominates $G(\cdot)$.
(ii) $\forall x_0 \in [0, \infty)$,

$$\int_0^{x_0} F(x)\, dx \le \int_0^{x_0} G(x)\, dx.$$

(iii) For any nondecreasing concave function $u : \mathbb{R}^{+} \to \mathbb{R}$,

$$\int_0^{\infty} u(x)\, dF(x) \ge \int_0^{\infty} u(x)\, dG(x).$$

A few remarks are in order. First, proposition 5.1.1 (iii) implies that if $F(\cdot)$ first-order stochastically dominates $G(\cdot)$, then $\mathbb{E}_F[x_j] \ge \mathbb{E}_G[x_j]$. However, $\mathbb{E}_F[x_j] \ge \mathbb{E}_G[x_j]$ does not tell anything about first-order stochastic dominance. Second, first-order stochastic dominance implies second-order stochastic dominance, but not vice versa. This is straightforward by comparing statement (iii) of proposition 5.1.2 with statement (iii) of proposition 5.1.1. Third, if $\mathbb{E}_F[x_j] = \mathbb{E}_G[x_j]$, $F(\cdot)$ second-order stochastically dominates $G(\cdot)$ if and only if $G(\cdot)$ is a mean-preserving spread of $F(\cdot)$. Note that if $G(\cdot)$ is a mean-preserving spread of $F(\cdot)$, then $Var_G(x_j) \ge Var_F(x_j)$, but not vice versa. Comparing only variance says little about the mean-preserving spread.

5.2 Classical Search-Theoretic Models: Sequential Search and Simultaneous Search

We review classical consumer search-theoretic models in this section. Classical models of consumer search, dating back to Stigler (1961), are motivated by observed price dispersion of a product even when the product is identical. It was considered a major challenge to the classical Walrasian demand model's law-of-one-price prediction. Our purpose here is not to give a comprehensive review of the search theory literature; rather, we intend to give a concise overview of the extent to which they are employed in the recent empirical literature.

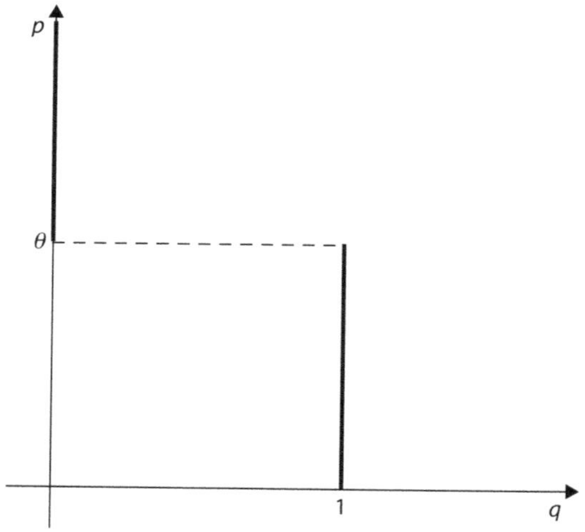

FIGURE 5.2.1. Unit inelastic individual demand curve

The classical consumer search models use two major schemes: sequential search and simultaneous search.[1] In sequential search, consumers draw one price at each period and decide whether to keep searching for one more or to stop searching. The sequential search problem boils down to the optimal stopping problem. In simultaneous search, consumers commit to the search set ex ante before engaging in the actual search. Then, they draw all the prices in the search set, collect the prices, and then choose an alternative that has the lowest price.

The baseline assumptions common to the search models that we study in this section are as follows:

AS(1) Each consumer has a unit inelastic demand.
AS(2) A continuum of consumers have the identical choke price θ.
AS(3) Consumers know their own search-cost function.
AS(4) Consumers know the common price distribution $F(p)$, which is exogenous, nondegenerate, and homogeneous over the set of infinitely many stores $\mathcal{J}$.[2]
AS(5) Each price draw is independent.[3]

The shape of consumers' common unit inelastic demand, AS(1) and AS(2) combined, is depicted in figure 5.2.1. AS(3) and AS(4) are about the prior knowledge

1. Chronologically simultaneous search was developed first. However, we study sequential search first for illustrative purposes.

2. It implies the price distribution $F(p)$ is not indexed by the stores, which we relax in section 5.2.2.2.

3. An independent price draw is closely related to the assumption that consumers' learning about price distribution over the price draws does not occur.

of the consumers. The actual price distribution and the search cost are considered to be prior knowledge of consumers; it is assumed that learning about the price distribution or the search cost does not occur during the search procedure. Assumption AS(5) implies no spillover of information in search. We stick to the assumptions AS(3)–AS(5) because the majority of empirical works to date do not seem to incorporate search with learning about price distributions or search costs.

5.2.1 *Sequential Search*

5.2.1.1 SEQUENTIAL SEARCH WITH HOMOGENEOUS EX-ANTE PRICE DISTRIBUTION AND PERFECT RECALL

The sequential search framework originated in McCall (1970)'s wage-search problem, which was later adapted to the consumers' price-search context. In sequential search, consumers decide whether to stop or keep searching after each price draw. In addition to assumptions AS(1)–AS(5), we impose the following three assumptions for the sequential search:

AS(SEQ1) At the beginning of each period t, the consumer randomly draws one price out of the infinitely many stores, and then decide whether to stop searching or keep searching for one more.

AS(SEQ2) The consumer's marginal cost of searching one more price is $c > 0$ except for the first price draw, which is given for free. Here, c is common across $\mathcal{J}$.

AS(SEQ3) Consumers can revisit any of the previously searched stores costlessly.

Assumption AS(SEQ1) is the sequential search assumption, assumption AS (SEQ2) specifies the structure of constant marginal cost of search, and assumption AS(SEQ3) is the perfect recall assumption. The problem of determining which stores to visit first is irrelevant when the ex-ante price distributions are the same across all the stores.

Let p_t^B be the minimum price searched thus far at period t; that is,

$$p_t^B := \min_{1 \leq s \leq t} \{p_s\}.$$

For each period, consumers can collect p_t^B for sure or try to search one more store by paying the marginal cost of search c. If consumers are searching once more, the search result p_{t+1} would be such that either $p_{t+1} \geq p_t^B$ or $p_{t+1} < p_t^B$. Consumers will stick to p_t^B in the former case.

To formalize, denote $v\left(p_t^B\right)$ as the value of p_t^B. The period t decision problem becomes

$$v\left(p_t^B\right)=\min\left\{p_t^B, c+\mathbb{E}\left[v\left(p_{t+1}^B\right)\right]\right\}. \tag{5.2.1}$$

First, notice that the range of the function $v(\cdot)$ cannot be negative. Second, $\mathbb{E}\left[v\left(p_{t+1}^B\right)\right]$ is a constant function in p_t^B because the new price draw at $t+1$ is not affected by the realization of the current price draw p_t. Therefore, the second term in the min operator is a constant function in p_t^B. On the other hand, the first argument p_t^B is a linear function of p_t^B. Therefore, the optimal solution for this decision problem has a reservation price structure (i.e., there is a unique price level p^* such that consumers accept p_t^B if $p_t^B \leq p^*$ and reject p_t^B if $p_t^B > p^*$, and p^* does not change over t). Because p_t^B is the minimum of the price draws up to period t, this solution structure implies that once one price draw realization is below p^*, then the consumer accepts it and quits the market forever. Interestingly, recall never occurs even if it is allowed in this setup where all the price draws are from the same distribution.

Denote $\bar{V}=\mathbb{E}\left[v\left(p_{t+1}^B\right)\right]$. The optimal reservation price level p^* is such that the two terms in the min operator equalizes; that is,

$$p^*=c+\bar{V}. \tag{5.2.2}$$

Given that the solution has a reservation price structure, we can characterize the shape of $v(\cdot)$ further in terms of reservation price p^* as follows:

$$v\left(p_t^B\right)=\begin{cases} p_t^B & p_t \leq p^* \\ c+\bar{V} & p_t > p^* \end{cases}.$$

Using this characterization, let us now write $\bar{V}$ in terms of the reservation price p^*:

$$\bar{V}=\int_0^{p^*} p dF(p)+\left(c+\bar{V}\right)\int_{p^*}^{\bar{p}} dF(p). \tag{5.2.3}$$

We have two equations (5.2.3) and (5.2.2), and two unknowns, $\left(\bar{V}, p^*\right)$. To eliminate $\bar{V}$, we plug equation (5.2.2) back into equation (5.2.3), which gives

$$p^*-c=\int_0^{p^*} p dF(p)+p^*\int_{p^*}^{\bar{p}} dF(p).$$

Rearranging, we get

$$c = \int_0^{p^*} \left(p^* - p\right) dF(p). \tag{5.2.4}$$

The reservation price p^* is characterized as the solution for equation (5.2.4), but we are unsure yet whether the solution p^* is well defined. Also, notice that other components of equation (5.2.4) are the price distribution $F(\cdot)$ and the marginal cost of search c. Next, we would like to examine the effects c and $F(\cdot)$ if a solution p^* is well defined.

Now, let us define a function $\psi\left(p_t^B\right)$ as follows, which takes the current best price p_t^B as its argument:

$$\psi\left(p_t^B\right) := \int_0^{p_t^B} \left(p_t^B - p\right) dF(p). \tag{5.2.5}$$

It can be easily verified that $\psi(\cdot)$ is continuous and monotonically increasing,[4] $\lim_{p_t^B \to 0+} \psi\left(p_t^B\right) = 0$, and $\lim_{p_t^B \to +\infty} \psi\left(p_t^B\right) = \infty$. Because $c > 0$, $\psi\left(p_t^B\right)$ crosses c just once. Hence, a unique solution for equation (5.2.4) exists, and thus for the equivalent problem, equation (5.2.1), as well. We define p^* implicitly as the solution for

$$\psi\left(p^*\right) = c, \tag{5.2.6}$$

which is well defined, as we have just shown. We refer to p^* as the reservation price henceforth.

The left panel of figure 5.2.2 illustrates how p^* is implicitly determined. When the consumer has $p_t^B < p^*$ in hand, collecting the current p_t^B and quitting is better than drawing one more price in the next period. The consumer therefore will choose the first option in the choice problem (5.2.1). When the consumer has $p_t^B > p^*$ in hand, drawing one more price is better than just collecting p_t^B and quitting, so the consumer will choose the second option in equation (5.2.1). Now it becomes clear that we can rewrite the original problem in equation (5.2.1) equivalently as follows:

$$\min\left\{\psi\left(p_t^B\right), c\right\} = \min\left\{\int_0^{p_B} \left(p_B - p\right) dF(p), c\right\}. \tag{5.2.7}$$

4. Under some regularity conditions,

$$\frac{\partial}{\partial p_B} \psi\left(p_B\right) = \frac{\partial}{\partial p_B} \int_0^{p_B} \left(p_B - p\right) dF(p),$$

and it can be easily verified that the second part $\frac{\partial}{\partial p_B} \int_0^{p_B} \left(p_B - p\right) dF(p)$ is simply $F\left(p_B\right)$ by using the Leibniz integral rule. Then, it is also straightforward that $\frac{\partial^2}{\partial p_B^2} \psi\left(p_B\right) > 0$, thereby implying $\psi(\cdot)$ is convex.

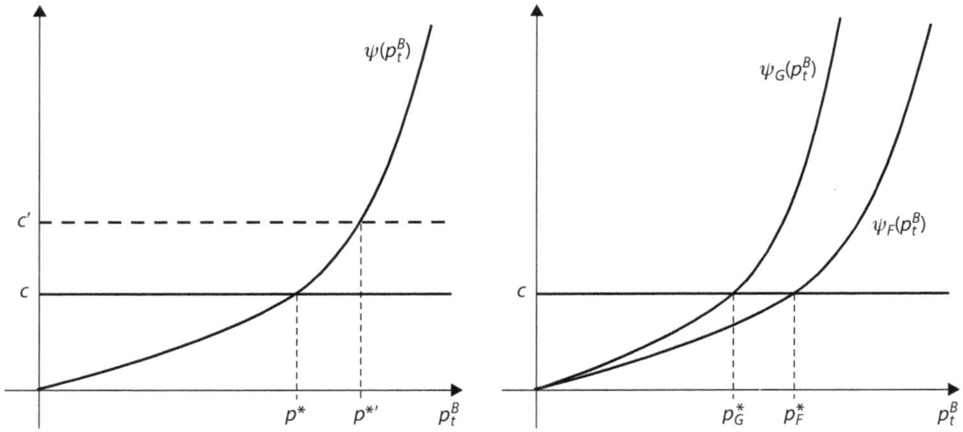

FIGURE 5.2.2. Determination of reservation price p^*

Notice that a higher marginal cost of search c' will induce a higher reservation price, and therefore, consumers will accept higher price draws then before. Such a prediction is consistent with the intuition that consumers want to stop the search earlier because of the increased search cost.

We further examine what happens to the reservation price when the underlying price distribution $F(\cdot)$ changes in a specific way: first- and second-order stochastic dominance. Suppose that a price distribution $G(\cdot)$ exists such that $F(\cdot)$ first- or second-order stochastically dominates $G(\cdot)$. For any $p_t^B > 0$, define $\left(p - p_t^B\right)^- = \min\left\{p - p_t^B, 0\right\}$, which is an increasing and weakly concave function of p. Then, the following holds from propositions 5.1.1 and 5.1.2:

$$\begin{aligned}\int_0^{p_t^B} \left(p - p_t^B\right) dF(p) &= \int_0^{\infty} \left(p - p_t^B\right)^- dF(p) \geq \int_0^{\infty} \left(p - p_t^B\right)^- dG(p) \\ &= \int_0^{p_t^B} \left(p - p_t^B\right) dG(p) \qquad (5.2.8)\end{aligned}$$

Now let us index $\psi(\cdot)$ by F and G, respectively, and then subtract:

$$\begin{aligned}\psi_F\left(p_t^B\right) - \psi_G\left(p_t^B\right) &= -\left\{\int_0^{p_t^B} \left(p - p_t^B\right) dF(p) - \int_0^{p_t^B} \left(p - p_t^B\right) dG(p)\right\} \\ &\leq 0.\end{aligned}$$

This inequality implies $\psi_F(\cdot)$ will always be below $\psi_G(\cdot)$ at the same p_t^B value. As a result, the associated p_G^* would be lower than p_F^*. Determination of p^* with respect to the ex ante price-distribution change is depicted in the right panel of figure 5.2.2.

Recall from propositions 5.1.1 and 5.1.2 in section 5.1.2 that $\mathbb{E}_F\left[x_j\right] \geq \mathbb{E}_G\left[x_j\right]$ when equation (5.2.8) holds. Furthermore, if the equality holds so that $\mathbb{E}_F\left[x_j\right] = \mathbb{E}_G\left[x_j\right]$, then $Var_G\left(x_j\right) \geq Var_F\left(x_j\right)$. An immediate result is that a better ex ante distribution[5] in the sense of first-order stochastic dominance will decrease the reservation price. Intuitively, consumers will have higher standards on the draws from $G(\cdot)$ than from $F(\cdot)$. If the expectations of the two ex ante price distributions are identical, a "riskier" distribution will decrease the reservation price. All else being equal, consumers have "more to gain by searching" when the underlying price distribution is riskier. These intuitions will carry over when the ex ante price distribution is heterogeneous.

5.2.1.2 AN EXCURSUS: SEQUENTIAL SEARCH WITH HOMOGENEOUS EX-ANTE PRICE DISTRIBUTION AND NO RECALL

Assumption AS(SEQ3) allows a perfect recall. However, consumers never actually return to a previously visited store to collect p_s for $s < t$ in the problem structure presented here, where the price distribution is homogeneous across alternatives. That is, a price draw that is rejected once will never be accepted in the future. One may conjecture even more: reservation price p^* might be identical regardless of whether recall is allowed, and we show here that such a conjecture is indeed true.[6]

We begin our discussion from an alternative characterization of the reservation price p^* in equation (5.2.6) that will be used here. Since we now know that the problem in equation (5.2.1) has a reservation price structure, reservation price p^* is the level of p_t^B such that the two terms in the min operator in the original problem in equation (5.2.1) is equalized; that is,

$$p^* = c + \int_0^{p^*} p dF(p) + p^* \int_{p^*}^{\bar{p}} dF(p). \tag{5.2.9}$$

Now let us replace assumption AS(SEQ3) by the following:

AS(SEQ3') Consumers cannot revisit any of the previously searched stores.

When recall of the previous price offers is not allowed, consumers must either take the current price draw p_t or abandon p_t to search for one more price. To formalize, consumers again solve

5. "Better" means that the chance of low price realization is higher. In this case, $G(\cdot)$ is better than $F(\cdot)$.
6. This is the original wage-search model setup studied by McCall (1970).

$$v\left(p_t\right) = \min\left\{p_t, c + \mathbb{E}\left[v\left(p_{t+1}\right)\right]\right\}$$
$$= \min\left\{p_t, c + \int_0^{\bar{p}} v(p)dF(p)\right\}, \qquad (5.2.10)$$

where $\mathbb{E}\left[v\left(p_{t+1}\right)\right]$ is the expected value of the one-period-ahead price draw p_{t+1}. Because p_t is linearly increasing in p_t and $c + \int_0^{\bar{p}} v(p)dF(p)$ is a positive constant function in p_t,[7] the solution for the problem in equation (5.2.10) also has a reservation price structure.

Let p^{**} be the reservation price of the problem in equation (5.2.10). Here, p^{**} is a price level such that the two terms in equation (5.2.10) are equalized (i.e., $p^{**} = c + \int_0^{\bar{p}} v(p)dF(p)$). Then, the minimum value $v\left(p_t\right)$ in equation (5.2.10) is

$$v\left(p_t\right) = \begin{cases} p_t & \text{for } 0 \le p_t < p^{**} \\ p^{**} \equiv c + \int_0^{\bar{p}} v(p)dF(p) & \text{for } p_t \ge p^{**}. \end{cases}$$

Using the above display equation, (5.2.10) can be reformulated as

$$v\left(p_t\right) = \min\left\{p_t, c + \int_0^{p^{**}} v(p)dF(p) + \int_{p^{**}}^{\bar{p}} v(p)dF(p)\right\}$$
$$= \min\left\{p_t, c + \int_0^{p^{**}} pdF(p) + p^{**}\int_{p^{**}}^{\bar{p}} dF(p)\right\}. \qquad (5.2.11)$$

Furthermore, the two terms inside the minimum operator in equation (5.2.11) are equal when $p_t = p^{**}$. In other words, p^{**} is the solution for the implicit equation

$$p^{**} = c + \int_0^{p^{**}} pdF(p) + p^{**}\int_{p^{**}}^{\bar{p}} dF(p),$$

which is identical to equation (5.2.9). Hence, solution p^{**} for this equation is also identical to p^*. Because the problem structure and the solution are identical, we can reformulate the problem in equation (5.2.10) in terms of p_t as follows:

$$\min\left\{\int_0^{p_t} \left(p_t - p\right) dF(p), c\right\}. \qquad (5.2.12)$$

7. Here, $v\left(p_t\right) = \sum_{\tau=t}^{\infty} y_\tau$ where $y_\tau = c$ if the consumer chooses to search one more time in period τ, and $y_\tau = p_\tau$ if the consumer chooses to buy at price p_τ and then $y_{\tau+s} = 0$ for all $s > 0$. Hence, $v\left(p_t\right)$ is positive.

Equating the two terms inside the min operator gives the same equation that characterizes reservation price p^{**}. Now notice that the equation characterizing the reservation price is identical to equation (5.2.7). Therefore, so long as c and $F(p)$ are the same, reservation price p^{**} for this problem must be identical to the problem with recall.

5.2.1.3 SEQUENTIAL SEARCH WITH HETEROGENEOUS EX-ANTE PRICE DISTRIBUTIONS

In this subsection, we relax the homogeneity assumptions AS(4) and AS(SEQ2), keeping assumptions AS(1), AS(2), AS(3), AS(5), AS(SEQ1), and AS(SEQ3) intact. The relaxed assumptions are as follows:

AS(4') Consumers know price distribution $F_j(p)$, which is exogenous and non-degenerate. Also, $F_j(p)$ may differ over store index j, and the set of stores $\mathcal{J}$ is finite.

AS(SEQ2') Consumers' constant marginal cost of searching one more price is $c_j(>0)$. Here, c_j may differ over the store index j $(\in \mathcal{J})$.

The price distribution and the marginal cost of search are alternative specific. Because alternatives are heterogeneous, consumers' sequential decision problem entails an extra component: which alternative to search first. Weitzman (1979) proved the optimal decision rule in this setup follows three simple criteria using the reservation prices: ordering, stopping, and choice rule.

Before presenting these criteria, recall how the reservation-price structure was determined in the homogeneous case in equation (5.2.7). In this heterogeneous alternative case, equation (5.2.7) is converted to

$$\min\left\{\int_0^{p_B}(p_B - p)\, dF_j(p), c_j\right\}, \tag{5.2.13}$$

where p_B is the lowest price in hand. Notice reservation price p_j^* itself, which is determined implicitly by equating the two terms in equation (5.2.13), is alternative specific. Here, p_j^* can be thought of as a function of $\left(F_j(\cdot), c_j\right)$, and it is not affected by which alternative is searched first. We present Weitzman's optimal decision rule next, which corresponds to the ordering, stopping, and choice rule, respectively:

WS(1) Calculate the reservation price p_j^* for $j = 1, \ldots, J$. Without losing generality, order $\mathcal{J}$ such that $p_1^* < p_2^* < \cdots < p_J^*$. Search from alternative 1 to J sequentially in increasing order.

Table 5.1. An example of recall when alternatives are ex-ante heterogeneous

Order of Draw	0	1	2	3	4
Reservation price	—	10	20	30	40
Actual draw	—	25	28	—	—
Current best draw	∞	25	25	—	—

WS(2) Stop at j if the actual price draw $p_j < p^*_{j+1}$; that is, stop if the actual price draw is lower than all the reservation prices of the unsearched alternatives.

WS(3) Collect the alternative with the lowest price among those searched.

We briefly discussed in section 5.2.1.1 that consumers' higher standards for the ex ante price distributions will boil down to the form of a lower reservation price in the sequential search models with homogeneous ex ante price distributions. When the ex ante price distribution is heterogeneous over alternatives, ordering rule WS(1) states that consumers draw prices first from the alternatives where "better outcomes are expected." The rule seems intuitive, and the proof is rather technical, so we do not go over it here.

Allowing or not allowing perfect recall is no longer innocuous. That is, consumers may return to a foregone alternative to collect p_s for $s < t$. To see why, consider the example in table 5.1, with four alternatives. The consumer stops at $t = 2$, returns to the first alternative, and collects 25. The search ceases at $t = 2$ even if the current best draw is not smaller than alternative 2's reservation price. The reason is that when the consumer proceeds to $t = 3$, the best draw before drawing the price of store 3 is already smaller than 30. There is no reason for the consumer to wait for another period to collect 25, which is the current best draw.[8] Finally, we note that Salop (1973) shows a similar implication to Weitzman (1979)—namely, that the reservation price increases over the order of the draw, even when recall is not allowed.

5.2.2 *Simultaneous Search*

5.2.2.1 SIMULTANEOUS SEARCH WITH HOMOGENEOUS EX-ANTE PRICE DISTRIBUTIONS

Simultaneous search, often referred to as "fixed-sample search" or "nonsequential search," was pioneered by Stigler (1961). We assume the following in addition to assumptions AS(1)–AS(5):

8. This is especially true if we introduce the time discounts to the model as in the original setup of Weitzman (1979).

AS(SIM1) Consumers choose and commit to the search set $\mathcal{S}\ (\subset \mathcal{J})$ ex ante before engaging in search.

AS(SIM2) The marginal cost of search c is constant and common across consumers.

Notice that choosing the search set $\mathcal{S}$ ex ante is equivalent to choosing $n := |\mathcal{S}|$, the size of the search set, when the price distribution is homogeneous.

Let $F(p)$ be the prior distribution that has a compact support $[0, \bar{p}]$ and a density $f(p)$.[9] Before engaging in search, consumers choose the size of price draws n and commits to it. Consumers choose n to minimize the expected minimum price plus the total cost of search. The marginal cost of search c is constant. Consumers solve

$$\begin{aligned} n^* &= \arg\min_n \left\{ \mathbb{E}\left[\min_{1\leq k\leq n} p_k \right] + cn \right\} \\ &= \arg\min_n \left\{ \int_0^{\bar{p}} np\left(1 - F(p)\right)^{n-1} f(p)dp + cn \right\}. \end{aligned} \tag{5.2.14}$$

Equation (5.2.14) follows from the fact that the density of the minimum-order statistics among n i.i.d. draws is given by $np\left(1 - F(p)\right)^{n-1} f(p)$.[10]

It is immediate that increasing n involves a trade-off: the expected minimum price decreases while the cost of search increases. To see the fact more clearly, let us convert the cost-minimization problem in equation (5.2.14) as the net benefit maximization problem by using a negative sign and replacing the minimum operator with the maximum operator as follows:

$$\begin{aligned} n^* &= \arg\max_n \left\{ -\mathbb{E}\left[\min_{1\leq k\leq n} p_k \right] - cn \right\} \\ &= \arg\max_n \left\{ \mathbb{E}\left[-\min_{1\leq k\leq n} p_k \right] - cn \right\} \end{aligned}$$

9. Extension of the argument to domain $[0, \infty)$ is straightforward.

10. Because

$$\begin{aligned} \Pr\left(p_1 > p, p_2 > p, \ldots, p_n > p\right) &= \prod_{k=1}^{n} \Pr\left(p_k > p\right) \\ &= \left(1 - F(p)\right)^n, \end{aligned}$$

the cumulative distribution function of the minimum price is $1 - \left(1 - F(p)\right)^n$, with density $n\left(1 - F(p)\right)^{n-1} f(p)$. Similarly, the cumulative distribution function of the maximum price is simply $\left(F(p)\right)^n$, with density $n\left(F(p)\right)^{n-1} f(p)$.

$$= \arg\max_{n} \left\{ \mathbb{E}\left[\max_{1 \le k \le n} \{-p_k\} \right] - cn \right\}$$

$$= \arg\max_{n} \left\{ \mathbb{E}\left[\max_{1 \le k \le n} u_k \right] - cn \right\}, \tag{5.2.15}$$

where we use the utility specification $u_k = w - p_k$ with the location adjustment w in equation (5.2.15), which will not change the solution of the original problem. Denote M_n by the benefit of drawing n prices:

$$\begin{aligned} M_n &:= -\mathbb{E}\left[\min_{1 \le k \le n} p_k \right] \\ &= -\int_0^{\bar{p}} np\left(1 - F(p)\right)^{n-1} f(p)dp \\ &= -\int_0^{\bar{p}} \left(1 - F(p)\right)^n dp.^{11} \end{aligned} \tag{5.2.16}$$

Then, the marginal benefit of drawing one more price is

$$M_{n+1} - M_n = \int_0^{\bar{p}} \left(1 - F(p)\right)^n F(p)dp. \tag{5.2.17}$$

The right-hand side of equation (5.2.17) is monotonically decreasing, converging to zero as $n \to \infty$.

The search cost, on the other hand, is linearly increasing over n.[12] Figure 5.2.3 depicts how the optimal search is determined. The left panel illustrates the original

11. The following lemma is used:

Lemma 5.2.1. Let $G_{(n)}(\cdot)$ be a cumulative distribution function with a density $g_{(n)}(\cdot)$ that has a support $[0, \bar{p}]$. Then,

$$\int_0^{\bar{p}} pg_{(n)}(p)dp = \int_0^{\bar{p}} \left(1 - G_{(n)}(p)\right) dp.$$

Proof. It is straightforward from integration by parts:

$$\int uv' = uv - \int u'v,$$

and letting $u = 1 - G_{(n)}(p)$ and $v = p$. □

12. Search cost does not need to be linear over n; it only has to be strictly increasing and convex over n to draw the same implications.

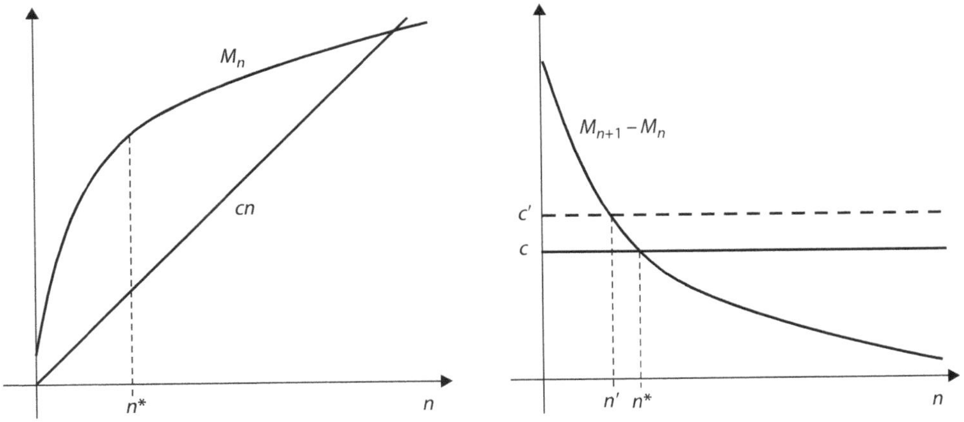

FIGURE 5.2.3. Determination of the optimal search size in Stigler's model

problem in equation (5.2.14),[13] and the right panel shows the fact that the optimal search size n^* is determined at the level at which the marginal benefit of search equals the marginal cost of search. When the marginal cost of search c increases, the optimal search size n^* decreases.

5.2.2.2 SIMULTANEOUS SEARCH WITH HETEROGENEOUS EX-ANTE PRICE DISTRIBUTIONS

Vishwanath (1992) and Chade and Smith (2005, 2006) study generalized versions of the simultaneous search problem, where each store may have a different ex ante distribution of prices. That is, assumptions AS(1), AS(2), AS(3), AS(5), and AS(SIM) remain intact, but assumption AS(4) is changed as follows:

AS(4') Consumers know the price distribution $F_j(p)$, which is exogenous and nondegenerate. $F_j(p)$ may differ over store index j, and the set of stores $\mathcal{J}$ is finite.

Consumers choose the set to search $\mathcal{S}$ $(\subset \mathcal{J})$ ex ante, draw the prices of all the alternatives in $\mathcal{S}$, and then choose the best draw from $\mathcal{S}$. The cost function of search $c(\cdot)$ is assumed to depend only on the cardinality of $\mathcal{S}$. Because $F_j(p)$ differs by j, the problem of choosing $\mathcal{S}$ now entails two distinct factors: choosing the composition and size of $\mathcal{S}$. Chade and Smith (2005, 2006) consider both (1) choosing $n^* \equiv |\mathcal{S}|$ first and then the composition of $\mathcal{S}$, and (2) choosing $|\mathcal{S}|$ and

13. We assume that the benefit of searching for at least one alternative is high enough in drawing the left panel (i.e., $w \gg 0$ in the utility specification $u_j = w - p_j$). The assumption can be understood as a positive location adjusted to M_n, which will not change the solution of the original problem so long as w is sufficiently large. This assumption $w \gg 0$ is often replaced by the assumption that the first search is free.

the composition of $\mathcal{S}$ simultaneously. Options (1) and (2) can be achieved simply by adjusting the cost function $c(|\mathcal{S}|)$. In case (1),

$$c(|\mathcal{S}|) = \begin{cases} 0 & \text{if } |\mathcal{S}| \leq n^* \\ \infty & \text{otherwise} \end{cases},$$

and in case (2),

$$c(|\mathcal{S}|) = c\,|\mathcal{S}|.$$

Now let us formalize the problem. Consumers solve

$$\begin{aligned} \mathcal{S}^* &= \arg\min_{\mathcal{S} \subset \mathcal{J}} \mathbb{E}\left[\min_{k \in \mathcal{S}} \{p_k\} + c(|\mathcal{S}|)\right] \\ &= \arg\min_{\mathcal{S} \subset \mathcal{J}} \left\{\mathbb{E}\left[\min_{k \in \mathcal{S}} \{p_k\}\right] + c(|\mathcal{S}|)\right\} \end{aligned} \qquad (5.2.18)$$

to find the optimal search set $\mathcal{S}^*$. Consumers' search problem to find $\mathcal{S}^*$ entails two intertwined choice problems: the size and the composition of $\mathcal{S}^*$. Simple formulas such as in equation (5.2.14) do not exist because now all the price distributions are indexed by j. In principle, consumers have to consider every possible subset of $\mathcal{J}$ and then compare each possible subset to find the optimal set $\mathcal{S}^*$. The cardinality of the set to be compared is $2^{|\mathcal{J}|}$. This brute-force comparison is inefficient, and the computing time explodes because the number of comparisons increases exponentially over $|\mathcal{J}|$.

Chade and Smith (2005, 2006) provide a simple recursive algorithm with a polynomial computing time and the sufficient conditions for the algorithm to find the optimal set $\mathcal{S}^*$. We first describe the algorithm, which is called the Marginal Improvement algorithm (MIA). Let $\mathcal{S}_t$ denote the optimal search set at stage t. At stage t do the following:[14]

MIA(1) Choose l_{t+1} such that it improves the expected price the most; that is,

$$l_{t+1} = \arg\min_{l \in (\mathcal{J} \setminus \mathcal{S}_t)} \mathbb{E}\left[\min_{k \in (l \cup \mathcal{S}_t)} \{p_k\}\right].$$

MIA(2) Stop if the marginal benefit is less than the marginal cost; that is, if

14. We assume that $c(1)$ is low enough, or u in $u_k := w - p_k$ is high enough, to ensure that consumers engage in searching.

$$\mathbb{E}\left[\min_{k\in\mathcal{S}_t}\{p_k\}\right]-\mathbb{E}\left[\min_{k\in(l_{t+1}\cup\mathcal{S}_t)}\{p_k\}\right]<c\,(t+1)-c\,(t),$$

Compare $\mathbb{E}\left[\min_{k\in\mathcal{S}_t}\{p_k\}+c\,(|\mathcal{S}_t|)\right]$ with $\mathbb{E}\left[\min_{k\in\mathcal{S}_{t+1}}\{p_k\}+c\,(|\mathcal{S}_{t+1}|)\right]$, and take $\mathcal{S}^*$ as the set that returns a smaller value.[15]

MIA(3) Otherwise, take $\mathcal{S}_{t+1}:=\mathcal{S}_t\cup l_{t+1}$ and go back to MIA(1).

The algorithm resembles Weitzman (1979)'s rules in sequential search, particularly because it sorts the alternative set $\mathcal{J}$ ex ante. The crucial difference is, however, the ordering criteria: Weitzman's rule sorts the alternatives by the reservation price, whereas the MIA sorts the alternatives by the order of better improving the expected minimum price. Now we state some sufficient conditions for the MIA to be optimal.

Theorem 5.2.1. *(Sufficient Conditions for the Optimality of the MIA)* MIA(1)–MIA(3) find the search set $\mathcal{S}^*$ that solves equation (5.2.18) if either of the following is met:

(i) *(First-Order or Quasi-Second-Order Stochastic Dominance)* $\mathcal{J}$ can be ordered in a way that for each $j=1,\ldots,J-1$, $\forall r\in[0,\bar{p}]$ where $[0,\bar{p}]$ contains the union of the supports of $\{F_j(\cdot)\}$,

$$\int_0^r F_{j+1}(p)dp\leq\int_0^r F_j(p)dp \tag{5.2.19}$$

with strict inequality at $r=0$.

(ii) (Binary Success) For each $j\in\mathcal{J}$, the cumulative distribution function $F_j(p)$ takes the following form:

$$F_j(p)=\begin{cases}0 & \text{if } p<p_j^0\\ \alpha & \text{if } p_j^0\leq p<\bar{p}\\ 1 & \text{if } p>\bar{p}\end{cases}$$

with $0<\alpha<1$ and $p_j^0\in(0,\bar{p})$.

Notice that first-order stochastic dominance over j is sufficient for equation (5.2.19), in which case part (1) states that MIA(1)–MIA(3) finds the optimal search set $\mathcal{S}^*$. Part (2) states that if the price draw has a gamble structure such that for some positive probability, the draw is the highest possible price (failure),[16] MIA(1)–MIA(3) find the optimal search set $\mathcal{S}^*$.

15. This comparison is necessary because t can take only integer values.

16. This is the case when $\alpha<1$, where the failure probability is $1-\alpha$.

MIA(1)–MIA(3) reduce the order of the number of comparisons from $2^{|\mathcal{J}|}$ to $(|\mathcal{J}| - 1) + \ldots + 1$, by introducing the ex ante optimal ordering of $\mathcal{J}$. To see why, notice that MIA(1) compares $\mathbb{E}\left[\min_{k \in \mathcal{J}} \{p_k\}\right]$ for each k at $t = 1$, and therefore, the maximum number of comparisons is $(|\mathcal{J}| - 1)$. The same logic applies downward for $t = 2, \ldots, J$. An important implication of theorem 5.2.1 is that when first-order or quasi-second-order stochastic dominance of the underlying price distribution can be assumed, one can simplify the search algorithm substantially. We study some examples of empirical applications in section 5.4. As a last remark, similar to the homogeneous price-distribution case from Stigler (1961), it is immediate from MIA(2) that an upward shift/pivot of the cost function $c(\cdot)$ will decrease the size of $\mathcal{S}^*$.

5.3 Price Dispersion in the Market Equilibrium and Search Cost Identification with Price Data

5.3.1 Critiques of Classical Consumer Search Models as Explanations of the Observed Price Dispersion

We studied the sequential and simultaneous search models in sections 5.2.1 and 5.2.2, respectively. Stigler (1961)'s original motivation for developing the search model was to explain the observed, persistent price dispersion of even an identical product. Roughly speaking, by introducing the search friction, the simple search models we have studied in this chapter might successfully generate an elastic, downward-sloping, nondegenerate market demand function from a collection of homogeneous, degenerate demand functions.[17] One of the common core assumptions imposed in the search models was that the price distribution $F(\cdot)$ is exogenously given to be a nondegenerate, well-behaving distribution.[18] The supplier-side problem from which $F(\cdot)$ is generated, however, is left unresolved: an observed price dispersion should not exist if it is optimal for the suppliers to sell at the identical price. It turns out that it is indeed optimal for the suppliers to set a single price in the simple search models we studied here, which leads to a "paradox." Next, we provide a brief overview of the arguments for why such a paradox arises, and discuss what adjustments to the models can possibly resolve it.

17. A prominent example of a homogeneous, degenerate demand function is the unit-inelastic demand curve illustrated in figure 5.2.1.

18. Weitzman (1979) and Chade and Smith (2005, 2006), which allow $F(\cdot)$ to be heterogeneous across suppliers, do not say much about how the heterogeneous price distribution can be sustained as an equilibrium behavior.

This paradox was raised by Diamond (1971) and Rothschild (1973). They argue that firms' optimal pricing has no price dispersion if consumers are searching, and therefore the assumption that $F(\cdot)$ is a nondegenerate distribution leads to a contradiction in the equilibrium. We describe the essential logic of their critiques in a simplified static setup where firms engage in price competition to maximize their own profits. Let $q(p_j)$ and $c(p_j)$ be the demand and cost functions that firm j faces, respectively, and let

$$\pi(p_j) := p_j q(p_j) - c(p_j)$$

be the profit function of firm j. Then, suppose that a single joint profit-maximizing price level $\bar{p} > 0$ exists such that for any $p_j \neq \bar{p}$, $\pi(p_j) < \pi(\bar{p})$.

The argument for consumers engaging in simultaneous search is as follows: Consumers have the same c and the same $F(\cdot)$, and therefore the same optimal search size n^*. Let p_j be the price that firm j charges. A consumer will purchase from the firm if j is in the searched set $\mathcal{S}$[19] and

$$p_j \leq \min_{k \in \mathcal{S}} \{p_k\}.$$

Let I be the measure of consumers in the market. The ex ante (expected) demand curve that a firm faces is

$$\begin{aligned} q(p_j) &= I \Pr\left(\{j \in \mathcal{S}\} \cap \left\{p_j \leq \min_{k \in \mathcal{S}} \{p_k\}\right\}\right) \\ &= I \Pr(j \in \mathcal{S}) \Pr\left(p_j \leq \min_{k \in \mathcal{S}} \{p_k\} \,\middle|\, j \in \mathcal{S}\right) \\ &= I \frac{n^*}{|\mathcal{J}|} \left(1 - F(p_j)\right)^{n^*-1}.^{20} \end{aligned} \tag{5.3.1}$$

19. Recall that $|\mathcal{S}| = n^*$.

20. The derivation of equation (5.3.1) is as follows:

$$\begin{aligned} \Pr\left(p_j \leq \min_{k \in \mathcal{S}} \{p_k\} \,\middle|\, j \in \mathcal{S}\right) &= \Pr\left(\min_{k \in \{\mathcal{S} \setminus j\}} \{p_k\} > p_j \,\middle|\, j \in \mathcal{S}\right) \\ &= \prod_{k \in (\mathcal{S} \setminus j)} \Pr(p_k > p_j) \qquad (5.3.2) \\ &= \prod_{k \in (\mathcal{S} \setminus j)} \left(1 - \Pr(p_k \leq p_j)\right) \\ &= \left(1 - F(p_j)\right)^{n^*-1}. \end{aligned}$$

Note that we invoked the assumption of independent draws in equation (5.3.2).

Knowing this demand curve, firms will charge the price that maximizes expected profit. Because all the firms will charge the same price, we should see no persistent equilibrium price dispersion.[21]

An argument for consumers engaging in sequential search is as follows: Because every consumer has the same cost of marginal search c, the associated reservation price p^* is identical across consumers. Note that p^* is strictly between 0 and $\bar{p}$. Consider any firm that charges $p < p^*$. The firm will have an incentive to charge $p+\epsilon$, where $0 < \epsilon < c$. Consumers will still accept $p+\epsilon$ because the search cost c is higher than ϵ. The same logic yields that $p+\epsilon$, $p+2\epsilon$, $p+3\epsilon$, $p+4\epsilon$, and so on cannot be the equilibrium price. Now that all the firms will charge p^*, consumers' new reservation price should shift up to somewhere between p^* and $\bar{p}$. On the other hand, no firm will have an incentive to charge any price higher than $\bar{p}$. Repeating this logic, it turns out that the only possible price at the equilibrium is $\bar{p}$, which is the joint profit-maximizing price. The existence of the homogeneous search cost c in the sequential search actually induces a stable collusion.

The key factor causing this "paradox" is the homogeneity of the suppliers. To resolve this paradox to allow an equilibrium price dispersion within the consumer search context, the following is usually necessary: (1) a downward-sloping market demand curve with search friction and (2) an upward-sloping supply curve. Next, we illustrate a few different ways that the literature uses to derive the equilibrium price dispersion.

5.3.2 Equilibrium Price-Dispersion Models and Search-Cost Distribution Identification Using Market-Level Price Data

In this subsection, we study models that explain the sustained price dispersion in a market equilibrium. Price dispersion can be an equilibrium outcome if different firms charge different prices and firms have no incentive to change the current pricing strategy. As mentioned previously, firm-side heterogeneity is required for a price dispersion to be sustained as a market equilibrium. The models studied in this section show the existence of a price-dispersion equilibrium, along with one or multiple single-price equilibria. Specific assumptions that lead to a price-dispersion equilibrium differ by individual model.

Two remarks about equilibrium price-dispersion models that we discuss next are noteworthy. The first is about the equilibrium selection. The theory models that we study prove the existence of a price-dispersion equilibrium under different

21. Furthermore, the price that the firms charge will not equal the Bertrand price in general, because an ϵ deviation from the optimal price does not make the firm lose all of its demand. Exactly what price is optimal depends on the shape of $F(\cdot)$. However, investigating the property of $F(\cdot)$ is not informative in this context, because in equilibrium, the assumption that $F(\cdot)$ is a nondegenerate distribution is contradictory anyway.

setups, but they provide little information about when and how the price-dispersion equilibrium is realized. The second is about dynamics and stationarity. Consumer search models, especially sequential search models, entail dynamics by their very nature. In the context of dynamics, the equilibrium concepts employed throughout this subsection assume stationarity, where the same (downward-sloping) demand and (upward-sloping) supply functions replicate over time.

Throughout this subsection, we denote $F_p(\cdot)$ as the distribution of prices charged by firms, $F_r(\cdot)$ as the distribution of firms' marginal cost or production, $G_c(\cdot)$ as the distribution of consumers' marginal cost of search, and $G_{p^*}(\cdot)$ as the distribution of consumers' reservation price. Here, $f_p(\cdot)$, $f_r(\cdot)$, $g_c(\cdot)$ and $g_{p^*}(\cdot)$ denote their densities. All the models studied in this subsection assume the heterogeneity of consumers' search costs, which ensures that $G_c(\cdot)$ is a nondegenerate distribution. The world from which the data are generated is assumed to be in a stationary price-dispersion equilibrium; distributions $F_p(\cdot)$, $F_r(\cdot)$, $G_c(\cdot)$, and $G_{p^*}(\cdot)$ represent the stationary equilibrium distributions of $(p, r, c,$ and $p^*)$, respectively.

5.3.2.1 SEQUENTIAL SEARCH OF CONSUMERS, DOWNWARD-SLOPING INDIVIDUAL DEMAND, HETEROGENEOUS MARGINAL COST OF FIRMS

Consider the sequential search framework. Reinganum (1979) relaxes the unit inelastic demand assumption of consumers and cost-function homogeneity of suppliers. For consumers, Reinganum introduces a downward-sloping individual demand curve when the price is smaller than the reservation price. To this end, AS(1) and AS(2) are replaced with the following:

AS(R1) Each consumer has a downward-sloping individual demand function given by $q(p)$, where $q(p)$ has the constant own-price elasticity $\varepsilon < -1$.

AS(R2) A continuum of consumers exists with the identical demand function. The measure of consumers in the market is I.

Consumers engage in sequential search. When $p_j < p^*$, the demand function for firm j when it is searched is given by

$$q\left(p_j\right) = \begin{cases} q\left(p_j\right) & \text{if } p_j \leq p^* \\ 0 & \text{if } p_j > p^* \end{cases}.$$

Because firms are ex ante homogeneous, the share of consumers who sample each firm is identical for each firm.[22] The equilibrium share of consumers that each firm being sampled is denoted as λ. Accordingly, firms' profits are given by

22. This is because the $F_p(\cdot)$ that a firm faces is homogeneous across firms.

$$\pi\left(p_j; r_j\right) = \begin{cases} \lambda I\left(p_j - r_j\right) q\left(p_j\right) & \text{if } p_j \leq p^* \\ 0 & \text{if } p_j > p^* \end{cases}.$$

Firms' marginal costs are exogenously given, distributed over $[\underline{r}, \bar{r}]$, with cumulative distribution function $F_r(\cdot)$. Each firm maximizes the profit $\pi\left(p_j; r_j\right)$ taking other firms' strategies as given.

Reinganum (1979) shows that the following $F_p(\cdot)$ can be sustained as the price-dispersed equilibrium price distribution:

$$F_p(r) = \begin{cases} F_r\left(p\frac{1+\varepsilon}{\varepsilon}\right) & \text{for } p < p^* \\ 1 & \text{for } p = p^*. \end{cases}$$

The equilibrium range of price is $\left[\underline{r}\left(\frac{\varepsilon}{1+\varepsilon}\right), p^*\right]$. Notice that $F_p(p)$ has a mass point at $p = p^*$, which is problematic for an empirical application. Models that we review here suggest equilibria with nondegenerate price distributions over their supports, and therefore they have been employed as bases of recent empirical works.

5.3.2.2 SIMULTANEOUS SEARCH WITH RESERVATION PRICE AND HOMOGENEOUS MARGINAL COST OF FIRMS

Burdett and Judd (1983) establish the existence of a price-dispersion equilibrium when homogeneous consumers engage in simultaneous search and consumers have common reservation price p^*. If all the revealed prices are higher than p^*, consumers search again. Building upon Burdett and Judd's price-dispersion equilibrium, Hong and Shum (2006)[23] develop a nonparametric identification result of consumers' search-cost distribution from the observed price-distribution data. Assumptions AS(1)–AS(5) remain intact, but assumptions AS(SIM1)–AS(SIM2) are modified as follows:

AS(HS1) Consumers choose and commit to the search set $\mathcal{S}_n\ (\subset \mathcal{J})$ ex ante before engaging in search. However, if all the searched prices are higher than the reservation price, consumers search again from the beginning.

AS(HS2) Consumers' marginal cost of search c_n[24] may differ across consumers.

23. This was in the first part of the paper.

24. The reason why c is indexed by search size n, not simply i, becomes clear next. This setup in which search costs are heterogeneous across consumers is an extension made by Hong and Shum (2006). Burdett and Judd's original setup is such that consumers' search cost is homogeneous, and the paper shows that a price-dispersion equilibrium, where consumers search up to two prices, can exist.

Identification of Search-Cost Distribution from Observed Price Dispersion

An econometrician observes $\bar{k}$ distinct prices $\{p_k\}_{k=1}^{\bar{k}}$ [25] and its equilibrium distribution $\{F_p(p_k)\}_{k=1}^{\bar{k}}$. The goal of search-cost distribution identification is to find mapping $\Phi : \left(\{p_k, F_p(p_k)\}_{k=1}^{\bar{k}}\right) \to \left(\{c_n, G_c(c_n)\}_{n=1}^{\bar{n}}\right)$, a mapping from the observed equilibrium price dispersion to the search-cost distribution. As an identification condition, we assume that $\bar{n} \leq \bar{k} - 1$. In practice, during the estimation, $\bar{n}$ is treated as a tuning parameter set a priori by an econometrician because it is assumed that the search size is not directly observed.

Each consumer, whose optimal search size is n, has consumer-specific heterogeneous search cost c_n,[26] whereas the ex ante price distribution $F_p(\cdot)$ is common across consumers. Recall equations (5.2.16) and (5.2.17), which specify the (marginal) benefit of search:

$$\begin{aligned} M_n &= -\mathbb{E}\left[\min_{1\leq l\leq n}\{p_l\}\right] \\ &= -\int_0^{\bar{p}} \left(1 - F_p(p)\right)^n dp \qquad (5.3.3) \\ M_{n+1} - M_n &= \int_0^{\bar{p}} \left(1 - F_p(p)\right)^n F_p(p) dp \\ &=: \Delta_n. \end{aligned}$$

We showed that Δ_n is monotonically decreasing over n in section 5.2.1. Furthermore, the optimality condition for the consumers states that

$$\Delta_n = c_n.$$

That is, the indifferent consumers' marginal cost of search equals the marginal benefit. Consumers with $c_i > \Delta_1$ will draw only one price, $\Delta_2 \leq c_i < \Delta_1$ will draw two prices, and so on.[27] Constructing the mapping Φ proceeds in three stages:

25. Without loss of generality, $\{p_k\}_{k=1}^{\bar{k}}$ is indexed in ascending order, $p_1 < p_2 < \ldots < p_{\bar{k}}$. If a tied price is observed, one can give ϵ-perturbation on either of the observations.

26. The setup of heterogeneous search costs, across consumers is an extension made by Hong and Shum (2006). The original setup of Burdett and Judd's original setup is such that consumers' search cost is homogeneous, and they showed that a price-dispersion equilibrium, where consumers search up to two prices, can exist.

27. This is under the running assumption that either the first search is free or $u_j = w - p_j$ with $w \gg 0$.

Stage 1. The first stage is to construct the mapping from the proportion of consumers who searched for n prices $\{\phi_n\}_{n=1}^{\bar{n}}$ to the consumers' search-cost distribution $\{G_c(\Delta_n)\}_{n=1}^{\bar{n}}$. By construction, we have a set of equations as follows:

$$
\begin{aligned}
\phi_1 &= \Pr(c_i > \Delta_1) = 1 - G_c(\Delta_1) \\
\phi_2 &= \Pr(\Delta_2 \leq c_i < \Delta_1) = G_c(\Delta_1) - G_c(\Delta_2) \\
&\vdots \\
\phi_{\bar{n}-1} &= \Pr(\Delta_{\bar{n}-1} \leq c_i < \Delta_{\bar{n}-2}) = G_c(\Delta_{\bar{n}-2}) - G_c(\Delta_{\bar{n}-1}) \\
\phi_{\bar{n}} &= \Pr(\Delta_{\bar{n}} \leq c_i < \Delta_{\bar{n}-1}) = G_c(\Delta_{\bar{n}-1}) - G_c(\Delta_{\bar{n}}).
\end{aligned} \tag{5.3.4}
$$

Here, ϕ_n is an intermediate parameter that is not directly observable to the econometrician in this setup. An additional step is required to link $\{\phi_n\}_{n=1}^{\bar{n}}$ with $\left\{p_k, F_p(p_k)\right\}_{k=1}^{\bar{k}}$.

Stage 2. The second stage is to construct the mapping from $\left\{p_k, F(p_k)\right\}_{k=1}^{\bar{k}}$ to $\{\phi_n\}_{n=1}^{\bar{n}}$. To that end, Hong and Shum (2006) consider the equilibrium pricing equation of Burdett and Judd (1983). Let r be the firms' common marginal cost. Assume that the market is in the price-dispersion equilibrium. Burdett and Judd show that the following pricing equation should hold in the equilibrium:

$$
\begin{aligned}
\left(p_{\bar{k}} - r\right)\phi_1 &= \left(p_k - r\right)\left[\sum_{n=1}^{\bar{n}} \phi_n n \left(1 - F_p(p_k)\right)^{n-1}\right] \qquad \text{for } k = 1, \ldots, \bar{k} - 1 \\
\phi_{\bar{n}} &= 1 - \sum_{n=1}^{\bar{n}-1} \phi_n,
\end{aligned} \tag{5.3.5}
$$

where $0 < \phi_1 < 1$ and $p^* > r$. Because we assumed $\bar{n} \leq \bar{k} - 1$, we have $\bar{k}$ equations for $\bar{n}$ unknowns, which allows us to solve for $\left\{r, \{\phi_n\}_{n=1}^{\bar{n}-1}\right\}$. Combining stages 1 and 2, we have a mapping from $\left\{p_k, F_p(p_k)\right\}_{k=1}^{\bar{k}}$ to $\{G(\Delta_n)\}_{n=1}^{\bar{n}}$ via $\left\{r, \{\phi_n\}_{n=1}^{\bar{n}-1}\right\}$. The only remaining part that is missing is $\{\Delta_n\}_{n=1}^{\bar{n}}$.

Stage 3. The last stage is to construct $\{c_n\}_{n=1}^{\bar{n}} = \{\Delta_n\}_{n=1}^{\bar{n}}$ from the right-hand side of equation (5.3.3) and their differences over n. Because the prices and their distribution $F_p(\cdot)$ are observed, the calculation of M_n, the expected minimum price by drawing n prices, is straightforward, done by inverting the distribution function: $\Delta_n = F_p^{-1}(G_c(\Delta_n))$. Calculating sequentially from $n=1$ to $\bar{n}$, we have $\{\Delta_n\}_{n=1}^{\bar{n}}$, and thus $\{c_n\}_{n=1}^{\bar{n}}$.

Estimation of Search-Cost Distribution Let $\hat{F}_p(p) := \frac{1}{\bar{k}} \sum_{k=1}^{\bar{k}} \mathbf{1}(p_k \leq p)$ be the empirical distribution function of the price. We treat $\hat{F}_p(p)$ as a discrete distribution with support $\{p_k\}_{k=1}^{\bar{k}}$. The data consist of $\{p_k, \hat{F}_p(p_k)\}_{k=1}^{\bar{k}}$, where $F_p(p_1) = 0$ and $F_p(p_{\bar{k}}) = 1$. The mapping that was just constructed, $\Phi : \left(\{p_k, F_p(p_k)\}_{k=1}^{\bar{k}}\right) \to \left(\{c_n, G_c(c_n)\}_{n=1}^{\bar{n}}\right)$, has $\bar{k}$ observations[28] for $\bar{n}+1$ unknowns, where $\bar{k} \geq \bar{n}+1$ by construction. The estimation procedure proceeds backward from stage 3 to 1.[29]

For stage 3, replacing $F_p(p)$ with its empirical distribution $\hat{F}_p(p_k)$ and plugging the result back in to equation (5.3.3) yields, for $n = 1, 2, \ldots, \bar{n}$,

$$\hat{\Delta}_n = \sum_{j=1}^{\bar{k}} \left\{ 1 - \frac{1}{\bar{k}} \sum_{k=1}^{\bar{k}} \mathbf{1}(p_k \leq p_j) \right\}^n \left\{ \frac{1}{\bar{k}} \sum_{k=1}^{\bar{k}} \mathbf{1}(p_k \leq p_j) \right\}$$
$$=: \hat{c}_n.$$

We estimate $\left(\hat{r}, \hat{\phi}_1, \ldots, \hat{\phi}_{\bar{n}}\right)$, which corresponds to Stage 2. Abbreviate $\hat{\boldsymbol{\theta}} := \left(\hat{r}, \hat{\phi}_1, \ldots, \hat{\phi}_{\bar{n}}\right)$ and write the empirical counterpart of equation (5.3.5) as

$$(p_{\bar{k}} - r)\hat{\phi}_1 = (p_k - r)\left[\sum_{n=1}^{\bar{n}} \hat{\phi}_n n \left(1 - \left[\frac{1}{\bar{k}} \sum_{k=1}^{\bar{k}} \mathbf{1}(p_k \leq p_j) \right] \right)^{n-1} \right]$$
$$\text{for } k = 1, \ldots, \bar{k}-1 \qquad (5.3.6)$$

$$\hat{\phi}_{\bar{n}} = 1 - \sum_{n=1}^{\bar{n}-1} \hat{\phi}_n. \qquad (5.3.7)$$

By using the fact that $F_p(p_1) = \hat{F}_p(p_1) = 0$, evaluate equation (5.3.6) at p_1 to obtain

28. There is one observation for each equation.

29. For the asymptotics, we assume that $\bar{k}$ grows to infinity while $\bar{n}$ is fixed.

$$r = \frac{p_1\left(\sum_{n=1}^{\bar{n}} \hat{\phi}_n n\right) - p_{\bar{k}}\hat{\phi}_1}{\left(\sum_{n=1}^{\bar{n}} \hat{\phi}_n n\right) - \hat{\phi}_1}. \tag{5.3.8}$$

Plugging equation (5.3.8) back into each k of equation (5.3.6) eliminates firms' common marginal cost r. Then, we can use equations (5.3.6) and (5.3.7) as a moment condition to proceed with the GMM or the empirical likelihood. Hong and Shum (2006) use the empirical likelihood and provide the corresponding asymptotics.

The remaining step of estimation, which corresponds to stage 1, is to use the one-to-one mapping in equation (5.3.4) sequentially from top to bottom, which maps $\{\hat{\phi}_n\}_{n=1}^{\bar{n}}$ to $\{\hat{G}_c(\hat{c}_n)\}_{n=1}^{\bar{n}}$.

5.3.2.3 SEQUENTIAL SEARCH OF CONSUMERS AND HOMOGENEOUS MARGINAL COST OF FIRMS

Identification Argument of Consumers' Reservation-Price Distribution from Observed Price Dispersion Rob (1985) establishes a price-dispersion equilibrium by employing the Nash-Stackelberg equilibrium concept between a continuum of profit-maximizing firms with zero marginal cost[30] when consumers search sequentially. Hong and Shum (2006)[31] establish an argument to identify the search-cost distribution, building upon Rob's setup. Assumption AS(SEQ2) is modified as follows:

AS(RS2) Consumers' constant marginal cost of searching for one more price is $c_k\ (>0)$. Here, c_k follows a nondegenerate distribution $G_c(\cdot)$ that has density $g_c(\cdot)$.

Note that the only difference between this and section 5.2.1.1 is that we introduced the search-cost distribution $G_c(\cdot)$. All the results and implications from section 5.2.1.1 carry over. In particular, recall the indifference equation that determines consumers' reservation price:

$$c_k = \int_0^{p_k^*} \left(p_k^* - p\right) dF_p(p). \tag{5.3.9}$$

Note that the reservation price p_k^* is indexed by k because it is determined as an implicit function of c_k. We showed in section 5.2.1 that for each given $c_k > 0$, equation (5.3.9) has a unique solution, p_k^*. Furthermore, p_k^* is a strictly increasing

30. This can be easily extended to a positive, constant-marginal-cost case.

31. This was done in the second part of the paper.

function of c_k, provided that $F_p(\cdot)$ is well behaving. This construes a one-to-one mapping from consumers' reservation price to consumers' marginal cost of search, and therefore, the remaining task is to construct a mapping between the distribution of the observed prices $\{p_k\}_{k=1}^{\bar{k}}$ and consumers' reservation price $\{p_k^*\}_{k=1}^{\bar{k}}$.

Let $[p_1, p_{\bar{k}}]$ be the support of $F_p(\cdot)$, and let $\{p_k\}_{k=1}^{\bar{k}}$ be the observed price data.[32] It is immediate that $F_p(p_1) = 0$ and $F_p(p_{\bar{k}}) = 1$. Let r be the firms' common, constant marginal cost. In equilibrium, each participating firm in the market must not have any incentive to deviate to charge a different price. Rob's key equilibrium assumption is the nonnegative equal-profit condition over the support of the equilibrium price distribution $F_p(\cdot)$. That is, for any observed price $p_k\ (\neq p_{\bar{k}})$,

$$(p_{\bar{k}} - r)\, q(p_{\bar{k}}) = (p_k - r)\, q(p_k) \tag{5.3.10}$$

should hold, which gives us $\bar{k} - 1$ effective equations for $k = 1, \ldots, \bar{k} - 1$. Furthermore, using the fact that consumers will employ the reservation-price strategy in sequential search, the demand function $q(p_{\bar{k}})$ is defined such that

$$\begin{aligned} q(p) &= I \Pr(p^* > p) \\ &= I\left(1 - G_{p^*}(p)\right), \end{aligned} \tag{5.3.11}$$

where I is the measure of consumers. Plugging equation (5.3.10) back, equation (5.3.10) can be transformed into the form of consumers' reservation-price distribution $G_{p^*}(\cdot)$ as follows:

$$(p_{\bar{k}} - r)\left(1 - G_{p^*}(p_{\bar{k}})\right) = (p_k - r)\left(1 - G_{p^*}(p_k)\right). \tag{5.3.12}$$

Parametric Estimation of Search-Cost Distribution $\{G_{p^*}(p_k)\}_{k=1}^{\bar{k}}$, which is the distribution of the reservation price of the consumers, is an intermediate object that will be eliminated eventually. A nonparametric estimation as in section 5.3.2.2, however, is not feasible here because we have only $\bar{k} - 1$ equations for $\bar{k}$ objects.[33] Therefore, Hong and Shum (2006) proceed with parameterizing

32. In the corner case when c_k is too large, the reservation price is taken to be $\min\{p_k^*, p_{\bar{k}}\}$.

33. Even though we set $G_{p^*}(p_1) = 0$ so that we have $\bar{k} - 1$ effective equations for $\bar{k} - 1$ objects, it is still insufficient because the number of objects to be estimated grows at the same rate as the number of equations. For asymptotics, we need the number of equations to grow at a faster rate than the number of parameters to be estimated.

$G_c(\cdot)$ as a gamma distribution to derive the likelihood and construct a mapping between $G_c(\cdot)$ and $G_{p^*}(\cdot)$. Let $\boldsymbol{\theta}$ be the finite-dimensional parameter vector that dictates the behavior of distribution $G_c(\cdot;\boldsymbol{\theta})$. The goal is to write the likelihood of observing $\{p_k\}_{k=1}^{\bar{k}}$ in terms of $g_c(\cdot;\boldsymbol{\theta})$.

Determination of α We solve for $\alpha := 1 - G_{p^*}(p_{\bar{k}})$ first. As an initial condition, we impose $\Pr(p^* \leq p_1) = G_{p^*}(p_1) = 0$, implying that

$$\begin{aligned} 1 - G_{p^*}(p_{\bar{k}}) &= \frac{(p_1 - r)}{(p_{\bar{k}} - r)} \\ &= 1 - \Pr(p^* \leq p_{\bar{k}}) \\ &=: \alpha. \end{aligned} \tag{5.3.13}$$

Rearranging, we have

$$\alpha\,(p_{\bar{k}} - r) = p_1 - r. \tag{5.3.14}$$

Plugging equation (5.3.13) back into equation (5.3.12) and rearranging, we have

$$G_{p^*}(p_k) = 1 - \alpha\frac{(p_k - r)}{(p_{\bar{k}} - r)}. \tag{5.3.15}$$

Deriving the Expression of $F_p(\cdot;\boldsymbol{\theta})$ in Terms of $g_c(\cdot;\boldsymbol{\theta})$ Denoting $\tau_k := G_{p^*}(p_k)$ by the percentile of p_k, equation (5.3.12) becomes

$$(p_{\bar{k}} - r)\,\alpha = \left(G_{p^*}^{-1}(\tau_k) - r\right)(1 - \tau_k),$$

which yields

$$G_{p^*}^{-1}(\tau_k) = \alpha\frac{(p_{\bar{k}} - r)}{(1 - \tau_k)} + r \tag{5.3.16}$$

for $k = 1, \ldots, \bar{k} - 1$. Then, by the reservation-price equation,

$$G_c^{-1}(\tau_k;\boldsymbol{\theta}) = \int_{p_{k_1}}^{G_{p^*}^{-1}(\tau_k)} F_p(p)\,dp.$$

Differentiating with respect to τ_k yields

$$\frac{\partial G_c^{-1}(\tau_k;\boldsymbol{\theta})}{\partial \tau_k} = \alpha \frac{(p_{\bar{k}} - r)}{(1-\tau_k)^2} F_p\left(\alpha \frac{(p_{\bar{k}} - r)}{(1-\tau_k)} + r\right). \tag{5.3.17}$$

Let $\iota(\tau_k;\boldsymbol{\theta})$ be the τ_kth percentile of $G_c(\cdot;\boldsymbol{\theta})$ such that $G_c(\iota(\tau_k;\boldsymbol{\theta});\boldsymbol{\theta}) = \tau_k$. By the inverse function theorem,

$$\frac{\partial G_c^{-1}(\tau_k;\boldsymbol{\theta})}{\partial \tau_k} = \frac{1}{g_c(\iota(\tau_k;\boldsymbol{\theta});\boldsymbol{\theta})}. \tag{5.3.18}$$

Combining equations (5.3.17) and (5.3.18) yields

$$\frac{1}{g_c(\iota(\tau_k;\boldsymbol{\theta});\boldsymbol{\theta})} = \alpha \frac{(p_{\bar{k}} - r)}{(1-\tau_k)^2} F_p\left(\alpha \frac{(p_{\bar{k}} - r)}{(1-\tau_k)} + r\right).$$

Substituting equations (5.3.15) and (5.3.16) to the display equation above, eliminate $\tau_k \equiv G_{p^*}(p_k)$, we finally have

$$F_p(p_k;\boldsymbol{\theta}) = \frac{\alpha(p_{\bar{k}} - r)}{(p_k - r)^2 g_c\left(\iota\left(1 - \alpha\frac{(p_k - r)}{(p_{\bar{k}} - r)};\boldsymbol{\theta}\right);\boldsymbol{\theta}\right)}. \tag{5.3.19}$$

Notice that $F_p(p_k;\boldsymbol{\theta})$ inherits $\boldsymbol{\theta}$ from $g_c(\cdot;\boldsymbol{\theta})$.

Determination of r Because $F_p(p_{\bar{k}};\boldsymbol{\theta}) = 1$ has to be satisfied, by combining equation (5.3.14) with equation (5.3.19), we get

$$1 \equiv F_p(p_{\bar{k}};\boldsymbol{\theta}) = \frac{(p_1 - r)}{(p_{\bar{k}} - r)^2 g_c\left(\iota\left(1 - \frac{(p_1 - r)}{(p_{\bar{k}} - r)};\boldsymbol{\theta}\right);\boldsymbol{\theta}\right)},$$

which determines r.

Parameterization and MLE Estimation Finally, taking the first-order derivative on equation (5.3.19) with respect to p_k gives $f_p(p_k;\boldsymbol{\theta})$. The likelihood of observing the entire price data is simply

$$\prod_{k=1}^{\bar{k}} f_p(p_k;\boldsymbol{\theta}).$$

By parameterizing $g_c(\cdot;\boldsymbol{\theta})$ as a gamma density, plugging back into equation (5.3.19) and running the maximum likelihood estimation (MLE) will give a consistent estimate for $\boldsymbol{\theta}$. Hong and Shum (2006) note that they employ a gamma distribution due to restrictions that the equilibrium condition in Rob (1985) implies.[34]

5.3.2.4 SEQUENTIAL SEARCH OF CONSUMERS AND HETEROGENEOUS MARGINAL COST OF FIRMS

Carlson and McAfee (1983) derive equilibrium price dispersion from consumers searching sequentially without recall. Consumers have heterogeneous search costs, and firms have heterogeneous marginal costs of production. Based on Carlson and McAfee, Hortaçsu and Syverson (2004) develop the identification results and the estimation method of consumers' search-cost distribution. Allen et al. (2019) study the search market in a similar setup, but with prices being negotiated, rather than posted.

One key advance that Hortaçsu and Syverson make is that they utilize the quantity data $\{q_k\}_{k=1}^{\bar{k}}$ in addition to the price-distribution data for identification. Hortaçsu and Syverson's setup is the utility search with linear utility specification, whereas we stick to the price-search setup in the following illustration for simplicity. Carlson and McAfee and Hortaçsu and Syverson assume that the price distribution has discrete support $\{p_k\}_{k=1}^{\bar{k}}$.[35] The price distribution $F_p(\cdot)$ can be summarized as a probability mass function that takes the following form:

$$f_p(p) = \begin{cases} \rho_k & p = p_1, \ldots, p_{\bar{k}} \\ 0 & \text{otherwise} \end{cases}, \tag{5.3.20}$$

with $\rho_k > 0$ and $\sum_{k=1}^{\bar{k}} \rho_k = 1$. The price distribution $\{p_k, \rho_k\}_{k=1}^{\bar{k}}$ is taken to be the prior knowledge of the consumers. Here, ρ_k is interpreted as the ex ante probability of consumers' sample price p_k.

Derivation of Downward-Sloping Market Demand from Search-Cost Distribution

Identification of Cutoff Search Costs Suppose that consumer i already has p_k in her hand. Recall from equation (5.2.12) that the consumer's per-period choice problem can be expressed as follows:

34. Namely, the density has to be decreasing over the support.

35. As before, p_k is ordered in a way that $p_1 < p_2 < \ldots < p_{\bar{k}}$ without loss of generality.

$$\min\left\{\int_0^{p_k}\left(p_k-p\right)dF_p(p),c_i\right\}.$$

The indifference condition of this problem states that consumers should stop searching if the marginal cost of searching exceeds the marginal benefit; that is,

$$\begin{aligned} c_i &> \int_0^{p_k}\left(p_k-p\right)dF_p(p) \\ &=: \psi_k. \end{aligned} \tag{5.3.21}$$

By combining equation (5.3.21) with equation (5.3.20), the discrete version of equation (5.3.21) applies. The marginal benefit of searching for one more price ψ_k is

$$\psi_k=\sum_{k'=1}^{k}\rho_k\left(p_k-p_{k'}\right), \tag{5.3.22}$$

where ψ_k is simply the sum of the marginal benefit of drawing $p_{k'}$ for each $k'\leq k$, weighted by its sampling probability $\rho_{k'}$. It is straightforward that $\psi_1=0$[36] and $\{\psi_k\}_{k=2}^{\bar{k}}$ can be identified, given that $\{\rho_k\}_{k=1}^{\bar{k}}$ can be either parametrically or non-parametrically estimated.[37] This procedure identifies the cutoff value of $\{\psi_k\}_{k=1}^{\bar{k}}$, and thus that of c_i.

Identification of Downward-Sloping Market Demand Function from Search-Cost Distribution An individual consumer's reservation price p_i^* is a monotonically increasing implicit function of c_i.[38] Furthermore, a consumer will buy from anywhere, provided that the visited firm offers a price less than the reservation price p_i^*. Thus, the cutoff rule gives a downward-sloping demand function.

Our goal now is to write the demand function for each firm k, $\left\{q_k\right\}_{k=1}^{\bar{k}}$, in terms of the consumers' search-cost distribution, $G_c\left(\cdot\right)$. We begin from the most expensive product $\bar{k}$. For product $\bar{k}$, only the consumer with $c_i\geq\psi_{\bar{k}}$ will buy it. Demand

36. If a consumer already knows that she has the lowest possible price, searching for one more price provides no benefit.

37. Hortaçsu and Syverson (2004) assume the following functional form during the estimation:

$$\rho_j=\frac{z_j^{\alpha}}{\sum_{k=1}^{\bar{k}}z_k^{\alpha}},$$

where z_j is an index of product-level observables that influence the probability that a firm is sampled.

38. Recall figure 5.2.2.

for firm $\bar{k}$ is therefore the measure of consumers that have a search cost higher than $\psi_{\bar{k}}$ multiplied by its sampling probability $\rho_{\bar{k}}$:

$$q_{\bar{k}} = I\rho_{\bar{k}}\left(1 - G_c\left(\psi_{\bar{k}}\right)\right),$$

where I is the mass of consumers. Demand for product $\bar{k}-1$ is composed of two terms as follows:

$$\begin{aligned} q_{\bar{k}-1} &= I\left\{\rho_{\bar{k}-1}\left(1 - G_c\left(\psi_{\bar{k}}\right)\right) + \frac{\rho_{\bar{k}-1}}{1-\rho_{\bar{k}}}\left(G_c\left(\psi_{\bar{k}}\right) - G_c\left(\psi_{\bar{k}-1}\right)\right)\right\} \qquad (5.3.23)\\ &= I\rho_{\bar{k}-1}\left\{1 + \frac{\rho_{\bar{k}}}{1-\rho_{\bar{k}}}G_c\left(\psi_{\bar{k}}\right) - \frac{1}{1-\rho_{\bar{k}}}G_c\left(\psi_{\bar{k}-1}\right)\right\}. \end{aligned}$$

The first term of equation (5.3.23), $\rho_{\bar{k}-1}\left(1 - G_c\left(\psi_{\bar{k}}\right)\right)$, is the probability that consumers with a search cost higher than $\psi_{\bar{k}}$ has sampled $\bar{k}-1$ times. The second term is the sum of the probability that consumers with search costs between $\psi_{\bar{k}-1}$ and $\psi_{\bar{k}}$ has sampled $\bar{k}-1$ times, after sampling only $\bar{k}$ in the previous periods. Notice the stationary probability of drawing $\bar{k}$ in the previous periods, $\left(1-\rho_{\bar{k}}\right)^{-1} = 1 + \rho_{\bar{k}} + \rho_{\bar{k}}^2 + \ldots$, is multiplied to the second term of the second equality in equation (5.3.23). Analogous calculations yield the expression for q_j for $1 \leq j \leq \bar{k}-2$:

$$\begin{aligned} q_j &= I\rho_j\left\{\left(1 - G_c\left(\psi_{\bar{k}}\right)\right) + \frac{1}{1-\rho_{\bar{k}}}\left(G_c\left(\psi_{\bar{k}}\right) - G_c\left(\psi_{\bar{k}-1}\right)\right) + \ldots\right.\\ &\quad\left. + \frac{1}{1-\rho_{\bar{k}} - \ldots \rho_{j+1}}\left(G_c\left(\psi_{j+1}\right) - G_c\left(\psi_j\right)\right)\right\}\\ &= I\rho_j\left\{1 + \frac{\rho_{\bar{k}}}{1-\rho_{\bar{k}}}G_c\left(\psi_{\bar{k}}\right) + \frac{\rho_{\bar{k}-1}}{\left(1-\rho_{\bar{k}}\right)\left(1-\rho_{\bar{k}}-\rho_{\bar{k}-1}\right)}G_c\left(\psi_{\bar{k}-1}\right)\right.\\ &\quad + \sum_{k=\bar{k}-2}^{j+1}\frac{\rho_k}{\left(1-\rho_{\bar{k}} - \ldots - \rho_{k+1}\right)\left(1-\rho_{\bar{k}} - \ldots - \rho_k\right)}G_c\left(\psi_k\right)\\ &\quad\left. - \frac{1}{\left(1-\rho_{\bar{k}} - \ldots - \rho_{j+1}\right)}G_c\left(\psi_j\right)\right\}. \qquad (5.3.24) \end{aligned}$$

It can be shown that $\frac{dq_j}{dp_j} < 0$.

We assume that an econometrician has the market share data $\{q_k\}_{k=1}^{\bar{k}}$, and therefore $I = 1$. The system in equation (5.3.24) then gives $\bar{k} - 1$ equations for $\bar{k} - 1$ objects—namely, $\{G_c(\psi_k)\}_{k=2}^{\bar{k}}$. Combined with the fact that search cost cannot be negative ($G_c(\psi_1) = G_c(0) = 0$), we have all the necessary cutoff points for the search-cost distribution. Another possibility is to parameterize distribution $G_c(\cdot;\boldsymbol{\theta})$ to a family of distributions and estimate a value of $\boldsymbol{\theta}$ that governs $G_c(\cdot;\boldsymbol{\theta})$.

Supply Side and Equilibrium One of the sufficient conditions, although it is not exhaustive, for the existence of the persistent price dispersion of a homogeneous product from Carlson and McAfee (1983) is that $g_c(\cdot)$ is nondecreasing over its support. Hortaçsu and Syverson (2004) do not impose or test the condition because their setup is the utility search in a differentiated-products market. In the context of utility search with heterogeneous alternatives, the existence of the persistent price dispersion is trivial. Instead, Hortaçsu and Syverson utilized additional conditions from the suppliers' pricing equation to estimate the levels of search cost, and then to derive the slope of the demand function, $\frac{\partial q_j}{\partial p_j}$. We omit the part that the suppliers' pricing equation plays in estimating the level of search costs in the context of utility search.

5.4 Empirical Frameworks with Search-Set Data or Their Proxy

In this section, we study empirical frameworks of consumer search that use more granular data compared to the market-level price-quantity data. The goal is to write the likelihood under the relevant search assumptions with the available data. Ideally, an econometrician should be able to observe all the utility orderings of the alternatives, the search sequence, and the choice. Because observing all the components of this ideal data is virtually impossible, we study how the lack of a component is reflected in writing the likelihood.

The models studied in this section are based on the utility search in a differentiated-products market. Nevertheless, all the results and implications of the optimal search rules on price search, which we studied in section 5.2.1, apply.

5.4.1 *Empirical Frameworks of Sequential Search*

Kim et al. (2010, 2017) develop an empirical framework of consumer search based on Weitzman (1979)'s theoretic setup on sequential search. Consumers search sequentially on heterogeneous alternatives with recall in order to find the alternative with the highest utility among the choice set $\mathcal{J}_i$.

5.4.1.1 SETUP AND BASIC RESULTS

Let the alternative-specific utility of consumer i choosing $j \in \mathcal{J}_i$ be

$$\begin{aligned} u_{i,j} &:= \bar{u}_{i,j}\left(\boldsymbol{\beta}_i, \alpha_i\right) + \epsilon_{i,j} \\ &= \mathbf{x}_j' \boldsymbol{\beta}_i - \alpha_i p_j + \epsilon_{i,j}, \end{aligned} \tag{5.4.1}$$

where the parameter vectors are assumed to follow

$$\begin{aligned} \boldsymbol{\beta}_i &\sim \mathcal{N}\left(\boldsymbol{\beta}, \boldsymbol{\Sigma}_{\boldsymbol{\beta}}\right) \\ \ln\left(\alpha_i\right) &\sim \mathcal{N}\left(\alpha, \sigma_\alpha^2\right) \\ \epsilon_{i,j} &\sim \mathcal{N}\left(0, \sigma_{i,j}^2\right). \end{aligned} \tag{5.4.2}$$

In the original setup of Kim et al. (2010), each consumer knows their own $\left(\boldsymbol{\beta}_i, \alpha_i\right)$, and the goal of search is to resolve the uncertainty of $\epsilon_{i,j}$. If alternative j is searched, no uncertainty remains in the utility term $u_{i,j}$. The econometrician, however, does not observe $\left(\boldsymbol{\beta}_i, \alpha_i\right)$, and estimating them is part of the goal of the estimation procedure. Here, $\sigma_{i,j}$ can be heterogeneous across individuals, which reflects the difference between more knowledgable and less knowledgable consumers and/or alternatives. When $\sigma_{i,j}$ is heterogeneous across individuals or alternatives, it will be further parameterized as following a parametric distribution.

The baseline assumption is that consumers search sequentially over heterogeneous alternatives. Weitzman (1979)'s rules, which were studied in section 5.2.1.3, apply here. The only difference is that now consumers try to find an alternative that yields the maximum utility, not the minimum prices, but the principle behind the rules are the same. For each alternative $k \in \mathcal{J}_i$, the reservation utility $u_{i,k}^*$ can be calculated implicitly by the following equation:

$$c_{i,k} = \int_{u_{i,k}^*}^{\bar{u}_{i,k}} \left(u_{i,k} - u_{i,k}^*\right) dF_{\epsilon_{i,j}}\left(\epsilon_{i,j}\right).$$

Let us first sort $\mathcal{J}_i$ in the descending order of $u_{i,k}^*$ (i.e., higher reservation utility has lower index) without losing generality. Recall the Weitzman's rule proceeds in three stages:

(1) (Ordering) Sort the alternatives in the descending order of the reservation utility $u_{i,k}^*$ and search sequentially from the order made in the previous step.

(2) (Stopping) At each stage $t \in \mathcal{J}_i$, compare $\max_{1 \leq k \leq t} \{u_{i,k}\}$ with $u^*_{i,t+1}$ and stop if $\max_{1 \leq k \leq t} \{u_{i,k}\} > u^*_{i,t+1}$, and define $\mathcal{S}_i \ (\subset \mathcal{J}_i)$[39] as the searched set thus far.

(3) (Choice) If stopped, collect the alternative j such that $j = \arg\max_{k \in \mathcal{S}_i} \{u_{i,k}\}$.

The individual-product-specific search cost $c_{i,j}$ is further parameterized as follows:

$$c_{i,j} \propto \exp\left(\mathbf{w}'_{i,j}\boldsymbol{\gamma}_i\right)$$
$$\boldsymbol{\gamma}_i \sim \mathcal{N}\left(\boldsymbol{\gamma}, \boldsymbol{\Sigma}_{\gamma}\right), \tag{5.4.3}$$

where $\mathbf{w}_{i,j}$ is the individual and/or product-specific search-cost shifter,[40] which contains 1, and therefore the coefficient of 1 will represent the mean search cost over individuals. Under the model assumptions with the given parameterizations in equations (5.4.1), (5.4.2), and (5.4.3), it can be shown that the reservation utility has the following closed-form solution:

$$u^*_{i,j} = \bar{u}_{i,j}\left(\boldsymbol{\beta}_i, \alpha_i\right) + \sigma_{i,j}\zeta\left(\frac{c_{i,j}\left(\boldsymbol{\gamma}_i\right)}{\sigma_{i,j}}\right)$$
$$= \mathbf{x}'_j\boldsymbol{\beta}_i - \alpha_i p_j + \sigma_{i,j}\zeta\left(\frac{c_{i,j}\left(\boldsymbol{\gamma}_i\right)}{\sigma_{i,j}}\right),$$

where $\zeta\ (t)$ is a function defined implicitly by the following equation:

$$t = \left(1 - \Phi\left(\zeta\right)\right)\left(\frac{\phi\left(\zeta\right)}{1 - \Phi\left(\zeta\right)} - \zeta\right).$$

A straightforward application of the implicit function theorem shows $\zeta\ (t)$ is a monotone function, strictly decreasing over its domain.

Let $\boldsymbol{\theta} := \left(\boldsymbol{\beta}, \boldsymbol{\Sigma}_{\boldsymbol{\beta}}, \alpha, \sigma_{\alpha}, \boldsymbol{\gamma}, \boldsymbol{\Sigma}_{\gamma}, \left\{\sigma_{i,j}\right\}_{i \in \mathcal{I}, j \in \mathcal{J}_i}\right)$ be the vector of model parameters. The goal of the estimation is now to estimate $\boldsymbol{\theta}$ consistently with the given data. The availability of different variables in data restricts the path that an

39. Notice that $\mathcal{S}_i$ has the same order as $\mathcal{J}_i$.

40. Ursu (2018), notably, uses the randomized ranking of the alternatives in $\mathbf{w}_{i,j}$. By utilizing the experimental variation on the ranking determination, the study removes the endogeneity when the ranking is determined.

econometrician can take substantially, and we study a few paths that can be taken or have already been taken in the literature in what follows.

5.4.1.2 IDEAL-CASE LIKELIHOOD WHEN INDIVIDUAL-LEVEL SEARCH SEQUENCE AND CHOICE ARE OBSERVED

Let us consider an ideal-case likelihood of observing the order of search set $\mathcal{S}_i = \{1, 2, \ldots, S_i\}$ out of the available alternatives $\mathcal{J}_i = \{1, 2, \ldots, S_i, S_i + 1, \ldots, J_i\}$. Again, without loss of generality, $\mathcal{S}_i$ and $\mathcal{J}_i$ are ordered according to the reservation utility, so the consumer searches from index 1 first and then sequentially moves to the next index, stops at S_i, and collects j.

The unconditional probability of observing $\mathcal{J}_i$ and the choice $j \in \mathcal{S}_i$ is such that

$$\begin{aligned}
&\Pr\left(\{j \in \mathcal{S}_i \text{ chosen}\} \cap \{\text{stopped at } S_i\} \cap \{\mathcal{J}_i \text{ ordered}\}; \boldsymbol{\theta}\right) \\
&= \Pr\left(j \in \mathcal{S}_i \text{ chosen} |\ \{\text{stopped at } S_i\} \cap \{\mathcal{J}_i \text{ ordered}\}; \boldsymbol{\theta}\right) \\
&\quad \times \Pr\left(\text{stopped at } S_i | \mathcal{J}_i \text{ ordered}; \boldsymbol{\theta}\right) \\
&\quad \times \Pr\left(\mathcal{J}_i \text{ ordered}; \boldsymbol{\theta}\right). \qquad (5.4.4)
\end{aligned}$$

Here, "$\mathcal{J}_i$ ordered" is shorthand for $\mathcal{J}_i$ being ordered as $\{1, 2, \ldots, S_i, S_i + 1, \ldots, J_i\}$. The equality in equation (5.4.4) is obtained simply by repeatedly applying the law of total probability.

Ordering Rule In this ideal case, the search sequence of each consumer $\mathcal{S}_i = \{1, 2, \ldots, S_i\}$ is observed, with the actual choice $j \in \mathcal{S}_i$. This S_i-tuple contains the information about the results from $\frac{1}{2} S_i (S_i - 1)$ pairwise comparisons. Furthermore, the S_i-tuple contains information about $S_i (J_i - S_i)$ pairs of information on $\mathcal{J}_i \backslash \mathcal{S}_i$ because for each $k \in \mathcal{S}_i$ and $m \in \mathcal{J}_i \backslash \mathcal{S}_i$, the ordering should be such that $k < m$.

According to Weitzman's ordering rule, we have three restrictions. Each restriction is for $\mathcal{S}_i$, between $\mathcal{S}_i$ and $\mathcal{J}_i \backslash \mathcal{S}_i$, and for $\mathcal{J}_i$, respectively. The restrictions are as follows:

(1) For each $k, l \in \mathcal{S}_i$ such that $k < l$, $u^*_{i,k} > u^*_{i,l}$ holds.
(2) For each $k \in \mathcal{S}_i$, $m \in \mathcal{J}_i \backslash \mathcal{S}_i$, $u^*_{i,k} > u^*_{i,m}$ holds.
(3) For each $m, n \in \mathcal{J}_i \backslash \mathcal{S}_i$ such that $m < n$, $u^*_{i,m} > u^*_{i,n}$ holds.

The ordering problem is deterministic for the consumers, but it is stochastic for the econometrician. From the econometrician's perspective, the source of stochasticity is the uncertainty in $(\boldsymbol{\beta}_i, \alpha_i, \boldsymbol{\gamma}_i, \sigma_{i,j})$. The ideal-case likelihood of observing an ordered sequence $\mathcal{J}_i$, which is infeasible to implement because the order of $\mathcal{J}_i \backslash \mathcal{S}_i$ is never observed, is

$$\begin{aligned}\Pr\left(\mathcal{J}_i \text{ ordered}; \boldsymbol{\theta}\right) = &\left\{\prod_{\{k,l \in \mathcal{S}_i : k<l\}} \Pr\left(u^*_{i,k} - u^*_{i,l} > 0; \boldsymbol{\theta}\right)\right\}\\ &\times \left\{\prod_{\{k \in \mathcal{S}_i, m \in \mathcal{J}_i \backslash \mathcal{S}_i\}} \Pr\left(u^*_{i,k} - u^*_{i,m} > 0; \boldsymbol{\theta}\right)\right\}\\ &\times \left\{\prod_{\{m,n \in \mathcal{J}_i \backslash \mathcal{S}_i : m<n\}} \Pr\left(u^*_{i,m} - u^*_{i,n} > 0; \boldsymbol{\theta}\right)\right\}.\end{aligned}$$

Instead, in an ideal data set, the search order within $\mathcal{S}_i$ can be observed. Observing $\mathcal{S}_i$ out of $\mathcal{J}_i$ is

$$\begin{aligned}\Pr\left(\mathcal{S}_i\ (\subset \mathcal{J}_i)\ \text{ ordered}; \boldsymbol{\theta}\right) = &\left\{\prod_{\{k,l \in \mathcal{S}_i : k<l\}} \Pr\left(u^*_{i,k} - u^*_{i,l} > 0; \boldsymbol{\theta}\right)\right\}\\ &\times \left\{\prod_{\{k \in \mathcal{S}_i, m \in \mathcal{J}_i \backslash \mathcal{S}_i\}} \Pr\left(u^*_{i,k} - u^*_{i,m} > 0; \boldsymbol{\theta}\right)\right\}. \qquad (5.4.5)\end{aligned}$$

To back out $\Pr\left(\mathcal{J}_i \text{ ordered}; \boldsymbol{\theta}\right)$ using $\Pr\left(\mathcal{S}_i\ (\subset \mathcal{J}_i)\ \text{ ordered}; \boldsymbol{\theta}\right)$, in principle, one can construct all the possible orders of $\mathcal{J}_i \backslash \mathcal{S}_i$ and then use the probability-weighted sum to derive the expression $\Pr\left(\mathcal{J}_i \text{ ordered}; \boldsymbol{\theta}\right)$ from only $\Pr\left(\mathcal{S}_i\ (\subset \mathcal{J}_i)\ \text{ ordered}; \boldsymbol{\theta}\right)$. In practice, calculating all the permutation orders can be further simplified by using the simulation methods.

Stopping Rule If the consumer decided to stop at S_i, the following two conditions must hold: (1) $\max_{1 \leq k \leq t}\left\{u_{i,k}\right\} \leq u^*_{i,t+1}$ for all the previous periods $t\ (< S_i)$, and (2) $\max_{1 \leq k \leq S_i}\left\{u_{i,k}\right\} \geq u^*_{i,S_i+1}$ for period S_i. Combined with the fact $u_{i,j} = \max_{1 \leq k \leq S_i}\left\{u_{i,k}\right\}$, the infeasible conditional probability of the consumer stopped at S_i, conditional on the order $\mathcal{J}_i$, is

$$\begin{aligned}&\Pr\left(\text{stopped at } S_i | \mathcal{J}_i \text{ ordered}; \boldsymbol{\theta}\right)\\ &= \Pr\left(\left\{\bigcap_{t=1}^{S_i-1}\left\{\max_{1 \leq k \leq t}\left\{u_{i,k}\right\} < u^*_{i,t+1}\right\}\right\} \cap \left\{u_{i,j} \geq u^*_{i,S_i+1}\right\}; \boldsymbol{\theta}\right).\end{aligned}$$

However, because the order of $\mathcal{J}_i \backslash \mathcal{S}_i$ is never observed, any alternative in $\mathcal{J}_i \backslash \mathcal{S}_i$ can be in the $S_i + 1$th reservation utility order. Thus, the feasible version would be

$$\begin{aligned}
&\Pr\left(\text{stopped at } S_i | \mathcal{J}_i \text{ ordered}; \boldsymbol{\theta}\right) \\
&= \Pr\left(\left\{\bigcap_{t=1}^{S_i-1}\left\{\max_{1\le k\le t}\left\{u_{i,k}\right\} < u^*_{i,t+1}\right\}\right\} \cap \left\{\max_{1\le k\le S_i}\left\{u_{i,k}\right\} \ge u^*_{i,S_i+1}\right\}; \boldsymbol{\theta}\right) \\
&= \sum_{l\in\{\mathcal{J}_i\backslash\mathcal{S}_i\}} \Pr\left(u_{i,l} = \max_{S_i+1\le m\le J_i}\left\{u_{i,m}\right\}; \boldsymbol{\theta}\right) \\
&\quad \Pr\left(\left\{\bigcap_{t=1}^{S_i-1}\left\{\max_{1\le k\le t}\left\{u_{i,k}\right\} < u^*_{i,t+1}\right\}\right\} \cap \left\{u_{i,j} \ge u^*_{i,l}\right\}; \boldsymbol{\theta}\right). \qquad (5.4.6)
\end{aligned}$$

In practice, one can use simulation methods to calculate the probability $\Pr\left(u_{i,l} = \max_{S_i+1\le m\le J_i}\left\{u_{i,m}\right\}\right)$.

Choice Rule When the searched set $\mathcal{S}_i$ and the chosen alternative $j \in \mathcal{S}_i$ are observed, the choice rule states that for the chosen item j,

$$u_{i,j} = \max_{k\in\mathcal{S}_i}\left\{u_{i,k}\right\}$$

should hold.

The conditional choice probability of j out of $\mathcal{S}_i$, conditioned on the two events $\left\{\text{stopped at } S_i\right\}$ and $\{\mathcal{J}_i \text{ ordered}\}$, is

$$\begin{aligned}
&\Pr\left(j \in \mathcal{S}_i \text{ chosen}|\left\{\text{stopped at } S_i\right\} \cap \{\mathcal{J}_i \text{ ordered}\}; \boldsymbol{\theta}\right) \\
&= \Pr\left(\left\{k \in \mathcal{S}_i : u_{i,j} \ge \max_{k\in\mathcal{S}_i}\left\{u_{i,k}\right\}\right\}; \boldsymbol{\theta}\right) \\
&= \Pr\left(\left\{k \in \mathcal{S}_i : u_{i,j} \ge u_{i,k}\right\}; \boldsymbol{\theta}\right).
\end{aligned}$$

Estimation of Parameterized Search-Cost Distribution Using Ordered Individual-Level Search-Set Data Chen and Yao (2016) utilize a clickstream data set, which is the closest possible instance to the ideal case in the literature. Although the essence is the same, their likelihood representation is slightly different from equation (5.4.4), combining the events $\left\{\text{stopped at } S_i\right\} \cap \{\mathcal{J}_i \text{ ordered}\}$ in one expression.

Estimation of Parameterized Search-Cost Distribution Using Unordered Individual-Level Search-Set Data Honka and Chintagunta (2017) and Ursu (2018) use individual-level, unordered search-set data to identify and estimate the parameterized search-cost distribution. All other components of the likelihood are identical to what is illustrated in section 5.4.1.2. Because the search order even in $\mathcal{S}_i$ is not observed, it makes the permutation problems in equations (5.4.5) and (5.4.6) more complicated than when $\mathcal{S}_i$ is fully observed.

5.4.1.3 ESTIMATION OF PARAMETERIZED SEARCH-COST DISTRIBUTION USING MARKET-LEVEL VIEW-RANK DATA

Commonality Index Data and Construction of the Model Counterpart Kim et al. (2010) use Amazon's pairwise conditional view-rank data that record the view rank of all other alternatives $\mathcal{J}\backslash j$ for each alternative j.[41] Amazon's commonality index between products j and k is defined as

$$CI_{jk} := \frac{n_{jk}}{\sqrt{n_j}\sqrt{n_k}}, \tag{5.4.7}$$

where n_{jk} is the number of consumers who viewed j and k in the same session, n_j and n_k only j and k in the same session, respectively. The commonality index is defined to reflect the viewing preferences in such a way that for each j, if (j,k) is viewed more than (j,l), then $CI_{jk} > CI_{jl}$, and vice versa. The estimation proceeds with constructing a model counterpart of equation (5.4.7), and then implementing either moment matching or maximum likelihood.

Weitzman (1979)'s optimal stopping rule dictates that the inclusion probability of product j in the searched set is

$$\begin{aligned}\Pr\left(\left\{j \in \mathcal{S}_i\right\};\boldsymbol{\theta}\right) &= \Pr\left(\max_{k\in\{1,2,\ldots,j-1\}}\left\{u_{i,k}\right\} < u^*_{i,j};\boldsymbol{\theta}\right)\\ &= \prod_{k=1}^{j-1} F_{\epsilon_{i,j}}\left(u^*_{i,j} - u_{i,k};\boldsymbol{\theta}\right).\end{aligned}$$

Note that $\boldsymbol{\theta} := \left(\boldsymbol{\beta}, \boldsymbol{\Sigma}_{\boldsymbol{\beta}}, \alpha, \sigma_\alpha, \boldsymbol{\gamma}, \boldsymbol{\Sigma}_{\boldsymbol{\gamma}}, \left\{\sigma_{i,j}\right\}_{i\in\mathcal{I}, j\in\mathcal{J}_i}\right)$ contains all the utility parameters and search-cost parameters. $\Pr\left(\{1 \in \mathcal{S}_i\};\boldsymbol{\theta}\right) = 1$ by the assumption that consumers search at least once. In other words, the possibility of an outside option

41. Notice that the individual index i is taken out because only market-level data are observed.

is not allowed here. Then, it is trivial to show that for any pair (j, j') such that $j < j'$,

$$\Pr\left(\left\{j \in \mathcal{S}_i\right\}; \boldsymbol{\theta}\right) > \Pr\left(\left\{j' \in \mathcal{S}_i\right\}; \boldsymbol{\theta}\right)$$

and

$$\begin{aligned}\Pr\left(\left\{j \in \mathcal{S}_i\right\} \cap \left\{j' \in \mathcal{S}_i\right\}; \boldsymbol{\theta}\right) &= \min\left\{\Pr\left(\left\{j \in \mathcal{S}_i\right\}; \boldsymbol{\theta}\right), \Pr\left(\left\{j' \in \mathcal{S}_i\right\}; \boldsymbol{\theta}\right)\right\} \\ &= \Pr\left(\left\{j' \in \mathcal{S}_i\right\}; \boldsymbol{\theta}\right)\end{aligned}$$

hold. Also, note that

$$\Pr\left(\mathcal{S}_i = \{1, \ldots, S_i\}; \boldsymbol{\theta}\right) = \Pr\left(\{S_i \in \mathcal{S}_i\}; \boldsymbol{\theta}\right) - \Pr\left(\{(S_i + 1) \in \mathcal{S}_i\}; \boldsymbol{\theta}\right).$$ [42]

The model-side $\widehat{CI}_{jk}(\boldsymbol{\theta})$ is defined as follows:

$$\widehat{CI}_{jk}(\boldsymbol{\theta}) := \frac{\hat{n}_{jk}(\boldsymbol{\theta})}{\sqrt{\hat{n}_j(\boldsymbol{\theta})}\sqrt{\hat{n}_k(\boldsymbol{\theta})}}, \tag{5.4.8}$$

where $\hat{n}_j(\boldsymbol{\theta}) = \sum_{i \in \mathcal{I}} \Pr\left(\left\{j \in \mathcal{S}_i\right\}; \boldsymbol{\theta}\right)$ and $\hat{n}_{jk}(\boldsymbol{\theta}) = \sum_{i \in \mathcal{I}} \min\left\{\Pr\left(\left\{j \in \mathcal{S}_i\right\}; \boldsymbol{\theta}\right), \Pr\left(\{k \in \mathcal{S}_i\}; \boldsymbol{\theta}\right)\right\}$.

Estimation: Moment Matching or MLE The remaining step of estimation is either moment matching or MLE. Moment matching can be carried out by minimizing the squared difference of the model commonality index (5.4.8) and data (5.4.7):

$$\min_{\boldsymbol{\theta}} \sum_{j,k \in \mathcal{J}} \left\{\widehat{CI}_{jk}(\boldsymbol{\theta}) - CI_{jk}\right\}^2.$$

MLE can be carried out by further assuming the parametric distribution of ϵ_{jk}; that is,

$$CI_{jk} = \widehat{CI}_{jk}(\boldsymbol{\theta}) + \epsilon_{jk} \qquad \epsilon_{jk} \sim i.i.d.\, \mathcal{N}\left(0, \frac{\nu^2}{2}\right).$$

Then, the building block for the likelihood becomes

$$\Pr\left(CI_{jk} - CI_{jl} \geq 0; \boldsymbol{\theta}, \nu\right) = \Phi\left(\frac{1}{\nu}\left(\widehat{CI}_{jk}(\boldsymbol{\theta}) - \widehat{CI}_{jl}(\boldsymbol{\theta})\right)\right).$$

42. Recall that $\mathcal{S}_i$ is sorted by the decreasing order of the reservation utility.

Therefore, the MLE problem is as follows:

$$\max_{(\boldsymbol{\theta},\nu)} \prod_{j,k,l\in\mathcal{J}} \Pr\left(\widehat{CI}_{jk}(\boldsymbol{\theta}) - \widehat{CI}_{jl}(\boldsymbol{\theta}) \geq ; \boldsymbol{\theta}, \nu\right)^{\iota_{j,kl}},$$

where $\iota_{j,kl} := \mathbf{1}\left(\left\{CI_{jk} - CI_{jl} \geq 0\right\}\right)$.

5.4.1.4 REMARKS AND FURTHER READING

Kim, Albuquerque, and Bronnenberg (2017) and Moraga-González, Sándor, and Wildenbeest (2018) derive additional results on the building blocks of the likelihood under different scenarios of data availability and under different distributional assumptions. Kim et al. rely on the Gaussian assumption, and Moraga-González et al. rely on the T1EV assumption and augment the sequential search likelihood on Berry et al. (1995)'s demand-estimation framework.

5.4.2 Empirical Frameworks of Simultaneous Search

5.4.2.1 SETUP AND DATA

Honka (2014) combines the simultaneous search and sorting rule based on Chade and Smith (2005, 2006) with consideration-set data. The context is consumers choosing automobile insurance, and some of the setups given here are specific to that context. The consumer connects the simultaneous search to the consideration-set formation. The data are an unordered individual-level consideration set without a search sequence, in which case it is natural to consider simultaneous search rather than sequential search. Consumers are assumed to choose characteristics first, lock in to the characteristics, and then search to reveal the uncertainty of only the prices. In other words, elasticity of substitution between the price component and characteristics component is zero.

Consumer i's utility of choosing alternative j is specified as

$$\begin{aligned} u_{i,j} &:= \bar{u}_{i,j}\left(\boldsymbol{\beta}, \alpha, \eta_{i,j}\right) + \gamma_i \mathbf{1}\left(i \text{ chose } j \text{ at } t-1\right) + \epsilon_{i,j} \\ &= \mathbf{x}_{i,j}'\boldsymbol{\beta} - \alpha p_{i,j} + \eta_{i,j} + \gamma_i \mathbf{1}\left(i \text{ chose } j \text{ at } t-1\right) + \epsilon_{i,j}, \end{aligned}$$

where

$$\begin{aligned} \epsilon_{i,j} &\sim i.i.d.\ T1EV\,(0,1) \\ \boldsymbol{\eta}_i &\sim \mathcal{N}\left(\boldsymbol{\eta}, \boldsymbol{\Sigma}_{\eta}\right) \\ \gamma_i &= \gamma_0 + \mathbf{w}_i'\boldsymbol{\gamma}_1. \end{aligned}$$

Here, $\mathbf{x}_{i,j}$ contains consumer-specific attributes, demographics, psychographic factors, and region-fixed effects that are common across j. Note that the region-fixed effects drop out of the within-region choice decision, conditional on search and consideration, but they may play a role in the search and consideration decisions. Here, $p_{i,j}$ is the quoted price, and we assume that $p_{i,j} \sim T1EV\left(\mu_{i,j}, \sigma_p\right)$, where σ_p is constant across alternatives; and $\boldsymbol{\eta}_i$ captures consumer-specific brand intercepts. The term $\mathbf{1}\left(i \text{ chose } j \text{ at } t-1\right)$ reflects the choice inertia, and $\mathbf{w}_i$ contains demographics, psychographic factors, and customer satisfaction with the previous insurer, and therefore, γ_i captures the interaction between the consumer characteristics with the inertia.

Consumers get a quote from the previous insurer for free. We assume that consumers know the characteristics vector $\mathbf{x}_{i,j}$ without cost.[43] The only variable subject to searching is the price, which is a setup adopted from Mehta et al. (2003). Consumers observe $\mathbb{E}_p\left[u_{i,j}\right]$, given by

$$\mathbb{E}_p\left[u_{i,j}\right] = \mathbf{x}_{i,j}'\boldsymbol{\beta} - \alpha\mu_{i,j} + \eta_{i,j} + \gamma_i \mathbf{1}\left(i \text{ chose } j \text{ at } t-1\right) + \epsilon_{i,j},$$

whereas $\left(\epsilon_{i,j}, \eta_{i,j}\right)$ is not directly observable to the econometrician.

5.4.2.2 MARGINAL IMPROVEMENT ALGORITHM AND THE LIKELIHOOD

A specific form of the first-order stochastic dominance among the (belief) distribution of $p_{i,j}$ across j is assumed to implement Chade and Smith (2005, 2006)'s MIA. The price-belief distribution $p_{i,j} \sim T1EV\left(\mu_{i,j}, \sigma_p\right)$ has the same variance over alternatives, but different means. This assumption of price belief that follows the exact same shape of distribution allows Honka to calculate the optimal order of the alternative set $\mathcal{J}_i$ by using the MIA discussed in section 5.2.2.2. By the virtue of the MIA, the derivation of the likelihood discussed next resembles what was studied in section 5.4.1 for the sequential search.

The search and choice rule is as follows. Let 0 denote the previous insurer. Consumers, as well as the econometrician, sort $\mathcal{J}_i$ in the descending order of $\mathbb{E}_p\left[u_{i,j}\right]$.[44] Without loss of generality, let $\mathcal{J}_i \backslash 0 = \left\{1, \ldots, J_i\right\}$ follow this order. Let

43. This assumption might be applicable in only some restricted contexts such as insurance-premium searching, where the majority of consumers lock in to their coverage first and then search only for the prices.

44. The search rule described in this discussion is, in fact, slightly simpler than the original MIA because it is assumed that the distribution $p_{i,j}$ follows the same shape. If the shape of the distribution that $p_{i,j}$ follows is heterogeneous, comparing only the mean is no longer sufficient because what matters in the MIA is the tail behavior of the price distribution.

$\mathcal{S}_i$ contain the previous insurer as index 0.[45] Consumers know the realization of $\left\{\epsilon_{i,j}\right\}_{j\in\mathcal{J}_i}$ already.

Ordering Rule The ordering rule, combined with the data availability, contains the following information:

$$\min_{k\in\mathcal{S}_i}\left\{\mathbb{E}_p\left[u_{i,k}\right]\right\} \geq \max_{k\in\mathcal{J}_i\setminus\mathcal{S}_i}\left\{\mathbb{E}_p\left[u_{i,k}\right]\right\}. \tag{5.4.9}$$

Using the extreme-value assumption on the price distributions, the likelihood calculation becomes much simpler.

Stopping Rule Recall the net benefit of searching the set $\mathcal{S}_i = \{0, 1, \ldots, S_i\}$ is given by

$$\Gamma\left(S_i\right) := \mathbb{E}_p\left[\max_{k\in\mathcal{S}_i}\left\{u_{i,k}\right\}\right] - c_i S_i.$$

Furthermore, for the observed search set $\mathcal{S}_i$, for all $1 \leq s \leq J_i$,

$$\Gamma\left(S_i\right) \geq \Gamma\left(s\right) \tag{5.4.10}$$

should hold.

Choice Rule Conditional on $\mathcal{S}_i$ being observed, the choice rule is as usual:

$$j = \arg\max_{k\in\mathcal{S}_i} u_{i,k}. \tag{5.4.11}$$

Likelihood Now let us combine the events of ordering, stopping, and choice rule with the probability of observing the unordered consideration-set data with the choice to derive the likelihood. To simplify the notation, denote $\boldsymbol{\theta} := \left(\boldsymbol{\beta}, \alpha, \boldsymbol{\eta}, \boldsymbol{\Sigma}_{\eta}, \gamma_0, \boldsymbol{\gamma}_1\right)$ by the set of model parameters to be estimated. The event $\left\{\text{ordering } \mathcal{J}_i\right\} \cap \left\{\text{stopping at } \mathcal{S}_i\right\}$ is the event of observing $\mathcal{S}_i$ $(\subset \mathcal{J}_i)$. The likelihood of observing $\mathcal{S}_i$ and the choice $j \in \mathcal{S}_i$ is

$$\begin{aligned}
&\Pr\left(\left\{\text{ordering } \mathcal{J}_i\right\} \cap \left\{\text{stopping at } \mathcal{S}_i\right\} \cap \left\{\text{choose } j \in \mathcal{S}_i\right\}; \boldsymbol{\theta}\right)\\
&= \Pr\left(\left\{\text{ordering } \mathcal{J}_i\right\} \cap \left\{\text{stopping at } \mathcal{S}_i\right\}; \boldsymbol{\theta}\right)\\
&\quad \Pr\left(\text{choose } j \in \mathcal{S}_i \middle| \left\{\text{ordering } \mathcal{J}_i\right\} \cap \left\{\text{stopping at } \mathcal{S}_i\right\}; \boldsymbol{\theta}\right),
\end{aligned}$$

45. Inclusion of the "free" option reflects the specific context that the previous insurer sends the quote for free.

where

$$\begin{aligned}&\Pr\left(\left\{\text{ordering } \mathcal{J}_i\right\} \cap \left\{\text{stopping at } \mathcal{S}_i\right\}; \boldsymbol{\theta}\right)\\&= \Pr\left(\left\{\min_{k\in\mathcal{S}_i}\left\{E_p\left[u_{i,k}\right]\right\} \geq \max_{k\in\mathcal{J}_i\setminus\mathcal{S}_i}\left\{E_p\left[u_{i,k}\right]\right\}\right\}\cap\left\{1\leq s\leq J_i:\Gamma(S_i)\geq\Gamma(s)\right\};\boldsymbol{\theta}\right)\end{aligned}$$

and

$$\begin{aligned}&\Pr\left(\text{choose } j\in\mathcal{S}_i|\left\{\text{ordering } \mathcal{J}_i\right\} \cap \left\{\text{stopping at } \mathcal{S}_i\right\}; \boldsymbol{\theta}\right)\\&= \Pr\left(\left\{0\leq k\leq S_i : u_{i,j}\geq u_{i,k}\right\};\boldsymbol{\theta}\right).\end{aligned}$$

Here, $\left(\epsilon_{i,j}, \eta_{i,j}\right)_{i\in\mathcal{I}, j\in\mathcal{J}_i}$ are observable to the consumers, but not to the econometrician. Only their distributions are parameterized. The MLE problem solves the following to take into account the variables unobservable to the econometrician:

$$\begin{aligned}\arg\max_{\boldsymbol{\theta}}\prod_{i\in\mathcal{I}}\int&\left[\prod_{\mathcal{S}_i\subset\mathcal{J}_i}\prod_{j\in\mathcal{S}_i}\Pr\left(\left\{\text{ordering } \mathcal{J}_i\right\} \cap \left\{\text{stopping at } \mathcal{S}_i\right\}; \boldsymbol{\theta}\right)^{\mathbf{1}(\mathcal{S}_i \text{ Observed})}\right.\\&\left.\times\Pr\left(\text{choose } j\in\mathcal{S}_i|\left\{\text{ordering } \mathcal{J}_i\right\} \cap \left\{\text{stopping at } \mathcal{S}_i\right\}; \boldsymbol{\theta}\right)^{\mathbf{1}(j\in\mathcal{S}_i \text{ Chosen})}\right]\\&d\Pr\left(\epsilon_{i,j}, \eta_{i,j}; \boldsymbol{\theta}\right).\end{aligned}$$

Note that $\prod_{\mathcal{S}_i\subset\mathcal{J}_i}$ means all the possible combinations of subset $\mathcal{S}_i$ of $\mathcal{J}_i$.

5.4.3 Testing the Modes of Search and Further Reading

5.4.3.1 SEQUENTIAL OR SIMULTANEOUS?

We presented the theoretical and empirical framework of consumer search under two large assumptions on the consumers' thought process: sequential search and simultaneous search. In the beginning of this chapter, we mentioned that little research to date has taken account of the consumers' thought process on the search modes. However, if *all* other assumptions hold for the respective search modes, sequential search and simultaneous search yield different patterns on the observed search sequence or searched set, allowing for an econometrician to test whether consumers search sequentially or simultaneously. Next, we provide a brief overview of the key ideas behind De los Santos et al. (2012) and Honka and Chintagunta (2017), who attempted to test the modes of search using individual-level data. Both De los Santos et al. and Honka and Chintagunta conclude that consumers' search pattern is closer to simultaneous search.

De los Santos et al. (2012) use ComScore (partial) sequence data of browsing and purchase. The following patterns from the data are shown, which can be considered a reduced-form test on search modes. First, recall occurs often, suggesting that the benchmark model of sequential search assuming the homogeneous ex ante price distribution is rejected. Second, even when allowing for the ex ante heterogeneity over price distributions, search size does not depend on the revealed prices. That is, if consumers are searching sequentially, consumers searching once are more likely to have found a relatively low price, and consumers searching twice are likely to have found a relatively high price in the first search. This pattern is not discovered in this study's data.

Honka and Chintagunta (2017) use the unordered consideration-set data from Honka (2014) and suggest examining the mean of the prices over the consideration set. If consumers employ the simultaneous search strategy, the mean price over the consideration set would be equal to the mean price over the population. On the other hand, if consumers employ the sequential search strategy, the mean price over the searched set can be different from the population average because consumers adaptively decide whether to stop searching at each period t. That is, they argue that the mean price over the searched set is lower than the mean over the population when consumers search sequentially. Honka and Chintagunta show that the prediction from the sequential search holds true for the the subset of consumers who ended up searching only once.

A possible common criticism of these comparisons concerns whether the violation of the pattern in the sequential search originates from consumers' search mode or from other assumptions that are imposed in the search models. Consumers might employ a mixed search strategy, or learning and spillover on the price distribution of unsearched alternatives might occur. Many more assumptions are involved in deriving the predictions from the sequential/simultaneous search models studied in this chapter, which constitute the arena for future research as more granular and/or experimental data become available.

5.4.3.2 FURTHER READINGS

Three recent literature reviews have been published on the subject. Baye, Morgan, and Scholten (2006) give an overview in the perspective of equilibrium price dispersion and its sustainability. Ratchford (2009)'s review focuses more on the empirical evidence of search. A recent review by Honka, Hortaçsu, and

Wildenbeest (2019) focuses the empirical frameworks and the relation between search and consideration-set models.

Bibliography

Allen, J., R. Clark, & J.-F. Houde (2019). "Search frictions and market power in negotiated-price markets." *Journal of Political Economy*, 127, 1550–1598.

Anderson, S. P., & R. Renault (1999). "Pricing, product diversity, and search costs: A Bertrand-Chamberlin-Diamond model." *RAND Journal of Economics*, 30, 719–735.

Anderson, S. P., & R. Renault (2000). "Consumer information and firm pricing: Negative externalities from improved information." *International Economic Review*, 41, 721–742.

Athey, S., & G. Imbens (2011). "Position auction with consumer search." *Quarterly Journal of Economics*, 126, 1213–1270.

Baye, M. R., J. Morgan, & P. Scholten (2006). Chapter 6, "Information, search, and price dispersion." In vol. 1 of *Economics and Information Systems*, 323–375. Boston, MA: Elsevier.

Benabou, R. (1993). "Search market equilibrium, bilateral heterogeneity, and repeat purchases." *Journal of Economic Theory*, 60, 140–158.

Berry, S., J. Levinsohn, & A. Peakes (1995). "Automobile prices in market equilibrium." *Econometrica*, 63, 841–890.

Braverman, A. (1980). "Consumer search and alternative market equilibria." *Review of Economic Studies*, 47, 487–502.

Bronnenberg, B. J., J. B. Kim, & C. F. Mela (2016). "Zooming in on choice: How do consumers search for cameras online?" *Marketing Science*, 35, 693–712.

Brown, J. R., & A. Goolsbee (2002). "Does the internet make markets more competitive? Evidence from the life insurance industry." *Journal of Political Economy*, 110, 481–507.

Burdett, K., & K. L. Judd (1983). "Equilibrium price dispersion." *Econometrica*, 51, 955–969.

Butters, G. R. (1977a). "Equilibrium distributions of sales and advertising prices." *Review of Economic Studies*, 44, 465–491.

Butters, G. R. (1977b). "Market allocation through search: Equilibrium adjustment and price dispersion—A comment." *Journal of Economic Theory*, 15, 225–227.

Carlson, J. A., & R. P. McAfee (1983). "Discrete equilibrium price dispersion." *Journal of Political Economy*, 91, 480–493.

Chade, H., & L. Smith (2005). "Simultaneous search." Working paper, University of Wisconsin-Madison.

Chade, H., & L. Smith (2006). "Simultaneous search." *Econometrica*, 74, 1293–1307.

Chen, Y., & S. Yao (2016). "Sequential search with refinement: Model and application with click-stream data." *Management Science*, 63, 4345–4365.

De los Santos, B., A. Hortaçsu, & M. R. Wildenbeest (2012). "Testing models of consumer search using data on web browsing and purchasing behavior." *American Economic Review*, 102, 2955–2980.

De los Santos, B., A. Hortaçsu, & M. R. Wildenbeest (2017). "Search with learning for differentiated products: Evidence from e-commerce." *Journal of Business and Economic Statistics*, 35, 626–641.

Diamond, P. A. (1971). "A model of price adjustment." *Journal of Economic Theory*, 3, 156–168.

Dixit, A. K., & J. E. Stiglitz (1977). "Monopolistic competition and optimum product diversity." *American Economic Review*, 67, 297–308.

Ellison, G., & S. F. Ellison (2009). "Search, obfuscation, and price elasticities on the internet." *Econometrica*, 77, 427–452.

Goeree, M. S. (2008). "Limited information and advertising in the U.S. personal computer industry." *Econometrica*, 76, 1017–1074.

Goldmanis, M., A. Hortaçsu, C. Syverson, & Önsel Emre (2009). "E-commerce and the market structure of retail industries." *Economic Journal*, 120, 651–682.

Hong, H., & M. Shum (2006). "Using price distributions to estimate search costs." *RAND Journal of Economics*, 37, 257–275.

Honka, E. (2014). "Quantifying search and switching costs in the US auto insurance industry." *RAND Journal of Economics*, 45, 847–884.

Honka, E., & P. Chintagunta (2017). "Simultaneous or sequential? Search strategies in the U.S. auto insurance industry." *Marketing Science*, 36, 21–42.

Honka, E., A. Hortaçsu, & M. A. Vitorino (2017). "Advertising, consumer awareness, and choice: evidence from the U.S. banking industry." *RAND Journal of Economics*, 48, 611–646.

Honka, E., A. Hortaçsu, & M. Wildenbeest (2019). Chapter 4, "Empirical search and consideration sets." In Vol. 1, *Handbook of the Economics of Marketing*, Amsterdam. Elsevier

Hortaçsu, A., & C. Syverson (2004). "Product differentiation, search costs, and competition in the mutual fund industry: A case study of S&P 500 index funds." *Quarterly Journal of Economics*, 119, 403–456.

Ioannides, Y. M. (1975). "Market allocation through search: Equilibrium adjustment and price dispersion." *Journal of Economic Theory*, 11, 247–262.

Kim, J. B., P. Albuquerque, & B. J. Bronnenberg (2010). "Online demand under limited consumer search." *Marketing Science*, 29, 1001–1023.

Kim, J. B., P. Albuquerque, & B. J. Bronnenberg (2011). "Mapping online consumer search." *Journal of Marketing Research*, 48, 13–27.

Kim, J. B., P. Albuquerque, B. J. Bronnenberg (2017). "The Probit choice model under sequential search with an application to online retailing." *Marketing Science*, 63, 3911–3929.

Koulayev, S. (2014). "Search for differentiated products: Identification and estimation." *RAND Journal of Economics*, 45, 553–575.

MacMinn, R. D. (1980). "Search and market equilibrium." *Journal of Political Economy*, 88, 308–327.

McCall, J. J. (1970). "Economics of information and job search." *Quarterly Journal of Eocnomics*, 84, 113–126.

Mehta, N., S. Rajiv, & K. Srinivasan (2003). "Price uncertainty and consumer search: A structural model of consideration set formulation." *Marketing Science*, 22, 58–84.

Moraga-González, J. L., Z. Sándor, & M. R. Wildenbeest (2018). "Consumer search and prices in the automobile market." *Review of Economic Studies*. Accessed: https://academic.oup.com/restud/advance-article-abstract/doi/10.1093/restud/rdac047/6651084?redirectedFrom=fulltext&login=true.

Morgan, P., & R. Manning (1985). "Optimal search." *Econometrica*, 53, 923–944.

Pires, T. (2016). "Costly search and consideration sets in storable goods markets." *Quantitative Marketing and Economics*, 14, 157–193.

Ratchford, B. T. (2009). "Consumer Search Behavior and Its Effect on Markets." *Foundations and Trends in Marketing*, 3, 1–74.

Rauh, M. T. (2009). "Strategic complementarities and search market equilibrium." *Games and Economic Behavior*, 66, 959–978.

Reinganum, J. F. (1979). "A simple model of equilibrium price dispersion." *Journal of Political Economy*, 87, 851–858.

Rob, R. (1985). "Equilibrium price distributions." *Review of Economic Studies*, 52, 487–504.

Rothschild, M. (1973). "Models of market organization with imperfect information: A survey." *Journal of Political Economy*, 81, 1283–1308.

Rothschild, M. (1974). "Searching for the lowest price when the distribution of prices is unknown." *Journal of Political Economy*, 82, 689–711.

Salop, S. C. (1973). "Systematic job search and uneomplyment." *Review of Economic Studies*. 40, 191–201.

Salop, S., & J. Stiglitz (1977). "Bargains and ripoffs: A model of monopolistically competitive price dispersion." *Review of Economic Studies*, 44, 493–510.

Seiler, S. (2013). "The impact of search costs on consumer behavior: A dynamic approach." *Quantitative Marketing and Economics*, 11, 155–203.

Stahl II, D. O. (1989). "Oligopolistic pricing with sequential consumer search." *American Economic Review*, 79, 700–712.

Stigler, G. J. (1961). "The economics of information." *Journal of Political Economy*, 69, 213–225.

Ursu, R. M. (2018). "The power of rankings: Quantifying the effect of rankings on online consumer search and purchase decisions." *Marketing Science*, 37, 530–552.

Varian, H. R. (1980). "A model of sales." *American Economic Review*, 70, 651–659.

Vishwanath, T. (1992). "Parallel search for the best alternative." *Economic Theory*, 2, 495–507.

Weitzman, M. L. (1979). "Optimal search for the best alternative." *Econometrica*, 47, 641–654.

Wolinsky, A. (1986). "True monopolistic competition as a result of imperfect information." *Quarterly Journal of Economics*, 101, 493–512.

6

Auctions: Theory and Empirics

Auctions are used in a wide variety of contexts to allocate goods and services. Governments, central banks, internet selling platforms such as eBay, stock exchanges, treasuries, electricity markets, search engines, and ad-supported social media platforms all use them. Designing and optimizing auctions are important for both buyers and sellers, and the aim is typically to maximize the sellers' revenue, allocate goods to the buyers who need them most, or both. Large sums of money are at stake in many auctions, and economists have played a central role in their design.

This is a setting in which strategic behavior is of utmost importance, so game theorists and mechanism designers have built up a rich body of theoretical literature over the last few decades. There are also plenty of data available on real-life auctions and their outcomes for empirical economists to analyze. Moreover, constructing one's own data set using experimental auctions can be relatively simple for a researcher. Hence, experimental economists, econometricians, and empirical industrial organization economists have developed and used a variety of techniques to (1) test the predictions of auction theory and (2) recover structural parameters of interest from real life auctions. This empirical work is crucial for auctioneers trying to implement optimal auctions that maximize revenue, allocate goods efficiently, or both.

This chapter will provide a short primer/review of the basic theory behind single-unit auctions with both independent and interdependent values, and some leading models of multiunit auctions as well. After discussing the canonical models, we will cover empirical work that develop structural techniques for auction analysis, in addition to some applications of those techniques. Our treatment of the topic is by no means comprehensive. A standard reference on empirical work on auctions is Hendricks and Porter (2007). For a survey of more recent work, see Hortaçsu and Perrigne (2021). For book-length treatments on auctions, Paarsch and Hong (2006) explain many of the leading structural econometric methods until that point in time, and Krishna (2009) covers much of the theory and canonical models with far more depth and breadth than we do here. This chapter should essentially be viewed as a complement, not a substitute, for the papers and textbooks referenced herein.

6.1 Bidders' Valuations

Just as microeconomic theory texts generally begin with people's preferences or utility, here we begin with bidders' *values* for the goods up for auction. Values lie at the heart of how people choose to bid: the structure of people's values is a key input to theoretical modeling, while structural econometrics of auctions is often focused on trying to estimate the properties of bidders' values. We now consider several important aspects of the value structure.

6.1.1 Private Values versus Interdependent Values

Arguably, the most salient consideration when looking at bidders' values is whether they are private or interdependent with one another. This topic will be discussed next.

6.1.1.1 PRIVATE VALUES

Consider the following situation: One hot summer day, a classmate brings an unopened bottle of water to school. He is willing to sell it to the student who is willing to pay the most for it. A thirsty student may be willing to pay more than a fellow student who is not thirsty. Learning that another bidder is thirsty does not affect one's own thirst level, however. If, as in this context, bidders' valuations of the auctioned object do not depend on others' valuations of it, then we say that the bidders have *private values*. In real life, private values tend to arise when (1) bidders solely derive value from the good due to the utility that they can get from consuming it directly, as opposed to when the good's value is affected by its market/resale or social value; and (2) bidders clearly know their value for the good. Section 6.2 discusses private values in greater detail.

6.1.1.2 INTERDEPENDENT VALUES

Now, suppose a farmer owns farmland that is thought to be situated on top of an oil well and decides to put up the development rights of the land to auction. The bidders for the land will likely send seismic engineering crews to conduct their own geological surveys, trying to assess how much oil is underground. This is a situation where bidders would want to learn what other bidders think about the value of the object, which is hence known as the *interdependent values* framework. Indeed, one may argue that this example is an instance of the *common values* framework, where the value of the good being sold is the same for all bidders. The key in these auctions is that bidders don't know the exact valuation of the good at the time of the auction—only an estimate of it based on any information they may have—so other bidders' information and behavior can affect one's own expectation of a good's value. Section 6.4 discusses interdependent values in greater detail.

6.1.2 Symmetry versus Asymmetry of Bidders

Each person is different and thus may have different values for different goods. However, we can group certain types of people together: for example, in the scenario with the water bottle, a classroom of children could be divided into (1) those without a water bottle and (2) those with one.

Intuitively, when everyone who bids in an auction can be thought of as belonging to the same group, we can say that they have *symmetric* values. More formally, we would say that each bidder's value is drawn from the same distribution. However, if there are different groups of bidders in the auction, then it might make sense to consider them *asymmetric*: their values are drawn from different distributions, each corresponding to a different group. For example, although the students who did not bring water bottles may have different levels of thirst, it might make sense to group them as having their values drawn from the same distribution. However, the group of students who brought their own water bottles will have values drawn from a different distribution, such as one with a lower mean. In real life, this group-based asymmetry argument often arises when different types of firms compete in government procurement auctions, such as large firms versus small firms or firms whose production facilities are close to versus those far from a job site.

In theory, one could assume complete asymmetry, where each individual bidder has their value drawn from a unique distribution. However, as we will explain in section 6.2.3, asymmetry can make models complicated, if not altogether intractable. Therefore, in many parts of our discussion, we will assume symmetry to make the models more tractable, both analytically and computationally.

6.2 Single-Unit Auctions with Independent Private Values: Theory

The baseline auction setup involves a single unit of an indivisible good, where each bidder is symmetric and has an *independent private valuation* for the good (i.e., the private values are drawn independently from the same distribution). This section will focus on the basic theory behind this setup. Suppose that a single unit of a good is up for auction. The seller places zero value on the good, and it is indivisible. There are N bidders, each of whom has valuation $v_i \in [0, 1]$ for $i \in \mathcal{I} \equiv \{1, \ldots, N\}$, which other bidders do not know. Since bidders are symmetric, each bidder's private value v_i is independently drawn from a common, strictly increasing distribution $F(\cdot)$, with pdf $f(\cdot)$. This distribution $F(\cdot)$ is common knowledge to all bidders. Furthermore, each bidder is risk-neutral: if bidder i wins and must pay b, then their payoff is $v_i - b$. We note that the models we discuss here assume that bidders have no budget constraints. In other words, bidders are able to pay up to their respective values.[1][2]

6.2.1 The Four Standard Auctions and Their Equilibrium Strategies

We consider four standard auction formats that find wide use in applications, and as with any game, we want to figure out the equilibrium strategies therein. We will define each game and then provide a bidder's optimal strategy and some intuition for it.[3] As a preview, these auction are known as the "sealed-bid first-price auction (FPA): sealed-bid second-price auction (SPA)," "descending/Dutch auction," and "ascending/English auction."

6.2.1.1 SEALED-BID SPAS

We begin with the SPA, as its equilibrium strategy is simpler than that of the FPA. In an SPA, each bidder submits a private bid to the auctioneer; no other bidder can see it. The winning bidder (the one with the highest bid) gets the good and has to pay only the amount of the second-highest bid. So if bidder 2 has the second-highest bid (b_2), and bidder 1 is the highest bidder (with bid $b_1 > b_2$), then bidder 1 receives a payoff of $v_1 - b_2$, while losing bidders receive a payoff of 0. We now characterize the equilibrium bidding strategy of the SPA.

Suppose that you are in an SPA, with value v_i for the good. First, suppose that you bid $b_i > v_i$. Then suppose that the highest bidder among your opponents submits a bid of $b_2 \in (v_i, b_i)$. This means that you get a negative payoff, $v_i - b_2 < 0$, and you would rather have lost the auction. On the other hand, suppose that the highest bidder among your opponents submits $b_2 < v_i$. Then your payoff is

1. Unless noted otherwise, we will ignore the event of ties in equilibrium bids, which turns out to be a probability-zero event because we assumed $F(\cdot)$ to be continuous. In practice, tie-breaking rules can be applied, such as selecting the winner randomly from those who placed the highest bids.

2. Risk-averse or risk-seeking bidders would instead have payoff $u(v_i - b)$, where the utility function $u(\cdot)$ adds concavity or convexity. Risk aversion is discussed briefly in section 6.2.3.

3. For those who want more rigorous proofs, see, for example, Krishna (2009).

$v_i - b_2 > 0$. But notice how $b_i > v_i$ accomplishes the same payoff as $v_i = b_i$, so there is no benefit from submitting a bid higher than your value. There is only a risk of winning the good at a loss. So an optimal bid must satisfy $b_i \leq v_i$.

Now, suppose that you bid $b_i < v_i$ and the highest bidder among your opponents bids $b_2 \in (b_i, v_i)$. Then you would lose the auction and receive the payoff of 0, when you would rather receive $v_i - b_2 > 0$. On the other hand, suppose that you have the highest bid (i.e., $b_2 < b_i$). Then you receive the payoff $v_i - b_2$; however, your payoff from submitting $b_i < v_i$ is the same as your payoff from submitting $b_i = v_i$. So there is no gain from submitting a bid lower than your value, but you risk losing when you would have preferred to win. This means that at an optimum, $b_i \geq v_i$. Hence, putting these arguments together, the optimal SPA bid for bidder i is

$$b_i^{SPA} = v_i.$$

This is a weakly dominant strategy,[4] and in a Nash equilibrium, all bidders will bid their true valuations.

6.2.1.2 ASCENDING/ENGLISH AUCTIONS

Unlike an SPA, where sealed bids are submitted simultaneously, an English auction is mechanically dynamic. The seller starts at a price of 0, which all bidders with positive value are obviously willing to pay. The seller proceeds to raise the price over time until all but one bidder drops out.[5] The winning bidder (whom we denote as bidder 1, with value v_1) then pays the price at which the second-to-last bidder (which we denote as p_2) drops out, so their payoff is $v_1 - p_2$. As always, all the other bidders receive a payoff of 0.

Now, suppose that you are in an English auction, where you choose the price p_i at which you drop out of the auction. Again, you have some value of v_i. As the price rises, you will not drop out when the price is below v_i, since if everyone else happens to drop out by the time the price hits $p_2 < v_i$, you would win $v_i - p_2 > 0$. Conversely, you obviously want to drop out before the price is above v_i because if

4. If the highest bidder among your opponents bids b_2 above your value v_i in equilibrium, then you are indifferent for all $b_i \in [0, b_2)$.

5. This is done either by a continuous price clock in which the price steadily rises over time, or by each bidder openly calling out a higher price. We will use the price clock framework, although in empirical settings, we often switch to open outcry. Note that the price clock framework is a special case of what is known as a "Japanese auction," which is different from an English auction. A canonical English auction is when the bidders call out a higher price, whereas a Japanese auction is when the auctioneer raises the price over time and bidders must keep signaling their willingness to stay in until their reservation price is reached. So it is technically incorrect to refer to an ascending price clock auction as an "English auction," but since the terminology has become a convention in the literature, we will follow the convention to avoid confusion.

every remaining competitor drops out by the time the price hits $p_2 > v_i$, then you win the auction with $v_i - p_2 < 0$. Therefore, you should drop out at price $p_i^E = v_i$. An important consideration is that in this independent private values setting, an English auction is equivalent to an SPA: at an optimum,

$$p_i^E = v_i = b_i^{SPA}.$$

Therefore, we will use the notation b instead of p when discussing English auctions.[6]

6.2.1.3 SEALED-BID FPA

In FPAs, each bidder submits a bid to the auctioneer; each bidder knows only their own bid. The bidder with the highest bid (bidder 1) wins the good and pays their own bid, for a payoff of $v_1 - b_1$, while losers pay nothing and receive a payoff of 0. In SPAs and English auctions, bidder *i*'s bid b_i did not affect *i*'s ex post payoff after winning the auction, and it was optimal to simply bid *i*'s true valuation. However, now the bidder must pay their own bid, meaning that bidding one's true value in an FPA will guarantee a zero payoff whether the bidder wins or loses.

Since an optimal bid clearly depends on each bidder's valuation of the good, the bidding function $b(\cdot)$ can be formulated as an assumed continuous, strictly increasing function:

$$b(v) : [0, 1] \to [0, 1].$$

Intuitively, $b(0) = 0$. By the symmetry of our model setup, if an equilibrium bidding function $b(\cdot)$ exists, each bidder will use the same $b(\cdot)$. Thus, function $b(\cdot)$ constitutes an equilibrium if no bidder can do better by choosing a different bidding function $\tilde{b}(\cdot)$, given that all the other bidders use $b(\cdot)$. So the bidder's expected utility function if they have value v_i and uses $b(\cdot)$ but bids as though they have a value of $r \in [0, 1]$ is

$$u(r, v_i) = \Pr(i \text{ wins} | b(r)) (v_i - b(r)).$$

Then, we can rewrite this objective function more formally:

$$\begin{aligned}
\Pr(i \text{ wins} | b(r)) (v_i - b(r)) &= \Pr\left(\text{all other } b\left(v_j\right) < b(r), j \neq i\right) (v_i - b(r)) \\
&= \Pr\left(v_j < r, \forall j \neq i\right) (v_i - b(r)) \\
&= F^{N-1}(r) (v_i - b(r)).
\end{aligned}$$

6. When bidders' valuations are interdependent, English auctions and SPAs are not equivalent. We discuss interdependent-value English auctions in section 6.4.

The second equality is because we assume a strictly increasing bidding function (i.e., $x > y \Longleftrightarrow b(x) > b(y)$). The third equality follows from the probability of bidder i's stated value r being greater than all others' true values, given that everyone's value is drawn from a common distribution of $F(\cdot)$. Now, note that $b(\cdot)$ is a symmetric equilibrium bidding function, meaning that $b(v_i)$ is the equilibrium bid for any $i \in \{1, 2, \ldots, N\}$. Then, the first-order condition is an ordinary differential equation (ODE), which can be solved to derive the optimal bid:

$$\left. \frac{dF^{N-1}(r)(v_i - b(r))}{dr} \right|_{r=v_i} = 0$$

$$\Leftrightarrow \quad \left. \frac{dF^{N-1}(r)\, b(r)}{dr} \right|_{r=v_i} = \left(\left. \frac{dF^{N-1}(r)}{dr} \right|_{r=v_i} \right) \cdot v_i$$

$$\Leftrightarrow \quad \left. \frac{dF^{N-1}(r)\, b(r)}{dr} \right|_{r=v_i} = (N-1) F^{N-2}(v_i) f(v_i)\, v_i$$

$$\Leftrightarrow \quad F^{N-1}(v_i)\, b(v_i) = \int_0^{v_i} (N-1) F^{N-2}(x) f(x)\, x dx$$

$$\Leftrightarrow \quad b^{FPA}(v_i) = \frac{1}{F^{N-1}(v_i)} \int_0^{v_i} (N-1)\, x F^{N-2}(x) f(x)\, dx. \tag{6.2.1}$$

If Y_1 is the highest valuation of all other bidders (i.e., the highest-order statistic among the remaining $N-1$ valuations), we have

$$b^{FPA}(v_i) = \mathbb{E}[Y_1 | Y_1 < v_i]$$

because the term in the integral, $(N-1) F^{N-2}(\cdot) f(\cdot)$, is the probability density function of the highest-order statistic among $N-1$ valuations. The denominator term adjusts to condition on $Y_1 < v_i$.

In addition, one can use integration by parts in equation (6.2.1) to show that

$$b^{FPA}(v_i) = v_i - \frac{\int_0^{v_i} F^{N-1}(x)\, dx}{F^{N-1}(v_i)}.\text{[7]} \tag{6.2.2}$$

In other words, the optimal bid in an FPA has two convenient interpretations. $\mathbb{E}[Y_1 | Y_1 < v_i]$ implies that the optimal bid is your expectation of the highest value among the other bidders, conditional on your value being the highest among all bidders. This is intuitive: since you pay your own bid in an FPA, you want to pay the minimum possible bid such that you still win the item, and the highest value among the other bidders provides an upper bound on the highest bid among the other bidders. Another related interpretation from equation (6.2.2) is that the optimal bid shades your value, according to the number of other bidders in the auction.

6.2.1.4 DESCENDING/DUTCH AUCTION

In Dutch auctions, the seller begins by fixing a high price at which, ideally, no bidder would want to buy the good. The seller proceeds to drop the price until a bidder signals that they are willing to pay the current price.[8] That bidder wins and pays the current price, so if we denote the current price (at which the bid wins) as p_1, then their payoff is $v_1 - p_1$. Losers receive a zero payoff. As the clock ticks down, you have to decide at what price p_i you will shout your willingness to pay the price. Not only are you willing to pay that price, but you *must* pay that price if you shout it out, so the price again affects your ex post payoff.

Put differently, the Dutch auction could be considered as one where all the players have written on a piece of paper the price at which they will shout out their willingness to pay. The game structure is the same as that of an FPA,[9] except that players shout out the bid they wrote down instead of submitting the piece of paper to the auctioneer. So the optimal dropout price is

$$p_i^D = b^{FPA}(v_i).$$

As with the English auction, we will drop p notation in favor of b when discussing Dutch auctions later in this chapter.

6.2.2 Revenue Equivalence and Allocative Efficiency

6.2.2.1 THE REVENUE EQUIVALENCE THEOREM

We now study the auctioneer's perspective. The auctioneer wants to maximize the expected revenue (which equals profit, since we assume the seller faces no cost for creating/procuring the good). What auction format should the auctioneer use? First, remember that in the current setup, FPA bids equal Dutch auction bids in equilibrium, and the same holds for SPA and English auction bids. Therefore,

7. Specifically, note that you can (1) rewrite $\int_0^{v_i}(N-1)\,xF^{N-2}(x)f(x)\,dx$ as $\int_0^{v_i} x dF^{N-1}(x)$, (2) use integration by parts, (3) plug the resulting expression back into the overall expression for $b^{FPA}(v_i)$, and (4) simplify to the desired form.

8. This is done either continuously (i.e., by a continuously falling price clock) or by the seller calling out a lower price in discrete steps. We will use the price clock framework here.

9. Learning other bidders' valuation over time does not occur since we assumed that $F(\cdot)$ is common knowledge.

when considering a revenue-maximizing auction, we can simply compare expected revenues between SPAs and FPAs.

Define R^{FPA} and R^{SPA} as the respective expected revenues of an FPA and an SPA. We can define the expected revenues as follows:

$$\begin{aligned}
R^{FPA} &= \int_0^1 b^{FPA}(v)\, g_{1,N}(v)\, dv \\
&= \int_0^1 b^{FPA}(v)\, NF^{N-1}(v) f(v)\, dv \\
R^{SPA} &= \int_0^1 v g_{2,N}(v)\, dv \\
&= \int_0^1 vN(N-1)\, F^{N-2}(v) f(v)\,(1-F(v))\, dv,
\end{aligned}$$

where $g_{1,N}(v)$ and $g_{2,N}(v)$ are the probability densities for the highest and second-highest valuations (derived using order statistics), respectively.[10] We can now show that FPAs yield the same expected revenue as SPAs. Substituting in our expression for $b^{FPA}(v)$ from equation (6.2.1), we get

$$\begin{aligned}
R^{FPA} &= \int_0^1 b^{FPA}(v)\, NF^{N-1}(v) f(v)\, dv \\
&= N(N-1) \int_0^1 \int_0^v xF^{N-2}(x) f(x) f(v)\, dx dv \\
&= N(N-1) \int_0^1 \int_x^1 xF^{N-2}(x) f(x) f(v)\, dv dx \\
&= N(N-1) \int_0^1 xF^{N-2}(x) f(x) \left[\int_x^1 f(v)\, dv \right] dx \\
&= N(N-1) \int_0^1 xF^{N-2}(x) f(x)\,(1-F(x))\, dx \\
&= R^{SPA}
\end{aligned}$$

In other words, since $R^{SPA} = R^{FPA}$, and since we have explained how English (Dutch) auctions are equivalent to SPAs (FPAs), the result here implies that all

10. The highest and second-highest value density among N bidders are given by

$$\begin{aligned}
g_{1,N}(v) &\equiv NF^{N-1}(v) f(v) \\
g_{2,N}(v) &\equiv N(N-1)\, F^{N-2}(v) f(v)\,(1-F(v)).
\end{aligned}$$

four auction formats yield the same expected revenue. The result is known as the "revenue equivalence theorem" in the literature (Vickrey, 1961; Myerson, 1981).

6.2.2.2 ALLOCATIVE EFFICIENCY

Researchers have studied allocative efficiency of auction outcomes as well (i.e., whether the good is allocated to the bidder who has the highest valuation). In our current setup, all four standard auctions achieve allocative efficiency when bidders follow the equilibrium strategies; it follows from the fact that the equilibrium bidding functions are strictly increasing in bidder values. Hence, the bidder with the highest value submits the highest bid and wins the good. However, allocative efficiency may break down when, for example, bidders are asymmetric or when the auction is a multiunit auction. We will study these topics later in this chapter.

6.2.3 *Extensions*

Having discussed the important results from the bidders' side (bidding strategies) and the seller's side (expected revenue and efficiency), we now consider some extensions to our framework.

6.2.3.1 SELLER'S OPTIMAL RESERVE PRICES

A seller may be unwilling to sell below a certain price; they may place a positive value on the good, such that receiving a price below that value would actually cause them to incur a loss. Hence, sellers often impose a reserve price that is at or above their value: for a bidder to win the good, not only must they beat all other bidders, but their bid must also be above the reserve price.

Denote the reserve price by r, and assume that this is public and common knowledge. In an SPA, all bidders again have the weakly dominant strategy of simply bidding their values. Meanwhile, in the FPA, the optimal bid for a bidder with value $v_i \geq r$ (obviously, a bidder with value $v_i < r$ will refuse to participate) is

$$\begin{aligned} b^{FPA}(v_i) &= \mathbb{E}\left[\max\{Y_1, r\} \,|Y_1 < v_i\right] \\ &= \frac{1}{F^{N-1}(v_i)}\left(rF^{N-1}(r) + \int_r^{v_i} x\,(N-1)\,F^{N-2}(x) f(x)\,dx\right).^{11} \end{aligned}$$

Furthermore, in an FPA and an SPA, it can be shown that the expected payment of a bidder with a value $v_i \geq r$ is simply

11. Recall that Y_1 denotes the highest value among the other bidders.

$$rF^{N-1}(r) + \int_r^{v_i} x(N-1)F^{N-2}(x)f(x)\,dx.$$

Thus, we have revenue equivalence in the standard setup with reserve prices. Now, the problem a seller faces is to figure out what reserve price to set such that expected revenue is maximized. First, suppose that the seller values the good at level v_0. Then the overall expected payoff of the seller if they set a reserve price $r \geq v_0$ is

$$F^N(r)\,v_0 + N\int_r^1 \left[rF^{N-1}(r) + \int_r^{v_i} x(N-1)F^{N-2}(x)f(x)\,dx\right] f(y)\,dy. \tag{6.2.3}$$

In other words, the seller's expected payoff is the expected value of keeping the good (no bidder meets the reserve price) plus the sum of the expected payments if bidders bid at least the reserve price. Taking the first-order condition of equation (6.2.3) gives the optimal reserve price, characterized by

$$r^* - \frac{1-F(r^*)}{f(r^*)} = v_0. \tag{6.2.4}$$

In fact, sellers that want to maximize their revenue should always set a reserve price that exceeds their value. That said, this does have the consequence of introducing potential inefficiency: even if the highest bidder values the object more than the seller, that bidder may still go home with nothing if they fail to meet the reserve price.

6.2.3.2 BIDDERS' RISK AVERSION

We discuss the consequences of risk-averseness of bidders here, where the payoff of the winning bidder is now $u(v_i - b)$, with $u(\cdot)$ being strictly concave. An important result from bidders' risk aversion is that revenue equivalence no longer holds. In particular, the expected revenue from an FPA is higher than that of an SPA.

Note first that even under risk aversion, the same strategic considerations hold in an SPA: risk-averse bidders have no incentive to do anything but bid their value in an SPA. However, because they must pay their bid in an FPA, the bidders behave differently. Their expected utility function in an FPA is

$$F^{N-1}(v_i)\cdot u(v_i - \gamma(v_i))$$

for a new bidding function under risk aversion, $\gamma(\cdot)$. If we define $F^{N-1}(v_i) = G(v_i)$, then we can show that for $g(v) = \frac{dG}{dv}$,

$$\gamma'(v_i) = \frac{u(x - \gamma(v_i))}{u'(v_i - \gamma(v_i))} \frac{g(v_i)}{G(v_i)}.$$

On the flip side, in our risk-neutral setup, one can show that

$$b'(v_i) = (v_i - b(v_i)) \frac{g(v_i)}{G(v_i)}.$$

Krishna (2009) shows that with these first-order conditions, it must be the case that $\gamma(v_i) > b(v_i)$. In other words, risk aversion makes people submit higher bids when they must pay them, since the loss in utility from a slightly higher payment is not as bad as losing the auction. Since people submit higher bids in the FPA under risk aversion, whereas people submit the same bids in the SPA under both risk aversion and risk neutrality, expected revenue must be higher for an FPA under risk aversion.

With regard to efficiency, Hu, Matthews, and Zou (2010) show that when considering reserve prices, FPAs are ex post more efficient than SPAs if bidders are risk averse because the optimal reservation price in an FPA turns out to be lower than that of an SPA. Hence, if a sale (to the bidder with the highest value) occurs in an SPA, it would likewise occur in an FPA, but not vice versa.

Asymmetric Bidders Suppose that bidders are no longer symmetric (i.e., they do not draw their values from the same common distribution anymore). For a simple example, consider two bidders. Bidder 1's value is drawn from $F_1(\cdot)$ on $[0, \omega_1]$ and bidder 2's value is drawn from $F_2(\cdot)$ on $[0, \omega_2]$. Denote the inverse of their respective bidding functions as $\psi_i(\cdot) \equiv b_i^{-1}(\cdot)$. Bidder i's objective function is

$$F_j(\psi_j(b_i))(v_i - b_i).$$

The first-order condition is

$$\psi_j'(b_i) = \frac{F_j(\psi_j(b_i))}{f_j(\psi_j(b_i))} \frac{1}{\psi_i(b_i) - b_i}.$$

It is very difficult to solve this first-order condition analytically to find a general solution. However, Maskin and Riley (2000) show that for a special case where $\omega_1 \geq \omega_2$ and $\frac{f_1(x)}{F_1(x)} > \frac{f_2(x)}{F_2(x)}$, $b_2(x) > b_1(x)$ holds for any $x \in [0, \omega_2]$: the bidder with the lower upper bound on their distribution of values actually bids more aggressively than the one with the higher upper bound.

The auctions with symmetric bidders were allocatively efficient since the bidder with the highest valuation won the auction; it no longer holds necessarily in an auction with asymmetric bidders. Furthermore, one can construct examples where $R^{SPA} > R^{FPA}$ or $R^{SPA} < R^{FPA}$: revenue equivalence breaks down with asymmetric bidders.

6.2.3.3 COLLUSION BY BIDDERS

Collusion is prevalent in auctions because bidders who join collusive bidding rings can extract a high surplus in auctions. The Sherman Antitrust Act has been invoked many times in cases dealing with auction markets. When analyzing collusive behavior in auctions, consider our standard framework, but let $I < N$ denote the number of bidders in a bidding ring. Furthermore, for a set $\mathcal{I}$ of bidders in a ring, let $V_1^{\mathcal{I}}$ denote the highest value among all ring members. Finally, let bidders be asymmetric: each bidder i's value is drawn from a distribution F_i over a common interval $[0, 1]$.[12]

Here, we will consider only one ring targeting an SPA.[13] For the ring member who wants to win, it is weakly dominant to bid $V_1^{\mathcal{I}}$. All other members submit the minimum bid possible: either 0 or the reserve price r (if there is one). Thus, competition is limited, and there are circumstances in which the winning ring member pays a lower price for the good than otherwise would have happened without collusion. More formally, let $\mathcal{N}$ denote the set of all bidders. The price that a winning ring member i has to pay is

$$\hat{b}_i \equiv \max\left\{V_1^{\mathcal{N}\backslash\mathcal{I}}, r\right\} \leq \max\left\{V_1^{\mathcal{N}\backslash i}, r\right\} \equiv b_i,$$

where $\hat{b}_i$ denotes i's payment with a ring and b_i denotes the same i's payment without a ring. The difference between $\hat{b}_i$ and b_i is the source of the ring's profits. Let $m_i(v_i)$ denote the expected payment of bidder i with value v_i without a ring, and $\hat{m}_i(v_i)$ denote the expected payment with a ring. Then the ex ante expected profits of the ring are

$$\sum_{i \in \mathcal{I}} \mathbb{E}\left[m_i(v_i) - \hat{m}_i(v_i)\right].$$

On the other hand, for bidder $j \notin \mathcal{I}$, it is weakly dominant to bid their value v_j. The probability that they win the good does not depend on whether or not there

12. Note that assuming a common interval is not necessary and done only for simplicity in this exposition.

13. We confine our interests to an SPA because many auctions conducted in real life are English auctions. See, e.g., Krishna (2009) for a discussion on collusion in FPAs.

is a collusive ring, because it is simply the probability that they have the highest value among all bidders. In addition, note that if j wins, then they pay

$$\hat{b}_j \equiv \max\left\{V_1^{\mathcal{I}}, V^{\mathcal{N}\setminus\mathcal{I}\setminus j}, r\right\} = \max\left\{V^{\mathcal{N}\setminus j}, r\right\} \equiv b_j.$$

So nonring bidders pay the same bid if they win, meaning that whether or not there is a ring, the expected payment is the same for a nonring bidder. Furthermore, it is clear that the expected payment of the ring to the auctioneer falls weakly as more bidders in $\mathcal{N}$ join $\mathcal{I}$.

A natural follow-up question would be how the ring ensures that cartel members truthfully reveal their private values to the other members of the ring so at the actual auction, only the ring member with the highest member submits a serious bid. One method is for the ring to conduct some sort of "preauction knockout (PAKT)" prior to the actual auction. In the PAKT, each ring member is asked to reveal their private value for the good. The ring member i with the highest value will then submit the ring's only serious bid at the auction, while the PAKT losers submit noncompetitive bids (such as the reserve price). If i wins the auction, then they pay $b_i - \hat{b}_i$ to the ring, which is the difference between what they paid versus what they would have paid without a ring.

Finally, the ring makes a side payment to each of the losing members. With a well-chosen way of defining each member's side payment, the PAKT will be incentive compatible since it will be weakly dominant for each member to report their true value, and it will also be individually rational since no ring member would be better off by not participating.[14]

To finish our analysis, let us briefly discuss the seller's side. As more bidders join the ring, a seller's expected revenues fall due to the reduced competition. Without appealing to antitrust authorities, and with a fixed auction format, the only thing that sellers can do to save their revenues is to impose an optimal reserve price to offset the reduced competition. It can be proved that the optimal reserve price for the seller is larger when there is a ring than when there is no ring, and as a bidding ring gains more members, the optimal reserve price for the seller must increase. When it comes to efficiency, a bidding ring may introduce inefficiency into the auction, depending on the structure of the PAKT. In particular, if the bidding ring uses a mechanism that incentivizes bidders to bid above their values in the PAKT,[15]

14. For example, the ring can give each member i a side payment of $m_i(v_i) - \hat{m}_i(v_i)$. This would make the PAKT incentive compatible and individually rational. However, it has issues in terms of budget balancing: it is balanced in expected terms, but in reality, the sum of side payments may be greater or less than its gains from the target auction. See Krishna (2009) for further details.

15. This can arise due to the side payment structure.

then goods in the target auction may actually go to bidders without the highest valuations.

6.3 Single-Unit Auctions with Independent Private Values: Empirics and Econometrics

The tight structure that auction theory provides makes it very appealing for empirical economists using structural estimation to test predictions and estimate parameters. Generally, the main unknown that we want to estimate is the distribution of bidder values, given that we only observe bidding data. This is because we can see bidding data plus other observable auction characteristics (e.g., the number of bidders), but not bidders' underlying values, so combining estimates of distributions with the bidding (and other auction) data allows us to back out estimates of values. In turn, we can use these estimates to run counterfactual analyses.

6.3.1 *Empirics and Econometrics for SPAs*

6.3.1.1 IDENTIFICATION AND ESTIMATION OF BIDDER VALUATION DISTRIBUTION IN SPAS

Athey and Haile (2002) provide an excellent overview of identification of symmetric independent private value models. We focus here on SPAs due to the prevalence of English auctions in real life and the equivalence between the two formats.

Let $F_{V_i}(\cdot)$ denote the distribution of the value of bidder i, and V_i the corresponding random variable. Assuming symmetry, we can drop the notation i and write the distribution as $F_V(\cdot)$. It is often the case that the econometrician only observes the transaction price of the good in a given auction. Recall that the dominant strategy for bidders is $b_i = v_i$ in SPAs. Athey and Haile prove that even with just the transaction price data, one can nonparametrically identify $F_V(\cdot)$.

The identification argument is as follows. First, note that the ith order statistic from an i.i.d. sample of size N from a distribution $F(\cdot)$ is given by the formula

$$F_{i:N}(x) = \frac{N!}{(N-i)!\,(i-1)!} \int_0^{F(x)} t^{N-i}(1-t)^{i-1}\, dt.^{16}$$

The right-hand side is strictly monotonic in $F(x)$, implying that for any (i, N), $F(x)$ is uniquely determined by $F_{i:N}(x)$. Thus, since the transaction price gives $F_{V,2:N}(\cdot)$, we can identify $F_V(\cdot)$ from a strictly monotonic mapping $\phi[\cdot|N]$, defined as follows:

16. See Arnold et al. (1992).

$$F_{V,2:N}(v) = N(N-1)\int_0^{F_V(v)} t^{N-2}(1-t)\,dt \tag{6.3.1}$$

$$\equiv \phi\left[F_V(v)\,|N\right]. \tag{6.3.2}$$

Assuming symmetric independent private values implies that values of $F_V(v)$ implied by different order statistics should be identical for all v, which is a testable prediction. Therefore, we can test the SPA model if we either observe a set of auctions that have exogenously varying numbers of bidders or if we observe multiple bids in one auction.

Paarsch and Hong (2006) discuss a few possibilities for estimators within this framework. Suppose that we observe a sample of T independent auctions, each with N bidders, and we see all their bids. One could simply use the sample analog for the population quantity, or the empirical distribution function, as an estimator for $F_V(v)$:

$$\hat{F}_V(v) = \frac{1}{TN}\sum_{t=1}^{T}\sum_{i=1}^{N}\mathbf{1}(b_{it} \leq v)$$

where $\mathbf{1}(\cdot)$ is the indicator function. Furthermore, in the situation where we only observe the winning bid across T auctions, and if N does not vary across auctions, one could exploit equation (6.3.2) from the display equation above and use

$$\hat{F}_{V;2,N}(v) \equiv \frac{1}{T}\sum_{t=1}^{T}\mathbf{1}\left(v_{t,2:N} \leq v\right),$$

which yields

$$\hat{F}_V(v) = \phi^{-1}\left[\hat{F}_{V,2:N}(v)\,|N\right].$$

That is, first estimate the empirical distribution function (EDF) of the winning bids/second-highest valuations across the T auctions, and then use the inverse of the order statistic formula to obtain the underlying $F_V(\cdot)$.

6.3.1.2 ESTIMATION WITH WEAKER ASSUMPTIONS

A large body of literature in experimental economics has tested how laboratory subjects, often selected from college students, bid in various auction mechanisms, and has shown that bidders do not bid exactly at their valuation in SPAs. Motivated by the experimental evidence, Haile and Tamer (2003) analyze SPAs using only the following weaker behavioral assumptions:

HT(1) Bidders do not pay more than their valuation.
HT(2) Bidders do not allow opponents to win at a price below their valuation.

Derivation of the Bounds for Bidder's Valuation Distribution $F(v)$ HT(1) can be written as $b_i \leq v_i$ for all i. If $G(x) \equiv \Pr(b_i \leq x)$, then we get a first-order stochastic dominance relation:

$$G(v) \geq F(v) \qquad \forall v \geq 0.$$

This dominance relation provides an upper bound on bidders' valuation distribution $F(\cdot)$. Moreover, this dominance relation also applies to all order statistics of bids and valuations (i.e., $G_{i:N}(v) \geq F_{i:N}(v)$ for all i and v). These will let us attain tighter bounds. HT(2) can be written as $v_{2:N} \leq b_{1:N} + \Delta$, where Δ denotes the *minimum bid increment*. Thus, we get the dominance relation

$$F_{2:N}(v) \geq G^{\Delta}_{1:N}(v) \qquad \forall v \geq 0,$$

where $G^{\Delta}_{1:N}(\cdot)$ denotes the distribution of the highest bid plus the bid increment, $b_{1:N} + \Delta$. This provides us with a lower bound on $F(v)$.

Now suppose that the econometrician observes bids in T auctions, each of which has between 2 and M bidders. Then one can use the following empirical distribution functions as estimators:

$$\hat{G}_{i:N}(v) = \frac{1}{T_N}\sum_{t=1}^{T} \mathbf{1}\left(N_t = N, b_{i:N_t} \leq v\right)$$

$$\hat{G}^{\Delta}_{1,N}(v) = \frac{1}{T_N}\sum_{t=1}^{T} \mathbf{1}\left(N_t = N, b_{1:N_t} + \Delta_t \leq v\right),$$

where $T_N = \sum_{t=1}^{T} \mathbf{1}(N_t = N)$. While each of these estimated EDFs can be used to construct upper and lower bounds, one can also take the minimum and maximum across the individual EDFs to construct even sharper bounds. That is, one can construct upper and lower bounds of $F(v)$ using

$$\hat{F}_U(v) = \min_{N\in\{2,\ldots,M\}, i\in\{1,\ldots,N\}} \phi^{-1}\left[\hat{G}_{i:N}(v)\,|i, N\right]$$

$$\hat{F}_L(v) = \max_{N\in\{2,\ldots,M\}} \phi^{-1}\left[\hat{G}^{\Delta}_{1:N}(v)\,|i = 2, N\right], \quad \text{respectively.}$$

Bounds for the Seller's Profit Function and the Optimal Reserve Prices Haile and Tamer (2003) then consider how to calculate the optimal reserve price. Consider the function

$$\pi(r) \equiv (r - v_0)[1 - F(r)].$$

Assuming that $\pi(r)$ is strictly pseudoconcave in r on an interval $(\underline{v}, \overline{v})$, and also keeping the same two behavioral assumptions as before, one can show that the optimal reserve price maximizes $\pi(r)$:

$$r^* = \arg\max_r (r - v_0)[1 - F(r)].$$[17]

We can use the estimated bounds on $F(\cdot)$ to analyze

$$\pi_U(r) = (r - v_0)[1 - F_U(r)]$$
$$\pi_L(r) = (r - v_0)[1 - F_L(r)].$$

Because $\hat{F}_L(v) \leq \hat{F}(v) \leq \hat{F}_U(v)$, for each r, we have

$$\pi_U(r) \leq \pi(r) \leq \pi_L(r);$$

that is, we have found bounds for the profit function. Now, define

$$r_1^* = \arg\sup_r \pi_U(r)$$
$$\pi_U^* = \sup_r \pi_U(r).$$

Finally, we can define bounds on the optimal reserve price:

$$r_L^* \equiv \sup\left\{r < r_1^* : \pi_L(r) \leq \pi_U^*\right\}$$
$$r_U^* \equiv \inf\left\{r > r_1^* : \pi_L(r) \leq \pi_U^*\right\}.$$

Figure 6.3.1 illustrates the bounds for profit function and the characterizations of (r_L^*, r_U^*). Notice that the unknown true profit function $\pi(r)$ attains a maximum

17. The strategy to directly exploit the formula in equation (6.2.4),

$$r^* - \frac{1 - F(r^*)}{f(r^*)} = v_0,$$

does not work because it involves $f(\cdot)$ that is not restricted by placing restrictions on $F(\cdot)$.

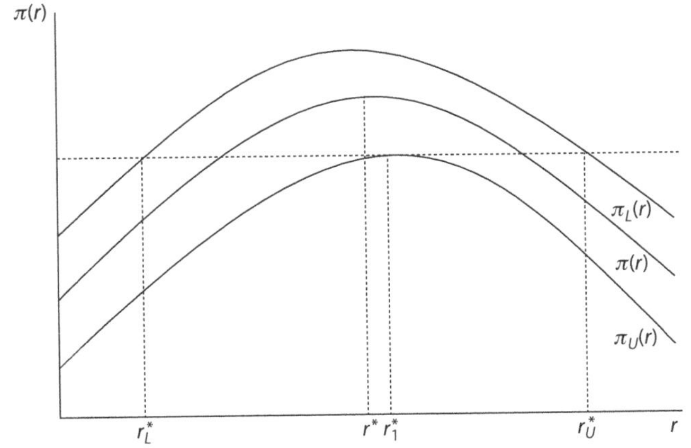

FIGURE 6.3.1. Construction of the optimal reserve price bounds

that is weakly higher than π_U^*, the maximum of $\pi_U(r)$. However, the maximand r^* of $\pi(r)$ should be between r_L^* and r_U^* since $\pi(r)$ is always below $\pi_L(r)$. Therefore, the optimal reserve price for the unknown $F_V(\cdot)$ should lie between r_L^* and r_U^*.[18]

Estimation of the Model Primitives For estimation, Haile and Tamer (2003) first use the sample analogs $\hat{\pi}_U(r) = (r - v_0)\left[1 - \hat{F}_U(r)\right]$ and $\hat{\pi}_L(r) = (r - v_0)\left[1 - \hat{F}_L(r)\right]$. Then they define the following estimators:

$$\hat{\pi}_U^* = \sup_r \hat{\pi}_U(r)$$

$$\hat{r}_1^* = \arg\sup_r \hat{\pi}_U(r)$$

$$\hat{r}_L^* \equiv \sup\left\{r < \hat{r}_1^* : \min_{\pi \in \hat{\pi}_L^c(r)} \left(\pi - \hat{\pi}_U^*\right)^2 \leq \epsilon_T\right\}$$

$$\hat{r}_U^* \equiv \inf\left\{r > \hat{r}_1^* : \min_{\pi \in \hat{\pi}_L^c(r)} \left(\pi - \hat{\pi}_U^*\right)^2 \leq \epsilon_T\right\},$$

where $\hat{\pi}_L^c(r)$ is a correspondence defined by

$$\pi \in \hat{\pi}_L^c(r) \Longleftrightarrow \pi \in \left[\lim_{r' \uparrow r} \hat{\pi}_L(r'), \lim_{r' \downarrow r} \hat{\pi}_L(r')\right]$$

18. Haile and Tamer also prove that r_L^* and r_U^* provide sharp bounds on the optimal reserve price. In other words, there exist possible $F_V(\cdot)$ satisfying the behavioral restrictions that have either r_L^* or r_U^* as their optimal reserve price. See their theorem 4.

and $\epsilon_T > 0$ approaches 0 at an appropriate rate as the number of markets T approaches infinity. The authors prove that $\hat{r}_L^*$ and $\hat{r}_U^*$ are consistent estimators of the optimal reserve price bounds.[19]

6.3.2 Empirics and Econometrics for FPAs

Bids are nonlinear functions of bidder valuations in FPAs (i.e., $b_i = b(v_i)$). Therefore, identification and estimation of FPAs are fundamentally more difficult than those of SPAs where bids b_i and bidders' valuations v_i coincide. One possibility is to approach the problem parametrically (i.e., define $F_V(v;\theta)$ as a known function and implement maximum likelihood estimation). To do this, define the inverse bid function as $\psi(b(v)) \equiv b^{-1}(b(v))$. Then, for a given value of θ, one can take each bid b_i and find the value $v_i = \psi(b_i;\theta)$ that rationalizes b_i by solving an ordinary differential equation, and subsequently use maximum likelihood estimation (MLE) with the parameterized distribution. Unfortunately, there are several key disadvantages to implementing this parametric method, including that we have to argue that the parametric assumption on $F_V(\cdot)$ is a good fit for reality, and we have to solve the ODE for each θ, which can be computationally costly.

6.3.2.1 GUERRE ET AL. (2000)'S NONPARAMETRIC IDENTIFICATION AND ESTIMATION OF BIDDER VALUATION DISTRIBUTION IN FPAS

In an influential paper, Guerre, Perrigne, and Vuong (2000) propose a nonparametric approach to identify and estimate bidders' valuations in FPAs. They begin by considering bidder i's objective:

$$\max_b (v_i - b) \Pr(i \text{ wins}|b) \tag{6.3.3}$$

The first-order condition for equation (6.3.3) is:

$$v_i - b = \left(\frac{\partial \Pr(i \text{ wins}|b)}{\partial b}\right)^{-1} \Pr(i \text{ wins}|b). \tag{6.3.4}$$

In an FPA, we can rewrite equation (6.3.4) as

$$v_i - b = \frac{1}{N-1}\frac{F(\psi(b))}{f(\psi(b))\,\psi'(b)}$$

19. They also consider how to introduce observable heterogeneity in auctions, where each good being sold may differ in observable characteristics. We refer interested readers to section V in their paper.

$$\equiv \frac{1}{N-1}\frac{G(b)}{g(b)},$$

where $g(\cdot)$ is the density of the CDF of bids, $G(\cdot)$. Now, $G(\cdot)$ and $g(\cdot)$ can be nonparametrically estimated from observed bids, giving rise to a two-step estimator. First, we use the nonparametric estimates of $G(\cdot)$ and $g(\cdot)$ to back out private values $\hat{v}$. Next, we use the empirical distribution of $\hat{v}$ to estimate $F_V(v)$.

Specifically, if we have T auctions with N bidders each, the first step can be estimated using

$$\tilde{G}(b) = \frac{1}{NT}\sum_{t=1}^{T}\sum_{i=1}^{N}\mathbf{1}(B_{it} \le b)$$

$$\tilde{g}(b) = \frac{1}{NTh_g}\sum_{t=1}^{T}\sum_{i=1}^{N}K_g\left(\frac{b-B_{it}}{h_g}\right)\mathbf{1}\left(B_{\min}+h_g \le B_{it} \le B_{\max}-h_g\right), \tag{6.3.5}$$

where h_g is a bandwidth parameter, B_{it} is an observed bid from bidder i in auction t, $K_g(\cdot)$ is a kernel function with compact support, and the indicator function $\mathbf{1}\left(B_{\min}+h_g \le B_{it} \le B_{\max}-h_g\right)$ trims the observations outside the bandwidth to eliminate bias.[20] Here, v_i can be estimated using

$$\hat{v}_i - b = \frac{1}{N-1}\frac{\tilde{G}(b)}{\tilde{g}(b)}.$$

Finally, $\hat{F}_V(v)$ can be estimated using the empirical CDF of $\hat{v}$.

Guerre et al. (2000) then generalize their method to auctions with observed heterogeneity. Let $\mathbf{x}_t$ denote a d-dimensional vector of observable characteristics for the good in auction t. In addition, N_t denotes the number of bidders in auction t, and the distribution of bidder values V_{it} is a conditional distribution $F(\cdot|\mathbf{x}_t, N_t)$, while the distribution of observed bids is $G(\cdot|\mathbf{x}_t, N_t)$. We have

$$V_{it} - B_{it} = \frac{1}{N_t - 1}\cdot\frac{G(B_{it}|\mathbf{x}_t, N_t)}{g(B_{it}|\mathbf{x}_t, N_t)},$$

and the estimators in equation (6.3.5) become

20. See Li and Racine (2007) for a general discussion of trimming sequences for kernel estimation. See Campo et al. (2011), Marmer and Shneyerov (2012), and especially Hickman and Hubbard (2015) for more on trimming and boundary-corrected estimation approaches following Guerre et al. (2000).

$$\tilde{G}(b, \mathbf{x}, n) = \frac{1}{Th_G^d} \sum_{t=1}^{T} \frac{1}{N_t} \sum_{i=1}^{N_t} \mathbf{1}(B_{it} \leq b) K_G \left(\frac{\mathbf{x} - \mathbf{x}_t}{h_G}, \frac{n - N_t}{h_{GN}} \right)$$

$$\tilde{g}(b, \mathbf{x}, n) = \frac{1}{Th_g^{d+1}} \sum_{t=1}^{T} \frac{1}{N_t} \sum_{i=1}^{N_t} K_g \left(\frac{b - B_{it}}{h_g}, \frac{\mathbf{x} - \mathbf{x}_t}{h_G}, \frac{n - N_t}{h_{GN}} \right).$$

Unfortunately, as the number of observable covariates d grows larger, these estimators begin to require very large amounts of data due to their slow convergence properties; this also known as the "curse of dimensionality problem."[21] Due to this problem, Paarsch and Hong (2006) argue that parametric approaches can be better for dealing with large numbers of covariates. One strategy that a researcher can use is to homogenize bids by making the bidding function (multiplicatively) separable in a base bid, b_{it}^0, and a function of auction characteristics, $\gamma(\mathbf{x}_t, N_t)$:

$$b_{it} = b_{it}^0 \cdot \gamma(\mathbf{x}_t, N_t).$$

Bid homogenization is typically carried out by regressing logged bids (and logged reserve prices) on auction characteristics, and then subtracting that regression's predicted values from the logged bids (and logged reserve prices). We note that parameterization creates a trade-off with the aforementioned issues that parametric methods have.

6.3.2.2 COLLUSION AND UNOBSERVED HETEROGENEITY IN FPAS

Asker (2010) applies Guerre et al. (2000)'s method to study the effect of collusion in auctions, specifically the effect of a bidding ring on buyers' and sellers' welfare.[22] His data comes from eleven target SPA auctions in 1996–1997, which document a bidding ring that participated in collectible stamp auctions. The ring had eleven members, and there are detailed data on their activity, including bids, side payments, wins, and target prices.

The bidding ring utilized knockout auctions, as described in section 6.2.3, to determine who had the right to bid on the good at the final auction. Furthermore, the ring utilized a side payment system. Suppose that one member of the ring won

21. More details on the curse of dimensionality can be found in any nonparametrics textbook, such as Silverman (1986). This may also be referred to as the "empty space phenomenon," as in Pagan and Ullah (1999), 59–60.

22. Another interesting paper that studies collusion in auctions is Porter and Zona (1999), which seeks to identify collusion in procurement auctions for school milk. Porter and Zona use reduced form methods as opposed to structural ones, though, and therefore we will not discuss it further in this chapter.

a good at the target auction. Any members of the ring who bid below the sale price at the target auction would receive nothing. Any members whose knockout bid was above the sale price at the auction, but did not win the knockout auction, would receive payments from the winning bidder, such that the higher the bid, the higher the payment that the bidder would receive.[23] It turns out that this side payment structure actually makes it optimal for a bidder to overbid in the knockout auction: unlike in the standard SPA model, one's payoff can increase if one bids above one's value. Due to this structure, the auctioneer may actually benefit from the presence of a bidding ring with this knockout auction format: although the goal of the ring is to set winning prices below those in the absence of the ring, some target auctions may have had the price bid higher than it otherwise would have gone. Note that the rising prices harm nonring bidders, in conjunction with inefficient allocations caused by the ring's existence.

The bidding problem of each ring member in knockout auction t is

$$\max_b \int_{-\infty}^{b} (v_{it} - x)\, h_r(x)\, dx F_{-i}(\psi(b))$$
$$-\frac{1}{2}\int_{-\infty}^{b}\int_{x}^{b} (y-x)\, h_r(x) f_{-i}(\psi(y))\, dy dx$$
$$+\frac{1}{2}\int_{-\infty}^{b} (b-x)\, h_r(x)\, dx\, (1 - F_{-i}(\psi(b))),$$

where v_{it} is the value of winning the good in the target auction, r is the highest value among the nonring bidders in the target auction, and $\{H_r(\cdot), h_r(\cdot)\}$ denotes the CDF and density of r, respectively. If α_j is the probability of bidder j participating,[24] then $F_{-i}(\psi(b)) = \frac{\sum_{j\neq i}\alpha_j F_j(\psi_j(b))}{\sum_{j\neq i}\alpha_j}$ and $f_{-i}(\psi(b)) = \frac{\partial F_{-i}(\psi(b))}{\partial b}$, where $F_j(\cdot)$ is bidder j's value distribution as always. In the two-bidder case, the corresponding first-order condition is given by

$$v = b - \frac{\frac{1}{2}H_r(b)(1 - G_{-i}(b))}{h_r(b)\, G_{-i}(b) + H_r(b)\, g_{-i}(b)}, \tag{6.3.6}$$

23. Specifically, suppose that I ring members bid above the actual sale price but lost the knockout auction. Order these members as $\{1, 2, \ldots, I\}$, where I denotes the ring bidder with the highest bid who lost the knockout auction, while 1 denotes the ring bidder with the lowest bid who lost the knockout auction (while, again, bidding above the actual sale price). Let b_i denote bidder i's bid, and let b_0 denote the actual sale price at the target auction. Bidder i's side payment would consist of $\sum_{j=1}^{i}\left(\frac{b_j - b_{j-1}}{2}\right)\frac{1}{I-j+1}$. In turn, the bidder who won the knockout auction and the target auction would pay the ring $\sum_{j=1}^{I}\left(\frac{b_j - b_{j-1}}{2}\right)$.

24. Ring members know the *number* of bidders in the knockout, but not their *identities*.

where $F_{-i}(\psi(b)) = G_{-i}(b)$ and $f_{-i}(\psi(b)) = g_{-i}(b)$. We further define the inverse function of equation (6.3.6) as follows:

$$b = \beta(v), \tag{6.3.7}$$

which will be used later in this chapter.

To calculate damages and inefficiencies resulting from the ring, Asker's structural estimation approach adapts Guerre et al. (2000) and a method proposed by Krasnokutskaya (2011) to account for unobserved heterogeneity across auctions. Asker only uses data from two-bidder knockout auctions; hence we only consider the two-bidder first-order condition. There are five primary steps in the procedure:

Step 1: Accounting for Observed Auction Heterogeneity Define v_{it} as the true value of bidder i in knockout auction t. Here, v_{it} can be modeled as

$$v_{it} = \Gamma(\mathbf{x}_t) \cdot u_{it} \cdot \epsilon_t,$$

where $\mathbf{x}_t$ are observable characteristics, u_{it} is the private component of bidder i's valuation in knockout t, and ϵ_t is a factor that affects bidders' valuations and is observable by bidders, but not by the econometrician (i.e., unobserved heterogeneity).[25] Specifying the functional form $\Gamma(\mathbf{x}_t) = \exp\left(\mathbf{x}_t'\boldsymbol{\gamma}\right)$ leads to the following first-stage regression:

$$\ln b_{it} = \mathbf{x}_t'\boldsymbol{\gamma} + \eta_{it} + \sigma_{it},$$

where η_{it} is a set of dummies for the target auction and individual ring members and σ_{it} is an error term. Intuitively, this is regressing logged bids on logged values, where η_{it} and σ_{it} correspond to u_{it}. In turn, it leads to the normalized bid

$$\ln \hat{b}_{it} = \ln b_{it} - \mathbf{x}_t\hat{\boldsymbol{\gamma}}.$$

Step 2: Unobserved Common Bid Heterogeneity Density Estimation Now that we have accounted for observed heterogeneity, the second step is to separate the idiosyncratic elements from the unobserved common heterogeneity in bids, and then to estimate the densities of these bid components. This relies heavily on Krasnokutskaya (2011) and Li and Vuong (1998).

25. Lemma 3 of Asker (2010) states that if values are scaled by a constant, then bids are also scaled by the same constant. That is, if the optimal knockout bid when $v_{it} = u_{it}$ is b_{it}, then the optimal bid when $v_{it} = \Gamma(\mathbf{x}_t) \cdot u_{it}$ is $\Gamma(\mathbf{x}_t) \cdot b_{it}$.

First, note that lemma 3 of Asker (2010) also allows us to write the homogenized bids as multiplicative functions of common and idiosyncratic components. Indeed, if we see two homogenized bids in auction t, we can write them as

$$\ln \hat{b}_{1t} = \ln(\epsilon_t) + \ln \beta(\nu_{1t})$$

$$\ln \hat{b}_{2t} = \ln(\epsilon_t) + \ln \beta(\nu_{2t}),$$

where the inverse of $\beta(\nu)$ is given in equation (6.3.7), corresponding to the component of bids that are attributable to the idiosyncratic variation in bidders' valuations. Intuitively, the distribution of $\ln(\epsilon_t)$ can be estimated using variation across auctions, while the distributions of $\ln \beta(\nu_1)$ and $\ln \beta(\nu_2)$ can be estimated using the variation of bids within auctions.

Our goal is to back out the density of $\{\ln(\epsilon), \ln \beta(\nu_1), \ln \beta(\nu_2)\}$ from $\ln(\epsilon_t) \perp\!\!\!\perp \{\beta(\nu_{1t}), \beta(\nu_{1t})\}$ and the known distribution of $\ln \hat{b}_{1t}$, $\ln \hat{b}_{2t}$, and $\ln(\epsilon)$. To operationalize this, we use characteristic functions and Kotlarski (1966)'s theorem.[26] In this setting, we have three independent, real-valued random variables, $\ln(\epsilon)$, $\ln \beta(\nu_1)$, and $\ln \beta(\nu_2)$, with characteristic functions $\Phi_{\ln(\epsilon)}$, $\Phi_{\ln \beta(\nu_1)}$, and $\Phi_{\ln \beta(\nu_2)}$. Furthermore, we have $\ln \hat{b}_1 = \ln(\epsilon) + \ln \beta(\nu_1)$ and $\ln \hat{b}_2 = \ln(\epsilon) + \ln \beta(\nu_2)$, with a joint characteristic function Ψ. If the characteristic functions are nonzero almost everywhere, then we can invoke Kotlarski's theorem and conclude

26. **Definition.** (Characteristic Function) The characteristic function of a scalar random variable X with density $f_X(\cdot)$ is

$$\Phi_X(t) = \mathbb{E}[\exp(itX)] = \int_{\mathbb{R}} \exp(itx) f_X(x)\, dx,$$

where $i = \sqrt{-1}$. A characteristic function can fully define a random variable's probability distribution.

Of particular interest to us here are *inversion formulas*: if X has distribution $F_X(\cdot)$, then these two integrals allow us to back out $F_X(\cdot)$ and $f_X(\cdot)$ using $\Phi_X(\cdot)$:

$$F_X(b) - F_X(a) = \frac{1}{2\pi} \lim_{T\to\infty} \int_{-T}^{+T} \frac{\exp(-ita) - \exp(-itb)}{it} \Phi_X(t)\, dt$$

$$f_X(b) = \frac{1}{2\pi} \int_{\mathbb{R}} \exp(-itb)\, \Phi_X(t)\, dt.$$

Theorem 6.3.1. (Kotlarski) Let Y, ϵ, and η be mutually independent random variables with respective characteristic functions Φ_Y, Φ_ϵ, and Φ_η. Let the characteristic functions be nonzero almost everywhere and let $\mathbb{E}[\epsilon] = 0$. Furthermore, let $X = Y + \epsilon$ and $Z = Y + \eta$, and denote the joint characteristic function of X and Z with Ψ. Then

$$\Phi_Y = \exp\left(\int_0^t \frac{\Psi_1(0, t_2)}{\Psi(0, t_2)} dt_2\right).$$

Corollary. $\Psi(x, 0) = \Phi_Y(x)\, \Phi_\epsilon(x)$ and $\Psi(0, x) = \Phi_Y(x)\, \Phi_\eta(x)$.

Proof. See Kotlarski (1966), 131–134. □

$$\Phi_{\ln(\epsilon)}(x) = \exp\left(\int_0^x \frac{\Psi_1(0,u_2)}{\Psi(0,u_2)} du_2\right).$$

With this background knowledge, we can estimate densities by first applying Kotlarski's theorem and then using the characteristic function density inversion formula. First, the empirical characteristic function of the joint distribution of $\ln \hat{b}_1$ and $\ln \hat{b}_2$ can be estimated as (following step 2 on p. 303 of Krasnokutskaya (2011)):

$$\hat{\Psi}(z_1, z_2) = \frac{1}{n}\sum_{k=1}^{K} \exp\left(iz_1 \ln \hat{b}_{1k} + iz_2 \ln \hat{b}_{2k}\right).$$

We can then invoke Kotlarski's theorem and its corollary to estimate the characteristic functions of the marginal distributions as (following Krasnokutskaya's step 3)

$$\hat{\Phi}_{\ln(\epsilon)}(x) = \exp\left(\int_0^x \frac{\hat{\Psi}_1(0,u_2)}{\hat{\Psi}(0,u_2)} du_2\right)$$

$$\hat{\Phi}_{\ln\beta(v_1)}(x) = \frac{\hat{\Psi}(x,0)}{\hat{\Phi}_{\ln(\epsilon)}(x)}$$

$$\hat{\Phi}_{\ln\beta(v_2)}(x) = \frac{\hat{\Psi}(0,x)}{\hat{\Phi}_{\ln(\epsilon)}(x)}.$$

Finally, characteristic function inversion lets us estimate the densities as (following Krasnokutskaya's step 4):

$$\hat{g}_Y(x) = \frac{1}{2\pi}\int_{-T_n}^{T_n} d(t) \exp(-itx)\, \hat{\Phi}_Y(t)\, dt,$$

where $Y \in \{\ln(\epsilon), \ln\beta(v_1), \ln\beta(v_2)\}$ and $d(t)$ is a damping function (Diggle and Hall, 1993).

Now, let r^* denote the price paid at a target auction. When the ring wins, this reflects the highest value among nonring bidders. This procedure, especially using characteristic function inversion to estimate densities, can be applied to $\{\ln\beta(r^*), \ln\beta(v_1)\}$, in addition to $\{\ln\beta(v_2), \ln\beta(v_1)\}$, since we can identify the distribution of $\ln(\epsilon)$ using $\ln(r^*) = \ln(\epsilon) + \ln(r)$.

Step 3: Correcting for Selection Bias The third step is to correct for the selection bias in r^*. Ideally, the r^* observed in the data would reflect the highest value among nonring bidders, r; the issue is that r^* reflects r only when the ring wins the auction. We would like to estimate the unconditional distribution of the highest nonring value when we only have data on the highest nonring bid conditional on the ring winning the auction. To do this, let $G(\cdot)$ denote the distribution of the highest bid in general, with $g(\cdot)$ as its density. Let $\mathcal{I}$ denote the set of ring members. Then we can define the following:

$$\overline{H}_r(x) \equiv H_r\left(x \middle| \max_{i\in\mathcal{I}} b_i > x\right)$$

$$\overline{h}_r(x) \equiv h_r\left(x \middle| \max_{i\in\mathcal{I}} b_i > x\right)$$

$$G_m(b) \equiv G\left(\max_{i\in\mathcal{I}} b_i\right)$$

$$g_m(b) = g\left(\max_{i\in\mathcal{I}} b_i\right).$$

Given this, one can derive the following:

$$H_r(r) = A\int_{-\infty}^{r} \frac{\overline{h}_r(x)}{[1 - G_m(x)]}dx$$

$$h_r(r) = A\frac{\overline{h}_r(r)}{[1 - G_m(r)]},$$

where A is a scaling factor that can be computed numerically as $\left[\int_{-\infty}^{\infty} \frac{\overline{h}_r(x)}{[1-G_m(x)]}dx\right]^{-1}$.

Steps 4–5: Bidder-Valuation Distribution and Counterfactual Simulation Step 4 is to recover the distribution of v_i, which can be done using Guerre et al. (2000) and our estimates of the distributions/densities from Asker's step 2. And finally, step 5 is to run a set of simulated auctions using our estimated distributions and constructions of valuations; these allow one to estimate damages and efficiency losses.

Using the outlined procedure, Asker finds that the ring mechanism (namely, the incentive to overbid due to the side payment structure), created inefficiency in the market; the overbidding harmed ring members from time to time, but overall, the ring benefited from the coordinated bidding. However, nonring members were harmed by the ring due to inefficient allocations and prices being driven to higher-than-competitive levels. Sellers, on the other hand, had ambiguous welfare effects: the ring's coordinated bidding acted as a harm, but this was mitigated, and possibly outweighed, by the ring's potential to overbid.

6.3.2.3 COMPARING OPEN AND SEALED-BID AUCTIONS

Athey, Levin, and Seira (2011) apply the methods from Guerre et al. (2000) to a setting with bidder asymmetry. Specifically, the study looks into timber auctions in California and northern (Oregon and Washington) forests where bidders are asymmetric, both open and sealed formats are utilized, and bidders must decide whether or not to enter an auction. The auctions are either FPAs or English auctions. They seek to analyze differences in participation decisions, timber allocation, and revenue between the two formats.

In these auctions, bidders are risk neutral and asymmetric. There are two types of bidders: "mills," who have manufacturing capacity, and "loggers," who have no such capacity. With this setting, they first set up a model and generate multiple theoretical predictions. Then they estimate the mills' and loggers' valuations using data on FPAs and use the estimated model parameters to simulate outcomes in the English auctions in their data.

To estimate bidder valuations' rationalizing observed FPA bids, Athey et al. (2011) build on Guerre et al. (2000). Given estimated bidders' valuation distributions, they estimate entry costs using observed entry behavior and zero profit conditions. The authors also find it necessary to account for possible unobserved (to the econometrician) heterogeneity in sale characteristics; without doing so, the estimated bidder valuations yield implausibly high bid margins. Let $\mathbf{x}$ denote a vector of auction characteristics known to both the researcher and the agents, while u denotes a characteristic known to bidders but unknown to the researcher. $M = M_l + M_m$ denotes the potential number of bidders (loggers and mills, respectively) and $N = N_l + N_m$ denotes the number of participating bidders. The entry cost as a function of characteristics and potential participants is $c(\mathbf{x}, M)$; if one enters, they learn the unobserved (to the econometrician) auction characteristic, u, and, the number of participating bidders, N. Thus, the value distributions can be written as $F_l(\cdot|\mathbf{x}, u, M)$ and $F_m(\cdot|\mathbf{x}, u, M)$, while the corresponding bid distributions are $G_l(\cdot|\mathbf{x}, u, M, N)$ and $G_m(\cdot|\mathbf{x}, u, M, N)$. A bidder's value v_i must be related to their observed bid via

$$v_i = \psi_i(b_i; \mathbf{x}, u, M, N) = b_i + \frac{1}{\sum_{j \in n \setminus i} \frac{g_j(b_i|\mathbf{x},u,M,N)}{G_j(b_i|\mathbf{x},u,M,N)}}.$$

To avoid the curse of dimensionality, the authors pursue a parametric approach to account for the large number of auction-level covariates. Specifically, they assume Weibull bid distribution: for $k \in \{l, m\}$,

$$G_k(b|\mathbf{x}, u, M, N) = 1 - \exp\left(-u \cdot \left(\frac{b}{\lambda_k(\mathbf{x}, M, N)}\right)^{\rho_k(N)}\right)$$

$$\ln \lambda_k(\mathbf{x}, M, N) = \mathbf{x}'\boldsymbol{\beta}_{\mathbf{x}} + M\beta_M + N\beta_{N,k} + \beta_{0,k}$$

$$\ln \rho_k(N) = N\gamma_{N,k} + \gamma_{0,k},$$

where $\lambda_k(\cdot)$ is the scale parameter and $\rho_k(\cdot)$ is the shape parameter. Furthermore, instead of adopting a nonparametric approach to address unobserved heterogeneity as in Krasnokutskaya (2011), u is assumed to have a gamma distribution with mean 1 and variance θ, and to be independent of $(\mathbf{x}, M, N)$. Then the parameters $(\boldsymbol{\beta}, \boldsymbol{\gamma}, \theta)$ can be estimated using MLE, where the log-likelihood function is

$$l_t = \left(N_{l_t} + N_{m_t}\right)\ln\theta + \ln\Gamma\left(\frac{1}{\theta} + N_{l_t} + N_{m_t}\right) - \ln\Gamma\left(\frac{1}{\theta}\right)$$
$$+ \sum_{i=1}^{N_{l_t}+N_{m_t}} \ln\left(p_{it}\lambda_{it}\left(\frac{b_{it}}{\lambda_{it}}\right)^{p_{it}-1}\right) + \left(\frac{1}{\theta} + N_{l_t} + N_{m_t}\right)$$
$$\ln\left(1 + \theta\sum_{i=1}^{N_{l_t}+N_{m_t}}\left(\frac{b_{it}}{\lambda_{it}}\right)^{p_{it}}\right).$$

The value distributions can be recovered via

$$F_k(v|\mathbf{x}, u, M) = G_k\left(\psi_k^{-1}(v, \mathbf{x}, u, M, N)\,|\mathbf{x}, u, M, N\right).$$

Entry costs are then estimated using equilibrium conditions for optimal entry behavior.

Once bidders' valuation distributions and entry costs are estimated, Athey et al. simulate bids and auction outcomes in the English auctions in their data, assuming that bidders are behaving competitively. They find that the simulated bids fit moments of the observed English auction bids in the California forests in their data set well. However, the simulated bids are higher than observed bids in the northern forests, suggesting that a departure from competitive conduct may be possible in this region. They also find that sealed bidding induces more participation by loggers, and loggers are also more likely to win sealed-bid auctions.

6.4 Single-Unit Auctions with Interdependent Values

As explained in section 6.1, many auctions deal with goods where the true value to a bidder is unknown at the time of the auction. Instead, bidders have expected values for the good, and these expectations depend not only on one's own information about the good, but on other bidders' information as well. Bidders' valuations become interdependent, which is the key subject of this section.

6.4.1 Theory

The theory behind auctions with interdependent values is not a straightforward extension of the case with independent private values, and certain theoretical predictions that we have already discussed may no longer hold. Therefore, we have more theory to develop before getting to the empirics and econometrics of such auctions.

6.4.1.1 INTERDEPENDENCE: COMMON AND AFFILIATED VALUES

As before, there is a single unit of an indivisible good up for auction. However, bidders no longer know their own valuation for the good. Bidder i's unknown valuation is treated as a random variable V_i, and he privately observes a signal $S_i \in \mathbb{R}$ that allows him to estimate his true valuation, v_i.

For N bidders, we have the random variables $\{V_1, \ldots, V_N\}$ and $\{S_1, \ldots, S_N\}$. We assume that all of these are correlated. Define $g\left(v_1, \ldots, v_n; s_1, \ldots, s_N\right)$ as the probability density that $(V_1, \ldots, V_N; S_1, \ldots, S_N)$ equals $(v_1, \ldots, v_N; s_1, \ldots, s_N)$. Naturally, we assume that V_i and S_i are positively correlated—higher signals mean that higher values are more likely.

The simplest form of interdependent models is the *common values model*, where there is one true value of good v which each bidder is trying to estimate.[27] One variant of the common values model takes the form $s_i = v + \epsilon_i$, where $\mathbb{E}\left[\epsilon_i\right] = 0$. Then $\mathbb{E}\left[S_i | V = v\right] = v$. This variant is also known as the *mineral rights model*.

We can actually impose a strong form of positive correlation, known as *affiliation*. Mathematically, affiliation means that for all i, and for all $\underline{\mathbf{v}} \equiv \left(\underline{v}_1, \ldots, \underline{v}_N\right) \leq (\bar{v}_1, \ldots, \bar{v}_N) \equiv \bar{\mathbf{v}}$ and $\underline{\mathbf{s}} \equiv \left(\underline{s}_1, \ldots, \underline{s}_N\right) \leq (\bar{s}_1, \ldots, \bar{s}_N) \equiv \bar{\mathbf{s}}$,[28] $\frac{g(v_i, \bar{\mathbf{v}}_{-i}, \bar{\mathbf{s}})}{g(v_i, \underline{\mathbf{v}}_{-i}, \bar{\mathbf{s}})}$ is nondecreasing in v_i and $\frac{g(\bar{\mathbf{v}}, s_i, \bar{\mathbf{s}}_{-i})}{g(\underline{\mathbf{v}}, s_i, \underline{\mathbf{s}}_{-i})}$ is nondecreasing in s_i. In essence, if all other

27. For example, suppose that everyone is bidding over an oil tract. There is a true amount of oil, and each bidder has a signal that allows the bidder to estimate that amount.

28. These inequalities are element wise.

bidders' true valuations/signals are high, then it is more likely that one's own valuation/signal will be high.

In the general interdependent (also called "correlated" or "affiliated") values model, where signals and values are correlated, there is a component of value v that is common to all bidders, and ex post utility takes the form $v_i(s_1, \ldots, s_N, v)$. This begets two special cases. One extreme of the general interdependent values model is the *affiliated private values model*, where the ex post utility for bidder i is $v_i(s_1, \ldots, s_N, v) = s_i$. In the affiliated private values model, values/signals across bidders are jointly distributed with one another, but (1) there is no common component, and (2) other bidders' signals do not affect one's own ex post utility directly.[29] The other extreme is the *common values model*, where signals are correlated but ex post utility is simply the common value term: $v_i(s_1, \ldots, s_N, v) = v$.

From now on, we will use the term "interdependent values" to refer only to cases where there is either a common value component v present, or one's ex post utility depends on at least one other bidder's signal. In other words, we rule out the affiliated private value model from the interdependent values model in our discussion, wherein one's own signal may be informative of other bidders' signals due to affiliation of the signals, but knowing another bidder's signal does not affect one's expected valuation of the good. The distinction will become crucial in the following sections.

6.4.1.2 WINNER'S CURSE

An immediate consequence of interdependent values is that bidders do not want to condition only on their own signal. Higher signals mean higher bids, so consider the person with the highest signal in an auction with common values, whom we will denote as bidder 1. His expected value of the good, conditioning on his own signal, is $\mathbb{E}[V|S_1 = s_1]$. Since he has the highest signal, he submits the highest bid and wins the good. But as he look around the room after winning, he suddenly realizes that his expected value is now $\mathbb{E}\left[V|S_1 = s_1, S_{i \neq 1} \leq s_1 \ \forall i\right]$, which is less than $\mathbb{E}[V|S_1 = s_1]$ by affiliation of the signals. Everyone else had a lower signal than the winner, meaning that he may have overbid the good's true worth based on an unusually high signal. The fact that he may have overpaid for the item is known as the *winner's curse*. Furthermore, the more bidders there are, the worse the winner's curse is. If one competed against one other person and won, there is a decent chance that the winner did not actually overbid, but even if the winner did, he may

29. Note that the affiliated private values model is distinct from the independent private values model. In the independent private model, values are independently distributed, whereas, in the affiliated private values model, signals can be correlated.

not have overbid by that much. But if one won an auction with 100,000 bidders, then the winner probably had a wildly high signal, and if the winner simply conditioned on his own signal, he would feel far worse since he probably also submitted a wildly high bid.

As a simple example, take the mineral rights model, where everyone has an unbiased signal. Note that because the max operator is a convex function, by Jensen's inequality,

$$\mathbb{E}\left[\max_i S_i | V = v\right] \geq \max_i \mathbb{E}\left[S_i | V = v\right] = \mathbb{E}\left[S_i | V = v\right] = v.$$

In other words, although each signal is an unbiased estimator of the good's true value, the *maximum* of the signals is not, and the person with the highest signal who simply conditions on it is bidding according to $\mathbb{E}\left[\max S_i | V = v\right]$.

Hence, we would like to derive equilibrium bidding strategies for the various auction formats that do not fall prey to the winner's curse. In particular, we discuss how conditioning on other bidders' signals may resolve the problem of winner's curse.

6.4.1.3 SYMMETRIC BIDDERS IN INTERDEPENDENT VALUE MODEL

Let us first focus on the symmetric bidders case as before. In the independent private values model, symmetry meant that each value is drawn from the same distribution. When the bidder valuations are interdependent, both the joint density of values/signals and one's expected value conditional on others' signals need to be the same across the bidders for symmetry, defined precisely as follows.

Symmetry of the Joint Density of Value and Signal Let $\mathbf{v} = (v_1, \ldots, v_N)$, and denote $\mathbf{v}' = \left(v'_1, \ldots, v'_N\right)$ by a permutation of $\mathbf{v}$. Define $\mathbf{s} = (s_1, \ldots, s_N)$, and let $\mathbf{s}' = \left(s'_1, \ldots, s'_N\right)$ be the same exact permutation as $\mathbf{v}'$ (element wise). Under symmetry, we have

$$g\left(v_1, \ldots, v_N; s_1, \ldots, s_N\right) = g\left(v'_1, \ldots, v'_N; s'_1, \ldots, s'_N\right).$$

In other words, the order of bidders' values and signals do not matter when it comes to densities.

Irrelevance of the Identity of Bidders in Expected Own-Valuation Our second notion of symmetry is that which of a bidder's competitors has which signal. For example, if one is bidding against Will Smith and Chris Rock, then it does not matter if Will has signal s_2 while Chris has signal s_3, or vice versa. It only mattters that one of the competitors has signal s_2 while another has s_3. More formally, this three-bidder example can be written as

$$\mathbb{E}[V_1|S_2 = s_2, S_3 = s_3] = \mathbb{E}[V_1|S_2 = s_3, S_3 = s_2].$$

That being said, recall that in a standard auction, a bidder only needs to beat the highest bid among their competitors. This means that in some cases, a bidder may consider only the highest signal among their competitors. In such a scenario, this means that each bidder has the same expected value function:

$$\mathbb{E}[V_i|S_i, Y_1],$$

where Y_1 is the highest signal among the other bidders (and $Y_2, Y_3, \ldots, Y_{N-1}$ are defined accordingly). Symmetry means that it does not matter who has Y_1. All that matters is that somebody has it, and a bidder conditions on Y_1 no matter whom it belongs to.[30]

6.4.1.4 EQUILIBRIUM STRATEGIES IN INTERDEPENDENT VALUE MODELS

SPA In SPA with interdependent value, it is not an equilibrium strategy to bid $\mathbb{E}[V_i|S_i = s_i]$, since the second-highest estimate of the good's value will often be an overestimate, leading to the winner overpaying for the good. Instead, a bidder wants to consider $\mathbb{E}[V_i|S_i = s_i, Y_1 = y_1, \ldots, Y_{N-1} = y_{N-1}]$, since this mitigates the winner's curse: if one could condition on all other signals being the true realizations, then one's expected value would be the same before and after that bidder's was announced as the winner. However, as alluded in section 6.4.1.3, the bidder really cares about $\mathbb{E}[V_i|S_i = s_i, Y_1 = y_1]$ since in a sealed-bid auction, they learn about only one opponent's bid (and the corresponding signal) once the winning bid and transaction price are announced. Furthermore, if the bidder wins, then the price paid is determined by the bidder with signal Y_1.

Thus, suppose that you are in an SPA with signal s. By symmetry, you can be indexed as bidder 1. To think about your optimal strategy intuitively, let us do a thought experiment. How much would you need to bid, $b(s)$, such that you would *just* break even if you won the auction? This break-even point is determined by your expected value and the highest bid among the other bids; that break-even

30. Note that symmetry could be a restrictive assumption in real life. For example, suppose that you are bidding for a state-of-the-art, never-before-seen set of golf clubs, and your two competitors are Tiger Woods and an average weekend golfer. In scenario 1, Tiger says that the golf clubs look great, while the weekend golfer hates them. In scenario 2, Tiger hates the golf clubs, while the weekend golfer loves them. The expected value is unlikely to be the same between the two scenarios.

point would occur when the highest bid among the others is $b(s)$. From there, you would infer that $Y_1 = s$. Conditional on that information, your expected value would be $\mathbb{E}[V_1|S_1 = s, Y_1 = s]$, and because you do not want to bid above or below your break-even point,[31] the optimal bidding strategy is

$$b^{SPA}(s) = \mathbb{E}[V_1|S_1 = s, Y_1 = s].$$

To prove that this is the equilibrium strategy, suppose that all other bidders follow $b^{SPA}(\cdot)$. Let $w(x,y) \equiv \mathbb{E}[V_1|S_1 = x, Y_1 = y]$, and let $f_{Y_1}(y_1|s)$ denote the probability density that the highest signal among the other bidders is y_1, given that one's own signal is s. Note that your expected payoff when your signal is s and you bid p is

$$\int_0^{(b^{SPA})^{-1}(p)} \left(w(s,y) - b^{SPA}(y)\right) f_{Y_1}(y|s)\,dy$$
$$= \int_0^{(b^{SPA})^{-1}(p)} \left(w(s,y) - w(y,y)\right) f_{Y_1}(y|s)\,dy,$$

where w is increasing in the first argument, so for all $y < s$, we have $w(s,y) - w(y,y) > 0$, while for all $y > s$, we have $w(s,y) - w(y,y) < 0$. Thus, the marginal payoff is zero by choosing p such that $(b^{SPA})^{-1}(p) = s$ (i.e., choosing $p = b^{SPA}(s)$). Hence, $b^{SPA}(s) = w(s,s)$ maximizes your expected payoff and is the equilibrium bidding strategy.

To think about this proof more intuitively, suppose that you bid $b^{SPA}(s)$ and it wins. Then $s > y_1$, meaning your ex post expected payoff is $w(s,s) - w(y_1, y_1) > 0$. Increasing your bid here does nothing to change your ex post payoff, while it increases your risk of losing, so there is no reason to do so. On the flip side, suppose that your bid loses. Then $s < y_1$. Decreasing your bid does nothing to change your ex post expected payoff, while there is no incentive to deviate and bid above $w(y_1, y_1)$, as that is above your own ex post value.

Given this equilibrium bidding strategy, note that for all $y_1 \leq s$,

$$b^{SPA}(y_1) = \mathbb{E}[V_1|S_1 = y_1, Y_1 = y_1] \leq \mathbb{E}[V_1|S_1 = s, Y_1 = y_1]$$
$$\Rightarrow \quad \mathbb{E}\left[b^{SPA}(Y_1)\,|S_1 = s, Y_1 \leq s\right] \leq \mathbb{E}[V_1|S_1 = s, Y_1 \leq s]$$
$$\Rightarrow \quad \text{expected payment} \leq \text{expected value conditional on winning,}$$

31. As in the independent private values case, bidding below the break-even point means that you forgo opportunities to win at prices below your expected valuation of the good, while bidding above the break-even point means you might win at prices above your expected value.

where the second line invokes the law of iterated expectations. Hence, using this equilibrium bidding function helps a bidder avoid the winner's curse. Before, winning made him feel terrible, since upon winning and looking at the other bidders, he realized that his expected payment would be higher than his expected value due to his abnormally high signal. However, the equilibrium strategy explicitly makes sure that if he wins, his expected value is still greater than his expected payment, since now he is restricting the highest signal among the others to be at most his own. Thus, if he wins and looks around the room, he feels fine since he already took his signal being the highest into account.

FPA As in the private values case, bidders do not simply want to bid their conditional expected values in FPA, so we have to incorporate a shading factor. First, if bidder 1's signal is s,[32] and $Y_1 = y_1$, then the good's expected value is $\mathbb{E}[V_1|S_1 = s, Y_1 = y_1] \equiv w(s, y_1)$. In addition, let $b(x)$ denote the equilibrium bid of any bidder whose signal is x. As before, we want to derive a closed form of this bidding function.

Now define $u(x, s)$ to be a bidder's expected utility when they bid x, given that their signal is s and all other bidders bid according to $b(\cdot)$. Then, if they pretend their signal is $r \in \mathbb{R}_+, r \neq s$,

$$u(b(r), s) = \int_0^r [w(s, y) - b(r)] f_{Y_1}(y_1|s)\, dy;$$

that is, one's bid wins when $b(r) > b(y)$. By definition of $u(\cdot,\cdot)$ and $b(\cdot)$, $u(b(r), s)$ must be maximized when $r = s$. So taking the first-order condition and solving the resulting differential equation gives us the equilibrium bidding function:

$$\begin{aligned} b^{FPA}(s) &= \int_0^s w(y, y)\, h(y|s)\, dy \\ &= \int_0^s \mathbb{E}[V_1|S_1 = y, Y_1 = y]\, h(y|s)\, dy, \end{aligned}$$

where

$$h(y|s) \equiv \begin{cases} \frac{f_{Y_1}(y|y)}{F_{Y_1}(y|y)} \left(\exp\left(-\int_y^s \frac{f_{Y_1}(x|x)}{F_{Y_1}(x|x)} dx\right)\right) & \text{if } y \leq s \\ 0 & \text{if } y > s \end{cases}.$$

32. Again, we are taking bidder 1's point of view due to symmetry.

In addition, it can be shown that $\int_0^s h(y|s)\,dy = 1$ for all $s > 0$. Thus, $b^{FPA}(s)$ is a weighted average of $w(y,y)$ for $y \in [0,s]$. Furthermore, since $w(y,y)$ is strictly in increasing in y due to affiliation, then $b^{FPA}(s) < w(s,s) = \mathbb{E}[V_1|S_1 = s, Y_1 = s] = b^{SPA}(s)$. Therefore, just as in the private values case, the FPA bid takes the SPA bid and shades it by a factor.

Nonequivalence between the Standard Auction Formats When Values Are Interdependent In the independent private values case, of the four standard auctions, it sufficed to discuss only SPAs and FPAs, since SPAs were equivalent to English auctions while FPAs were equivalent to Dutch auctions. Is that still true when we have interdependent/common values?

First, consider a Dutch auction. As the auctioneer drops the price, one of two things can happen: you can shout out that you will pay the current price, or someone else can shout it out (assuming, of course, that bidders have positive values). In both cases, the auction ends. So yet again, with interdependent/common values, you can think of your Dutch auction strategy as writing the price that you will shout out your willingness to pay at on a piece of paper, then following through if the auctioneer gets to that price. Strategically, you are doing the same exact thing as in the private values case. Knowing someone else's bid (and hence, signal) might change your own expected valuation, but you only know the bid if the bidder shouts out a willingness to pay. But that would end the auction, so you cannot do anything with knowing someone else's signal. Thus, nothing changes from the independent private values setting, and so Dutch auctions are still equivalent to FPAs (i.e., equilibrium bids are the same).

Next, consider an English auction. As the auctioneer raises the price, bidders drop out of the auction. But this means that you can figure out what other people's signals are. Since values are now correlated, this is totally different from the private values case. Here, you constantly revise your own expected valuation as you see bidders drop out of the auction, whereas in the SPA, you have no way to figure out what other bidders' signals are. Thus, when values are correlated, SPAs and English auctions are *not* equivalent. There is one exception: an English auction is equivalent to an SPA if there are only two bidders.[33] But many auctions have more than two bidders, so now we will derive equilibrium bids in English auctions.

English Auctions The price starts at 0, and all N bidders are active. Every bidder knows who drops out, as well as the prices at which they drop out. Again, due to symmetry, all bidders use the same equilibrium bidding functions.

33. As soon as one bidder drops out of such an English auction, it ends.

Let $b_0(s)$ denote the price at which a bidder with signal s drops out when 0 bidders have dropped out so far. Let $b_1(s|p_1)$ denote the price at which a bidder with signal s drops out when 1 bidder has dropped out so far, at a price p_1. This goes on, so that in general, we let $b_k(s|p_1, p_2, \ldots, p_k)$ denote the price at which a bidder with a signal s drops out when $k \in \{1, \ldots, N-2\}$ bidders have dropped out so far, at a set of prices $p_1 \leq p_2 \leq \cdots \leq p_k$.[34] So an equilibrium bidding strategy in an English auction consists of $N-1$ functions $\{b_0^*(s), b_1^*(s|p_1), \ldots, b_{N-2}^*(s|p_1, \ldots, p_{N-2})\}$.

Let us start by finding an equilibrium bidding strategy $b_0^*(s)$ (i.e., your strategy when no bidder has dropped out yet). You now care about everybody's signal since in an English auction, you can see who drops out. However, you do not know anyone else's signal at this stage, let alone the highest signal among the others, $Y_1 = y$. Thus, a natural conjecture that you might have is to extend your SPA bidding strategy: $b_0(s) = \mathbb{E}[V_1|S_1 = s, Y_1 = \cdots = Y_{N-1} = s]$. Assuming that everyone else follows this strategy, you ask whether you have an incentive to deviate. Suppose that you deviate below $b_0(s)$. Then you may drop out before everyone else, at a price below your expected value; hence, you would forgo opportunities to win at a price where your expected payoff would be positive. On the other hand, suppose that you deviate above $b_0(s)$. If all other bidders suddenly drop out above $b_0(s)$ but below your new strategy, then you win the good at a loss. Furthermore, assuming that your bidding strategy is $b_0(s)$ and all other bidders suddenly drop out below that price (i.e., you win), then deviating upward does not affect your ex post payoff by the rules of an English auction. Hence, the equilibrium bidding function when nobody has dropped out yet is

$$b_0^*(s) = \mathbb{E}[V_1|S_1 = s, Y_1 = \cdots = Y_{N-1} = s].$$

Now, suppose that one person drops out of the auction and you are still in it. When following the equilibrium strategy, you know that this bidder dropped out at $p_1 = b_0^*(y_{N-1})$. In turn, you can recover the signal as $y_{N-1} = (b_0^*)^{-1}(p_1)$. So let us derive $b_1^*(s|p_1)$. This time, you know that the first bidder who dropped out had signal y_{N-1}, while the others' signals are still unknown to you. The process is exactly the same as before, and we end up with an equilibrium bidding function:

$$b_1^*(s|p_1) = \mathbb{E}[V_1|S_1 = s, Y_1 = \cdots = Y_{N-2} = s, Y_{N-1} = y_{N-1}].$$

34. To be clear on notation, note that we do not consider $k \in \{N-1, N\}$ because $b_{N-2}(s)$ covers the case when it is just a two-person auction. Once $N-1$ people drop out, the auction ends, so $b_{N-1}(s)$ does not exactly make sense, let alone $b_N(s)$.

The process repeats itself, so in the general case, when k bidders have dropped out, the equilibrium bidding function is

$$b_k^*\left(s|p_1,\ldots,p_k\right) = \mathbb{E}\left[V_1|S_1 = s, Y_1 = \cdots = Y_{N-1-k} = s, Y_{N-k} = y_{N-k},\ldots,Y_{N-1} = y_{N-1}\right].$$

The set of these $N-1$ functions forms the equilibrium bidding strategy in an English auction.

6.4.1.5 REVENUE COMPARISONS

Now, let us compare the expected revenue from the SPA, English auction, and FPA (again, we will ignore the Dutch auction since it is equivalent to the FPA). Does revenue equivalence still hold with interdependent values?

English Auction versus SPA Earlier, we remarked that SPAs are equivalent to English auctions if there are only two bidders. This helps us a lot when comparing the two formats' revenues.

Consider the following auction: we have an SPA with N bidders, but the seller somehow forces the bidders with the $N-2$ lowest signals to reveal them. Denote the order of the signals using X: X_i is the random variable of the ith highest signal and x_i is its realization. The seller then asks the bidders with the top two signals to play in an SPA, which we will denote as SPA_2. Using the same arguments as before, bidder 1 (invoking symmetry) bids

$$b^{SPA_2}(s) = \mathbb{E}\left[V_1|S_1 = s, Y_1 = s, X_3 = x_3,\ldots,X_N = x_N\right].$$

In other words, the two competitors bid as they would in a regular SPA, except they incorporate the signals of *all* bidders. Intuitively, since signals are affiliated, seeing others' signals will (on average) reduce the second-highest bidder's fear of the winner's curse, and hence bid less conservatively. And therefore, we have

$$R^{SPA_2} \geq R^{SPA}.$$ [35]

Now, note that $b^{SPA_2}(\cdot)$ is equivalent to one's bidding function in an English auction when $N-2$ bidders have dropped out. The price at which the English auction ends is $b_{N-2}^*\left(s|p_1,\ldots,p_{N-2}\right)$ when $s = x_2$. Likewise, $b^{SPA_2}(x_2)$ is the transaction

35. This is related to a famous result in auction theory known as the "linkage principle." See Krishna (2009) for more details.

price in SPA_2. This means the expected revenue is the same in SPA_2 and the English auction, implying

$$R^E = R^{SPA_2} \geq R^{SPA}.$$

SPA versus FPA (or Dutch) Recall the equilibrium bidding strategies for SPA and FPA, respectively, given by

$$b^{SPA}(s) = \mathbb{E}\left[V_1 | S_1 = s, Y_1 = s\right]$$
$$b^{FPA}(s) = \int_0^s b^{SPA}(y)\, h(y|s)\, dy.$$

The associated expected revenue for FPAs is simply the expectation of the highest bid. Conditional on s being the highest signal among the bidders, we have

$$R^{FPA} = \int_0^s b^{SPA}(y)\, h(y|s)\, dy.$$

For SPAs, the expected revenue is given by the expectation of the second-highest bid. Conditional on s being the highest signal among bidders,

$$R^{SPA} = \int_0^s b^{SPA}(y) \frac{f_{y_1}(y|s)}{F_{y_1}(s|s)} dy.$$

The $\frac{f_{y_1}(y|s)}{F_{y_1}(s|s)}$ term is included to condition on the second-highest signal being no more than s. In particular, this is achieved by dividing the integral by $F_{y_1}(s|s)$, so we consider the probability only in the $[0, s]$ interval, not the entire support.

We note that the SPA in interdependent value models yields higher expected revenue than the FPA. To see why, define $H(\cdot|\cdot)$ to be the CDF corresponding to the density $h(\cdot|\cdot)$. We have

$$\frac{F_{Y_1}(y|s)}{F_{Y_1}(s|s)} \leq H(y|s);$$

that is, $H(y|s)$ puts higher probability on lower values of $y \in [0, s]$ than $\frac{f_{y_1}(y|s)}{F_{y_1}(s|s)}$ does.[36]

36. If we let $H(y|s) = \int_0^y h(z|s)\, dz$, so $H'(y|s) = h(y|s)$, then we have

$$H(y|s) \equiv \exp\left(-\int_y^s \frac{f_{y_1}(x|x)}{F_{y_1}(x|x)} dx\right)$$

As a result, the hierarchy of expected revenues with correlated values is

$$R^E \geq R^{SPA} \geq R^{FPA} = R^D.$$

6.4.2 Empirics and Econometrics

It is much more difficult to build structural econometric models of interdependent/common value auctions, and in fact, most of the empirical literature has focused on private values. But there are still good methods for interdependent value analysis for us to look at.

6.4.2.1 CHALLENGES IN EMPIRICALLY TESTING FOR INTERDEPENDENT VALUES

A major difficulty with empirically testing for interdependent values is that even if bidders' values follow an interdependent values model (i.e., knowing others' signals affects one's own expected valuation), they could also be rationalized as belonging to an affiliated private values model. The reasoning is as follows: Suppose that we have data on bids and the underlying model follows interdependent values. Then one could simply normalize the signal distribution such that

$$w(s,s) = \mathbb{E}\left[V|S_1 = s, Y_1 = s\right] = s. \tag{6.4.1}$$

Equation (6.4.1) rationalizes the interdependent values with affiliated private values by rationalizing the observed joint distribution of bids with a joint distribution of affiliated private values. It allows one to write a model where each signal is actually an affiliated private value.

6.4.2.2 METHODS EXPLOITING VARIATION IN N

The argument of observational equivalence breaks down if we have variation in the number of bidders, N. This is because when values are interdependent, we know that bidders want to avoid the winner's curse, which gets worse when there are more bidders. It turns out we can exploit this change in the magnitude of the

---

$$\geq \exp\left(-\int_y^s \frac{f_{y_1}(x|s)}{F_{y_1}(x|s)} dx\right)$$

$$= \frac{F_{y_1}(y|s)}{F_{y_1}(s|s)}.$$

The inequality holds because $\frac{f_{y_1}(y|s)}{F_{y_1}(s|s)}$ is increasing in s.

winner's curse to check whether values are interdependent—namely, by checking if equilibrium bidding strategies change with the number of auction participants.

In an SPA with N bidders, once again taking bidder 1's perspective and supposing that they have the highest signal, we know that

$$
\begin{aligned}
w(s,s,N) &= \mathbb{E}\left[V|S_1 = s, X_2 = s, X_3 \leq s, \ldots, X_N \leq s\right] \\
&< \mathbb{E}_{X_N}\left[\mathbb{E}\left[V|S_1 = s, X_2 = s, X_3 \leq s, \ldots, X_{N-1} \leq s, X_N\right]\right] \\
&= \mathbb{E}\left[V|S_1 = s, X_2 = s, X_3 \leq s, \ldots, X_{N-1} \leq s\right] \\
&= w(s,s,N-1).
\end{aligned}
$$

Expressed in words, this means that given the same signal, the bid distribution in an SPA with N bidders is stochastically dominated by the bid distribution with only $N-1$ bidders, which is a testable restriction.

Laffont and Vuong (1996) and Athey and Haile (2002) provide more general identification results for tests of common versus private values. Laffont and Vuong show that if we extend our analysis to asymmetric bidders, an interdependent value model is observationally equivalent to an *independent* private value model. Furthermore, an asymmetric interdependent value model may not be distinguishable from a symmetric one. Assuming symmetry again, Athey and Haile provide an identification result for FPAs: if the top two bids are observed in auctions with N and $N-1$ bidders and $N \geq 3$, then one can test for the existence of interdependent values against affiliated private values. In addition, Athey and Haile study SPAs where the number of bidders is unknown to each bidder, but they observe some informative signal about N. They prove that one can test for interdependent values if the transaction price $b_{2,M}$ is observed in auctions with M bidders, and bids $b_{N-M+2,N}, \ldots, b_{2,N}$ are observed in auctions with $N > M \geq 2$ bidders.[37]

Haile et al. (2006) propose a nonparametric approach to test for interdependent versus private values in FPAs. First, a bidder's strictly increasing bidding strategy can be characterized as the ODE:

$$
w(x,x,N) = b(x,N) + \frac{b'(x,N)\,F_N(x|x)}{f_N(x|x)} \qquad \text{for all } x,
$$

37. A good mental image comes from supposing that you order two lists of bids in two auctions. One auction has M bidders and the other has N bidders. You order the bids such that the lowest bids in each auction are adjacent partners. Keep partnering bids together in ascending order until the highest bid in the auction with M bidders is next to the $(N-M+1)$th highest bid in the auction with N bidders. Then none of the higher bids in the auction with N bidders have partners. We want to collect the second-highest bid in the auction with M bidders, then collect every bid above and including its partner in the auction with N bidders, up until the second-highest bid in that auction.

and as a reminder, $w(x, x, N) \equiv \mathbb{E}[V_i|S_i = x, Y_1 = x, N]$. Now, due to the strict monotonicity of bidding functions, the joint distribution of signals is related to the joint distribution of bids through the relations

$$F_N(y|x) = G_N(b(y, N)|b(x, N))$$
$$f_N(y|x) = g_N(b(y, N)|b(x, N))\, b'(y, N),$$

where $G_N(\cdot|\cdot)$ is the equilibrium distribution of the highest bid among all non-i bidders, conditional on i's equilibrium bid being $b(x, N)$. Letting $b_i = b(x_i, N)$, we can rewrite the ODE as

$$w(x_i, x_i, N) = b_i + \frac{G_N(b_i|b_i)}{g_N(b_i|b_i)}.$$

We can then use nonparametric estimators of $G_N(b_i|b_i)$ and $g_N(b_i|b_i)$, per Guerre et al. (2000), to construct an estimate:

$$\hat{w}_{it} = b_{it} + \frac{\hat{G}_N(b_i|b_i)}{\hat{g}_N(b_i|b_i)}.$$

Now, we can implement a test of stochastic dominance. Let $F_{w,N}$ be the distribution of the random variable $W_{it} = w(X_{it}, X_{it}, N)$. The underlying principle of the test is that under independent private values,

$$F_{w,\underline{N}}(w) = F_{w,\underline{N}+1}(w) = \cdots = F_{w,\overline{N}}(w),$$

while under interdependent values,

$$F_{w,\underline{N}}(w) < F_{w,\underline{N}+1}(w) < \cdots < F_{w,\overline{N}}(w)$$

for all w. To test this, Haile et al. (2006) suggest comparing the means of the distributions of $F_{w,N}(\cdot)$ for different values of N. Since they use Guerre et al.'s estimator, the boundary effects are an issue, so they trim the boundary values of $\hat{w}_{it}$. Let $\hat{G}_N(\cdot)$ denote the empirical distribution of bids in auctions with N bidders, let $\hat{b}_{\tau,N}$ denote the τth quantile of $\hat{G}_N(\cdot)$, and let x_τ denote the τth quantile of $F_X(\cdot)$. Then they define a "quantile-trimmed mean":

$$\mu_{N,\tau} \equiv \mathbb{E}[w(X, X, N) \cdot \mathbf{1}(x_\tau \leq X \leq x_{1-\tau})].$$

This gives rise to the sample analog:

$$\hat{\mu}_{N,\tau} \equiv \frac{1}{NT_N} \sum_{t=1}^{T} \sum_{i=1}^{N} \hat{w}_{it} \cdot \mathbf{1}\left(\hat{b}_{\tau,N} \leq b_{it} \leq \hat{b}_{1-\tau,N}, N_t = N\right),$$

where T_N denotes the number of N-bidder auctions, and $T = \sum_N T_N$. One can then test the hypotheses

$$H_0 : \mu_{\underline{N},\tau} = \cdots = \mu_{\overline{N},\tau}$$

$$H_1 : \mu_{\underline{N},\tau} > \cdots > \mu_{\overline{N},\tau}.$$

The authors also consider (1) observed and unobserved heterogeneity and (2) endogenous participation in auctions. In particular, they discuss instrumental variable and control function methods. These ideas are further developed in Haile and Kitamura (2019) and Compiani et al. (2020).

6.4.2.3 EXPLOITING VARIATION IN EX POST OUTCOMES

Hendricks, Pinkse, and Porter (2003) propose a different method to test for bidder rationality in interdependent value settings where the common value is observed ex post: on average, rents (the difference between discounted net revenues and the winning bid) in an auction should be positive. Denote b_t and v_t by the winning bid and the estimate of the realization of V in auction t, respectively. We should expect

$$\frac{1}{T} \sum_{t=1}^{T} (v_t - b_t) > 0.$$

Another test is that bidders should expect positive rents conditional on submitting winning bids. Thus, define $\hat{v}_{it}$ as the estimate of bidder i's valuation in the auction conditional on winning with a bid b_{it}, which is acquired by estimating

$$R = \mathbb{E}\left[V_t | B_{it} = b, M_{it} < b, N_t \geq 1\right]$$

for a generic b, and then evaluating it at $b = b_{it}$, where $M_{it} = \max\{$highest rival bid, reserve price$\}$. If n_t^* denotes the number of bids in auction t, then the average profit margin for a sample of T auctions is

$$D = \frac{1}{T} \sum_{t=1}^{T} \sum_{i=1}^{n_t^*} \frac{1}{n_t^*} \left(\hat{v}_{it} - b_{it}\right) > 0.$$

Furthermore, for both of these tests, if there is a large difference in R or D when grouping auctions by the number of potential bidders in each auction, this would indicate that bidders are not anticipating the winner's curse. In addition, the authors consider the expected value of the good and the expected value of the good conditional on winning. Respectively, they test whether these are higher than their actual bids with these two equations:

$$\mathbb{E}\left[V_t | B_{it} = b, N_t \geq 1\right] > b$$
$$\mathbb{E}\left[V_t | B_{it} = b, M_{it} < b, N_t \geq 1\right] > b.$$

In addition, this provides a measure of the winner's curse:

$$\mathbb{E}\left[V_t | B_{it} = b, M_{it} < b, N_t \geq 1\right] - \mathbb{E}\left[V_t | B_{it} = b, N_t \geq 1\right].$$

We should expect the winner's curse to grow larger as more bidders enter an auction.

Hendricks et al. (2003) apply these tests to federal auctions for offshore leases, specifically wildcat leases, which deal with tracts whose geology is not well known. Each bidder is an oil firm. Running the tests, the authors find that most firms passed the tests of rational bidding and properly anticipated the winner's curse.

6.4.2.4 EMPIRICALLY STUDYING BIDDER BEHAVIOR

There are also multiple empirical papers that analyze bidder behavior in interdependent value auctions and compare them to theoretical predictions.

Hendricks and Porter (1988) study oil and gas drainage auctions, in which bidders have asymmetric information. In particular, some bidders have private knowledge of the value of the good being auctioned off, whereas other bidders only have noisy public signals; here, the neighbor firms (those that are adjacent to the drainage tract) can observe private signals of the good, whereas nonneighbor firms only have public signals. In this setup, the authors provide several predictions. Of particular interest are the following:

- Neighbor firms participate more frequently than nonneighbor firms.
- Neighbor firms will win more than 50 percent of the auctions.
- Expected profits for nonneighbor firms are zero, due to their bidding very conservatively.
- Due to the information asymmetry, neighbor firms have above-average expected profits.

The empirical results support these predictions. Neighbor firms participated in 83 percent of auctions, while nonneighbor firms participated in only 68 percent of auctions. Neighbor firms won 62 percent of the auctions that they bid on, and the average net profit for nonneighbor winning firms was roughly zero; in particular, their profit was positive on tracts where a neighbor bid and negative on tracts where no neighbor bid. On the other hand, neighbor firms received above-average profits, which did not vary based on whether nonneighbor firms chose to participate. In short, it is not a great idea to compete against agents with insider information.

Roth and Ockenfels (2002) study online auctions, specifically on eBay and Amazon.[38] The focus is how the two sites used different formats. Amazon used a traditional English auction format, where an item keeps receiving bids until nobody bids anymore, in classic "going-going-gone" style. On the other hand, eBay has been using a fixed ending time, so even if there are still bidders who would like to raise the price at the end of the auction, they are powerless to do anything once the deadline hits. Thus, the authors analyze the frequency of bid "sniping" across eBay and Amazon (i.e., bidding at the very last minute or second). They further break down the analysis by looking at antiques versus computer auctions on each site.

Multiple reasons have been proposed for why one might bid snipe instead of simply submitting an early bid, especially against the risk of the late bid not processing in the website's system, which Roth and Ockenfels discuss. Most relevant to this section is one involving interdependent values: bid sniping is a way to prevent competing bidders from learning one's information on the good's value. For example, if a sports card is up for auction and one submits a bid far higher than the current maximum bid, competing bidders will see that someone has a stated willingness to pay, and hence revise their expectation of the good's value. On the other hand, sniping the sports card in the final seconds of an auction gives competitors very little time to revise their expectation of the good's value, then submit their own bid in response. This might be especially prevalent among auctions with fixed deadlines when there is information asymmetry. Continuing the sports card example, a specialist in this area who can accurately assess the card's value would rather not reveal their information to any nonspecialist pawn shop owners who may be bidding against them. This information asymmetry, on the other hand, is mitigated or may even be eliminated under a "going-going-gone" rule. In particular, Amazon's auctions allowed new bids up to ten minutes after the previous bid was submitted, which is plenty of time to submit a counterbid.

38. Amazon used to run auctions from 1999 to 2001. However, the site stopped promoting their auctions just a year after they were launched.

Bajari and Hortaçsu (2003) provide a model in which bid sniping on eBay constitutes a symmetric Nash equilibrium under interdependence. Each bidder is risk neutral and assumed to be ex ante symmetric. Let v_i be the utility to bidder i of winning the auction, and let s_i be a bidder's private information on the object's value. The authors assume a common value model (i.e., $v_i = v$), which seems to be a fair assumption for goods such as antique coins (which Bajari and Hortaçsu study). Then private information takes the form $s_i = v + \epsilon_i$, where the ϵ_i are i.i.d. across i.

The authors partition an eBay auction into two stages. If an auction's time duration is T, then the first stage takes up most of it: it lasts for $T - \epsilon$, where $\epsilon > 0$ denotes the tiny time frame in which bidders cannot update their bids in response to others anymore. The second stage thus has a time duration of ϵ. The first stage is an English auction, and most bidders' dropout points can be openly observed as $\theta_1 \leq \theta_2 \leq \cdots \leq \theta_N$; only θ_N is unobservable.[39] The second stage is simply an SPA[40] where every bidder, including anyone who ostensibly dropped out in the first stage, is allowed to submit a bid b. The highest bidder in the second stage wins the good.

Bajari and Hortaçsu (2003) first prove that in equilibrium, first-stage dropout points cannot monotonically increase in a bidder's signal. The intuition is simple: since signals are correlated, bidder i choosing to drop out earlier makes other bidders lower their expected value of the good, which increases bidder i's probability of winning the good in the second stage. This is a lemma that leads to the following proposition: it is an equilibrium for bidders to bid 0 (or nothing at all) in the first stage, and then participate in the second stage as though it were a pure SPA. This essentially makes an eBay auction an SPA, so bidders will want to snipe. Note that Amazon's format cannot be reduced to an SPA: for any ϵ, submitting a b in a second stage would turn the auction back into an English auction. Hence, one would not expect bid sniping to be as prevalent.

The theoretical analysis given here appears corroborated by the data. Roth and Ockenfels (2002) report that eBay had far more cases of bid sniping than Amazon: 20 percent of all final bids on eBay were submitted in the last hour, compared to just 7 percent on Amazon. Furthermore, at least one bidder was active in the final hour

39. One can see anonymized bidder names next to each bid on an eBay auction. Hence, most bidders' dropout points can be observed as the points at which they stop bidding. Only the highest bidder's dropout point in the first stage cannot be observed.

40. This is an SPA and not an FPA because eBay uses what is known as "proxy bidding." Suppose that you place a bid, which becomes the current highest bid. Then eBay allows you to place an even higher proxy bid. Then, if another bidder enters and bids above the first bid you made, eBay's system will automatically bid one increment above your competitor's bid until your proxy bid is reached. The proxy bid system is roughly an SPA, except that the highest proxy bidder wins at a price one increment above the second-highest bidder.

of two-thirds of eBay auctions, compared to just one-quarter of Amazon auctions. When looking at computers and antiques specifically, the discrepancy between websites continues: on eBay, 16 percent of antiques bidders submit their bids in the last five minutes, and 9 percent do so for computers. On Amazon, only 1 percent of bidders bid in the last few minutes in both categories.[41] Furthermore, the 7 percent difference between antiques and computers on eBay suggests that there may be a significant effect of information asymmetry on bid sniping. Antiques require more specialized information than computers: anyone can easily search for computer specifications and check market values, whereas expertise is needed to appraise antiques accurately.

6.5 Multiunit and Multi-Good Auctions

Thus far, we have discussed auctions with only one good being auctioned off. However, auctions often feature multiple units of a homogeneous good (multiunit auctions) or multiple heterogeneous goods being auctioned off (multi-good auctions). This section will provide a brief overview of some theoretical and empirical work in this area, though again, it is not a comprehensive guide to the literature. We will not divide this section into theory and econometrics; this time, we will show a handful of canonical models and then discuss some of their applications.

For a guide to the theory, we again recommend Krishna (2009). Paarsch and Hong (2006) also discuss some models that we leave out.

6.5.1 *The Wilson Model and Its Applications*

6.5.1.1 SETUP AND CHARACTERIZATION OF THE OPTIMAL BIDDING SCHEDULE

First, we consider a symmetric, independent private values version of the share auction model by Wilson (1979). The auction has Q units of an identical good for sale; alternatively, one can think of a measure Q of a homogeneous good for sale. Bidder i's marginal valuation at the qth unit is $v_i\left(q; s_i\right)$, which increases in signal $s_i \in \mathbb{R}$.[42] Signals are i.i.d. across bidders and auctions. The bidder also has a bid function $y_i\left(p, s_i\right)$ for a price p, which maps their signal s_i onto a demand curve; the corresponding inverse demand function is $y_i^{-1}\left(q; s_i\right)$.[43]

41. Amazon extended the auction deadline to ten minutes whenever someone makes a bid at the end, and hence the time data is recorded as a bidder's submission relative to the *current* deadline (before submitting their bid), not the actual time that an auction finally ends.

42. In turn, the total value for q units is $\int_0^q v_i\left(z, s_i\right) dz$.

43. It would be helpful to think of bidding as submitting a price-quantity schedule. Each bidder tells the auctioneer several price-quantity pairs that they would be willing to pay.

Bidder i faces the residual supply curve RS_i, which is the sum of competing bidders' bid functions, subtracted from the total quantity available: $RS_i\left(p, s_{-i}\right) = Q - \sum_{j \neq i} y_j\left(p, s_j\right)$. The intersection of residual supply with her bidding function determines the market clearing price, P^c.

Given this, the expected surplus of a risk-neutral bidder who bids $y_i\left(p\right)$ can be written as

$$\max_{y_i(p)} \int_{\underline{p}}^{\overline{p}} \underbrace{\left(\int_0^{y_i(p)} v_i\left(q, s_i\right) - y_i^{-1}\left(q\right) dq \right)}_{\text{Surplus conditional on } P^c = p} dH_i\left(p, y_i\left(p\right)\right),$$

where $\left[\underline{p}, \overline{p}\right]$ is the support of the market clearing price distribution and $H_i\left(\cdot, \cdot\right)$ is defined as

$$\begin{aligned} H_i\left(p, y_i\left(p\right)\right) &= \Pr\left(y_i\left(p\right) \leq RS_i\left(p\right)\right) \\ &= \Pr\left(P^c \leq p\right). \end{aligned}$$

There are two intuitive interpretations of this probability. The first is that $H_i\left(p, y_i\left(p\right)\right)$ is the probability that bidder i wins $y_i\left(p\right)$ units when bidding the price p for them. Alternatively, this is the probability that the $y_i\left(p\right)$ units that the bidder is requesting at price p are inframarginal (i.e., that the market clearing price P^c is less than or equal to p when bidder i has bidding function $y_i\left(p\right)$). The equivalence between the two interpretations can be seen by considering $y_i\left(p\right) + \sum_{j \neq i} y_j\left(p\right) \leq Q = y_i\left(P^c\right) + \sum_{j \neq i} y_j\left(P^c\right)$, which occurs if and only if $P^c \leq p$.

We discussed some primitives thus far. Next, we analyze two primary selling mechanisms: the discriminatory auction and the uniform price auction.

Discriminatory Auction In the *discriminatory auction*, also known as a *pay-as-bid auction*, bidder i pays their own inframarginal (winning) bids.[44] Thus, the total payment for i is $\int_0^{y_i(P^c, s_i)} y_i^{-1}\left(q\right) dq$, the area under the bid function up to the quantity won in the auction. In turn, i's expected payoffs can be expressed as

$$\int_0^{Q} \left(v_i\left(q, s_i\right) - y_i^{-1}\left(q\right)\right) dH_i\left(y_i^{-1}\left(q\right), q\right).$$

44. In the discrete case, if each bidder places a bid on each of the Q items (and assuming decreasing marginal value, bids for each successive unit will decrease), then the seller simply takes the Q highest bids among all bidders, gives each bidder the amount that they won, and makes each bidder pay their bids.

The integrand is the expected payoff that i gets from winning a qth unit at price $y_i^{-1}(q)$, which occurs with probability $H_i\left(y_i^{-1}(q), q\right)$ when i uses $y_i^{-1}(\cdot)$ as their bidding function.

Uniform Price Auction In the *uniform price auction*, the realized market clearing price is charged to *all* inframarginal units.[45] In this case, the total ex post payment by a bidder is given by $P^c \cdot y_i(P^c, s_i)$. However, the expected payoff has a slightly more complicated expression:

$$\int_0^{\infty}\left(\int_0^{y_i(p)}\left(v_i(q, s_i) - p\right) dq\right)\frac{dH_i\left(p, y_i(p)\right)}{dp}dp.$$

The inner integral gives bidder i's payoff from winning $y_i(p)$ units at price p. The term $\frac{dH_i(p, y_i(p))}{dp}$ gives weights, akin to density for the event that p is greater than or equal to the realized market-clearing price, provided that bidder i submits bidding schedule $y_i(\cdot)$. Intuitively, the expression can be understood as integrating i's expected payoff among their submitted demand curve $y_i(p)$, with respect to the distribution of the realized market-clearing outcome along the curve.

Euler Equations for the Optimal Bidding Function Given these mechanisms, Wilson (1979) derives the corresponding Euler equations to characterize the optimal $y_i(p)$. The discriminatory auction's Euler equation is

$$v_i\left(y_i(p)\right) = p + \frac{H_i\left(p, y_i(p)\right)}{\frac{\partial H_i(p, y_i(p))}{\partial p}},$$

whereas the uniform price auction's Euler equation is

$$v_i\left(y_i(p)\right) = p - y_i(p)\frac{\frac{\partial H_i(p, y_i(p))}{\partial y}}{\frac{\partial H_i(p, y_i(p))}{\partial p}}.$$

Both Euler equations take the form of bids with a shading factor added. Reny (1999) proves that the discriminatory auction (in our risk-neutral setup) has a monotone pure-strategy equilibrium (MPSE), and McAdams (2006) proves that

45. In the discrete case, the market clearing price is any price between the Qth and $(Q+1)$th-highest bid, and this per-unit price gets charged to all winning bidders. A common convention is to make the market-clearing price equal the Qth highest bid.

all mixed-strategy equilibria are outcome equivalent to an MPSE. The uniform price auction also has these properties. However, whether an equilibrium in this model is unique remains an open question; indeed, in the uniform price auction model where there is no uncertainty about bidder values or the supply of auctioned goods, multiple equilibria have been shown to exist, as in Wilson (1979), LiCalzi and Pavan (2005), and McAdams (2006).

6.5.1.2 ESTIMATING BIDDER VALUATIONS

When estimating the Wilson model, one should note that the right-hand sides of the Euler equations have empirically observed quantities: we can identify and estimate bidders' $v_i\left(y_i\left(p\right)\right)$ values if we can estimate their equilibrium probability of winning at least $y_i\left(p\right)$, which is $H_i\left(p, y_i\left(p\right)\right)$. In an experimental setting, bidders would receive different i.i.d. s_i draws in each period, meaning that one can observe the empirical distribution of equilibrium bid functions $y_i\left(p, s_i\right)$, and hence one can simulate draws of $RS_i\left(p\right)$ to simulate $H_i\left(p, y_i\left(p\right)\right)$. On the other hand, in real-world auctions, bidder valuations across the auctions are probably not always drawn from the same distribution; however, bidder valuations may be i.i.d. *conditional* on covariates.

Hortaçsu and McAdams (2010) analyze discriminatory auctions; they describe how to augment the aforementioned simulation to account for auction-level covariates, as well as also how to modify the estimation method to account for ex-ante known asymmetries across bidders.

Define, as in the Wilson model, the probability that bidder i wins quantity y as

$$H_{it}\left(y; p\right) = \Pr\left(Q_t - \sum_{j \neq i} y_{jt}\left(p, v_{jt}\left(\cdot\right)\right) \geq y\right),$$

which can be reduced to $H_t\left(y; p\right)$ in each auction t if we assume bidders play symmetric pure strategies. Strategies constitute a Bayesian Nash equilibrium, and interim expected payoffs take the form

$$\sum_{y=1}^{y^{max}} H_t\left(y; p\left(y\right)\right)\left(v_{it}\left(y\right) - p\left(y\right)\right).$$

The issue here is that in most real-world discriminatory auctions, bidders submit discrete price-quantity pairs that define their bids, and price-quantity bids may be specified only in discrete increments. This may lead to marginal values not being point-identified: one bid can be a best response given different marginal value schedules.

Discrete Price-Quantity Bids and Bounds of Marginal Values Therefore, we will focus on estimating bounds on marginal valuations based on discrete deviations in bid strategies. In particular, consider prices $p^h \in (p(y), p(y-1))$ and $p^l \in (p(y+1), p(y))$. Raising a bid on the yth unit from $p(y)$ to p^h is a profitable deviation if $(v(y) - p^h) H(y; p^h) > (v(y) - p(y)) H(y; p(y))$. And in particular, $p(y)$ can be a best response only if the bidder's marginal value is bounded above by

$$v(y) \leq p(y) + \left(p^h - p(y)\right) \frac{H(y; p^h)}{H(y; p^h) - H(y; p(y))}.$$

Likewise, lowering the yth unit bid from $p(y)$ to p^l is profitable if $v(y)$ is bounded below by

$$v(y) \geq p(y) + \left(p(y) - p^l\right) \frac{H(y; p^l)}{H(y; p(y)) - H(y; p^l)}.$$

These are discrete analogs of the discriminatory Wilson's Euler equation derived previously.

Now, suppose that we have data on T auctions with N potential bidders each, all bids are observed, and there is a vector of observable auction covariates $\mathbf{x}_t$, which are i.i.d. across auctions. Furthermore, there is no unobserved heterogeneity, so equilibrium bids are i.i.d. across auctions conditional on $\mathbf{x}_t$. To estimate the upper and lower bounds described in this section, we first need to estimate a bidder's probability of winning a given quantity with a unit bid equal to a given price, for a finite set of prices and quantities. In particular, the bounds and probabilities we want to estimate take the form

$$v(y) \leq \bar{v}(y; p(\cdot)) = p(y) + \Delta + \frac{\Delta \sum_{q=\underline{y}}^{y} H(q; p(y))}{\sum_{q=\underline{y}}^{y} \left[H[q; p(y) + \Delta] - H(q; p(y))\right]}$$

$$v(y) \geq \underline{v}(y; p(\cdot)) = p(y) + \frac{\Delta \sum_{q=y}^{\bar{y}} H(q; p(y) - \Delta)}{\sum_{q=y}^{\bar{y}} \left[H(q; p(y)) - H(q; p(y) - \Delta)\right]},$$

where $y \in \left[\underline{y}, \bar{y}\right]$ and $0 \leq \Delta \leq \min\left\{p\left(\underline{y} - 1\right) - p(y), p(\bar{y}) - p(\bar{y} + 1)\right\}$.

Estimating the Bounds of Marginal Values To estimate these bounds, we need to estimate the $H(\cdot;\cdot)$ terms, which in turn require estimating the distribution of the residual supply. First, note that since bidders are presumed to have private values, each bidder i cares about others' bidding strategies only insofar as their bids affect the residual supply for i. Thus, we can estimate this distribution using a resampling approach on the observed bids, and in turn back out $H(\cdot;\cdot)$.

Suppose that all T auctions have identical covariates. The resampling approach can be outlined as follows:

1. Fix bidder i and her bid, $p_i(\cdot)$.
2. Draw a random subsample of $N-1$ bid vectors with replacement from the sample of NT bids in the data.
3. Construct bidder i's realized residual supply, assuming that the other $N-1$ bidders in the auction make those bids, to determine the realized market-clearing price given $p_i(\cdot)$, as well as whether bidder i would have won quantity y at price p for all (y,p).
4. Repeat this process many times to consistently estimate each of bidder i's winning probabilities $H(y;p)$ as the fraction of all subsamples in which i would have won a yth unit at price p.

Now we can estimate the bounds. Let $y(\cdot, v(\cdot), \mathbf{x}, N)$ denote each bidder's bid, given the private marginal value schedule, covariates $\mathbf{x}$, and N bidders. If the bidders are symmetric and supply is known, the winning probabilities can be expressed as

$$
\begin{aligned}
H(y;p|\mathbf{x},N) &= \Pr\left(\sum_{j=1}^{N-1} y_t\left(p, v_j(\cdot), \mathbf{x}\right) \le Q - y \,\middle|\, \mathbf{x}\right) \\
&= \underbrace{\int \cdots \int}_{N-1} \mathbf{1}\left(\sum_{j=1}^{N-1} y_j \le Q - y\right) \prod_{j=1}^{N-1} dF\left(y_j; p|\mathbf{x}, N\right), \qquad (6.5.1)
\end{aligned}
$$

where $F(y;p|\mathbf{x}) = \Pr\left(y\left(p, v(\cdot), \mathbf{x}\right) \le y|\mathbf{x}\right)$; that is, the probability a bidder demands at most quantity y at price p, and $dF(y;p|\mathbf{x}) = \Pr\left(y\left(p, v(\cdot), \mathbf{x}\right) = y|\mathbf{x}\right)$. If all T auctions have identical covariates and N bidders, we can simply estimate $F(y;p)$ using

$$
\hat{F}^T(y;p) = \frac{1}{NT}\sum_{t=1}^{T}\sum_{j=1}^{N} \mathbf{1}\left(y_{jt}(p) < y\right). \qquad (6.5.2)
$$

Then equation (6.5.2) can be plugged into equation (6.5.1) to obtain the following estimator:

$$\hat{H}^T(y;p) = \underbrace{\int \cdots \int}_{N-1} \mathbf{1}\left(\sum_{j=1}^{N-1} y_j \leq Q - y\right) \prod_{j=1}^{N-1} d\hat{F}^T(y_j;p)$$

$$= \frac{1}{(NT)^{N-1}} \sum_{j_1=1}^{NT} \cdots \sum_{j_{N-1}=1}^{NT} \mathbf{1}\left(y_{j_1}(p) + \cdots + y_{j_{N-1}}(p) \leq Q - y\right).$$

In other words, the EDF $\hat{F}^T(y;p)$ makes the estimator $\hat{H}^T(y;p)$ an average of all possible $(N-1)$–fold sums of the NT bids, $\{y_{jt}(p), j = 1 \ldots N, t = 1 \ldots T\}$. $\hat{H}^T(y;p)$ is pointwise (in y) consistent and asymptotically normal.[46] Note that this method can be easily extended to allow asymmetric bidders: one would simply estimate the bidder-specific winning probabilities $H_{it}(y;p|\mathbf{x},N)$ in terms of bidder-specific $F_{jt}(y;p|\mathbf{x},N)$ for all $j \neq i$.

Incorporating Auction Characteristics Now, suppose that auctions vary in the covariates $\mathbf{x}_t$ and number of bidders N_t. We have to estimate conditional CDFs $F(y;p|x,n)$:

$$\hat{F}^T(y;p|\mathbf{x},n) = \sum_{t=1}^{T} \frac{K\left(\frac{\mathbf{x}-\mathbf{x}_t}{h_T^{\mathbf{x}}}, \frac{n-N_t}{h_T^n}\right)}{\sum_{t'=1}^{T} K\left(\frac{\mathbf{x}-\mathbf{x}_{t'}}{h_T^{\mathbf{x}}}, \frac{n-N_{t'}}{h_T^n}\right)} \sum_{j=1}^{N_t} \frac{\mathbf{1}\left(y_{jt}(p) < y\right)}{N_t},$$

where $K(\mathbf{x},n)$ is a kernel function, and $h_T^{\mathbf{x}}$ and h_T^n are bandwidth parameters. Then the estimated winning probability is

$$\hat{H}^T(y;p|\mathbf{x},n) = \underbrace{\int \cdots \int}_{n-1} 1\left\{\sum_{j=1}^{n-1} y_j \leq Q - y\right\} \prod_{j=1}^{n-1} d\hat{F}^T(y;p|\mathbf{x},n)$$

$$= \frac{\sum_{j_1=1}^{\overline{N}(T)} \cdots \sum_{j_{n-1}=1}^{\overline{N}(T)} 1\left(y_{j_1}(p) + \cdots + y_{j_{n-1}}(p) \leq Q - y\right) \prod_{k=1}^{n-1} K\left(\frac{\mathbf{x}-\mathbf{x}_{j_k}}{h_T^{\mathbf{x}}}, \frac{n-N_{j_k}}{h_T^n}\right)}{\sum_{j_1=1}^{\overline{N}(T)} \cdots \sum_{j_{n-1}=1}^{\overline{N}(T)} \prod_{k=1}^{n-1} K\left(\frac{\mathbf{x}-\mathbf{x}_{j_k}}{h_T^{\mathbf{x}}}, \frac{n-N_{j_k}}{h_T^n}\right)},$$

46. See Lehmann (1999). $\hat{H}^T(y;p)$ is known as a V-statistic with the kernel function $\mathbf{1}\left(\sum_{j=1}^{N-1} y_j(p) \leq Q - y\right)$.

where $\overline{N}(T)=\sum_{t=1}^{T} N_t$ and $(\mathbf{x}_{j_k}, N_{j_k})$ are the covariates and number of bidders that correspond to $y_{j_k}(p)$.[47] However, evaluating $\hat{H}^T(y;p|\mathbf{x},n)$ can be computationally infeasible due to the large number of combinations and permutations. Hence, one can approximate it by resampling with replacement from the set of all observed bids across all auctions, then weighting each bid $y_{jt}(p)$ in a way that makes them more likely to be drawn from auctions with covariates closer to those in auction t:

$$\frac{1}{N_t}\frac{K\left(\frac{\mathbf{x}-\mathbf{x}_t}{h_T^{\mathbf{x}}}, \frac{n-N_t}{h_T^n}\right)}{\sum_{t'=1}^{T} K\left(\frac{\mathbf{x}-\mathbf{x}_{t'}}{h_T^{\mathbf{x}}}, \frac{n-N_{t'}}{h_T^n}\right)}.$$

Now, we can construct the bounds on bidders' marginal values as

$$\hat{\bar{v}}^T(y|p(\cdot)|x)=p(y)+\Delta+\frac{\Delta\sum_{q=\underline{y}}^{y}\hat{H}^T(q;p(y)|x)}{\sum_{q=\underline{y}}^{y}\left[\hat{H}^T(q;p(y)+\Delta|x)-\hat{H}^T(q;p(y)|x)\right]}$$

$$\hat{\underline{v}}^T(y|p(\cdot)|x)=p(y)+\frac{\Delta\sum_{q=y}^{\bar{y}}\hat{H}^T(q;p(y)-\Delta|x)}{\sum_{q=y}^{\bar{y}}\left[\hat{H}^T(q;p(y)|x)-\hat{H}^T(q;p(y)-\Delta|x)\right]}.$$

Consistency of the estimated bounds follows from consistency of $\hat{H}^T(q;p(y)|x)$, and one can use the delta method to compute bootstrap confidence intervals for $\hat{\underline{v}}^T(y|p(\cdot))$ and $\hat{\bar{v}}^T(y|p(\cdot))$.[48]

Counterfactuals The estimated $v(y_i(p))$ can be used to simulate certain counterfactuals. For example, consider allocative efficiency: are the bidders with the (estimated) highest marginal valuations the ones who receive the good, or does strategic bidding lead to losses in surplus? Hortaçsu and McAdams (2010) find little efficiency loss when studying Turkish treasury auctions, which utilized discriminatory auctions.[49] Kastl (2011) also finds low losses in his sample of Czech treasury auctions, which used uniform price auctions. Kang and Puller (2008) study Korean auctions, which use both mechanisms, and also find low efficiency losses; however, the discriminatory format has better allocational properties.

47. This is now a conditional *V-statistic*, and is closely related to the conditional U-statistic:

$$\hat{H}^T(y;p|\mathbf{x},n)=\frac{\sum_{(j_1,\ldots,j_{n-1})}\mathbf{1}\left(y_{j_1}(p)+\cdots+y_{j_{n-1}}(p)\leq Q-y\prod_{k=1}^{n-1}K\left(\frac{\mathbf{x}-\mathbf{x}_{j_k}}{h_T^{\mathbf{x}}}, \frac{n-N_{j_k}}{h_T^n}\right)\right)}{\sum_{(j_1,\ldots,j_{n-1})}\prod_{k=1}^{n-1}K\left(\frac{\mathbf{x}-\mathbf{x}_{j_k}}{h_T^{\mathbf{x}}}, \frac{n-N_{j_k}}{h_T^n}\right)}.$$

48. See van der Vaart (1998), theorem 23.5.

49. Treasury auctions are a very common application of the Wilson model.

One can also run counterfactual simulations of *Vickrey auctions* in order to compare revenues. A Vickrey auction is a generalization of the SPA to multiple units: namely, a bidder who wins k units of the good must pay the k lowest bids among her competing bids.[50] Since it is an extension of the SPA, it has the nice property that bidding one's true marginal valuations is a bidder's dominant strategy. Hence, one simply has to calculate the Vickrey payments, which correspond to the estimated marginal values. Kastl (2011) simulates this counterfactual with Czech treasury auctions, which were conducted in real life as uniform price auctions. Interestingly, Kastl finds that using Vickrey auctions would have yielded very low revenues.

Under some further assumptions, one can also conduct some counterfactual comparisons of discriminatory versus uniform price auctions. Friedman (1960) famously argued for switching US Treasury auctions from the discriminatory to the uniform price format: his reasoning was that the loss of revenue in inframarginal bids would be offset by a rise in bidders' bidding functions. This is further motivated by the fact that the revenue equivalence theorem does not hold in multiunit auctions where bidders have multiunit demands (Ausubel et al., 2014).

Hortaçsu and McAdams (2010) use the aforementioned bounding strategy to compare revenues from a discriminatory auction with those from a uniform price auction. Specifically, in a uniform price auction with no constraints on the number of bids that one can submit, bids will never exceed marginal valuations. Thus, the estimated marginal valuations in a discriminatory auction can be used to compute an upper bound on the revenue from a uniform price auction: if the upper bound is below the revenue from the real-life discriminatory auction, then clearly, the discriminatory auction was revenue-maximizing between the two formats. Hortaçsu and McAdams apply this strategy and find that switching to the uniform price format would not have led to a significant increase in revenues. On the other hand, Kastl (2011) finds that the bounding strategy may fail when there are constraints

50. Specifically, this is the set of opponent bids that would win a unit of the good if the bidder did not participate. For example, in a single-unit SPA, there is only one competing bid for any bidder: the highest bid among the other bidders. In a two-unit auction, there would be two competing bids. Thus, in an m-unit auction, there are m competing bids. The Vickrey auction will give you a unit of the good if your kth highest bid beats the kth-lowest competing bid. This means that winning one unit means your highest bid must beat the lowest competing bid, winning a second unit means your second-highest bid must beat the second-lowest competing bid, and so on. As a simple example, suppose that there are two units and you are bidding against two opponents. If opponent 1 submits a 2-tuple of bids (15,10) while opponent 2 submits (12, 8), your competing bids are (15, 12). To win one unit, your highest bid must beat 12, and to win a second unit, your second-highest bid must beat 15.

Making you pay the k lowest competing bids if you win k units can be considered a way of paying for other bidders' lost marginal welfare due to your participation. Equivalently, each bidder's payment is the area under the residual supply curve that the bidder faces, up to the quantity/price that the bidder is awarded.

on the number of bids that a bidder can place, in which case it may be optimal for bids to exceed marginal valuations. He finds that bidding above one's marginal valuation is quantitatively important in Czech auctions.

6.5.1.3 TESTING THE ASSUMPTIONS AND PREDICTIONS OF THE WILSON MODEL

The Wilson model makes a few strong assumptions. The first is that bidders maximize expected profits and play Bayesian Nash equilibrium strategies. The second is that bidders have private, not interdependent, values. It is certainly important to check whether these assumptions hold.

Testing Whether Bidders Use the Bayesian Nash Equilibrium (BNE) Strategy First, one may want to test whether bidders' strategies satisfy these Euler equations. However, for each quantity, there is a marginal value that can rationalize the observed bid. This necessitates outside information on marginal valuations or tests based on other restrictions placed on the data. McAdams (2006) suggests one test by showing that the empirical analogs of the Euler equations do not force the resulting marginal valuation estimates to be declining in quantity. Chapman, McAdams, and Paarsch (2007) then apply this to auctions conducted by the Canadian receiver general. In this setting, locally increasing marginal valuation curves are not plausible, so they can test whether estimated marginal values actually decline; they find statistically significant deviations from downward-sloping marginal valuation curves (although the resulting loss in surplus is small). Hortaçsu and Puller (2008) use a test based on outside information on marginal valuations/costs, with data from electricity auctions in Texas. They construct marginal cost schedules for each company observed in the data, and check whether companies' bids are the best responses given the constructed costs. They find that large firms with the most money at stake employ the best responses almost perfectly, whereas smaller firms that generate much smaller profits are more likely to deviate from optimal bids.

Testing the Private Values Assumption So far, we have only discussed private values; however, many real-life auctions could plausibly involve common value components. Testing for this is crucial. As discussed earlier, Laffont and Vuong (1996) and Athey and Haile (2002) show that interdependent value auctions can be observationally equivalent to affiliated private-value auctions. However, the two can yield vastly different comparative static predictions: for example, we discussed how an exogenous increase in the number of bidders leads to a first-order stochastic shift of the symmetric equilibrium of an SPA with interdependent values, whereas such an increase has no effect in an SPA with affiliated private values. Thus, one should test for private versus interdependent values using some sort of exogenous variation: variation in the number of bidders is one potential source of variation, but any exogenous variation that is excluded from bidders' valuations in the private values model should suffice.

In line with this idea, Hortaçsu and Kastl (2012) utilize a feature of Canadian Treasury auctions to test for interdependent values. In these auctions, a subset of bidders ("dealers") are allowed to observe the bids of another set of bidders ("customers"). The Canadian Treasury auction data set used by Hortaçsu and Kastl allows the observation of dealer bids before and after the observation of customer bids. An important complication that one needs to deal with, however, is the fact that the auction uses the discriminatory format.

In the case of a private-value SPA, observing the bid of another bidder should not lead to a revision of one's own bid, especially when one's bid exceeds the observed bid. On the other hand, if a common-value component is present, then observing another bidder's bid will lead to a revision of one's expected value of winning the SPA. This leads to a revision of one's bid, even if it originally exceeded the observed bid. However, in a private-value FPA, observation of a competitor's bid can lead to a revision in one's own bid. This is because observing a competitor's bid resolves some of the uncertainty regarding the competition that one faces in the auction, and hence the best response of the dealer observing the competing bid will change. Hence, the fact that the discriminatory auction is a multiunit analog of the FPA creates a difficulty in testing for interdependent values.

Under the null hypothesis of private values, one can account for this strategic source of revisions by utilizing the optimal bidding conditions in the discriminatory auction. Hortaçsu and Kastl utilize the first-order optimality conditions derived here using the Wilson model to account for the bid revisions that dealers would make upon seeing customers, assuming the null hypothesis that customer bids do not provide information about the value of the auctioned securities. Their statistical test for the null hypothesis of private values, then, is to see whether the observed bid revisions have a similar magnitude to what is predicted under the private values model. Their statistical tests fail to reject the null hypothesis of private values in their sample of three-month and twelve-month Canadian Treasury bills. The private values environment also allows them to estimate the surplus that dealers derive from observing customer bids in this auction: they calculate that close to one-third of dealer profits in these auctions can be attributed to their ability to observe customer information.

6.5.1.4 ELECTRICITY AUCTIONS

We have focused on treasury auctions so far, but the Wilson model has been used to analyze another important product market where multiunit auctions are used: wholesale electricity markets. In these auctions, electricity generators submit supply bids to provide electricity to their customers, which are typically electricity distribution companies or large industrial purchasers.

Setup and Notation This is a version of the Wilson model where bidders submit supply functions rather than demand functions. As such, we will introduce a little more notation, introduced by Hortaçsu and Puller (2008), that illustrates how electricity auctions work. There are N electricity generation firms in the market, each with a generation cost $C_i\left(q\right)$ for $i \in \{1, 2, \ldots, N\}$. Generation costs are heterogeneous across firms due to the type of technology they are using: wind turbines, for example, have zero marginal cost, but fossil fuel generation costs depend on fuel prices. Total demand is $\tilde{D}\left(p\right) = D\left(p\right) + \epsilon$ (i.e., the sum of a deterministic price-elastic component and a stochastic price-invariant component).

Another important aspect of electricity auctions is that, prior to the auction, generators typically sign forward contracts with some of their customers to deliver certain quantities of power every hour, denoted by QC_i, at a negotiated price PC_i.[51] This way, customers are less exposed to price volatility that arises from fluctuations in supply and demand. However, generation firms cannot send energy directly to their customers; rather, they have to use the power/transmission grid, which is a common resource for all firms. Hence, to allocate resources, an auctioneer determines which firms can produce/transmit what amount of electricity, and at what price they can do so.

In most electricity markets, auctions occur every hour of the day, or sometimes even more frequently, to allow spot prices to reflect supply and demand fluctuations within the day. In market-clearing auctions, forward contracts are sunk. Each firm submits a supply schedule $S_i\left(p\right)$ for each time period, based on its contractual obligation to supply QC_i. The auctioneer then sums all supply schedules to equate with demand and computes a market-clearing price P^c, i.e., a price such that $\sum_{i=1}^{N} S_i\left(P^c\right) = \tilde{D}\left(P^c\right)$. Under uniform pricing, which is the most common auction format in electricity markets, the auctioneer pays generation firms the market-clearing price, P^c, for all their inframarginal units, $S_i\left(P^c\right)$.

51. QC_i and PC_i are variables, and not, say, Q or P multiplied by cost C_i.

Bidders' Profits The ex post profit of generation firms is then given by

$$\pi_{it} = S_i\left(P^c\right)P^c - C_i\left(S_i\left(P^c\right)\right) - \left(P^c - PC_i\right)QC_i.$$

The last term follows from the firm's contract position: the firm must guarantee its customers the contract price PC_i for the contracted quantity QC_i. Hence, the firm loses profits if the auction market-clearing price P^c is higher than the contract price PC_i, since the firm could have sold these units for a higher price in the auction. If P^c is lower than the contract price PC_i, the firm makes a higher profit since it sells some of its units at the higher contract price.[52]

The auction market-clearing price P^c entails uncertainty for the following reasons. First, there is uncertainty about market demand $\tilde{D}$, which may depend on short-term fluctuations in such elements as temperature and fuel cost. Second, firms may also be uncertain about others' costs and contract positions. Although firms may have a pretty good idea about what their competitors' marginal costs are based on market prices of fuel, contract positions are typically private information since these are often negotiated in over-the-counter trades. Thus, bidder i's expected profit is

$$\max_{S_i(p)} \int_{\underline{p}}^{\overline{p}} \left[S_i(p)\,p - C_i\left(S_i(p)\right) - \left(p - PC_i\right)QC_i\right] dH_i\left(p, S_i(p); QC_i\right),$$

where again, $H_i(\cdot,\cdot;\cdot)$ is the probability distribution of the market-clearing price P^c:

$$H_i\left(p, S_i(p); QC_i\right) \equiv \Pr\left(P^c \leq p \mid QC_i, S_i^*(p)\right).$$

Bidders' Equilibrum Strategy The Euler-Lagrange condition for the optimal supply schedule $S_i^*(p)$ is

$$p - C_i'\left(S_i^*(p)\right) = \left(S_i^*(p) - QC_i\right)\frac{H_S\left(p, S_i^*(p); QC_i\right)}{H_p\left(p, S_i^*(p); QC_i\right)},$$

52. Since the auction outcome is uncertain, $S_i(P^c)$ typically does not exactly equal QC_i; however, the ex post profit expression still holds because:

1. If $S_i(P^c) > QC_i$ (i.e., the firm is *long* on its electricity supply relative to its obligations), then it sells QC_i units to the customer at PC_i, and $S_i(P^c) - QC_i$ units at P^c, yielding a revenue of $QC_iPC_i + (S_i(P^c) - QC_i)\,P^c = S_i(P^c)\,P^c - (P^c - PC_i)\,QC_i$. Subtract $C_i(S_i(P^c))$ from this to get the profit expression.
2. If $S_i(P^c) < QC_i$ (i.e., the firm is *short* of its contractual obligations), then it must make up the difference by buying $QC_i - S_i(P^c)$ units from the auctioneer for P^c, before selling it to the customer at PC_i. This yields a revenue of $S_i(P^c)\,PC_i + (PC_i - P^c)\,(QC_i - S_i(P^c)) = S_i(P^c)\,P^c - (P^c - PC_i)\,QC_i$. Again, subtract $C_i(S_i(P^c))$ to obtain profits.

where

$$H_p\left(p, S_i^*(p); QC_i\right) = \frac{\partial}{\partial p} \Pr\left(P^c \leq p | QC_i, S_i^*(p)\right)$$

$$H_S\left(p, S_i^*(p); QC_i\right) = \frac{\partial}{\partial S} \Pr\left(P^c \leq p | QC_i, S_i^*(p)\right).$$

The equations can be interpreted as markup expressions, where the price markup depends on the density of the market-clearing price $H_p(\cdot)$ and the ability of the firm to shift the market-clearing price distribution by increasing its supply, which is represented by $H_S(\cdot)$. Note that this equation is very similar (modulo the contract quantity term) to the Euler equation for the uniform price auction in the Wilson model that was derived previously.

Applications Electricity markets feature abundant bid data, and one can measure marginal costs with relative accuracy compared to many other production/manufacturing contexts. Green and Newbery (1992) apply this framework to the UK's then-newly restructured electricity market. They calibrate cost functions for any effective duopolists in the market, then solve for supply function equilibria (SFE). Because there are multiple SFE, they report a range of outcomes. They find that the highest-price/lowest-quantity equilibrium implies large markups above cost, although the prices do not appear to reflect such high markups. They also use their model to study entry incentives and outcomes, finding that entry incentives are highly dependent on demand elasticities and incumbents' pricing strategies.

Wolfram (1998, 1999) implements empirical tests of strategic behavior. On one hand, Wolfram (1999) utilizes marginal costs of production and documents the difference in supply functions and measured marginal costs; bidders appear to respond to demand after controlling for costs, suggesting strategic behavior. On the other hand, Wolfram (1998) focuses more on the multiunit aspects of bids, but also finds more evidence of strategic behavior: bidders seem to strategically withhold supply.

Borenstein, Bushnell, and Wolak (2002) utilize measurements of marginal costs to quantify inefficiencies generated by strategic behavior and exercise of market power in California; they find that market power was responsible for the majority of price increases during the summer of 2000. Hortaçsu and Puller (2008), as discussed earlier, study the Texas electricity market to analyze whether firms exhibit static best-response behavior in their bids, and find that larger firms with higher payoff stakes appear to bid much closer to the static best response than do smaller firms.

There is a rich body of literature on electricity markets that we encourage our readers to study further. Papers studying electricity auctions have also estimated generation costs (Wolak, 2003; Reguant, 2014), forward contracts and sequential markets (Wolak, 2007, Bushnell, Mansur, and Saravia, 2008, Borenstein et al., 2008, Ito and Reguant, 2016, Jha and Wolak, Forthcoming, and transmission constraints (Birge et al., 2018; Ryan, 2021; Mercadal, 2022).

6.5.2 *Sponsored Search Auctions*

We now consider the "ranked good auction" model, where bidders have single-object demand while the items for sale can be ranked in terms of quality. One of the most prominent real-life examples of ranked good auctions is the sponsored search auction, which is an auction for ad spots on an internet search engine. Search engines preserve spots on their sites for advertisers, and these spots can be easily ranked: for example, a prominent ad that immediately shows up at the top is better for advertisers than a small one near the bottom of the page. Thus, if ads placed in spot k are clicked with probability α_k and each click is worth v_i to bidder i, then bidder i's per-user value is $v_{i,k} = \alpha_k v_i$.

Equilibrium Bidding Strategy in GSPAs Sponsored search auctions are typically conducted as "generalized second price auctions (GSPAs)." In a GSPA, each bidder submits a single bid b_i, and the kth-highest bidder gets ad position k. However, the price that bidder pays is α_k times the $(k+1)$th–highest bid submitted in the auction. The literature generally models sponsored-search auctions as complete information games in which bidders all know each others' values, as opposed to auctions with i.i.d. private values.

Lahaie (2006); Varian (2007) and Edelman, Ostrovsky, and Schwarz (2007) develop a theory of equilibrium bidding in the GSPA under complete information. Suppose that bids $b_1 \geq b_2 \geq \cdots \geq b_N$ are made, so bidder i wins object i. In equilibrium, bidders must not prefer deviating to win another object. Also, note that bidder i can win any lower-ranked object $j > i$ with a bid slightly higher than b_{j+1}, but to win any higher-ranked object $j < i$, they need to outbid the current winner of j with a bid above b_j. Therefore, for winning bids to arise in a pure-strategy equilibrium, we must have that for each $i \in \{1, \ldots, K\}$:

$$v_{i,i} - \alpha_i b_{i+1} \geq v_{i,j} - \alpha_j b_{j+1} \quad \text{for all } j > i$$

$$v_{i,i} - \alpha_i b_{i+1} \geq v_{i,j} - \alpha_j b_j \quad \text{for all } j < i.$$

Conversely, if bidders' values satisfy these inequality conditions, then a pure strategy equilibrium exists that generates these bids. Granted, there is a multitude of equilibria in this context. To handle this, the literature has focused on an equilibrium selection criterion in which a stronger version of the second inequality holds:

$$v_{i,i} - \alpha_i b_{i+1} \geq v_{i,j} - \alpha_j b_{j+1} \text{ for all } j < i.$$

Empirics and Applications Using this equilibrium selection criterion, Hsieh, Shum, and Yang (2018) analyze GSPA sponsored-search auctions conducted by the largest online marketplace in China, assuming that bidders have complete information and play a symmetric equilibrium. They estimate bidder values, and then conduct a counterfactual analysis of how equilibrium outcomes would change if "bid scoring" were introduced (i.e., favoring bids from bidders whose ads are more likely to be clicked).[53] They find that scoring makes bidders more competitive, leading to higher prices for top positions; however, the effects of scoring on the platform's revenue and sorting rule are limited.

Börgers et al. (2013) look at GSPA data from the Overture search engine during one month in 2004, under the assumption that bids are generated in a pure-strategy (but not necessarily symmetric) equilibrium. They find that advertisers' willingness to pay for clicks is decreasing in ad position, an alternative auction format could have avoided significant welfare losses, and a fully rent-extracting mechanism would have raised 49 percent more revenue. In addition, they develop a method to test the joint hypothesis that (1) bids are generated in equilibrium, and (2) bidder *i*'s values are constant across some sample of auctions. If so, then bidder *i*'s values must satisfy the inequality conditions derived from the realized bids in those auctions; if there are no bidder values satisfying those conditions, then either (1) bidder *i* is not playing a best response, or (2) bidder *i*'s values vary across auctions. The authors find that for bidders submitting numerous bids, one can find a violation of this joint hypothesis every 1.34 days on average.

Ostrovsky and Schwarz (Forthcoming) analyze a sample of bids in Yahoo! GSPAs for over 460,000 keywords, using the GSPA equilibrium conditions to estimate the distribution of bidder values for each keyword. Their estimated distribution is then used to compute the optimal reserve price for each auction: they find that the optimal reserve price exceeded the actual reserve price for 90 percent of the keywords considered.[54] In addition, they ran an experiment to test their estimated optimal reserve prices, using 438,198 keywords as the

53. In general, a bidder's score is composed of (1) their bid and (2) a metric of its "quality." The highest score wins in an auction with bid scoring, so bidders with higher quality may win even with lower bids. For a very simple example, consider a multiplicative scoring rule. Suppose that bidder 1 has a quality of 1 while bidder 2 has a quality of 0.5, and that bidder 1 bids 10 while bidder 2 bids 15. Then bidder 1's score is 10 while bidder 2's is 7.5, so bidder 1 wins the auction despite submitting a lower bid.

54. Yahoo! set a uniform reserve price of only 10 cents for each keyword.

treatment and 22,989 as the control, while keeping the current reserve price. Using a difference-in-differences strategy, they find that the optimal reserve prices increased average revenue by 3.8 percent. On the other hand, when they compute the average revenue per search instead, they find that the new reserve prices led to a revenue *decrease* of 1.45 percent. This discrepancy arises because reserve prices negatively affect the revenue per search for rarely searched keywords while positively affecting that for frequently searched keywords. Hence, the fact that frequently searched keywords are responsible for most of the revenue while being much less common than rarely searched keywords drives the discrepancy.

6.5.3 Package Bidding and Spectrum Auctions

In this subsection, we discuss a setting in which a seller auctions off a set of nonidentical goods, and buyers may be interested in purchasing subsets, or "packages," of these goods.[55]

Setup and Equilibrium Strategy The setup is as follows: There are K dissimilar goods, and bids can be made on any package of these goods: $P \subset \{1, \ldots, K\}$. Each bid is a profile of package bids $\mathbf{b}_i = \left(b_{i,P}\right)_{P \in \mathcal{P}}$, where $\mathcal{P}$ is the power set of $\{1, \ldots, K\}$, and each $b_{i,P} \geq 0$. Bidders have values $v_{i,P}$ for each $P \subset \{1, \ldots, K\}$, where $\mathbf{v}_i = \left(v_{i,P} : P \subset \{1, \ldots, K\}\right)$ are i.i.d. across bidders. The auctioneer chooses a single package for each bidder (nonoverlapping and possibly empty) in a manner that maximizes total revenue, and each bidder pays their bid for the package received.

Bidder i's value when bidding $\mathbf{b}_i$ is $\mathbf{v}_i = \mathbf{v}_i^{PAC}(\mathbf{b}_i)$,[56] which is uniquely determined by the following system of equations for all packages P:

$$\sum_{P' \in \mathcal{P}} \left(v_{i,P'}^{PAC}(\mathbf{b}_i) - b_{i,P'}\right) \frac{dq_{i,P'}(\mathbf{b}_i)}{db_{i,P}} - q_{i,P}(\mathbf{b}_i) = 0,$$

where $q_{i,P}(\mathbf{b}_i)$ is bidder i's probability of winning package P when bidding $\mathbf{b}_i$.

Application to Spectrum Auctions Package auctions are most famously applied to auctions of radio spectrum rights, which are crucial for wireless communication industries; these have been conducted globally ever since the US Federal Communications Commission (FCC) introduced the first radio spectrum auction in 1994. As it turns out, the package auction framework fits these spectrum auctions well.

55. These "package auctions" are also referred to as "combinatorial auctions."

56. In this expression, *PAC* stands for package.

Spectrum licenses are most commonly sold using *simultaneous ascending bid auctions* (SAAs), in which prices for all goods start at 0 and rise simultaneously. Bidders can bid on any goods they are interested in, and the price of a good rises continuously if two or more bidders are actively bidding on it; the auction ends only when once one bidder remains active (has not dropped out) on each object.[57] Milgrom (2000) shows that so long as bidders choose (throughout the auction) to be active on whichever objects give them the most surplus at current prices, then the final prices and allocation will coincide with those of the efficient Vickrey auction. Now, package bids are not allowed in an SAA, but since bidders can bid on multiple objects at once, a bidder can obtain any package by outbidding others on every good in the desired package.

Fox and Bajari (2013) estimate bidders' valuations in the 1995–1996 FCC C-Block spectrum auction. They argue that the outcome of this auction should be pairwise stable in matches Ã la Gale and Shapley (1962) (i.e., no two bidders want to make a one-to-one exchange of licenses after the auction). This is implied by efficiency that occurs if bidders bid straightforwardly and there are no complementarities, as in Milgrom (2000). However, they show that this stability also occurs in collusive equilibria, à la Brusco and Lopomo (2002) and Engelbrecht-Wiggans and Kahn (2005).[58] This pairwise stability gives rise to a set of inequalities that the valuations of the final allocation have to satisfy; these valuations are decomposed into (1) a deterministic component capturing complementarity and bidder characteristics, (2) a fixed effect for each license, and (3) an idiosyncratic component. Fox and Bajari's estimator maximizes the number of inequalities that the deterministic component satisfies: these complementarities account for 24 percent of the total package value. In addition, they find that combining licenses into four large regions would increase efficiency over the realized allocation by 48 percent.

Xiao and Yuan (2022) seek to quantify the complementarity of spectrum licenses, and the effect of the "exposure problem" in FCC auctions: bidders who want a collection of complementary licenses are exposed to the risk of winning only some of those licenses due to tougher-than-expected competition. This exposure problem can lead to departures from straightforward bidding and give rise to strategic behavior, as shown by Szentes and Rosenthal (2003) and Bulow, Levin, and Milgrom (2009). One proposed solution to the problem is to allow bidders to place package bids (i.e., separate bids for different license packages), which allow them to express package-level preferences (including preferences for license

57. Note that a bidder who is currently inactive on an object may become active on it later, as the prices of other objects change.

58. This is corroborated by experimental evidence and the lack of observed trading after the FCC auction.

complementarities).[59] Xiao and Yuan tackle this by first noting that in FCC auctions, for each license and round, there is a minimum acceptable bid, which is an increment above the current high bid. In each rounds, most bidders (obviously) bid this amount if they choose to bid. Thus, they model the auction as a discrete choice entry/exit game. Bidders' beliefs about their winning probabilities change over the course of the auction, changing the expected marginal contribution of complementary licenses, leading bidders to enter and exit bidding for those licenses. These changes in bidding behavior allow the authors to identify and estimate the complementarities among licenses. Furthermore, a counterfactual analysis that they run finds that if an FCC auction included package bidding, it would alleviate the exposure problem and increase social surplus, but benefit large bidders at the expense of medium and small ones.

Recently, the FCC has begun conducting auctions to reallocate television broadcast licenses to mobile networks. These are known as "incentive auctions," which consist of (1) a reverse auction, where television broadcasters declare bids to sell their licenses; and (2) a forward auction, where wireless carriers bid to purchase spectrum. Milgrom and Segal (2020) develop the theory behind the incentive auctions, while Doraszelski et al. (2019) study these auctions empirically, focusing on strategic behavior by bidders.

Bibliography

Arnold, B. C., N. Balakrishnan, & H. N. Nagaraja (1992). *A First Course in Order Statistics*. Hoboken, NJ: Wiley-Interscience.

Asker, J. (2010). "A study of the internal organization of a bidding cartel." *American Economic Review*, 100, 724–62.

Athey, S., & P. A. Haile (2002). "Identification of standard auction models." *Econometrica*, 70, 2107–2140.

Athey, S., J. Levin, & E. Seira (2011). "Comparing open and sealed bid auctions: Evidence from timber auctions." *Quarterly Journal of Economics*, 126, 207–257.

Ausubel, L. M., P. Cramton, M. Pycia, M. Rostek, & M. Weretka (2014). "Demand reduction and inefficiency in multi-unit auctions." *Review of Economic Studies*, 81, 1366–1400.

Bajari, P., & A. Hortaçsu (2003). "The winner's curse, reserve prices, and endogenous entry: Empirical insights from eBay auctions." *RAND Journal of Economics*, 34, 329–355.

Bajari, P., & A. Hortaçsu (2005). "Are structural estimates of auction models reasonable? Evidence from experimental data." *Journal of Political Economy*, 113, 703–741.

Birge, J. R., A. Hortaçsu, I. Mercadal, & J. M. Pavlin (2018). "Limits to arbitrage in electricity markets: A case study of MISO." *Energy Economics*, 75, 518–533.

Borenstein, S., J. Bushnell, C. R. Knittel, & C. Wolfram (2008). "Inefficiencies and market power in financial arbitrage: A study of California's electricity markets." *Journal of Industrial Economics*, 56, 347–378.

59. Prior work related to package bidding includes Cantillon and Pesendorfer (2006), which studies auctions for London bus route operation licenses, and Kim, Olivares, and Weintraub (2014), which studies Chilean auctions to procure school meals.

Borenstein, S., J. B. Bushnell, & F. A. Wolak (2002). "Measuring market efficiencies in California's restructured wholesale electricity market." *American Economic Review*, 92, 1376–1405.

Börgers, T. (2015). *An Introduction to the Theory of Mechanism Design*. New York: Oxford University Press.

Börgers, T., I. Cox, M. Pesendorfer, & V. Petricek (2013). "Equilibrium bids in sponsored search auctions: Theory and evidence." *American Economic Journal: Microeconomics*, 5, 163–187.

Brusco, S., & G. Lopomo (2002). "Collusion via signalling in simultaneous ascending bid auctions with heterogeneous objects, with and without complementarities," *Review of Economic Studies*, 69, 407–436.

Bulow, J., J. Levin, & P. Milgrom (2009). "Winning play in spectrum auctions." Working paper, Stanford Institute for Economic Policy Research.

Bushnell, J. B., E. T. Mansur, & C. Saravia (2008). "Vertical arrangements, market structure, and competition: An analysis of restructured US electricity markets." *American Economic Review*, 98, 237–66.

Campo, S., E. Guerre, I. Perrigne, & Q. Vuong (2011). "Semiparametric estimation of first-price auctions with risk-averse bidders." *Review of Economic Studies*, 78, 112–147.

Cantillon, E., & M. Pesendorfer (2006). "Combination bidding in multi-unit auctions." Working Paper.

Chapman, J. T. E., D. McAdams, & H. J. Paarsch (2007). "Bounding revenue comparisons across multi-unit auction formats under ϵ-best response." *American Economic Review*, 97, 455–458.

Compiani, G., P. Haile, & M. Sant'Anna (2020). "Common values, unobserved heterogeneity, & endogenous entry in US offshore oil lease auctions." *Journal of Political Economy*, 128, 3872–3912.

Coppinger, V. M., V. L. Smith, & J. A. Titus (1980). "Incentives and behavior in English, Dutch and sealed-bid auctions." *Economic Inquiry*, 18, 1–22.

Cox, J., B. Roberson, & V. Smith (1982). "Theory and behavior of single object auctions." *Research in Experimental Economics*, 2, 1–43.

Diggle, P. J., & P. Hall (1993). "A Fourier approach to nonparametric deconvolution of a density estimate." *Journal of the Royal Statistical Society: Series B (Methodological)*, 55, 523–531.

Doraszelski, U., K. Seim, M. Sinkinson, & P. Wang (2019). "Ownership concentration and strategic supply reduction." *Working Paper*.

Edelman, B., M. Ostrovsky, & M. Schwarz (2007). "Internet advertising and the generalized second-price auction: Selling billions of dollars worth of keywords." *American Economic Review*, 97, 242–259.

Engelbrecht-Wiggans, R., & C. M. Kahn (2005). "Low-revenue equilibria in simultaneous ascending-bid auctions." *Management Science*, 51, 508–518.

Fox, J. T., & P. Bajari (2013). "Measuring the efficiency of an FCC spectrum auction." *American Economic Journal: Microeconomics*, 5, 100–146.

Friedman, M. (1960). *A Program for Monetary Stability*. New York: Fordham University Press.

Gale, D., & L. S. Shapley (1962). "College admissions and the stability of marriage." *American Mathematical Monthly*, 69, 9–15.

Green, R. J., & D. M. Newbery (1992). "Competition in the British electricity spot market." *Journal of Political Economy*, 100, 929–953.

Guerre, E., I. Perrigne, & Q. Vuong (2000). "Optimal nonparametric estimation of first-price auctions." *Econometrica*, 68, 525–574.

Guerre, E., I. Perrigne, & Q. Vuong (2009). "Nonparametric identification of risk aversion in first-price auctions under exclusion restrictions." *Econometrica*, 77, 1193–1227.

Haile, P., H. Hong, & M. Shum (2006). "Nonparametric tests for common values at first-price sealed-bid auctions." Working paper.

Haile, P. A., & Y. Kitamura (2019). "Unobserved heterogeneity in auctions." *Econometrics Journal*, 22, C1–C19.

Haile, P. A., & E. Tamer (2003). "Inference with an incomplete model of English auctions." *Journal of Political Economy*, 111, 1–51.

Hendricks, K., J. Pinkse, & R. H. Porter (2003). "Empirical implications of equilibrium bidding in first-price, symmetric, common value auctions." *Review of Economic Studies*, 70, 115–145.

Hendricks, K., & R. Porter (1988). "An empirical study of an auction with asymmetric information." *American Economic Review*, 78, 865–83.

Hendricks, K., & R. H. Porter (2007). Chapter 32, "An empirical perspective on auctions." In Vol. 3, *Handbook of Industrial Organization*, 2073–2143. Amsterdam: Elsevier.

Hickman, B. R., & T. P. Hubbard (2015). "Replacing sample trimming with boundary correction in nonparametric estimation of first-price auctions." *Journal of Applied Econometrics*, 30, 739–762.

Hortaçsu, A., & J. Kastl (2012). "Valuing dealers' informational advantage: A study of Canadian treasury auctions." *Econometrica*, 80, 2511–2542.

Hortaçsu, A., & D. McAdams (2010). "Mechanism choice and strategic bidding in divisible good auctions: An empirical analysis of the Turkish treasury auction market." *Journal of Political Economy*, 118, 833–865.

Hortaçsu, A., & I. Perrigne (2021). Chapter 11, "Empirical perspectives on auctions." In Vol. 5, *Handbook of Industrial Organization*, 81–175. Amsterdam: Elsevier.

Hortaçsu, A., & S. L. Puller (2008). "Understanding strategic bidding in multi-unit auctions: A case study of the Texas electricity spot market." *RAND Journal of Economics*, 39, 86–114.

Hsieh, Y.-W., M. Shum, & S. Yang (2018). "To score or not to score? Estimates of a sponsored search auction model." Working paper.

Hu, A., S. A. Matthews, & L. Zou (2010). "Risk aversion and optimal reserve prices in first- and second-price auctions." *Journal of Economic Theory*, 145, 1188–1202.

Hu, Y. (2008). "Identification and estimation of nonlinear models with misclassification error using instrumental variables: A general solution." *Journal of Econometrics*, 144, 27–61.

Hu, Y., D. McAdams, & M. Shum (2013). "Identification of first-price auctions with nonseparable unobserved heterogeneity." *Journal of Econometrics*, 174, 186–193.

Ito, K., & M. Reguant (2016). "Sequential markets, market power, and arbitrage." *American Economic Review*, 106, 1921–57.

Jehle, G. A., & P. J. Reny (2011). *Advanced Microeconomic Theory*. Harlow, UK: Financial Times/Prentice Hall.

Jha, A., & F. A. Wolak (Forthcoming). "Can forward commodity markets improve spot market performance? Evidence from wholesale electricity." *American Economic Journal: Economic Policy*.

Kagel, J. H., & A. E. Roth (1995). *The Handbook of Experimental Economics*. Princeton, NJ: Princeton University Press.

Kang, B.-S., & S. L. Puller (2008). "The effect of auction format on efficiency and revenue in divisible goods auctions: A test using Korean treasury auctions." *Journal of Industrial Economics*, 56, 290–332.

Kastl, J. (2011). "Discrete bids and empirical inference in divisible good auctions." *Review of Economic Studies*, 78, 974–1014.

Kim, S. W., M. Olivares, & G. Y. Weintraub (2014). "Measuring the performance of large-scale combinatorial auctions: A structural estimation approach." *Management Science*, 60, 1180–1201.

Kotlarski, I. (1966). "On some characterization of probability distributions in Hilbert spaces." *Annali di Matematica Pura ed Applicata*, 74, 129–134.

Krasnokutskaya, E. (2011). "Identification and estimation of auction models with unobserved heterogeneity." *Review of Economic Studies*, 78, 293–327.

Krishna, V. (2009). *Auction Theory*. Elsevier Monographs. Burlington, MA: Elsevier.

Laffont, J.-J., & Q. Vuong (1996). "Structural analysis of auction data." *American Economic Review*, 86, 414–20.

Lahaie, S. (2006). "An analysis of alternative slot auction designs for sponsored search," *Proceedings of the 7th ACM Conference on Electronic Commerce*, 218–227.

Lehmann, E. L. (1999). *Elements of Large-Sample Theory*. Springer Texts in Statistics. New York: Springer.

Li, Q., & J. S. Racine (2007). *Nonparametric Econometrics: Theory and Practice.* Princeton: Princeton University Press.

Li, T., & Q. Vuong (1998). "Nonparametric estimation of the measurement error model using multiple indicators." *Journal of Multivariate Analysis,* 65, 139–165.

LiCalzi, M., & A. Pavan (2005). "Tilting the supply schedule to enhance competition in uniform-price auctions." *European Economic Review,* 49, 227–250.

Marmer, V., & A. Shneyerov (2012). "Quantile-based nonparametric inference for first-price auctions." *Journal of Econometrics,* 167, 345–357.

Maskin, E., & J. Riley (2000). "Asymmetric auctions." *Review of Economic Studies,* 67, 413–438.

McAdams, D. (2006). "Monotone equilibrium in multi-unit auctions." *Review of Economic Studies,* 73, 1039–1056.

Mercadal, I. (2022). "Dynamic competition and arbitrage in electricity markets: The role of financial players." *American Economic Journal: Microeconomics,* 14, 665–699.

Milgrom, P. (2000). "Putting auction theory to work: The simultaneous ascending auction." *Journal of Political Economy,* 108, 245–272.

Milgrom, P., & I. Segal (2020). "Clock auctions and radio spectrum reallocation." *Journal of Political Economy,* 128, 1–31.

Myerson, R. B. (1981). "Optimal auction design." *Mathematics of Operations Research,* 6, 58–73.

Ostrovsky, M., & M. Schwarz (Forthcoming). "Reserve prices in internet advertising auctions: A field experiment." *Journal of Political Economy.*

Paarsch, H. J., & H. Hong (2006). *An Introduction to the Structural Econometrics of Auction Data.* MIT Press Books. Cambridge, MA: MIT Press.

Pagan, A., & A. Ullah (1999). *Nonparametric Econometrics.* Cambridge, UK: Cambridge University Press.

Porter, R. H., & J. D. Zona (1993). "Detection of bid rigging in procurement auctions." *Journal of Political Economy,* 101, 518–538.

Porter, R. H., & J. D. Zona (1999). "Ohio school milk markets: An analysis of bidding." *RAND Journal of Economics,* 30, 263–288.

Reguant, M. (2014). "Complementary bidding mechanisms and startup costs in electricity markets." *Review of Economic Studies,* 81, 1708–1742.

Reny, P. (1999). "On the existence of pure and mixed strategy Nash equilibria in discontinuous games." *Econometrica,* 67, 1029–1056.

Roth, A. E., & A. Ockenfels (2002). "Last-minute bidding and the rules for ending second-price auctions: Evidence from eBay and Amazon auctions on the internet." *American Economic Review,* 92, 1093–1103.

Ryan, N. (2021). "The competitive effects of transmission infrastructure in the Indian electricity market." *American Economic Journal: Microeconomics,* 13, 202–42.

Silverman, B. (1986). *Density Estimation for Statistics and Data Analysis.* Boca Raton, FL: Chapman and Hall.

Szentes, B., & R. W. Rosenthal (2003). "Three-object two-bidder simultaneous auctions: chopsticks and tetrahedra." *Games and Economic Behavior,* 44, 114–133.

van der Vaart, A. W. (1998). *Asymptotic Statistics.* Cambridge Series in Statistical and Probabilistic Mathematics. Cambridge, UK: Cambridge University Press.

Varian, H. R. (2007). "Position auctions." *International Journal of Industrial Organization,* 25, 1163–1178.

Vickrey, W. (1961). "Counterspeculation, auctions, and competitive sealed tenders." *Journal of Finance,* 16, 8–37.

Wilson, R. (1979). "Auctions of shares." *Quarterly Journal of Economics,* 93, 675–689.

Wolak, F. A. (2003). "Measuring unilateral market power in wholesale electricity markets: The California market, 1998-2000." *American Economic Review,* 93, 425–430.

Wolak, F. A. (2007). "Quantifying the supply-side benefits from forward contracting in wholesale electricity markets." *Journal of Applied Econometrics,* 22, 1179–1209.

Wolfram, C. D. (1998). "Strategic bidding in a multiunit auction: An empirical analysis of bids to supply electricity in England and Wales." *RAND Journal of Economics*, 29, 703–725.
Wolfram, C. D. (1999). "Measuring duopoly power in the British electricity spot market." *American Economic Review*, 89, 805–826.
Xiao, M., & Z. Yuan (2022). "License complementarity and package bidding: U.S. spectrum auctions." *American Economic Journal: Microeconomics*, 14, 420–464.

APPENDIX

Review of Basic Estimation Methods

In this appendix, we review some basic characteristics of the maximum-likelihood estimator, the generalized method of moments estimator, and some simulation-based estimators. The focus is to give a concise summary of the asymptotics (namely, consistency results and asymptotic normality). We recommend that readers consult the relevant econometrics textbooks and handbook chapters for a full treatment of the materials overviewed here.

A.1 Maximum Likelihood Estimation

Maximum likelihood estimation (MLE) is the primary way of estimating nonlinear models when the model is fully specified up to a set of finite-dimensional model parameters. Provided that the econometric model is correctly specified, the maximum-likelihood estimator is consistent and asymptotically efficient.

A.1.1 Definitions and Preliminary Results

We begin with presenting the definition of the maximum-likelihood estimator. Throughout this section, we assume that the parameter space $\Theta \subset \mathbb{R}^p$, the data $\mathbf{x}_i \in \mathbb{R}^k$, and the joint density of the true data-generating process is known up to a finite-dimensional parameter in the parameter space. We denote $\boldsymbol{\theta}_0 \in \Theta$ as the value of the true parameter. Also, we assume that all the regularity conditions for the differentiation under the integral sign are satisfied.

Definition. (Maximum-Likelihood Estimator) Let $\{\mathbf{x}_1, \mathbf{x}_2, \ldots, \mathbf{x}_n\}$ be the given data. Let $\mathcal{L}\left(\boldsymbol{\theta} \mid \{\mathbf{x}_i\}_{i=1}^n\right)$ be the joint density function corresponding to the true data-generating process known up to a finite-dimensional parameter $\boldsymbol{\theta} \in \Theta$. Then,

$$\hat{\boldsymbol{\theta}}_{MLE} := \arg\max_{\boldsymbol{\theta}} \mathcal{L}\left(\boldsymbol{\theta} \mid \{\mathbf{x}_i\}_{i=1}^n\right).$$

Proposition A.1.1. (MLE for i.i.d. Data) Let $\{\mathbf{x}_1, \mathbf{x}_2, \ldots, \mathbf{x}_n\}$ be the given data that are mutually independent and identically distributed. Let $f(\mathbf{x}_i|\boldsymbol{\theta})$ be the marginal density function corresponding to the true data-generating process known up to a finite-dimensional parameter $\boldsymbol{\theta} \in \Theta$. Then,

$$\hat{\boldsymbol{\theta}}_{MLE} = \arg\max_{\boldsymbol{\theta}} \prod_{i=1}^{n} f(\mathbf{x}_i|\boldsymbol{\theta}).$$

Corollary. (MLE for i.i.d. Data Using Log-Likelihood) Let $\{\mathbf{x}_1, \mathbf{x}_2, \ldots, \mathbf{x}_n\}$ be the given data that are mutually independent and identically distributed. Let $f(\mathbf{x}_i|\boldsymbol{\theta})$ be the marginal density function corresponding to the true data-generating process known up to a finite-dimensional parameter $\boldsymbol{\theta} \in \Theta$. Then,

$$\hat{\boldsymbol{\theta}}_{MLE} = \arg\max_{\boldsymbol{\theta}} \sum_{i=1}^{n} \ln f(\mathbf{x}_i|\boldsymbol{\theta}).$$

Throughout the remainder of this section, we implicitly consider an i.i.d. data-generating process, but generalizations to a non-i.i.d. data-generating process are straightforward.

Definition. (Score Function) Let $f(.|\boldsymbol{\theta})$ be the density function of the true data-generating process known up to a finite-dimensional parameter $\boldsymbol{\theta} \in \Theta$. A score function $\mathbf{s} : \mathbb{R}^p \times \mathbb{R}^k \to \mathbb{R}^p$ is defined by

$$\mathbf{s}(\boldsymbol{\theta}|\mathbf{x}_i) := \frac{\partial \ln f(\mathbf{x}_i|\boldsymbol{\theta})}{\partial \boldsymbol{\theta}}.$$

Proposition A.1.2. (Expectation of Score) Let $f(.|\boldsymbol{\theta})$ be the density function of the true data-generating process known up to a finite-dimensional parameter $\boldsymbol{\theta} \in \Theta$. Assume that the support of density $f(\mathbf{x}_i|\boldsymbol{\theta})$ does not depend on $\boldsymbol{\theta} \in \Theta$. Let $\mathbf{s}(\boldsymbol{\theta}|\mathbf{x}_i)$ be the corresponding score function. Then, $\mathbb{E}[\mathbf{s}(\boldsymbol{\theta}|\mathbf{x}_i)]\,|_{\boldsymbol{\theta}=\boldsymbol{\theta}_0} = \mathbf{0}$.

Proof.

$$\mathbb{E}[\mathbf{s}(\boldsymbol{\theta}|\mathbf{x}_i)]\,|_{\boldsymbol{\theta}=\boldsymbol{\theta}_0} = \mathbb{E}\left[\frac{\partial \ln f(\mathbf{x}_i|\boldsymbol{\theta})}{\partial \boldsymbol{\theta}}\right]\Bigg|_{\boldsymbol{\theta}=\boldsymbol{\theta}_0}$$

$$
\begin{aligned}
&= \left\{ \int \frac{\partial \ln f(\mathbf{x}_i|\boldsymbol{\theta})}{\partial \boldsymbol{\theta}} f(\mathbf{x}_i|\boldsymbol{\theta})\, d\mathbf{x}_i \right\} \bigg|_{\theta=\theta_0} \\
&= \left\{ \int \frac{\partial f(\mathbf{x}_i|\boldsymbol{\theta})}{\partial \boldsymbol{\theta}} \frac{f(\mathbf{x}_i|\boldsymbol{\theta})}{f(\mathbf{x}_i|\boldsymbol{\theta})} d\mathbf{x}_i \right\} \bigg|_{\theta=\theta_0} \\
&= \left\{ \frac{\partial}{\partial \boldsymbol{\theta}} \int f(\mathbf{x}_i|\boldsymbol{\theta}) \frac{f(\mathbf{x}_i|\boldsymbol{\theta})}{f(\mathbf{x}_i|\boldsymbol{\theta})} d\mathbf{x}_i \right\} \bigg|_{\theta=\theta_0} \\
&= \left\{ \frac{\partial}{\partial \boldsymbol{\theta}} \int f(\mathbf{x}_i|\boldsymbol{\theta})\, d\mathbf{x}_i \right\} \bigg|_{\theta=\theta_0} \\
&= \frac{\partial}{\partial \boldsymbol{\theta}} 1 \\
&= \mathbf{0}.
\end{aligned}
$$

Note that the fourth equality used the Leibniz integral rule, invoking the assumption of invariance of the support. The last equality used $f(\mathbf{x}_i|\boldsymbol{\theta})$ is a legitimate density that integrates to 1. □

This proposition asserts that MLE can be viewed as a subset of GMM; the moment condition that MLE imposes is $\mathbb{E}\left[\mathbf{s}(\boldsymbol{\theta}|\mathbf{x}_i)\right]|_{\theta=\theta_0} = \mathbf{0}$.

Proposition A.1.3. (MLE with Differentiability of the Log-Likelihood Function) Suppose $\forall \boldsymbol{\theta} \in \Theta$, $\ln f(\mathbf{x}_i|\boldsymbol{\theta})$ exists. Then, $\hat{\boldsymbol{\theta}}_{MLE}$ solves $\frac{1}{n}\sum_{i=1}^{n} \mathbf{s}(\boldsymbol{\theta}|\mathbf{x}_i) = \mathbf{0}$.

Remark. Proposition A.1.3 provides us with a justification for the first-derivative method through the GMM interpretation.

Definition. (Information Matrix) Let $\mathbf{s}(\boldsymbol{\theta}|\mathbf{x})$ be the score function for an i.i.d. data-generating process F. The Fisher information matrix $\mathbf{I}(\boldsymbol{\theta}_0)$ is defined by

$$\mathbf{I}(\boldsymbol{\theta}_0) := \mathbb{E}\left[\{\mathbf{s}(\boldsymbol{\theta}|\mathbf{x}_i)\}\{\mathbf{s}(\boldsymbol{\theta}|\mathbf{x}_i)\}'\right]|_{\theta=\theta_0},$$

where the expectation is taken against the distribution of $\mathbf{x}_i$.

Theorem A.1.1. (Information Matrix Equality) Let $\mathbf{s}(\boldsymbol{\theta}|\mathbf{x})$ be the score function for an i.i.d. data-generating process F. Then, under some regularity conditions,

$$\mathbf{I}(\boldsymbol{\theta}_0) = -\mathbb{E}\left[\frac{\partial}{\partial \boldsymbol{\theta}} \mathbf{s}(\boldsymbol{\theta}|\mathbf{x}_i)\right]\bigg|_{\theta=\theta_0}$$

$$= -\mathbb{E}\left[\frac{\partial^2}{\partial \boldsymbol{\theta} \partial \boldsymbol{\theta}'} \ln f(\mathbf{x}_i|\boldsymbol{\theta})\right]\Bigg|_{\boldsymbol{\theta}=\boldsymbol{\theta}_0}$$

$$\equiv -\mathbf{H}(\boldsymbol{\theta}_0).$$

Theorem A.1.2. (Cramer-Rao Lower Bound) Let $f(\mathbf{X}|\boldsymbol{\theta})$ be the joint density of $\mathbf{X} = \{\mathbf{x}_1, \mathbf{x}_2, \ldots, \mathbf{x}_n\}$ conditional on $\boldsymbol{\theta}$. For any $\boldsymbol{\theta} \in \Theta$, let $\tilde{\boldsymbol{\theta}}_{\boldsymbol{\theta}}(\mathbf{X})$ denote an unbiased estimator of $\boldsymbol{\theta}$, i.e., $\mathbb{E}\left[\tilde{\boldsymbol{\theta}}_{\boldsymbol{\theta}}(\mathbf{X})\right] = \boldsymbol{\theta}$. Then,

$$Var(\tilde{\boldsymbol{\theta}}_{\boldsymbol{\theta}}(\mathbf{X}))\big|_{\boldsymbol{\theta}=\boldsymbol{\theta}_0} \geq [\mathbf{I}(\boldsymbol{\theta}_0)]^{-1};$$

that is, $\left\{Var(\tilde{\boldsymbol{\theta}}_{\boldsymbol{\theta}}(\mathbf{X})) - [\mathbf{I}(\boldsymbol{\theta})]^{-1}\right\}\big|_{\boldsymbol{\theta}=\boldsymbol{\theta}_0}$ is positive semidefinite.

Proof. It suffices to show that

$$Var(\tilde{\boldsymbol{\theta}}_{\boldsymbol{\theta}}(\mathbf{X}))\mathbf{I}(\boldsymbol{\theta})\big|_{\boldsymbol{\theta}=\boldsymbol{\theta}_0} \equiv Var(\tilde{\boldsymbol{\theta}}_{\boldsymbol{\theta}}(\mathbf{X}))Var(\mathbf{s}(\boldsymbol{\theta}|\mathbf{X}))\big|_{\boldsymbol{\theta}=\boldsymbol{\theta}_0} \tag{A.1.1}$$

$$\geq \mathbf{I}_p, \tag{A.1.2}$$

where $\mathbf{I}_p$ is an $p \times p$ identity matrix.

The Cauchy-Schwartz inequality asserts $Var\left(\tilde{\boldsymbol{\theta}}_{\boldsymbol{\theta}}(\mathbf{X})\right)\mathbf{I}(\boldsymbol{\theta})\big|_{\boldsymbol{\theta}=\boldsymbol{\theta}_0} \geq \left\{Cov\left(\tilde{\boldsymbol{\theta}}_{\boldsymbol{\theta}}(\mathbf{X}), \mathbf{s}(\boldsymbol{\theta}|\mathbf{X})\right)\big|_{\boldsymbol{\theta}=\boldsymbol{\theta}_0}\right\}^2$. Invoking proposition A.1.2, the second term of the covariance is a zero matrix. The first term of the covariance reduces as follows:

$$\left\{Cov\left(\tilde{\boldsymbol{\theta}}_{\boldsymbol{\theta}}(\mathbf{X}), \mathbf{s}(\boldsymbol{\theta}|\mathbf{X})\right)\right\}\big|_{\boldsymbol{\theta}=\boldsymbol{\theta}_0}$$

$$= \left\{\int \tilde{\boldsymbol{\theta}}_{\boldsymbol{\theta}}(\mathbf{X})\left(\frac{1}{f(\mathbf{X}|\boldsymbol{\theta})}\frac{\partial f(\mathbf{X}|\boldsymbol{\theta})}{\partial \boldsymbol{\theta}}\right) f(\mathbf{X}|\boldsymbol{\theta})\, d\mathbf{X}\right\}\Bigg|_{\boldsymbol{\theta}=\boldsymbol{\theta}_0}$$

$$= \left\{\frac{\partial}{\partial \boldsymbol{\theta}}\int \tilde{\boldsymbol{\theta}}_{\boldsymbol{\theta}}(\mathbf{X}) f(\mathbf{X}|\boldsymbol{\theta})\, d\mathbf{X}\right\}\Bigg|_{\boldsymbol{\theta}=\boldsymbol{\theta}_0}$$

$$= \frac{\partial}{\partial \boldsymbol{\theta}}\mathbb{E}\left[\tilde{\boldsymbol{\theta}}_{\boldsymbol{\theta}}(\mathbf{X})\right]\Bigg|_{\boldsymbol{\theta}=\boldsymbol{\theta}_0}$$

$$= \mathbf{I}_p.$$

Hence, we have established the inequality in equation (A.1.2). □

A.1.2 Consistency and Asymptotic Efficiency

In this subsection, we establish the consistency of MLE and its asymptotic efficiency—MLE attains the Cramer-Rao lower bound when the sample size increases to infinity. Define

$$Q_0(\boldsymbol{\theta}) := \int \ln f(\mathbf{x}_i|\boldsymbol{\theta}) f(\mathbf{x}_i|\boldsymbol{\theta}_0)\, d\mathbf{x}_i$$

$$\hat{Q}_n(\boldsymbol{\theta}) := \frac{1}{n}\sum_{i=1}^{n} \ln f(\mathbf{x}_i|\boldsymbol{\theta}).$$ [1]

We further assume the following regularity conditions:

MLE(1) The support of the joint density $\mathcal{L}\left(\boldsymbol{\theta}|\{\mathbf{x}_i\}_{i=1}^n\right)$ does not depend on $\boldsymbol{\theta} \in \Theta$.
MLE(2) $\hat{Q}_n(\boldsymbol{\theta}) \Rightarrow_p Q_0(\boldsymbol{\theta})$ uniformly over Θ.[2]
MLE(3) If $Q_0(\boldsymbol{\theta})$ attains the maximum over $\boldsymbol{\theta} \in \Theta$, the maximizer is unique.
MLE(4) Θ is compact.
MLE(5) $Q_0(\boldsymbol{\theta})$ is continuous in $\boldsymbol{\theta}$.

Remark. The pointwise convergence in probability of $\forall\boldsymbol{\theta} \in \Theta$, $\hat{Q}(\boldsymbol{\theta}) \rightarrow_p Q_0(\boldsymbol{\theta})$ is guaranteed by the weak law of large numbers and the continuous mapping theorem. However, as we shall see, we need a stricter condition than the pointwise convergence to show the consistency of MLE.

Theorem A.1.3. (Consistency and Asymptotic Efficiency of MLE) Let $\hat{\boldsymbol{\theta}}_{MLE}$ be a maximum-likelihood estimator for a true parameter $\boldsymbol{\theta}$. Then, under assumption MLE(1)–(5),

(i) $\hat{\boldsymbol{\theta}}_{MLE} \rightarrow_p \boldsymbol{\theta}_0$ as $n \rightarrow \infty$.
(ii) $\sqrt{n}\left(\hat{\boldsymbol{\theta}}_{MLE} - \boldsymbol{\theta}_0\right) \rightarrow_d \mathcal{N}\left(\mathbf{0}, [\mathbf{I}(\boldsymbol{\theta}_0)]^{-1}\right)$.

Furthermore, $n\left(\hat{\boldsymbol{\theta}}_{MLE} - \boldsymbol{\theta}_0\right)\left(\hat{\boldsymbol{\theta}}_{MLE} - \boldsymbol{\theta}_0\right)' \rightarrow_p [\mathbf{I}(\boldsymbol{\theta}_0)]^{-1}$ as $n \rightarrow \infty$, so $\hat{\boldsymbol{\theta}}_{MLE}$ is asymptotically efficient.

1. Note the relationship when $\boldsymbol{\theta} = \boldsymbol{\theta}_0$:

$$Q_0(\boldsymbol{\theta}_0) = \mathbb{E}\left[\ln f(\mathbf{x}_i|\boldsymbol{\theta})\right]\big|_{\boldsymbol{\theta}=\boldsymbol{\theta}_0}.$$

However, $Q_0(\boldsymbol{\theta})$ is generally different from $\mathbb{E}\left[\ln f(\mathbf{x}_i|\boldsymbol{\theta})\right]\big|_{\boldsymbol{\theta}=\boldsymbol{\theta}_0}$.

2. We can replace this assumption with the boundedness of $Q_0(\boldsymbol{\theta})$.

Proof. (i) We first show that $\forall \boldsymbol{\theta} \neq \boldsymbol{\theta}_0$, $Q_0(\boldsymbol{\theta}) - Q_0(\boldsymbol{\theta}_0) < 0$.

$$\begin{aligned} Q_0(\boldsymbol{\theta}) - Q_0(\boldsymbol{\theta}_0) &= \int \ln\left(f(\mathbf{x}_i|\boldsymbol{\theta})\right) f(\mathbf{x}_i|\boldsymbol{\theta}_0)\, d\mathbf{x}_i - \int \ln\left(f(\mathbf{x}_i|\boldsymbol{\theta}_0)\right) f(\mathbf{x}_i|\boldsymbol{\theta}_0)\, d\mathbf{x}_i \\ &= \int \ln\left(\frac{f(\mathbf{x}_i|\boldsymbol{\theta})}{f(\mathbf{x}_i|\boldsymbol{\theta}_0)}\right) f(\mathbf{x}_i|\boldsymbol{\theta}_0)\, d\mathbf{x}_i \\ &\leq \ln \int \frac{f(\mathbf{x}_i|\boldsymbol{\theta})}{f(\mathbf{x}_i|\boldsymbol{\theta}_0)} f(\mathbf{x}_i|\boldsymbol{\theta}_0)\, d\mathbf{x}_i \qquad \text{(A.1.3)} \\ &= \ln \int f(\mathbf{x}_i|\boldsymbol{\theta})\, d\mathbf{x}_i \\ &= 0. \end{aligned}$$

The inequality in equation (A.1.3) is by invoking Jensen's inequality, using the fact that ln (.) is a concave function. Inequality (A.1.3) establishes $Q_0(\boldsymbol{\theta})$ attains its maximum when $\boldsymbol{\theta} = \boldsymbol{\theta}_0$. Invoking the assumption of MLE(3), the inequality in (A.1.3) becomes strict and $Q_0(\boldsymbol{\theta}_0)$ is the unique maximum of $Q_0(\boldsymbol{\theta})$.

MLE(2) then asserts:

$$\sup_{\boldsymbol{\theta}\in\Theta} \left\| \hat{Q}_n(\boldsymbol{\theta}) - Q_0(\boldsymbol{\theta}) \right\| \to_p 0,$$

which yields

$$\arg\max_{\boldsymbol{\theta}\in\Theta} \hat{Q}_n(\boldsymbol{\theta}) \equiv \hat{\boldsymbol{\theta}}_{MLE} \to_p \boldsymbol{\theta}_0.$$

This establishes the consistency.

(ii) Recall the definition of MLE—that MLE solves

$$\frac{1}{n}\sum_{i=1}^{n} \left.\frac{\partial \ln f(\mathbf{x}_i|\boldsymbol{\theta})}{\partial \boldsymbol{\theta}}\right|_{\boldsymbol{\theta}=\hat{\boldsymbol{\theta}}_{MLE}} = \mathbf{0}.$$

The mean value theorem asserts that $\exists \boldsymbol{\theta}^* \in \left[\boldsymbol{\theta}, \hat{\boldsymbol{\theta}}_{MLE}\right]$, such that

$$\frac{1}{n}\sum_{i=1}^{n}\left[\left.\frac{\partial \ln f(\mathbf{x}_i|\boldsymbol{\theta})}{\partial \boldsymbol{\theta}}\right|_{\boldsymbol{\theta}=\boldsymbol{\theta}_0} + \left.\frac{\partial^2 \ln f(\mathbf{x}_i|\boldsymbol{\theta})}{\partial \boldsymbol{\theta}^2}\right|_{\boldsymbol{\theta}=\boldsymbol{\theta}^*\in\left[\boldsymbol{\theta}_0, \hat{\boldsymbol{\theta}}_{MLE}\right]} \left(\hat{\boldsymbol{\theta}}_{MLE} - \boldsymbol{\theta}_0\right)\right] = \mathbf{0}.$$

Rearranging, we obtain

$$\hat{\boldsymbol{\theta}}_{MLE} - \boldsymbol{\theta}_0 = -\frac{\frac{1}{n}\sum_{i=1}^{n} \left.\frac{\partial \ln f(\mathbf{x}_i|\boldsymbol{\theta})}{\partial \boldsymbol{\theta}}\right|_{\boldsymbol{\theta}=\boldsymbol{\theta}_0}}{\frac{1}{n}\sum_{i=1}^{n} \left.\frac{\partial^2 \ln f(\mathbf{x}_i|\boldsymbol{\theta})}{\partial \boldsymbol{\theta}^2}\right|_{\boldsymbol{\theta}=\boldsymbol{\theta}^* \in \left[\boldsymbol{\theta}_0, \hat{\boldsymbol{\theta}}_{MLE}\right]}}$$

$$\rightarrow_p \mathbf{0}.^3$$

To invoke the central limit theorem, multiplying $\sqrt{n}$ and sending $n \rightarrow \infty$, we have

$$-\frac{\sqrt{n}}{n}\sum_{i=1}^{n} \left.\frac{\partial \ln f(\mathbf{x}_i|\boldsymbol{\theta})}{\partial \boldsymbol{\theta}}\right|_{\boldsymbol{\theta}=\boldsymbol{\theta}_0} \rightarrow_d \mathcal{N}(\mathbf{0}, \mathbf{I}(\boldsymbol{\theta}_0))$$

$$\frac{1}{n}\sum_{i=1}^{n} \left.\frac{\partial^2 \ln f(\mathbf{x}_i|\boldsymbol{\theta})}{\partial \boldsymbol{\theta}^2}\right|_{\boldsymbol{\theta}=\boldsymbol{\theta}^* \in \left[\boldsymbol{\theta}_0, \hat{\boldsymbol{\theta}}_{MLE}\right]} \rightarrow_p \mathbb{E}\left[\left.\frac{\partial^2}{\partial \boldsymbol{\theta}^2} \ln f(\mathbf{x}_i|\boldsymbol{\theta})\right]\right|_{\boldsymbol{\theta}=\boldsymbol{\theta}_0}$$
$$= \mathbf{I}(\boldsymbol{\theta}_0).$$

The last equality follows by the information equality. Therefore, the continuous mapping theorem asserts that

$$\sqrt{n}\left(\hat{\boldsymbol{\theta}}_{MLE} - \boldsymbol{\theta}_0\right) \rightarrow_d \mathcal{N}\left(\mathbf{0}, [\mathbf{I}(\boldsymbol{\theta}_0)]^{-1}\right),$$

which attains the Cramer-Rao efficiency bound. □

Remark. Note that if the model is misspecified as $g(\mathbf{x}_i|\boldsymbol{\theta})$ but the true data-generating process is $f(\mathbf{x}_i|\boldsymbol{\theta})$, then $\hat{\boldsymbol{\theta}}_{MLE}$ is not a consistent estimator of $\boldsymbol{\theta}_0$ because

$$Q_0(\boldsymbol{\theta}) = \int \ln g(\mathbf{x}_i|\boldsymbol{\theta}) f(\mathbf{x}_i|\boldsymbol{\theta}_0)\, d\mathbf{x}_i,$$

which is not necessarily maximized at $\boldsymbol{\theta}_0$.

However, the quasi-MLE (Q-MLE) estimator is consistent if $g(\mathbf{x}_i|\boldsymbol{\theta})$ and $f(\mathbf{x}_i|\boldsymbol{\theta})$ both belong to a linear exponential family. The Q-MLE estimator

3. Note that $\frac{1}{n}\sum_{i=1}^{n} \left.\frac{\partial \ln f(\mathbf{x}_i|\boldsymbol{\theta})}{\partial \boldsymbol{\theta}}\right|_{\boldsymbol{\theta}=\boldsymbol{\theta}_0} \rightarrow_p \frac{1}{n}\sum_{i=1}^{n} \mathbb{E}[\mathbf{s}(\mathbf{x}_i|\boldsymbol{\theta})] = \mathbf{0}$ by WLLN.

minimizes the following Kullback-Leibler information criterion:

$$\mathcal{I}\left(g,f;\boldsymbol{\theta},\boldsymbol{\theta}_0\right)=\int \ln\left[\frac{g\left(\mathbf{x}_i|\boldsymbol{\theta}\right)}{f\left(\mathbf{x}_i|\boldsymbol{\theta}_0\right)}\right] f\left(\mathbf{x}_i|\boldsymbol{\theta}_0\right) d\mathbf{x}_i.$$

Example A.1.1. (Sources of Stochasticity) Suppose that a researcher estimates the intertemporal elasticity of substitution to test the life-cycle consumption-saving hypothesis using MLE. Let $\boldsymbol{\theta}$ be the intertemporal elasticity of substitution, let $\mathbf{x}_i$ be the wage process, and let y_i be savings. We have obtained a data set on $\left(\mathbf{x}_i, y_i\right)$ to fit the model:

$$y_i = g\left(\mathbf{x}_i, \boldsymbol{\theta}\right) + u_i.$$

Four sources of stochasticity are possible here: (1) heterogeneity in the structural form $g_i\left(\boldsymbol{\theta}\right)$; (2) the dependence of the true $\mathbf{x}_i$ on some other factors, such as unexpected transfer income and wealth; (3) optimization failure, which is often observed in the lab experiments; and (4) measurement error on $\mathbf{x}_i$. In many cases, we let all the stochasticity comes from source 4 just to consistently estimate the parameters. However, if this is not the case, a significant bias can be involved in the estimates, model predictions, and/or counterfactuals.

A.2 Generalized Method of Moments

Structural econometric models often boil down to a set of moment conditions, especially when the researcher does not specify the distribution of unobservables. In such a case, the generalized method of moments by Hansen (1982) provides an integrated solution.

A.2.1 Motivation and Setup

Let $\mathbb{R}^n$ be the space of data. Let $\mathbb{P} \subset \mathbb{R}^k$ be the parameter space. We want to find $\boldsymbol{\beta}_{(k\times 1)} \in \mathbb{P}$, where we have $\mathbf{f}: \mathbb{P} \times \mathbb{R}^n \to \mathbb{R}^r$, such that

$$\mathbb{E}\left[\mathbf{f}\left(\mathbf{x}, \boldsymbol{\beta}\right)\right]\Big|_{\boldsymbol{\beta}=\boldsymbol{\beta}_0} = \mathbf{0}, \tag{A.2.1}$$

if and only if $\boldsymbol{\beta} = \boldsymbol{\beta}_0$ and $\boldsymbol{\beta}_0$ is the true parameter. The system of equation (A.2.1) has k unknowns and r equations. Equation (A.2.1) is called the "moment condition." We assume that $r \geq k$ so that the system in equation (A.2.1) is identified.

Let $\{\mathbf{x}_t\}_{t=1}^N \in \mathbb{R}^n$ be the observed data. It is immediate that we can formulate the sample analog of equation (A.2.1), defined by $\mathbf{g}_N : \mathbb{P} \times \mathbb{R}^n \to \mathbb{R}^r$ as

$$\mathbf{g}_N(\boldsymbol{\beta}) := \frac{1}{N}\sum_{t=1}^{N}\mathbf{f}(\mathbf{x}_t, \boldsymbol{\beta}) = \mathbf{0}. \tag{A.2.2}$$

If $r > k$, there might be no solution for equation (A.2.2) even if equation (A.2.1) has a solution.

We consider using a selection matrix $\mathbf{A}_{(k\times r)}$ to reduce the k-dimensional equations to the r dimension as

$$\mathbf{A}_{(k\times r)}\mathbf{g}_N(\boldsymbol{\beta}) = \mathbf{0} \tag{A.2.3}$$

and denote $\mathbf{b}_N$ as the solution for equation (A.2.3). The remaining task is to figure out a "good" choice of $\mathbf{A}$. As one changes the specification of $\mathbf{A}$, estimator $\mathbf{b}_N$ changes accordingly. Thus, the entire family of estimator $\{\mathbf{b}_N\}$ can be pinned down only by specifying $\mathbf{A}$. In other words, solution $\mathbf{b}_N$ is indexed by $\mathbf{A}$.

A.2.2 Efficiency Bound

A.2.2.1 LIMIT APPROXIMATIONS FOR $\boldsymbol{\beta}_0$

In this section, we want to establish the efficiency bound for the estimator $\mathbf{b}_N$ of $\boldsymbol{\beta}_0$. Let $\mathbf{g}_N(\boldsymbol{\beta}) = \frac{1}{N}\sum_{t=1}^{N}\mathbf{f}(\mathbf{x}_t, \boldsymbol{\beta})$, as before. We begin with the following assumptions:

GMM(1) The underlying data-generating process $\{\mathbf{x}_t\}_{t=1}^{N}$ is stationary and ergodic.[4]

GMM(2) (Central Limit Theorem) $\sqrt{N}\mathbf{g}_N(\boldsymbol{\beta}_0) \rightarrow_d \mathcal{N}(0, \mathbf{V})$.[5]

GMM(3) (Consistency of $\mathbf{b}_N$) $\mathbf{b}_N \rightarrow_{a.s.} \boldsymbol{\beta}_0$.[6]

4. Ergodicity can be relaxed.

5. We impose this central limit theorem as an assumption to rule out the case where the data-generating process $\{\mathbf{x}_t\}$ may be more strongly correlated than the assumption for the central limit theorem to hold. In other words, we want to rule out a strong dependence of the underlying process.

6. We assume that $\mathbf{b}_N \rightarrow_{a.s.} \boldsymbol{\beta}_0$ pointwise. To derive the consistency of $\mathbf{b}_N$, it is insufficient just to ensure the pointwise convergence of the following:

$$\mathbf{g}_N(\boldsymbol{\beta}) \equiv \frac{1}{N}\sum_{t=1}^{N}\mathbf{f}(\mathbf{x}_t, \boldsymbol{\beta}) \rightarrow_{a.s} \mathbb{E}\left[\mathbf{f}(\mathbf{x}_t, \boldsymbol{\beta})\right].$$

Instead, we should impose two additional restrictions:

1. For a compact parameter space $\mathbb{P}$,

$$\mathbf{g}_N(.) \rightarrow_{a.s.} \mathbb{E}\left[\mathbf{f}(\mathbf{x}_t, .)\right]$$

uniformly. This is the uniform convergence-type restriction.

GMM(4) (Differentiability of $\mathbf{f}$) $\mathbf{f}(\mathbf{x}_t, \boldsymbol{\beta})$ is continuously differentiable in $\boldsymbol{\beta}$.

GMM(5) (Differentiability of $\mathbf{f}$ at $\boldsymbol{\beta}_0$) $\exists\epsilon > 0$ such that $\mathcal{B}_\epsilon\left(\boldsymbol{\beta}_0\right) \subset \mathbb{P}$. That is, $\boldsymbol{\beta}_0$ is located in the interior of $\mathbb{P}$.[7]

GMM(6) (Smoothness of $\mathbf{f}$ around $\boldsymbol{\beta}_0$) $\mathbb{E}\left[\sup_{|\boldsymbol{\beta}-\boldsymbol{\beta}_0|<\epsilon}\left|\frac{\partial}{\partial\boldsymbol{\beta}}\mathbf{f}(\mathbf{x}_t, \boldsymbol{\beta}) - \frac{\partial}{\partial\boldsymbol{\beta}}\mathbf{f}\left(\mathbf{x}_t, \boldsymbol{\beta}_0\right)\right|\right] < \infty$.

Throughout the section, denote $\mathbf{D}_N := \frac{\partial}{\partial\boldsymbol{\beta}}\mathbf{g}_N(\mathbf{b}_N)$ and $\mathbf{D} := \mathbb{E}\left[\frac{\partial}{\partial\boldsymbol{\beta}}\mathbf{f}\left(\mathbf{x}_t, \boldsymbol{\beta}_0\right)\right]$.[8] Lemma A.2.1 is immediate from the assumptions.

Lemma A.2.1. (Consistency of Derivative Matrix) $\mathbf{D}_N \rightarrow_{a.s.} \mathbf{D}$.

Proof. We have

$$\begin{aligned}
\mathbf{D}_N &= \frac{\partial}{\partial\boldsymbol{\beta}}\mathbf{g}_N(\mathbf{b}_N) \\
&= \frac{1}{N}\sum_{t=1}^{N}\frac{\partial}{\partial\boldsymbol{\beta}}\mathbf{f}(\mathbf{x}_t, \mathbf{b}_N) \\
&\rightarrow_{a.s.} \mathbb{E}\left[\frac{\partial}{\partial\boldsymbol{\beta}}\mathbf{f}\left(\mathbf{x}_t, \boldsymbol{\beta}_0\right)\right] \\
&= \mathbf{D}.
\end{aligned}$$

The convergence follows GMM(3), (4), and (6), and the continuous mapping theorem that $\frac{\partial}{\partial\boldsymbol{\beta}}\mathbf{f}$ is continuous as well. □

Lemma A.2.2. (Mean Value Approximation) Under GMM(3)–(6),

$$\mathbf{g}_N(\mathbf{b}_N) \backsimeq \mathbf{g}_N\left(\boldsymbol{\beta}_0\right) + \mathbf{D}_N\left(\mathbf{b}_N - \boldsymbol{\beta}_0\right). \tag{A.2.4}$$

Lemmas A.2.1 and A.2.2, combined with GMM(2), yields theorem A.2.1.

---

2. $\exists\epsilon > 0$, such that

$$\mathbb{E}\left[\sup_{\left\|\boldsymbol{\beta}-\tilde{\boldsymbol{\beta}}\right\|<\epsilon,\tilde{\boldsymbol{\beta}}}\left\|\mathbf{f}(\mathbf{x}_t, \boldsymbol{\beta}) - \mathbf{f}\left(\mathbf{x}_t, \tilde{\boldsymbol{\beta}}\right)\right\|\right] < \infty.$$

Note that because $\mathbf{f}(\mathbf{x}_t, \boldsymbol{\beta})$ is a random function, we have integrated it out. Under this condition, the minimizer $\mathbf{b}_N$ of $\mathbf{g}_N(\boldsymbol{\beta})'\mathbf{W}\mathbf{g}_N(\boldsymbol{\beta})$ can be shown to converge almost surely to the true parameter.

7. This condition is required for the existence of the derivatives in the vicinity of $\boldsymbol{\beta}_0$.
8. $\mathbf{D}$ and $\mathbf{D}_N$ are $r \times k$ matrices.

Theorem A.2.1. (Central Limit Theorem for a GMM Estimator) Let $\mathbf{b}_N$ be a GMM estimator indexed by the selection matrix $\mathbf{A}$. Then,

$$\sqrt{N}\left(\mathbf{b}_N - \boldsymbol{\beta}_0\right) \rightarrow_d \mathcal{N}\left(0, Cov\left(\mathbf{A}\right)\right), \tag{A.2.5}$$

where $Cov\left(\mathbf{A}\right) = \left(\mathbf{AD}\right)^{-1}\mathbf{AVA}'\left(\mathbf{AD}\right)'^{-1}$.

Proof. Let $\mathbf{A}_{(k\times r)}$ be a selection matrix. From equation (A.2.3), we know that $\mathbf{b}_N$ is a solution for the equation $\mathbf{A}_{(k\times r)}\mathbf{g}_N\left(\boldsymbol{\beta}\right) = \mathbf{0}$, such that

$$\mathbf{A}_{(k\times r)}\mathbf{g}_N\left(\mathbf{b}_N\right) = \mathbf{0}$$

holds by definition.[9]

Recall equation (A.2.4) and suppose that N is large. Multiplying $\mathbf{A}_{(r\times k)}$ yields

$$\mathbf{A}\mathbf{g}_N\left(\boldsymbol{\beta}_0\right) + \mathbf{AD}\left(\mathbf{b}_N - \boldsymbol{\beta}_0\right) = \mathbf{A}\mathbf{g}_N\left(\mathbf{b}_N\right) \equiv \mathbf{0}.$$

So we have the equality

$$\mathbf{A}\mathbf{g}_N\left(\boldsymbol{\beta}_0\right) = -\mathbf{AD}\left(\mathbf{b}_N - \boldsymbol{\beta}_0\right).$$

Multiplying $\sqrt{N}$ yields

$$\mathbf{A}\sqrt{N}\mathbf{g}_N\left(\boldsymbol{\beta}_0\right) = -\mathbf{AD}\sqrt{N}\left(\mathbf{b}_N - \boldsymbol{\beta}_0\right).$$

By rearranging, we have

$$\sqrt{N}\left(\mathbf{b}_N - \boldsymbol{\beta}_0\right) = -\left(\mathbf{AD}\right)^{-1}\mathbf{A}\sqrt{N}\mathbf{g}_N\left(\boldsymbol{\beta}_0\right). \tag{A.2.6}$$

Notice that by A2, $\sqrt{N}\mathbf{g}_N\left(\boldsymbol{\beta}_0\right) \rightarrow_d \mathcal{N}\left(0, \mathbf{V}\right)$. So we have that

$$\sqrt{N}\left(\mathbf{b}_N - \boldsymbol{\beta}_0\right) \rightarrow_d \mathcal{N}\left(0, \left(\mathbf{AD}\right)^{-1}\mathbf{AVA}'\left(\mathbf{AD}\right)'^{-1}\right).$$[10]

□

9. Notice that $\mathbf{g}_N\left(\mathbf{b}_N\right)$ may not be $\mathbf{0}$.

10. Multiplying $\mathbf{D}$ yields

$$\sqrt{N}\mathbf{D}\left(\mathbf{b}_N - \boldsymbol{\beta}_0\right) = -\mathbf{D}\left(\mathbf{AD}\right)^{-1}\mathbf{A}\sqrt{N}\mathbf{g}_N\left(\boldsymbol{\beta}_0\right).$$

A.2.2.2 ASYMPTOTIC EFFICIENCY BOUND

The theorem that asserts the GMM estimator (theorem A.2.1) is asymptotically normally distributed leads our interests to the efficiency bound for the asymptotic variance of $\mathbf{b}_N$ and the way to achieve the bound, by selecting an adequate $\mathbf{A}$. We begin with showing that the asymptotic covariance matrix is unique up to invertible transformations.

Lemma A.2.3. (GMM Estimator and Its Asymptotic Variance Is Unique up to Invertible Linear Transformation) Let $\mathbf{B}_{(k\times k)}$ be invertible. Consider $\mathbf{BA}$ as our new selection-matrix choice. Then,

(i) $\mathbf{b}_N$ solves $\mathbf{A}_{(k\times r)}\mathbf{g}_N(\boldsymbol{\beta})=\mathbf{0}$ if and only if the same $\mathbf{b}_N$ solves $\mathbf{B}_{(k\times k)}\mathbf{A}_{(k\times r)}\mathbf{g}_N(\boldsymbol{\beta})=\mathbf{0}$.
(ii) $Cov(\mathbf{A})=Cov(\mathbf{BA})$.

Proof. (i) It is immediate by the definition of an invertible matrix.
(ii) Consider equation (A.2.6) again, replacing $\mathbf{A}$ with $\mathbf{BA}$:

$$\sqrt{N}\left(\mathbf{b}_N-\boldsymbol{\beta}_0\right)=-\left(\mathbf{BAD}\right)^{-1}\mathbf{BA}\sqrt{N}\mathbf{g}_N\left(\boldsymbol{\beta}_0\right)$$
$$\sqrt{N}\left(\mathbf{b}_N-\boldsymbol{\beta}_0\right)\rightarrow_d\mathcal{N}\left(\mathbf{0},(\mathbf{AD})^{-1}\mathbf{B}^{-1}\mathbf{BAVA}'\mathbf{B}'\mathbf{B}'^{-1}(\mathbf{AD})'^{-1}\right)$$
$$=_d\mathcal{N}\left(\mathbf{0},(\mathbf{AD})^{-1}\mathbf{AVA}'(\mathbf{AD})'^{-1}\right).$$

So the asymptotic covariance matrix is the same. □

By virtue of lemma A.2.3, we can pick $\mathbf{B}$ in a convenient way. Consider $\mathbf{B}=(\mathbf{AD})^{-1}$ so that $\mathbf{AD}=\mathbf{I}$. The asymptotic covariance matrix reduces to $\mathbf{AVA}'$ under the choice of $\mathbf{B}$. Thus, hereafter, without loss of generality, we can assume that $Cov(\mathbf{A})=\mathbf{AVA}'$. Theorem A.2.2 establishes the choice of $\mathbf{A}$ under which the lower bound of the asymptotic covariance matrix is achieved.

Theorem A.2.2. (Asymptotic Efficiency Bound of GMM Estimator) Suppose that $\mathbf{V}$ defined in GMM(2) is nonsingular. Let $\mathbf{A}^*=\left(\mathbf{D}'\mathbf{V}^{-1}\mathbf{D}\right)^{-1}\mathbf{D}'\mathbf{V}^{-1}$.[11]

Using equation (A.2.4) again, we obtain

$$\sqrt{N}\mathbf{g}_N(\mathbf{b}_N) = \left[\mathbf{I}-\mathbf{D}(\mathbf{AD})^{-1}\mathbf{A}\right]\sqrt{N}\mathbf{g}_N(\boldsymbol{\beta}_0)$$
$$\rightarrow_d\left[\mathbf{I}-\mathbf{D}(\mathbf{AD})^{-1}\mathbf{A}\right]\mathcal{N}(0,\mathbf{V}).$$

So we find that $\left[\mathbf{I}-\mathbf{D}(\mathbf{AD})^{-1}\mathbf{A}\right]$ is the adjustment term. Premultiplying $\mathbf{A}$ yields the both side $\mathbf{0}$, which is trivial by assumption.

11. Because $\left(\mathbf{D}'\mathbf{V}^{-1}\mathbf{D}\right)^{-1}$ is invertible, $\mathbf{A}^*$ can be replaced by $\mathbf{D}'\mathbf{V}^{-1}$ in practice, but not in this proof because we want to exploit the feature $\mathbf{AD}=\mathbf{I}$.

Then, $\mathbf{A}^*$ achieves the asymptotic efficiency bound of GMM estimator $\mathbf{b}_N$ with the asymptotic covariance matrix $Cov\,(\mathbf{A}^*) = \left(\mathbf{D}'\mathbf{V}^{-1}\mathbf{D}\right)^{-1}$; that is,

$$\sqrt{N}\left(\mathbf{b}_N - \boldsymbol{\beta}_0\right) \rightarrow_d \mathcal{N}\left(\mathbf{0}, \left(\mathbf{D}'\mathbf{V}^{-1}\mathbf{D}\right)^{-1}\right).$$

Furthermore, $\forall \mathbf{A}_{(k\times r)}$, $Cov\,(\mathbf{A}) - Cov\,(\mathbf{A}^*)$ is positive semidefinite.

Proof. Let $\mathbf{A}_{(k\times r)}$ be a selection matrix such that $\mathbf{AD} = \mathbf{I}$.

Guess $\mathbf{A}^* = \left(\mathbf{D}'\mathbf{V}^{-1}\mathbf{D}\right)^{-1}\mathbf{D}'\mathbf{V}^{-1}$. It is immediate that

$$\begin{aligned} Cov\left(\mathbf{A}^*\right) &= \mathbf{A}^*\mathbf{V}\left(\mathbf{A}^*\right)' = \left(\mathbf{D}'\mathbf{V}^{-1}\mathbf{D}\right)^{-1}\mathbf{D}'\mathbf{V}^{-1}\mathbf{V}\mathbf{V}^{-1}\mathbf{D}\left(\mathbf{D}'\mathbf{V}^{-1}\mathbf{D}\right)^{-1} \\ &= \left(\mathbf{D}'\mathbf{V}^{-1}\mathbf{D}\right)^{-1}. \end{aligned}$$

We have

$$\begin{aligned} \mathbf{AV}\left(\mathbf{A}^*\right)' &= \mathbf{AVV}^{-1}\mathbf{D}\left(\mathbf{D}'\mathbf{V}^{-1}\mathbf{D}\right)^{-1} \\ &= \mathbf{AD}\left(\mathbf{D}'\mathbf{V}^{-1}\mathbf{D}\right)^{-1} \\ &= \left(\mathbf{D}'\mathbf{V}^{-1}\mathbf{D}\right)^{-1}. \end{aligned}$$

The last equality is by our choice of $\mathbf{A}$ such that $\mathbf{AD} = \mathbf{I}$.

Now consider

$$\begin{aligned} Cov\,(\mathbf{A}) - Cov\left(\mathbf{A}^*\right) &= \mathbf{AVA}' - \mathbf{A}^*\mathbf{V}\left(\mathbf{A}^*\right)' \\ &= \mathbf{AVA}' - \left(\mathbf{DV}^{-1}\mathbf{D}'\right)^{-1} \\ &= \mathbf{AVA}' - \left(\mathbf{DV}^{-1}\mathbf{D}'\right)^{-1} + \left(\mathbf{DV}^{-1}\mathbf{D}'\right)^{-1} - \left(\mathbf{DV}^{-1}\mathbf{D}'\right)^{-1} \\ &= \mathbf{AVA}' - \mathbf{A}^*\mathbf{VA}' - \mathbf{AV}\left(\mathbf{A}^*\right)' + \mathbf{A}^*\mathbf{V}\left(\mathbf{A}^*\right)' \\ &= \left(\mathbf{A} - \mathbf{A}^*\right)\mathbf{V}\left(\mathbf{A} - \mathbf{A}^*\right)' \\ &= \left[\left(\mathbf{A} - \mathbf{A}^*\right)\sqrt{\mathbf{V}}\right]\left[\left(\mathbf{A} - \mathbf{A}^*\right)\sqrt{\mathbf{V}}\right]', \end{aligned}$$

which is a positive semidefinite matrix, because $\mathbf{V}$ is a positive definite matrix because $\mathbf{V}$ is nonsingular. □

Remark. Because $\mathbf{A}^* = \left(\mathbf{D}'\mathbf{V}^{-1}\mathbf{D}\right)^{-1}\mathbf{D}'\mathbf{V}^{-1}$ and $\left(\mathbf{D}'\mathbf{V}^{-1}\mathbf{D}\right)^{-1}$ is just a nonsingular matrix, the bound is attained if

$$\mathbf{A}^* = \mathbf{BD}'\mathbf{V}^{-1} \tag{A.2.7}$$

for a $\mathbf{B}$.

Remark. Notice the similarity of the proof structure with the Gauss-Markov theorem.

The results up to now can be summarized by the following four basic approximation equations:

$$\sqrt{N}\left(\mathbf{b}_N - \boldsymbol{\beta}_0\right) \approx -\left(\mathbf{AD}\right)^{-1}\mathbf{A}\sqrt{N}\mathbf{g}_N\left(\boldsymbol{\beta}_0\right) \tag{A.2.8}$$

$$\sqrt{N}\mathbf{g}_N\left(\mathbf{b}_N\right) \approx \left[\mathbf{I} - \mathbf{D}\left(\mathbf{AD}\right)^{-1}\mathbf{A}\right]\sqrt{N}\mathbf{g}_N\left(\boldsymbol{\beta}_0\right) \tag{A.2.9}$$

$$\sqrt{N}\mathbf{g}_N\left(\boldsymbol{\beta}_0\right) \to_d \mathcal{N}\left(0, \mathbf{V}\right) \tag{A.2.10}$$

$$Cov\left(\mathbf{A}^*\right) = \left(\mathbf{D}'\mathbf{V}^{-1}\mathbf{D}\right)^{-1}. \tag{A.2.11}$$

A.2.3 Tests of Overidentifying Restrictions

This subsection provides the asymptotic test of the validity of the moment conditions using the efficient selection matrix.

A.2.3.1 USING SELECTION MATRIX $\mathbf{A}^*$

We have determined that the efficiency bound is attained when we set $\mathbf{A}^*_{(k\times r)} = \mathbf{BD}'\mathbf{V}^{-1}$. Set $\mathbf{A}^* = \left(\mathbf{D}'\mathbf{V}^{-1}\mathbf{D}\right)^{-1}\mathbf{D}'\mathbf{V}^{-1}$ and factor $\mathbf{V}^{-1}_{(r\times r)} = \boldsymbol{\Lambda}'\boldsymbol{\Lambda}$ so that $\mathbf{V}_{(r\times r)} = \boldsymbol{\Lambda}^{-1}\boldsymbol{\Lambda}'^{-1}$.

Lemma A.2.4.

$$\sqrt{N}\boldsymbol{\Lambda}\mathbf{g}_N\left(\boldsymbol{\beta}_0\right) \to_d \mathcal{N}\left(0, \mathbf{I}_r\right)$$

Proof. It is straightforward from equation (A.2.10) and our construction of $\boldsymbol{\Lambda} = \sqrt{\mathbf{V}^{-1}}$. □

Now plugging back our construction of A^* into equation (A.2.9) yields

$$\sqrt{N}\mathbf{g}_N\left(\mathbf{b}_N\right) \approx \left[\mathbf{I} - \mathbf{D}\left(\mathbf{D}'\mathbf{V}^{-1}\mathbf{D}\right)^{-1}\mathbf{D}'\mathbf{V}^{-1}\right]\sqrt{N}\mathbf{g}_N\left(\boldsymbol{\beta}_0\right). \tag{A.2.12}$$

Premultiplying by $\boldsymbol{\Lambda}$ and substituting back $\mathbf{V}^{-1} = \boldsymbol{\Lambda}'\boldsymbol{\Lambda}$, we get

$$\sqrt{N}\boldsymbol{\Lambda}\mathbf{g}_N\left(\mathbf{b}_N\right) \approx \boldsymbol{\Lambda}\left[\mathbf{I} - \mathbf{D}\left(\mathbf{D}'\boldsymbol{\Lambda}'\boldsymbol{\Lambda}\mathbf{D}\right)^{-1}\mathbf{D}'\boldsymbol{\Lambda}'\boldsymbol{\Lambda}\right]\sqrt{N}\mathbf{g}_N\left(\boldsymbol{\beta}_0\right). \tag{A.2.13}$$

Defining $\boldsymbol{\Delta}_{(r\times k)} := \boldsymbol{\Lambda}_{(r\times r)}\mathbf{D}_{(r\times k)}$, equation (A.2.13) yields

$$\sqrt{N}\boldsymbol{\Lambda} g_N(\mathbf{b}_N) \approx \left[\boldsymbol{\Lambda} - \boldsymbol{\Lambda}\mathbf{D}\left(\mathbf{D}'\boldsymbol{\Lambda}'\boldsymbol{\Lambda}\mathbf{D}\right)^{-1}\mathbf{D}'\boldsymbol{\Lambda}'\boldsymbol{\Lambda}\right]\sqrt{N}\mathbf{g}_N(\boldsymbol{\beta}_0) \quad \text{(A.2.14)}$$

$$= \left[\boldsymbol{\Lambda} - \boldsymbol{\Delta}\left(\boldsymbol{\Delta}'\boldsymbol{\Delta}\right)^{-1}\boldsymbol{\Delta}'\boldsymbol{\Lambda}\right]\sqrt{N}\mathbf{g}_N(\boldsymbol{\beta}_0) \quad \text{(A.2.15)}$$

$$= \left[\mathbf{I}_r - \boldsymbol{\Delta}\left(\boldsymbol{\Delta}'\boldsymbol{\Delta}\right)^{-1}\boldsymbol{\Delta}'\right]\sqrt{N}\boldsymbol{\Lambda}\mathbf{g}_N(\boldsymbol{\beta}_0). \quad \text{(A.2.16)}$$

It is straightforward that

$$\sqrt{N}\boldsymbol{\Lambda}\mathbf{g}_N(\mathbf{b}_N) \rightarrow_d N\left(0, \mathbf{I}_r - \boldsymbol{\Delta}\left(\boldsymbol{\Delta}'\boldsymbol{\Delta}\right)^{-1}\boldsymbol{\Delta}'\right).$$

Lemma A.2.5. (Properties of $\mathbf{J}_1$ and $\mathbf{J}_2$) Define $\mathbf{J}_1 = \boldsymbol{\Delta}\left(\boldsymbol{\Delta}'\boldsymbol{\Delta}\right)^{-1}\boldsymbol{\Delta}'$ and $\mathbf{J}_2 = \mathbf{I} - \boldsymbol{\Delta}\left(\boldsymbol{\Delta}'\boldsymbol{\Delta}\right)^{-1}\boldsymbol{\Delta}'$.

(i) $\mathbf{J}_1$ and $\mathbf{J}_2$ are symmetric and idempotent.
(ii) $\mathbf{J}_1 + \mathbf{J}_2 = \mathbf{I}_r$.
(iii) $\mathbf{J}_1\mathbf{J}_2 = \mathbf{O}$.

Proof. Basic linear algebra yields the result. □

We are ready to characterize the limiting distribution for our overidentification test. The following theorem illustrates the limiting distribution of our squared objective function.

Theorem A.2.3. (Asymptotic Distributions of the GMM Test Statistics) Let $\mathbf{J}_1, \mathbf{J}_2$ be as defined in the display equation above. Let $\mathbf{g}_N(\boldsymbol{\beta}) = \frac{1}{N}\sum_{t=1}^{N}\mathbf{f}(\mathbf{x}_t, \boldsymbol{\beta})$. Let $\mathbf{A}^* = \mathbf{D}'\mathbf{V}^{-1}$ be an efficient selection matrix. Suppose that $\mathbf{b}_N$ is the GMM estimator that satisfies $\mathbf{A}^*\mathbf{g}_N(\mathbf{b}_N) = \mathbf{0}$. Then,

(i) $N\mathbf{g}_N(\boldsymbol{\beta}_0)'\mathbf{V}^{-1}\mathbf{g}_N(\boldsymbol{\beta}_0) \rightarrow_d \chi^2_r$.
(ii) $N\mathbf{g}_N(\mathbf{b}_N)'\mathbf{V}^{-1}\mathbf{g}_N(\mathbf{b}_N) \rightarrow_d \chi^2_{r-k}$.
(iii) $\begin{pmatrix}\mathbf{J}_1\\ \mathbf{J}_2\end{pmatrix}\sqrt{N}\boldsymbol{\Lambda}\mathbf{g}_N(\boldsymbol{\beta}_0) \rightarrow_d \mathcal{N}\left(\begin{pmatrix}\mathbf{0}\\ \mathbf{0}\end{pmatrix}, \begin{pmatrix}\mathbf{J}_1 & \mathbf{O}\\ \mathbf{O} & \mathbf{J}_2\end{pmatrix}\right)$.

Proof. (i)

$$N\mathbf{g}_N(\boldsymbol{\beta}_0)'\mathbf{V}^{-1}\mathbf{g}_N(\boldsymbol{\beta}_0) = \left[\sqrt{N}\boldsymbol{\Lambda}\mathbf{g}_N(\boldsymbol{\beta}_0)\right]'\left[\sqrt{N}\boldsymbol{\Lambda}\mathbf{g}_N(\boldsymbol{\beta}_0)\right], \quad \text{(A.2.17)}$$

and we have shown that $\left[\sqrt{N}\boldsymbol{\Lambda}\mathbf{g}_N(\boldsymbol{\beta}_0)\right] \rightarrow \mathcal{N}(\mathbf{0}, \mathbf{I}_r)$. Thus, we find that the test statistic converges in distribution to χ^2_r.

(ii) We begin from equation (A.2.17).

$$\left[\sqrt{N}\mathbf{\Lambda}\mathbf{g}_N(\boldsymbol{\beta}_0)\right]'\left[\sqrt{N}\mathbf{\Lambda}\mathbf{g}_N(\boldsymbol{\beta}_0)\right]=\left[\sqrt{N}\mathbf{\Lambda}\mathbf{g}_N(\boldsymbol{\beta}_0)\right]'\mathbf{J}_1\left[\sqrt{N}\mathbf{\Lambda}\mathbf{g}_N(\boldsymbol{\beta}_0)\right]$$
$$+\left[\sqrt{N}\mathbf{\Lambda}\mathbf{g}_N(\boldsymbol{\beta}_0)\right]'\mathbf{J}_2\left[\sqrt{N}\mathbf{\Lambda}\mathbf{g}_N(\boldsymbol{\beta}_0)\right]$$

by the previous lemma (A.2.5) that $\mathbf{J}_1+\mathbf{J}_2=\mathbf{I}_r$. From equations (A.2.12) and (A.2.16) we have

$$\left[\sqrt{N}\mathbf{\Lambda}\mathbf{g}_N(\mathbf{b}_N)\right]'\left[\sqrt{N}\mathbf{\Lambda}\mathbf{g}_N(\mathbf{b}_N)\right]\approx\left[\sqrt{N}\mathbf{\Lambda}\mathbf{g}_N(\boldsymbol{\beta}_0)\right]'\mathbf{J}_2\left[\sqrt{N}\mathbf{\Lambda}\mathbf{g}_N(\boldsymbol{\beta}_0)\right],$$

where we used $\mathbf{J}_2=\mathbf{J}_2\mathbf{J}_2=\mathbf{J}_2\mathbf{J}_2'$ from lemma A.2.5 (i), we have the desired convergence.

(iii) It is straightforward by the previous results and the fact that $\mathbf{J}_1\mathbf{J}_2=\mathbf{O}$. □

Remark. Notice the important difference between (i) and (ii) on the degree of freedom. When $\mathbf{b}_N$ is plugged in, the degree of freedom becomes $r-k$, while the actual $\boldsymbol{\beta}_0$ returns the degree of freedom r. The proof of the theorem was simple because of our selection of $\mathbf{A}^*=\mathbf{D}'\mathbf{V}^{-1}$.

In practice, $N\mathbf{g}_N(\mathbf{b}_N)'\mathbf{V}^{-1}\mathbf{g}_N(\mathbf{b}_N)\rightarrow_d \chi^2_{r-k}$ can be used for the overspecification test. If the test statistic is large, it can be considered as evidence that the model is somehow misspecified. That is, either the moment condition is wrong or some other restrictions are wrong. However, the literature has also documented that the test seems to reject overidentifying restrictions too often in practice.

A.2.4 Quadratic-Form Minimization and Implementation

We can think of the GMM estimator in a different way. Let $\mathbf{W}_{(r\times r)}$ be a weighting matrix. Consider the following minimization problem:

$$\min_{\boldsymbol{\beta}\in\mathbb{P}}\frac{1}{2}\mathbf{g}_N(\boldsymbol{\beta})'\mathbf{W}\mathbf{g}_N(\boldsymbol{\beta}). \tag{A.2.18}$$

The first-order condition is

$$\left[\frac{\partial}{\partial\boldsymbol{\beta}}\mathbf{g}_N(\boldsymbol{\beta})'\mathbf{W}\right]\mathbf{g}_N(\boldsymbol{\beta})=\mathbf{0}. \tag{A.2.19}$$

Let $\mathbf{b}_N$ denote the solution for equation (A.2.19). Notice $\frac{\partial}{\partial \boldsymbol{\beta}} \mathbf{g}_N(\mathbf{b}_N) \rightarrow_{a.s.} \mathbf{D}$. Thus, we find that the efficient choice for $\mathbf{W}$ is $\mathbf{V}^{-1}$.

Let K_N be the minimized objective function for equation (A.2.19), where $\mathbf{W} = \mathbf{V}^{-1}$; that is, $K_N := \frac{1}{2} \mathbf{g}_N(\mathbf{b}_N)' \mathbf{V}^{-1} \mathbf{g}_N(\mathbf{b}_N)$. Then,

$$N \mathbf{g}_N(\mathbf{b}_N)' \mathbf{V}^{-1} \mathbf{g}_N(\mathbf{b}_N) \rightarrow_d \chi^2_{r-k}, \tag{A.2.20}$$

as before.

In practice, one uses the consistent estimator of $\mathbf{V}^{-1}$ to find the estimator that solves equation (A.2.18). One way is do the estimation in two stages or, iteratively, begin from $\mathbf{W} = \mathbf{I}$. An alternative is the continuous-updating GMM, which uses the sample analog of the following covariance matrix estimator:

$$\mathbf{V}(\boldsymbol{\beta}) = \lim_{N \rightarrow \infty} \mathbb{E}\left[\frac{1}{\sqrt{N}} \left(\sum_{t=1}^{N} \mathbf{f}(\mathbf{x}_t, \boldsymbol{\beta}) - \frac{1}{N} \sum_{t=1}^{N} \mathbf{f}(\mathbf{x}_t, \boldsymbol{\beta}) \right) \frac{1}{\sqrt{N}} \left(\sum_{t=1}^{N} \mathbf{f}(\mathbf{x}_t, \boldsymbol{\beta}) - \frac{1}{N} \sum_{t=1}^{N} \mathbf{f}(\mathbf{x}_t, \boldsymbol{\beta}) \right)' \right],$$

which is a function of $\boldsymbol{\beta}$. Then, we can minimize the following:

$$\min_{\boldsymbol{\beta} \in \mathbb{P}} \frac{1}{2} \mathbf{g}_N(\boldsymbol{\beta})' (\mathbf{V}(\boldsymbol{\beta}))^{-1} \mathbf{g}_N(\boldsymbol{\beta}). \tag{A.2.21}$$

The solution $\mathbf{b}_N$ for the problem (A.2.21) also attains the efficiency bound.

A.3 Simulation-Based Estimation Methods

When a set of model parameters is point identified, most of the estimation method boils down either to MLE or GMM. As studied in this appendix, MLE is desirable when the likelihood is fully specified up to a finite-dimensional model parameter, by solving a structural model. GMM is semiparametric, in the sense that the distribution of the error term can be left unspecified. However, even if a set of likelihoods or moment conditions can be derived from solving a model, they often do not have an analytic expression or they may be practically impossible to evaluate. In some such instances, simulation-based methods can be useful.

A.3.1 A Starting Point: The Glivenko-Cantelli Theorem

Let $\{x_i\}_{i=1}^{n}$ be an i.i.d. sequence of random variables with distribution $F(.)$ on $\mathbb{R}$. The empirical distribution function is a function of $x \in \mathbb{R}$ defined as follows:

Definition. (Empirical Distribution Function) Let $\{x_i\}_{i=1}^{N} \sim$ i.i.d. $F(.)$. The empirical distribution function $\hat{F}(x)$ is defined by

$$\hat{F}_N(x) := \frac{1}{N}\sum_{i=1}^{N} \mathbf{1}(x_i \leq x).$$

For any given $x \in \mathbb{R}$, the strong law of large numbers asserts that $\hat{F}_N(x) \rightarrow_{a.s.} F(x)$, as $\hat{F}_N(x)$ is a form of sample mean.[12] The Glivenko-Cantelli theorem asserts more. $\hat{F}_N(x)$ is a reasonable estimate of $F(x)$ when both are viewed as functions of x.

Theorem A.3.1. (Glivenko-Cantelli) Let $\{x_i\}_{i=1}^{N}$ be an i.i.d. sequence of random variables with distribution function $F(.)$ on $\mathbb{R}$. Then,

$$\sup_{x\in\mathbb{R}} \left|\hat{F}_N(x) - F(x)\right| \rightarrow_{a.s.} 0.$$

McFadden (1989) and Pakes and Pollard (1989) generalize this theorem to a more general class of empirical measures and empirical process. Then, they give the consistency and asymptotic normality of the simulated GMM estimators. The key condition, other than the regularity conditions for the consistency and asymptotic normality of GMM, is that the simulation analog of the original moment condition converges fast enough to the true moment condition. In the following subsections, we illustrate the method of simulated moments and method of simulated likelihoods.

A.3.2 Method of Simulated Moments

Although the method of simulated moments can be used in a slightly more general setup, we consider the individual coefficients model in this subsection for the purpose of illustration. Consider a model that yields the unconditional moment

12. We only need to show that $\mathbb{E}[|\mathbf{1}(x_i \leq x)|] < \infty$, which is trivial because $\mathbf{1}(x_i \leq x)$ is bounded and N is finite.

condition

$$\mathbb{E}\left[g\left(y_j, \mathbf{x}_j; \boldsymbol{\theta}_i\right)\right] = \int \int g\left(y_j, \mathbf{x}_j; \boldsymbol{\theta}_i\right) d\Pr\left(\boldsymbol{\theta}_i\right) d\Pr\left(y_j, \mathbf{x}_j\right)$$
$$= 0,$$

where $\Pr(\boldsymbol{\theta}_i) =_d \mathcal{N}(\boldsymbol{\theta}, \boldsymbol{\Sigma}_\theta)$. The target model parameters are $(\boldsymbol{\theta}, \boldsymbol{\Sigma}_\theta)$. The GMM estimation solves, given sample $\left\{\left(y_j, \mathbf{x}_j\right)\right\}_{j=1}^{J}$,

$$\min_{\boldsymbol{\theta}, \boldsymbol{\Sigma}_\theta} \left\{ \frac{1}{J} \sum_{j=1}^{J} \int g\left(y_j, \mathbf{x}_j; \boldsymbol{\theta}_i\right) d\Pr\left(\boldsymbol{\theta}_i\right) \right\}^2 .$$

Given a candidate parameter $(\boldsymbol{\theta}, \boldsymbol{\Sigma}_\theta)$, it is practically infeasible to analytically evaluate

$$\int g\left(y_j, \mathbf{x}_j; \boldsymbol{\theta}_i\right) d\Pr\left(\boldsymbol{\theta}_i\right)$$

when $\dim(\boldsymbol{\theta})$ is larger than, say, 5. For the first and second derivatives, the problem gets even more serious.

The key idea is to replace $\int g\left(y_j, \mathbf{x}_j; \boldsymbol{\theta}_i\right) d\Pr\left(\boldsymbol{\theta}_i\right)$ with its simulation analog. For each $\left(y_j, \mathbf{x}_j\right)$, consider the simulation analog

$$\frac{1}{N_s} \sum_{i=1}^{N_s} g\left(y_j, \mathbf{x}_j; \boldsymbol{\theta}_i\right);$$

that is, we simulate $\Pr(\boldsymbol{\theta}_i)$ and take the mean. A variant of the Glivenko-Cantelli theorem asserts that $\frac{1}{N_s}\sum_{i=1}^{N_s} g\left(y_j, \mathbf{x}_j; \boldsymbol{\theta}_i\right)$ is uniformly consistent with $\int g\left(y_j, \mathbf{x}_j; \boldsymbol{\theta}_i\right) d\Pr\left(\boldsymbol{\theta}_i\right)$. An immediate limitation is that $\Pr(\boldsymbol{\theta}_i)$ has to be known up to the model parameters $(\boldsymbol{\theta}, \boldsymbol{\Sigma}_\theta)$.

Let $\boldsymbol{\phi} = \mathrm{vec}(\boldsymbol{\theta}, \boldsymbol{\Sigma}_\theta)$, and let $\boldsymbol{\phi}_0$ be the true parameter. Let $\hat{\boldsymbol{\phi}}_{GMM}$ and $\hat{\boldsymbol{\phi}}_{MSM}$ be GMM and maximum simulated likelihood (MSM) estimators, respectively. Let $\mathbf{V}_{GMM}$ be the GMM asymptotic variance. Pakes and Pollard (1989) show that for a fixed number N_s with a frequency simulator,

$$\sqrt{J}\left(\hat{\boldsymbol{\phi}}_{MSM} - \boldsymbol{\phi}_0\right) \to_d \mathcal{N}\left(\mathbf{0}, \left(1 + \frac{1}{N_s}\right)\mathbf{V}_{GMM}\right).$$

That is, the asymptotic variance is inflated by $\left(1 + \frac{1}{N_s}\right)$.

A.3.3 Maximum Simulated Likelihoods

The intuition of maximum simulated likelihoods, is similar to the method of simulated moments. Suppose that the likelihood or part of the likelihood is defined in terms of integrals:

$$f\left(y_j, \mathbf{x}_j; \boldsymbol{\theta}\right) = \int h\left(y_j, \mathbf{x}_j, \mathbf{u}_i; \boldsymbol{\theta}\right) d\Pr\left(\mathbf{u}_j\right).$$

Prominent examples include the multivariate normal $\mathbf{u}_i$, or the latent utility models, where the domain of integration is a strict subset of Euclidean space. The MLE objective function is

$$\sum_{j=1}^{J} \ln f\left(y_j, \mathbf{x}_j; \boldsymbol{\theta}\right) = \sum_{j=1}^{J} \ln \left\{ \int h\left(y_j, \mathbf{x}_j, \mathbf{u}_i; \boldsymbol{\theta}\right) d\Pr\left(\mathbf{u}_i\right) \right\}.$$

With N_s simulated draws of $\mathbf{u}_i$, approximate the right-hand side using

$$\sum_{j=1}^{J} \ln f\left(y_j, \mathbf{x}_j; \boldsymbol{\theta}\right) = \sum_{j=1}^{J} \ln \left\{ \frac{1}{N_s} \sum_{i=1}^{N_s} h\left(y_j, \mathbf{x}_j, \mathbf{u}_i; \boldsymbol{\theta}\right) \right\}.$$

The asymptotics are slightly different. Let $\hat{\boldsymbol{\theta}}_{MSL}$ be the method of the simulated likelihood estimator. Suppose that $N_s = O\left(\sqrt{J} + \delta\right)$ for $\delta > 0$. Let $\mathbf{I}\left(\boldsymbol{\theta}_0\right)$ be the Fisher information matrix. Then,

$$\sqrt{J}\left(\hat{\boldsymbol{\theta}}_{MSL} - \boldsymbol{\theta}_0\right) \rightarrow \mathcal{N}\left(\mathbf{0}, \mathbf{I}^{-1}\left(\boldsymbol{\theta}_0\right)\right).$$

That is, the method of simulated likelihoods is asymptotically equivalent to MLE when the number of simulation draws increase at a rate faster than $\sqrt{J}$.

A.3.4 Implementation Algorithms

The following four steps are typical in implementing the algorithm: (1) Draw N_s random vectors, (2) take the candidate parameter value, (3) calculate the simulation analog of the likelihood/moment condition, and (4) iterate over steps 2 and 3 to find the parameter value that maximizes/minimizes the objective function. In practice, one should never draw N_s again at each iteration to guarantee the numerical convergence.

Example A.3.1. (Berry, Levinsohn, and Pakes (1995)) $\Pr(\boldsymbol{\theta}_i) =_d \mathcal{N}(\boldsymbol{\theta}, \boldsymbol{\Sigma}_\theta)$. First, draw N_s standard normal random vectors $\boldsymbol{\eta}_i$. For each candidate parameter value, $\boldsymbol{\theta}_i = \boldsymbol{\theta} + \sqrt{\boldsymbol{\Sigma}_\theta}\boldsymbol{\eta}_i$, where $\left(\sqrt{\boldsymbol{\Sigma}_\theta}\right)\left(\sqrt{\boldsymbol{\Sigma}_\theta}\right)' = \boldsymbol{\Sigma}_\theta$. Calculate the simulation analog of the moment condition correspondingly. Then iterate over it.

Bibliography

Berry, S., J. Levinsohn, & A. Pakes (1995). "Automobile prices in market equilibrium." *Econometrica*, 63, 841–890.

Hansen, L. P. (1982). "Large sample properties of generalized method of moments estimators." *Econometrica*, 50, 1029–1054.

McFadden, D. (1989). "A method of simulated moments for estimation of discrete response models without numerical integration." *Econometrica*, 57, 995–1026.

Newey, W. K., & D. McFadden (1994). "Large sample estimation and hypothesis testing." In Vol. 4, *Handbook of Econometrics*, 2111–2245. Amsterdam: Elsevier.

Pakes, A., & D. Pollard (1989). "Simulation and the asymptotics of optimization estimators." *Econometrica*, 57, 1027–1057.

INDEX